Making Minds and Madness

Why do "maladies of the soul" such as hysteria, anxiety disorders, or depression wax and wane over time? Through a study of the history of psychiatry, Mikkel Borch-Jacobsen provocatively argues that most mental illnesses are not, in fact, diseases but the product of varying expectations shared and negotiated by therapists and patients. With a series of fascinating historical vignettes, stretching from Freud's creation of false memories of sexual abuse in his early hysterical patients to today's promotion and marketing of depression by drug companies, *Making Minds and Madness* offers a powerful critique of all the theories, such as psychoanalysis and biomedical psychiatry, that claim to discover facts about the human psyche while, in reality, producing them. Borch-Jacobsen proposes such objectivizing approaches should be abandoned in favor of a constructionist and relativist psychology that recognizes the artifactual and interactive character of psychic productions instead of attempting to deny or control it.

MIKKEL BORCH-JACOBSEN is Professor of French and Comparative Literature at the University of Washington. He is the author of highly influential books on the theory and history of psychiatry and psychoanalysis, and co-author of the best-selling *Le livre noir de la psychanalyse* (*The Black Book of Psychoanalysis*).

Making Minds and Madness

From Hysteria to Depression

Mikkel Borch-Jacobsen

CAMBRIDGE
UNIVERSITY PRESS

CAMBRIDGE UNIVERSITY PRESS
Cambridge, New York, Melbourne, Madrid, Cape Town, Singapore, São Paulo, Delhi

Cambridge University Press
The Edinburgh Building, Cambridge CB2 8RU, UK

Published in the United States of America by Cambridge University Press, New York

www.cambridge.org
Information on this title: www.cambridge.org/9780521716888

First published 2009

Printed in the United Kingdom at the University Press, Cambridge

A catalogue record for this publication is available from the British Library

Library of Congress Cataloguing in Publication data
Borch-Jacobsen, Mikkel.
   Making minds and madness : from hysteria to depression / Mikkel Borch-Jacobsen.
      p.   cm.
   Includes bibliographical references and index.
   ISBN 978-0-521-88863-9 (hardback) – ISBN 978-0-521-71688-8 (pbk.)   1. Psychotherapy.
   2. Psychoanalysis. I. Title.
   [DNLM: 1. Psychoanalytic Theory–Collected Works.   2. History, 20th Century–Collected
   Works.   3. Psychiatry–history–Collected Works.   4. Psychotherapeutic Processes–Collected
   Works.   WM 460 B726m 2009a]
   RC480.5.B664 2009
   616.89′14–dc22
   2009006853

ISBN 978-0-521-88863-9 hardback
ISBN 978-0-521-71688-8 paperback

Contents

Acknowledgments

Much of the material in this book was previously incorporated into papers that have appeared in a variety of periodicals and collections since the mid-1990s. I thank my earlier publishers for permission to use these texts. But several of this book's chapters are new in English, and one consists entirely of material published here for the first time. The chapters containing previously published material reflect revisions, augmentations, and abridgments undertaken to avoid repetition and streamline the book's argument.

Although these chapters were originally written as separate essays, weaving them together has not proved too artificial a task. They all address, from various angles, the same basic issues: the historicity of "mental illnesses," the co-production of psychic "facts" (what I call "artifacts"), and the performative character of our psychological and psychiatric theories.

The introduction began as a paper presented at the conference "History of psychiatry. New approaches, new perspectives," held in Lausanne in 1997, and it appeared under a slightly different title in *History of the Human Sciences*, vol. 14, no. 2. It offers a "discourse on method" of sorts, mapping out the general argument of the book.

The three chapters in Part I can be seen as illustrations of the methodological principles laid out there. Written in the 1990s, in the heyday of "recovered memory therapy" and "trauma theory" in North America, they trace the emergence and spread of the notions of "psychic trauma," "dissociation," and "repression" in order to highlight their historical, contingent, and ultimately artifactual nature. History, in these chapters, is used to critique claims to psychological universality and ahistoricity. Chapter 1 was first delivered as a lecture in Berkeley in 1996. It went on to be presented in various other venues and was eventually published in *History of Psychiatry*, 11, no. 41. It has benefited immensely from the observations and comments of Allen Esterson, Elizabeth Loftus, Mark Micale, Rosemarie Sand, Sonu Shamdasani, and Richard Skues; I am especially grateful to Malcolm "Mac" Macmillan for a long and detailed critique that filled several gaps in my argument. Chapter 2 started out as a talk presented in 1994 at All Souls College, Oxford, at the invitation of Malcolm Bowie, who is very much missed. Two years later, it came out in a longer version in *October*, 76; the postscript appended to this chapter originally appeared in Danish in *Kritik*, 131 (1998), after the *October* publication, in response to objections raised by Freud critics such as Frederick

Crews, Han Israëls, and Allen Esterson (Freud advocates did not raise any objections).

Chapter 3 was published in French in my book *Folies à plusieurs* (2002) and was adapted from a seminar given in December 2000 at the Ecole des Hautes Etudes en Sciences Sociales; it also takes up elements from a previous essay on multiple personality (1994c). The sections on Shirley Mason's biography are based on research done in 1998–99, in collaboration with Peter J. Swales, who accomplished in the process a truly amazing work of archival gathering and historical reconstruction to which I am heavily indebted. Swales and I have both presented our research in various venues (Boynton 1998–99; Croes 1999; Borch-Jacobsen 1999b; Swales 2000). I want to thank here all those who agreed to share their memories and/or personal archives with us: Virginia Flores Cravens and Graciela ("Mikki") Flores Watson; Harold, Cleo, and David Eichman; Dr. Herbert Spiegel; Dr. Dan Houlihan; and Dr. Mildred Bateman. Thanks also to my colleague Jennifer Bean for tracking down an obscure documentary film on narcosynthesis produced by Shirley Mason's therapist, Cornelia B. Wilbur.

Part II, also containing three chapters, focuses on what I see as the core of my argument, the co-production of psychological artifacts: people react in complex ways to ideas and to expectations about them, so that psychological and psychiatric theories inevitably influence and mold the "psychical reality" they claim to describe. Chapter 4, which first appeared in the *London Review of Books*, May 27, 1999, pays homage to Ian Hacking's kindred work on "interactive kinds" and "transient mental illnesses," Chapters 5 and 6 trace this idea of a co-construction of reality back to late nineteenth-century discussions about hypnosis and suggestion, and most notably to the wonderful work of the mathematician, philosopher, and hypnotist Joseph Delbœuf. Chapter 5 appeared first in French, in 1997, in a special issue of the journal *Corpus*, 32, edited by Jacqueline Carroy and Pierre-Henri Castel and devoted to Hippolyte Bernheim and Joseph Delbœuf, and then in English, in *Qui Parle?*, 16, no. 1. Chapter 6 was originally a paper presented at a conference held in Paris in March 2002, which centered on the work of my late friend Léon Chertok, MD (1911–91), an ardent advocate of hypnosis and hypnotherapy in a country, Freudian France, that at the time was utterly averse to it; John Forrester, a Freudian, gamely published the paper in English in *Psychoanalysis and History*, 7, no. 1.

Part III deals with Freud and psychoanalysis. Obviously, a book about the creation of psychological artifacts has to grapple with the question of how the unconscious, the Oedipus complex, penis envy, Freudian slips, and all the rest became realities for so many people in the twentieth century. Chapter 7 approaches this question from the angle of the narrative construction of psychoanalytic "data." It is a revised version of a paper presented at the "Narrative" conference held at Northwestern University in April 1998. The paper was later published in *Narrative*, 7, no. 1 (1999), where it was followed by a critical exchange with Claudia Brodsky-Lacour, which does not appear here. Chapter 8, originally a paper published in *History of the Human Sciences*, 21, no. 1 (2008), coins a new word, "interprefaction," to refer to the way in which Freud created facts with words, all the while denying that he was doing this. The paper was written in collaboration with Sonu Shamdasani and introduces an argument developed in our book on Freud (2006). Sonu has been an important interlocutor over the years, and I cannot begin to measure how much my own work owes to our collaboration. Chapter 9 is downright mean: it calls out psychoanalysis as a "zero theory" that has proliferated precisely because it is utterly devoid of stable content. Under a different title, the chapter was published as an essay in the *London Review of Books*, May 24, 2001; as a letter to the editor noted at the time, it elicited no rebuttals from psychoanalysts.

After psychoanalysis, Prozac® and Ritalin®: Part IV deals with the rise of biological psychiatry and its consequences. Chapter 10, originally published by Marcel Gauchet in *Le Débat*, 114, sets the stage for the discussion that follows. Chapter 11 appeared under a different title in the *London Review of Books*, July 11, 2002. It uses the example of depression to argue that biological psychiatry, no less than psychotherapy and psychodynamic psychiatry, also "makes minds and madness": our fin-de-siècle "depression," I claim with David Healy and Philippe Pignarre, is in large part a historical side effect of antidepressants. Chapter 12 is adapted from my contribution to a very exciting seminar, "Psychology, ideology and philosophy," held in Brussels in June 2006 under the auspices of the Université Libre de Bruxelles and subsequently aired on Radio France Culture. It reflects on the present situation of psychotherapy in the era of randomized, double-blind, placebo-controlled trials and mass production of new "mental illnesses." Chapter 13 takes up this discussion about the phenomenon of "disease mongering" and ends with some uncomfortable questions about the role of patients in the creation of their own illnesses. The chapter originated in a lecture given in October 2006 at a conference organized in Paris by the Centre Georges Devereux around the theme "Psychotherapy put to the test by its users" (*La psychothérapie à l'épreuve de ses usagers*). Members of several French patient-advocacy groups were present in the audience and on the podium; to my relief, most of them reacted positively to my remarks. The lecture was subsequently published in *Le Débat*, 152 (November–December 2008).

With one exception – the postscript to Chapter 2, originally published in Danish – all the chapters in this book have been translated or adapted from French, which remains my *langue de plume*. Douglas Brick translated the Introduction and Chapters 1, 2, 5, and 7. Jennifer Church translated Chapters 4, 8, 9, 10, and 11. Grant Mandarino translated Chapter 3. Kelly Walsh's translation of Chapters 12 and 13 was made possible by a grant from the Graduate School of the University of Washington, which is gratefully acknowledged. Lisa Appignanesi and John Forrester kindly offered to translate Chapter 6 at a moment when I could not do it myself. I thank them all for their contributions. I should add that I worked closely with them on the translations and often decided to rewrite passages to make them less Gallic. Sonu Shamdasani further emended our Chapter 8. Frances Brown, who ably edited the manuscript of this book for the publisher, added yet another layer of stylistic varnish. Therefore, any resemblance to the French originals is most likely to be coincidental.

In addition to those already mentioned, many other people contributed their help, advice, or friendly critiques to this book: Stéphane Barbéry, Odette Chertok, Frederick Crews, Todd Dufresne, Allen Esterson, Ernst Falzeder, Henri Grivois, Ian Hacking, Han Israëls, Michael G. Kenny, André LeBlanc, Patrick Mahony, Eric Michaud, Tobie Nathan, Michael Neve, Philippe Pignarre, Paul Roazen, François Roustang, Anthony Stadlen, and Isabelle Stengers. Warm thanks to all.

Introduction: making psychiatric history (questions of method)

Does the history of psychiatry have an object? And if so, what object? Let us assume for a moment that the first question can be answered positively. The answer to the second question will then seem obvious: the object of the history of psychiatry, we shall say, is the set of medical theories, social and institutional practices, and therapeutic methods that, since the end of the eighteenth century, have addressed madness (in the broadest and vaguest sense of the term). The history of psychiatry, on this score, would be the history not so much of madness, but of the various discursive practices that have accounted for it over time. In short, there would be three discrete, hierarchical levels: that of madness; that of the psychiatric theories and practices that take it as an object; and lastly, the historical metadiscourse that studies these theories and practices in their variable relationship with madness.

Consider now what this reassuring stratification of the mad, the psychiatrist, and the historian implies: a deeply ahistorical conception of madness, since madness is supposed to constitute the invariant of the many discourses that take it as an object. The historian of psychiatry, according to this conception, studies the different approaches to a psychopathology whose essence he refrains from addressing (since he is not a psychiatrist), but which he nonetheless takes for granted, never doubting that it exists "out there," independently of the psychiatric discourses and practices that attempt to define and to treat it. It should be obvious that this historian, however great the metadiscursive distance he takes in regard to the psychiatrist, shares in fact the same ideal of objectivity as the latter. For both, madness is an intangible x, existing on the horizon of their discourses. In the end, this historian and this psychiatrist have exactly the same object. This remains true, let us note in passing, even if that object be conceived, as in Michel Foucault's *Histoire de la folie*,[1] as a kind of mute, non-objectifiable experience, exceeding all discourse, all reason, and all history. Indeed, one would continue in this case to posit madness – "essential madness" – outside the various discourses that have attempted to account for it in history, thus lending it all the more objectivity as it is inaccessible and elusive.

This objectivist complicity between the psychiatrist and the historian of psychiatry becomes immediately evident if we stop speaking in vague terms of "madness," as we have been doing till now. Less ambitious than Foucault, the historian of psychiatry typically writes the history of specific syndromes – hysteria, depression, schizophrenia, anorexia, and the like. But where does he find the definition of these terms, if not in some psychiatric theory? To write the history of hysteria across the ages, as Ilza Veith,[2] for example, has done, presupposes that one knows what hysteria is, what symptoms define it, and how to differentiate it from other syndromes. The historian will thus have to start from a certain concept of hysteria (more or less Freudian, in the case of Ilza Veith), and then objectify it and follow its variations through history. Thus conceived, the history of psychiatry is a history written from the point of view of the psychiatrist or the psychoanalyst, whose categories the historian surreptitiously internalizes and ratifies, giving them the status of transhistorical and transcultural realities.

The limits of this iatrocentric conception are immediately apparent, and as a matter of fact very few historians of psychiatry would still allow it today. Indeed, what guarantees, unless it be some psychiatric theory, that there is such a thing as hysteria, depression, or schizophrenia? Such a certainty is justifiable only in the case of mental disorders with a clearly organic foundation (tumoral, neurological, endocrinal, toxic, or infectious), as, for example, epilepsy, neurosyphilis, or Alzheimer's disease. In these cases, we are confronted with disorders that escape (at least to a certain extent) from history and, once they are recognized, insistently impose themselves as objective clinical entities, or else simply disappear owing to the discovery of an appropriate treatment. These organic diseases are, by their very nature, ahistorical: one can, of course, write the history of the way they have been represented, theorized, and treated, perhaps the history of their propagation and their disappearance, and even the history of the way the sufferers experienced them (the history of their "illness narratives," as medical anthropologists say nowadays).[3] But these diseases are not historical *in themselves*: no matter what time period, a patient suffering from neurosyphilis will always develop the same psychic, neurological, and humoral symptoms.

Nevertheless, however fascinated psychiatrists have always been with organogenesis, and despite the ever more alluring promises of biochemistry and genetics, it is clear that the vast majority of psychiatric disorders escape from that reassuring model. If there really is a huge lesson to be learned from the history of psychiatry, it is the infinitely variable and fluctuating character of psychiatric entities. This is particularly true of what we call hysteria, whose protean character is such that we can legitimately ask ourselves, contrary to Ilza Veith and historians of psychoanalytic persuasion, if there ever was *a* hysteria: what is there in common between the "vapours" of eighteenth-century ladies, characterized by respiratory difficulties and a quasi lethargic immobility; Charcot's *grande hystérie*, with its attacks in four very distinct phases, its anesthesias and hemianesthesias, its contractures, its shrinking of the visual field; the "hysterical fugues" of the end of the nineteenth century; the varied symptoms of the "conversion hysteria" of Breuer and Freud's Viennese clients – coughs, facial neuralgias, phobias; the "shell shock" of soldiers in the

Great War, characterized mainly by aphonia and trembling; or again, the spectacular "Multiple Personality Disorders" of late twentieth-century North America? Clearly, we are dealing here not with one and the same syndrome, but with an array of "transient mental illnesses," to use Ian Hacking's term,[4] all of which are born, evolve, and disappear in accordance with very specific local and historical conditions.

This variability affects no less the other neuroses and psychosomatic illnesses in general. As the historian Edward Shorter has shown,[5] a neurotic person was most likely to have faintings and convulsive crises in the eighteenth century, most likely to suffer from some kind of paralysis or contracture in the nineteenth, and most likely today to suffer from depression, fatigue, psychosomatic complaints, or eating disorders. Likewise, the medical figures of the "pervert" and the "homosexual" began to appear, as such, only in the second half of the nineteenth century,[6] to be replaced in our time by new distributions and new roles: since the American Psychiatric Association's 1974 decision to strike homosexuality from the nosology of the DSM-III, hardly anybody still considers that "sexual preference" as a form of mental disease. Even depression, which one might believe is timeless and inherent in human nature, changes according to time and culture: what we consider as a pathology characterized by essentially psychical symptoms has taken in the past and still takes elsewhere[7] a somatic form, as in hypochondriacal melancholia; it has been endowed with a religious meaning, as in the acedia of medieval hermits and monks;[8] sometimes, it is even valued culturally and actively sought after through techniques of morose meditation, as in the Buddhist *pilikul bhavana* in Sri Lanka.[9] The same holds for female anorexia, which today is linked with a body image promoted by Western media, but which, according to the historian Caroline Bynum, was in medieval Italy (and still is in modern Portugal) a form of religious asceticism associated with bodily purification and sainthood.[10] As for what used to be called the "psychoses," it has long been commonplace in the anthropology of mental illnesses and ethnopsychiatry to emphasize their cultural relativity:[11] our paranoiac would, in other times, have been "possessed" or "obsessed" by demons; and in different climes our medicated schizophrenic would have been considered as a sacred being, have become a shaman, or have run murderously *amok*.

This is not to say that everyone agrees on this. There seems to be a growing consensus today to attribute schizophrenia and manic depression to genetic factors or biochemical imbalance. And the fact is that the symptomatic manifestations of these psychoses and of major depression can now be treated with psychotropic drugs whose effectiveness was undreamed of just a few decades ago. Is this not the proof, one might ask, that in these cases we are dealing with biological illnesses, which, as such, are immune to the vicissitudes of history and the influences of the environment? Yes, but how then are we to explain the variations noted by historians, sociologists, and anthropologists? How, for example, are we to explain that the symptoms classically associated with schizophrenia did not appear until the end of the eighteenth century, and that they affected an always growing number of patients throughout the nineteenth century?[12] How are we to explain that auditory hallucinations – the most important of these symptoms, if we are to believe Schneider's symptom profile – also evolved, as to both their content and the frequency with which they were reported by the patients?[13] Or again, that the Ibans of Borneo suffering from the "madmen illness" exhibit auditory hallucinations, but none of the disturbances of subjective thought so common among Western schizophrenics?[14] How come the average duration of schizophrenia is much shorter in the Third World than in industrialized countries, as has been shown by several epidemiological studies of the WHO, and that it is much more likely to present with an acute onset?[15] Why is there better recovery from schizophrenia in times of labor shortage,[16] or when there is some psychosocial preparation before release from the hospital?[17] How should we interpret the fact that Chinese "neurasthenics," whose symptoms correspond to those of a severe depression, hardly respond to antidepressants?[18] Obviously, genetics and biochemistry are far from explaining everything, and history, like anthropology, plays an important role here in correcting the biological psychiatrists' unwarranted generalizations. Even the mental illnesses that are presumably biological in nature do not, it appears, escape from the variations of history.

Under these circumstances, it would be foolhardy for historians to blindly place their trust in psychiatric categories when studying past psychopathologies or the cultural forms adopted in other societies by what *we* call "mental illness." To do so would amount to projecting categories that are themselves relative, as when Charcot read the stigmata of *grande hystérie* in those of demoniacal possession, or when Freud, under the name of "Oedipus complex," found in universal history the typical conflicts of the disintegrating nuclear family.[19] As a matter of fact, today's historians of psychiatry have become very aware of (and wary about) the snares of iatrocentrism. Generally, they tend to suspend all judgment on the validity of the psychiatric categories they deal with, in order to view them in strictly historical terms. They go beyond the narrow, specialized framework of the psychiatric field, situating the latter in its various social, political, and cultural contexts. For the study of the grand psychiatric theories, they substitute that of the actual practice of psychiatry – the daily practice of internment, clinical practice, diagnostic practice, and so forth. To the great founding cases, they prefer the study of psychiatric archives or epidemiological and statistical research. Lastly, and in a more general way, they are paying more attention to the patients and *their* experience of mental illness.

All these new approaches strongly contribute to the unmaking of the old theoretical complicity between the historian and the psychiatrist, by relativizing the till now dominant point of view of the latter. However, we may ask ourselves whether the new history of psychiatry does not remain, on one very specific point, subtly dependent on the psychiatric model that it elsewhere calls into question. Precisely because they take such care to extricate themselves from iatrocentrism, the new historians disallow themselves from making any judgment on what mental illness really is, thus enforcing the former separation of roles between the psychiatrist and his historiographer. This epistemic timidity is unwarranted, for historians of psychiatry are in fact in a position to say something capital on the subject of mental illness, namely that the latter is not, for the most part, an *object* of knowledge. If madness has a history, it is not only because each historical period, each society, each culture divides the reality of mental illness differently, as if the latter remained ideally the same "beneath" the various theories and practices that take it for an object. What the history of psychiatry teaches us daily is that so-called "mental illnesses" – including, to a certain extent, the organic or biological ones – vary in accordance with those theories and practices, to the point of disappearing before the gaze of the historian: one is not mentally ill in the same way here and there, and sometimes one isn't ill at all. Whatever comparisons, for example, we might be tempted to make between Siberian shamanism and the manifestations of hysteria, of epilepsy, or of schizophrenia, the fact is that the shamans are neither sick nor crazy. Just like the Greek bacchic celebrants, the Thonga "mad of the Gods,"[20] or the Hebrew *nabi*,[21] they are sacred beings whose behavior is accepted, recognized, and ritually sanctioned by the society as a whole, and whose subjective experience is thus entirely different from that of a hysteric or a schizophrenic patient. Mental illness, however real it may be, does not exist apart from the various discourses and practices that *make* it exist.

The history of psychiatry, just like the sociology of mental illnesses and ethnopsychiatry, thus fundamentally questions the objectivity of psychiatric discourse. Indeed, this discourse is not separated from the "object" it deals with, because it contributes powerfully to creating it: like psychiatrist, one might say, like psychotic, like pervert, like neurotic. This is not to say that we should demonize the psychiatrist or denounce the multiple forms of his power, after the fashion of an antipsychiatric tradition that is still quite strong among some historians and sociologists. That would still make of the mentally ill a purely passive object of psychiatric discourse and practices, whereas the global lesson that emerges from the work of historians of psychiatry is precisely that the patients, far from simply submitting to the psychiatric categories imposed upon them, very actively conform to them. If hysteria or neurasthenia, for example, gradually disappeared from the psychiatric landscape at the end of the nineteenth century and the beginning of the twentieth, it is not, as Mark Micale suggests, just because doctors stopped diagnosing them, dividing differently the map of neuroses and psychoses.[22] It is also because the patients themselves followed suit, migrating toward other symptomatic forms, such as catatonia, hebephrenia, psychasthenia, or obsessional neurosis, thus reinforcing the trend initiated by doctors and retroactively shoring up their new taxonomies. Similarly, if we have witnessed in the United States a spectacular comeback of multiple personality since the mid-1970s, it is not just because a growing number of psychiatrists and psychotherapists suddenly decided to apply that diagnosis instead of that of schizophrenia or "borderline personality." It is because the patients themselves, under the influence of best-selling books and films such as *Sybil*, opted for that new symptomology,[23] thus initiating a trend that was amplified in the early 1980s by the official introduction of the diagnosis of "Multiple Personality Disorder," or MPD, in the DSM-III.[24]

There are good reasons to believe that a similar process is at work behind the remarkable increase in depressive disorders since the late 1950s, which cannot simply and tautologically be attributed to a "depressive society"[25] or to the new forms of "fin de siècle individuality."[26] Indeed, as David Healy has brilliantly shown in *The Antidepressant Era*,[27] this explosion is strictly contemporaneous with the introduction of antidepressant medications. Far from their arriving on the market to treat a previously existing psychiatric disorder, these new drugs actually created it from scratch: modern depression, we might say, is a side effect of antidepressants. Now, this creation of a syndrome, which Healy describes a bit too readily as a result of marketing, obviously also requires a very active collaboration on the part of the patients. Indeed, unless we assume that depression was always there, waiting to be "revealed" by antidepressants, the patients must have recognized themselves in this new symptomatology and told themselves that they were indeed depressed. In choosing to become depressed, they seem therefore to have modeled their symptoms on the psychotropic medications that were reputed to act on those very symptoms.

Patients, in other words, are not passive. As Gregory Bateson[28] and the Palo Alto School,[29] and more recently Ian Hacking,[30] have emphasized, they react to the categories that describe them, either by rejecting them or by adopting new behaviors that in turn further confirm the categories, till, in a more or less random fashion, patients and doctors elaborate together a new psychopathological paradigm. The most striking example of this process is undoubtedly the American gay movement: classified as homosexuals at the end of the nineteenth century, certain individuals sharing the same type of sexual practices first recognized themselves in the medical category that was imposed on them; then organized themselves into a social group governed by a particular lifestyle; and finally, thanks to an intense lobbying effort, forced the American Psychiatric Association to abandon the very medicalization of homosexuality. In a more general way, the new phenomenon of patient advocacy groups, like the National Alliance for the Mentally Ill, has the great advantage of bringing to light an activism of the patients that was up till then concealed beneath the psychiatrists' frozen categories: today, one can hardly have any doubts anymore as to the always profoundly *negotiated* nature of psychiatric entities. Far from being indifferent to the theories elaborated about them by the psychiatrists, the patients have a profound interest in them and they interact with them by adopting, rejecting, or modifying them. In other words, they participate in the construction (or the deconstruction) of the pathologies from which they are said to suffer.

Now, if the patients thus collaborate in the discourse and practices of which they are the object, this clearly means that their mental illness is not some *thing* that we can observe and study from the outside. It is a behavior or idiom adopted by certain individuals to communicate (even if in the mode of non-communication) with some doctor or medical figure and, more largely, with the society that he represents. We must therefore avoid unduly objectivizing mental illness, as if it existed independently of the psychiatrist and surrounding culture. In reality, what we are dealing with most of the time are patients who interact with doctors and institutions, adopting their idiom or, on the contrary, creating a new one in order to have their complaint heard and their ill-being treated. This is true, not only of functional and "transient" mental illnesses, which are fundamentally relational, but also of organic or biological pathologies. Psychiatry deals neither solely nor even most frequently with sick bodies or brains, but rather with people with whom it interacts, and it is thus affected by all the familiar looping effects that mar the human sciences in general.

To take only one example of these looping effects, we know that experimental psychologists despair of ever eliminating artifacts from their experiments because of what Robert Rosenthal calls the "experimenter's effect"; that is, the propensity of experimental subjects to anticipate and confirm the experimenter's expectations.[31] Whatever one does, the experimental situation creates "demand characteristics" that influence the way in which the subjects react to the experiment.[32] It goes without saying that this type of looping effect, already noticeable in the most neutral and most controlled experimental setting, will come to full flower in a clinical or hospital setting, where the patients depend institutionally and/or emotionally upon their doctor. Here is where the familiar mechanisms of iatrogenic suggestion or mental contagion find their trivial explanation – as does, incidentally, the so-called "placebo effect" and the "transference" of psychoanalysts. However aberrant or incomprehensible they might appear at first glance, the patient's symptoms are always distress signals, calls for help, so they always have a tendency to conform in advance to the language of the doctor and the society from which the patient expects, if not a cure, at least the recognition of his ill-being.

This remains true even if the disorder is of a biological nature or is rooted in an experience of psychotic "centrality"[33] predating any psychiatric and/or cultural categorization. Even in these cases, the enigma represented by the illness for the patient will tend to be formulated in terms capable of being heard by the psychiatrist or the medicine-man. This is what the psychiatrist Henri Grivois calls the "narrative drift" of the psychotic experience: the patients cannot avoid conferring a signification to the unspeakable that is happening to them, for "such an abstinence would be impossible or superhuman,"[34] and they are led therefore to put forward delusional "explanations" which call upon themes borrowed from the ambient culture (be they religious, political, or scientific), and which conform to stereotypes of madness. From this point of view, the distinction made by Ian Hacking[35] between "transient" or historical mental illnesses and "real" or biological ones unnecessarily creates an opposition (an ontological dualism) where there really is a continuum. Patients suffering from a biophysical illness are no less affected by the way they are perceived and treated than patients suffering from so-called "functional" or "psychosomatic" illnesses. The fact that the action of psychotropic drugs depends so much on the context in which they are administered is a good illustration of this: the body itself reacts to the therapeutic situation; that is, to the expectations shared by the patient and the doctor.

All of this should be a warning for the psychiatrists: their diagnoses are an integral part of the "etiological equation" (as Freud called it) of the symptoms that they claim to observe. But this should also be a warning for historians of psychiatry. Indeed, they cannot claim to be immune to the looping effects that affect the psychiatric field in general. Whether it be in ratifying some psychiatric notion or, on the contrary, in relativizing and contextualizing it, historians, like it or not, intervene in turn in the global etiological equation that defines the psychiatric field at a given moment, especially if their work finds some echo among psychiatrists. To take only a single example, it seems clear that the publication in 1970 of Henri Ellenberger's *The Discovery of the Unconscious*,[36] with its reassessment of Janet and the "hypnotic" prehistory of psychoanalysis, was not without some influence on the return in the United States of the diagnosis of multiple personality and, more generally, of the traumatic-dissociative etiology of the neuroses.[37] So it is not only the psychiatrists but also the historians who interact with what they describe. To write the history of psychiatry is also, inevitably, to *make* it.

This performativity of the historians' work, once recognized, brings with it some important consequences. First of all, historians of psychiatry can no longer retain the attitude of neutrality and impartiality to which they normally confine themselves. No matter what, they are engaged – *engagés*, as the French existentialists used to say – in the field that they describe. In particular, they must realize that writing the history of psychiatry necessarily entails a critique, a calling into question of its claims to objectivity. Rather than deny this critical dimension, historians would do better to acknowledge fully that they are, by their work, engaged in a redefinition and, by the same token, a relativization of the very notion of "mental illness."

Then, historians must also elaborate a methodology in accord with that relativization, and one which, if one may say so, actively performs it. If indeed "mental illness" is at least in part an idiom developed *between* the patient, the doctor, and the surrounding culture, historians can no longer be content with describing the theories and practices of the psychiatrists, or, inversely, the subjective experience of the patients. They must show how both these objective theories and this subjective experience emerge from beliefs, preconceptions, and expectations that are shared, negotiated, and modified by both the theorist and his patients: madness is always a *folie à deux*, or rather a *folie à plusieurs*, the madness of several. Thus, the history of psychiatry and/or madness should ideally be the history of those complex interactions that give rise, through feedback, amplification, and crystallization, to new psychiatric concepts and symptomatic behaviors – in short, to a new reality common to the psychiatrist, the patient, and the surrounding society.

To be sure, these interactions can be studied at the level of entire psychiatric populations. The historian then becomes a statistician and an epidemiologist, showing, for example, how the recognition by the British army psychiatrists of the notion of "shell shock" in about 1915 vastly amplified the phenomenon they were describing;[38] or again, how the popularization and dissemination of the Freudian theory of neuroses paradoxically brought on a disaffection with them, favoring instead syndromes attributed to non-psychogenic and therefore non-guilt-producing causes, such as "post-traumatic stress disorder," "fibromyalgia," or "chronic fatigue syndrome."[39] But the historian can equally delve into the micro-historical level and analyze a particularly decisive interaction between a doctor and one (or more) of his patients in order to follow as closely as possible the emergence of a new theory or symptomology. This approach, which is similar to that of the epidemiologist trying to localize the source of an infectious illness, has the great advantage over the global approach of introducing us directly into the process of fabrication of new psychiatric notions and syndromes, prior to their crystallization into "facts." Unlike traditional psychiatric history, it studies not ready-made theories and syndromes, but those theories and syndromes *in the making* – what we might call, adopting a term proposed in another field by Bruno Latour,[40] "psychiatry in action."

Take for example a psychotherapeutic practice such as the talking cure of psychoanalytic inspiration, hinging on the recollection of repressed fantasies or memories. To be sure, the historian may adopt a global, statistical approach, analyzing the dissemination, evolution, and modifications of the psychoanalytic talking cure. But it would prove very difficult for this historian to highlight the constructed and historically relative character of the phenomenon, insofar as he would then be dealing with ready-made practices and behaviors. How can you put into perspective the therapeutic value of recollection when a whole culture believes in it, when thousands of patients all over the world daily confirm the theories of their therapists, bringing them memories and fantasies of a Freudian type, and being firmly convinced that they are feeling better for that reason? Here, statistical analysis runs the risk of adding grist to the mill of a self-confirming system, even reinforcing it through the prestige of large numbers. Only by migrating upstream, to the very first talking cure, does the historian have any chance of bringing to light the random nature of the interactions that gave birth to analytic therapy, somewhere *between* Anna O. (Bertha Pappenheim), Breuer, Freud, and his patients. The historian will then note that Bertha Pappenheim's "talking cure" initially centered around the telling of cute fairy-tales "in the style of Hans Andersen," then the acting out – the "tragedizing," writes Breuer[41] – of morbid hallucinations. Only after a long period of negotiation between the patient and her doctor did the treatment orient itself toward the recollection of past events, under the pressure of Breuer's theoretical interest in the notion of hypnotic hypermnesia. The historian will therefore conclude that it was not recollection as such that brought on the temporary lifting of the symptoms, but rather the interaction – the "rapport," as the magnetizers of old called it – between the patient and her doctor.

Then, continuing his inquiry, the historian will find that this alleged "talking cure" in reality ended up in a complete fiasco and that it was only by systematically finessing that disastrous conclusion, which contradicted his own Charcotian and Janetian hypotheses, that Freud, starting in 1889, could test the "Breuer method" on patients such as Fanny Moser and Anna von Lieben and obtain from them "confirmations" that allowed him finally to convince Breuer to rewrite (in every sense of the word) the case of "Fräulein Anna O." The historian will thus have showed how a treatment that initially had nothing whatsoever to do with recollection, and that, in addition, led to no long-term therapeutic result, was able to impose itself as the initial model of psychoanalytic treatment, at the end of a looping effect lasting thirteen years and involving no less than two doctors, two successive theories, and a whole pool of patients.[42] In paying minute attention to psychiatric systems in the making, following the unpredictable sequence of exchanges between the symptoms and behavior of the patients, on the one hand, and the theories and practices of the doctor, on the other, the historian is thus able to bring forth the randomness and contingency that these same systems conceal once they are stabilized and rigidified.

It is mainly in the domain of psychoanalysis, and more generally of what Henri Ellenberger has called "dynamic psychiatry," that this type of microhistorical approach has been used until now. There are several obvious reasons for this. Unlike hospital psychiatry, which embraces large populations of patients and whose approach is spontaneously classifying or quantitative, psychoanalysis and other systems of dynamic psychiatry mostly put faith in the detailed analysis of individual cases selected from a private clientele, and which are granted the status of veritable paradigms: Puységur's Joly, Morton Prince's Sally Beauchamp, Freud's Dora, Binswanger's Ellen West, Lacan's Aimée (not to mention Freud's self-analysis and Jung's personal confrontation with the collective unconscious). It is therefore quite natural that the attention of historians of dynamic psychiatry should bear primarily on these paradigmatic patients and their history, given the epistemological role they have been made to play. On this point, as on so many others, Henri Ellenberger's work has shown the way. In an article published in 1961 and reprinted by Mark Micale in the anthology *Beyond the Unconscious*,[43] Ellenberger emphasized the decisive contribution made by certain particularly gifted patients in the constitution of modern psychodynamic theories, insisting on the fruitful and creative nature of their encounter with some doctor who was receptive to their mythopoetic creations – the encounter of Fredericke

Hauffe with Justinus Kerner, of Anna O. with Breuer, of Helene Preisswerk with Jung, of Hélène Smith with Flournoy, and so on. Such an approach could certainly draw on some isolated statements of psychoanalysts such as Ferenczi or Lacan on the role of Anna O. or Emmy von N. in the invention of psychoanalysis, but it is likely that Ellenberger was more profoundly inspired by the work of Joseph Delbœuf who, at the end of the last century, had already emphasized the role played by the patients in the development of the theories of various schools of hypnotism.[44]

Whatever the case, Ellenberger launched with great panache the program of a "patient-centered" history of psychiatry, to use Roy Porter's phrase.[45] This research program has since been implemented by Albrecht Hirschmüller, Peter J. Swales, Ernst Falzeder, Sonu Shamdasani, Patrick Mahony, and Jacques Maître in their works on the patients of Freud, Janet, and Jung.[46] The lessons we can draw from their research are already numerous. Thanks to them we now better perceive the ambiguity of the rapport between the psychiatrist or psychotherapist and some of his patients, the interlacing of emotional and theoretical interests, the dimension of manipulation on the part of the patient, and the often considerable gullibility of the doctor. We also better realize the chancy and arbitrary character of the main psychodynamic theories, as well as the huge gap, sometimes bordering on deceit, between the published case histories and the actual progress of the treatments. By the same token, we better discern the many illusions inherent in the clinical method as a whole.

However, once these indispensable lessons have been assimilated, we may muse about possible future developments of the micro-historical method and formulate a few methodological caveats.

First of all, if we pay too much attention to the role of the patient, we risk neglecting the interactive dimension of the doctor–patient relationship. Ellenberger, for example, readily attributed the invention of the various systems of dynamic psychiatry to what he called, after Frederick Myers and Théodore Flournoy, the patients' "mythopoeic unconscious."[47] This was a welcome corrective to the iatrocentrism that had dominated the history of psychiatry up till then; but it was also giving too much credit to the doubtful notion of the unconscious, forgetting that its famed "productions" (as Lacan used to put it) have always been particularly prone to effects of suggestion and influence. One need only read Flournoy's *From India to the Planet Mars*,[48] for example, to realize how much Hélène Smith's mediumistic creations conformed themselves to Flournoy's expectations as well as to those of the spiritist milieu in which she evolved.[49] The same may be said of the "individuation" of Jung's patients in the gestation period of analytical psychology, as Sonu Shamdasani has shown,[50] or of the memories of incest and sexual abuse elicited by Freud during the years 1896–97, which were clearly the product of a *folie à plusieurs*, of a "madness" shared between the analyst and his patients.[51] From this point of view, unilaterally emphasizing the role of the patients and their subjective experiences amounts to disregard for the no less active intervention of the theorist in the phenomenon that he claims to observe.

Likewise, giving too much weight to the great founding cases risks acceding to the illusion of origin, as if each patient initiated a particular concept or practice – Fräulein Osterlin, Mesmerian "magnetism"; Victor Race, "lucid sleep"; Anna O., the "talking cure"; Emmy von N., "free association"; and so forth. In fact, what at first seems to be a singular and novel event most often turns out to be embedded in interactions and series of a much larger amplitude. For example, prior to the symptoms and "talking cure" of Bertha Pappenheim, we find the performances of the Danish stage hypnotist Carl Hansen; the German magnetic treatments of the beginning of the nineteenth century; Moriz Benedikt's speculations on hypnotic hypermnesia; and perhaps also the medical interpretation of Aristotle's catharsis proposed by Jakob Bernays – all this relayed to Bertha Pappenheim by newspapers, books, casual conversations, and Breuer's expectations. Far from being the stunning creation of Bertha Pappenheim's unconscious, the "talking cure" was the repetition and imitation of other treatments, other symptoms, and other theories, before itself becoming a paradigm for other doctors and other patients.

Furthermore, the founding event most often appears as such only after the fact, once other patients and other doctors have taken it up. We have already noted how Anna O.'s disastrous "talking cure" did not acquire its paradigmatic status until after it was imitated by Freud and some of his patients, such as Fanny Moser ("Emmy von N.") and Anna von Lieben ("Cäcilie M."). One can also show how the notion of hysterical post-traumatic amnesia, set forth in a purely speculative fashion by Charcot to relate the hysterias due to traumatic shock to the hypnotic state, went unheeded as far as his own patients were concerned and was not "confirmed" until later, when his disciples Janet and Freud, using hypnotism, "discovered" in their own patients traumatic memories of which they were unaware when awake.[52] In this case, as in many others, it was only after complex repetitions, amplifications, and feedbacks that the notion of hysterical post-traumatic amnesia (and later, of repression) took shape and acquired substance, as if it always takes several patients and several doctors to create an event in psychiatry.

Micro-historical analysis cannot, therefore, be content with substituting a patient-centered history for an iatrocentric one. If it wants to follow the formation of psychiatric theories and syndromes, it must extend its analysis beyond the individual case, even beyond the singular relation between a patient and a doctor, and take into consideration series, cycles, and interactions of a larger amplitude, implying more than two protagonists. For example, to understand how the notion of a traumatic sexual event emerged and evolved in psychoanalysis, we must follow step by step how Freud's first patients, in direct reaction to Freud's changing theories, first produced memories of non-sexual traumatic events, *à la* Janet; then memories of sexual traumas; then scenes of incest and perverse molestations going back to infancy; and finally, with Freud's gradual disenchantment with the seduction theory, infantile and Oedipal fantasies. Thus, a very simple chronology and accounting shows how

Freud's patients (at least those who did not leave his office slamming the door) collectively accompanied and confirmed his theoretical speculations of the moment, giving him the illusion of discovering in them what in fact he had suggested to them.

Then, widening the field of investigation, one could compare the evolution of Freud's theories with their diffusion or non-diffusion among other doctors and other patients. One could study, for example, how the patients in treatment with his students Felix Gattel and Emma Eckstein tended to corroborate his results, whereas Leopold Löwenfeld's contradicted them; or again, how at the beginning of the century the young psychiatrists of the Burghölzli team continued to obtain from their hysterical or dementia praecox patients scenes of sexual trauma, whereas Freud himself had already silently abandoned his seduction theory several years earlier.[53] By gradually extending the micro-historical model centered on the patient–doctor interaction to larger populations, we would give ourselves the means of studying the fabrication, diffusion, and crystallization of psychiatric ideas and the new symptoms that accompany them.

It is no accident that this last example is taken, once again, from psychoanalysis, since it is presently the field where micro-historical analysis is most advanced (this is what some people stigmatize today as "Freud bashing").[54] But there is no reason why this systemic and interactional approach, heedful of the constant transactions between doctors and their patients, could not be applied to other domains in the history of psychiatry, be it the study of syndromes, diagnoses and taxonomies, the social and institutional practices of internment, or methods of psychiatric treatment. Such an approach could take inspiration, for example, from anthropological fieldwork such as that of Robert Barrett or Allan Young, showing how schizophrenic patients learn, during clinical interviews, to speak the doctor's language,[55] or again, how the techniques used in the USA to diagnose Post-Traumatic Stress Disorder contribute to the formation of that syndrome.[56] Historians would then describe diachronically interactions that medical anthropologists, for their part, tend to describe synchronically. In this way, historians of psychiatry would become, as it were, epidemiologists of the soul, tracking the origin of the various psychic "infections," isolating the main vectors of propagation, analyzing the exchanges between the psychiatric categories and their host environment, the mutations of the former and the immunological responses of the latter.

We see, of course, what they would gain from this: a greater methodological sophistication, an aptitude to think in terms of process and production rather than in terms of result, and finally, the courage to confront the performativity of their own work. It is perhaps not so easy to see at first what they risk losing: their belief in the very idea of mental *illness* – for one might well imagine that the latter, in the end, will partly evaporate before their eyes, like a vast mirage interposed between the psychiatrist and his madman.

Translated by DOUGLAS BRICK

Notes

1 Translated into English as *Madness and Civilization: A History of Insanity in the Age of Reason* (Foucault 1965).
2 Veith 1965.
3 Kleinman 1988a; Good 1994.
4 Hacking 1998.
5 Shorter 1992.
6 Foucault 1978; 2003; Plummer 1981; Hansen 1992; Rosario 1997.
7 Kleinman 1977.
8 Jackson 1986; Forthomme 1999.
9 Obeyesekere 1985.
10 Bynum 1987; see also Bell 1985.
11 Benedict 1934; Devereux 1956; Bastide 1972; Lévi-Strauss 1987; Kleinman 1988a; Ellenberger 1995, Nathan, Stengers and Andréa 2000; pp. 431–447.
12 Shorter 1997, pp. 61–64.
13 Hacking 1999, pp. 113–114.
14 Barrett 2000.
15 World Health Organization 1979; Sartorius *et al.* 1986.
16 Warner 1985.
17 Harding *et al.* 1987.
18 Kleinman 1986.
19 Lacan 1984; Borch-Jacobsen 1994a.
20 Heusch 1971; Borch-Jacobsen 1992, pp. 106 ff.
21 Dhorme 1959.
22 Micale 1993.
23 See below.
24 Hacking 1995.
25 Roudinesco 2001.
26 Ehrenberg 2000.
27 Healy 1998.
28 Bateson 1972.
29 Watzlawick 1967.
30 Hacking 1999.
31 Rosenthal 1966.
32 Orne 1962; on the "construction" of the experimental subject as such, see Danziger 1991.
33 Grivois 1992.
34 Grivois 1998, pp. 46–48.
35 Hacking 1998.
36 Ellenberger 1970.
37 See Hacking 1995, p. 45.
38 Stone 1989; Merskey 1991.
39 Shorter 1992.
40 Latour 1987.
41 Breuer and Freud 1895.
42 Borch-Jacobsen 1996.
43 "Psychiatry and its unknown history," Micale 1993b, pp. 239–253.
44 Delbœuf 1886; Carroy 1997a; see also Chapter 6 below.
45 Porter 1985.
46 Mahony 1984; 1986; 1996; Swales 1986a; 1986b; 1988; Hirschmüller 1989; 1993; Shamdasani 1990; Maître 1993; Falzeder 1994.
47 Ellenberger 1993, pp. 56–57.
48 Flournoy 1994.

49 Cifali 1988; Shamdasani 2001.
50 Shamdasani 1997.
51 See Chapter 2 below.
52 See Chapter 1 below.
53 See Borch-Jacobsen and Shamdasani 2006, pp. 90–91.
54 Hale 1999; Borch-Jacobsen, Esterson, Macmillan, and Swales 1999.
55 Barrett 1990.
56 Young 1995.

PART I

Microhistories of trauma

ences, it is clear that the idea of psychic trauma implies a causal judgment

1   How to predict the past: from trauma to repression

Can a physical shock inflict a wound to the mind? This is, as we tend to forget, what "trauma" originally meant: an injury, an open wound, a violent rupture in the surface of the skin. Still today, military surgeons deal with traumas due to bullet or canon fire, and trauma units welcome all comers from the battlefields of highway and workplace. Yet this is not generally what we mean when we say that someone has suffered a trauma. What we mean, rather, is that some violent or unexpected event wounded this person spiritually, psychically: he suffers from depression and fits of rage ever since that terrible slaughter in Vietnam (Post-Traumatic Stress Disorder); she suffers from insomnia and anorexia ever since she was raped (Rape Trauma Syndrome); their personality split into pieces because they were sexually abused by their father (Multiple Personality Disorder).

How then did we get from the idea of a physical wound to that of a psychic wound (or "moral trauma," as they said in the nineteenth century)? It is a long story, one that starts on the battlefields of the American Civil War and the sites of the first great train wrecks, continuing to Charcot and Janet's Salpê-trière, and ending (provisionally) in the Viennese office of Sigmund Freud. Esther Fisher-Homberger describes it as a slow process of psychologization and dissolution of the mechanical shock,[1] Laplanche and Pontalis as a process of metaphorization: "The notion of trauma is applied in a metaphorical way to the psychical level, thus qualifying every event that suddenly breaks into the psychic organization of the individual."[2] Nonetheless, we see what this metaphor retains from the original meaning: just as the bullet is the direct *cause* of the hemorrhage treated by the surgeon, so a violent emotion is supposedly the *cause* of the phobia or bulimia treated by the psychiatrist. Even if we do not give "cause" the same strict sense that it has in experimental sciences, it is clear that the idea of psychic trauma implies a causal judgment of the type: "given certain conditions x, certain events y tend to provoke certain psychological problems z." Besides, it is this very idea of direct causality that makes the notion of psychic trauma so attractive to therapists and patients alike: in an area where complexities and uncertainty abound, the traumatic etiology of the neuroses has the advantage of procuring the same kind of simple and robust explanation as medicine. What could be more intellectually satisfying than knowing that a discrete, datable event is responsible for my anxiety, just as Koch's bacillus is responsible for tuberculosis? *Before* the terrible incident, everything was fine. *After*, my life became a nightmare.

And yet, how can we be sure that this is not a pseudo-causality? After all, the symptoms might as well have been caused by a biochemical imbalance or some latent psychological conflict, the traumatic shock being nothing more than an "agent provocateur," as Charcot put it. In order to establish with some certainty the traumatic etiology of such and such a psychological symptom, we would need to have a control group, perfectly comparable from the biological, social, and psychological points of view, but not having suffered the so-called "traumatic" event.

Obviously such conditions are impossible to fulfill in the laboratory, but we have a good approximation in a case of "accident neurosis," published in 1980 by the Australian psychiatrist Neville Parker.[3] Parker's study is of huge interest in this regard, for it deals with the parallel destiny of two identical twins, "Vince" and "Ernest." Not only were they perfectly identical from the genetic point of view, but Vince and Ernest had astonishingly similar biographies. Raised in a Christian fundamentalist setting, they both quit school at the age of 13, got married and became farmers at the age of 21, prospered financially and had numerous children. Both of them were excused from military service as conscientious objectors at 19. They had never shown the slightest tendency toward violence (not even toward animals: their religion forbade it). Psychologically, Parker describes them as "obsessive" personalities. Both of them suffered from asthma. In 1961, Ernest had consulted Parker for vague psychosomatic symptoms. Parker gave him a placebo, and that was the end of his psychiatric history.

Vince's began on June 28, 1975, when he was involved in an accident with a drunk driver (Vince himself was in no way responsible for the accident). Vince was not seriously injured, but two of his sons were trapped in the truck that was threatening to catch fire, and he was seized by an intense panic. His state of anxiety lasted for several days, and he was placed in a psychiatric hospital with a diagnosis of "traumatic neurosis." Upon his return, six weeks later, his family noted a marked personality change, characterized by depressive states, nightmares, and an uncharacteristic irritability. Despite Vince's being treated by a generalist specializing in the treatment of stress and then by a psychiatrist, his condition worsened, to the point that his wife separated from him temporarily, taking the children with her.

On July 20, 1977, Vince had a second accident. In this case, too, he was in no way responsible: a 36 foot metal girder, being carried by a truck in front of him, suddenly came loose, literally skewering his vehicle and missing him by inches. His anxiety having returned, more intense than ever, he was rehospitalized for two months in a private psychiatric clinic, and then again in December 1977 and June 1978 for relatively shorter periods of time. Each time, the diagnosis of the psychiatrists was the same: "traumatic neurosis." Meanwhile, Vince was taking tranquilizers and going to group therapy. On the evening of September 29, 1978, after a last quarrel with his wife, he strangled her, slit the throat of his 16-year-old daughter with a large bread knife, and then tried unsuccessfully to kill himself by driving his car into a lake (the water was not deep enough). During this whole time, his twin brother Ernest continued to lead the same untroubled life as before. Parker's conclusion:

> When the twins' background details are summarized . . . it seems reasonable to conclude that Vince would to-day be the same well controlled personality as his co-twin Ernest, but for the two life-threatening accidents . . . This unique example illustrates how . . . a neurosis [can] develop without the brain being damaged, and without any compensation motive (this was never considered in either accident).[4]

Note that Parker says that Vince's case "illustrates" the traumatic etiology of certain neuroses, not that it proves it. This prudence is welcome, for no matter how impressive this case might be, it proves, at best, a *correlation* between the two accidents and the neurosis, not a necessary relation of cause and effect. Every day, countless people come away from car accidents without developing psychological disorders like Vince's. Therefore, we can say with confidence that events of the type "car accident" are not, in the language of philosophers, a *sufficient* cause of neurotic symptoms of this type. Conversely, many people suffer from depression, sleep disorders, and irritability without ever having been involved in a car accident or any other similar incident, so events of that type cannot be considered as a *necessary* cause of such psychological problems. We must conclude that Vince's case cannot, in all rigor, be generalized as a law, "if *x*, then *y*."

Nonetheless, I doubt that this logical rigor will be sufficient to convince clinicians who are confronted daily with cases similar to Vince's. As Parker writes: "Among the most recent 1,000 consecutive cases of accident litigants with neurotic symptoms personally evaluated, 431 complained of difficulty in controlling the anger which developed shortly after the accident."[5] So let's grant the clinicians that traumatic events are *very often* followed by depression or irritability. Indeed, let's even suppose, ignoring for a moment what we just said, that this is *always* the case in our societies. Would such a statistic be sufficient to establish a relationship of cause and effect between those events and those symptoms? No, because those same symptoms are provoked, in other cultures, by very different "causes." An evil spell, a bewitchment, a breach in ritual can initiate states of prostration no less serious than those noted in our society in the victims of bombing or sexual abuse,[6] and in fact some of these beliefs strangely recall our own psychiatric etiologies.

Here, for example, is the description of an illness that the Quechua Indians of Peru call *Susto* ("fear" in Spanish). I quote the summary given by Henri Ellenberger of a study made by Federico Sal y Rosas:

> The Quechua Indians believe that the soul (or perhaps part of it) can leave the body, either spontaneously or through being forced. The *Susto* disease can

occur in two ways: either through fright caused, for instance, by thunder, the sight of a bull, a snake, and so on, or because of malevolent influences, not following upon fright (the latter being called "*Susto* without *Susto*")...The Quechuas show a great fear of certain slopes and caves, and especially of old Incan ruins...How can the disease be designated as *Susto* when it is not preceded by fright? It may be diagnosed as such when an individual loses weight and energy and becomes irritable, has disturbed sleep and nightmares, and especially when he falls into a state of physical and mental depression called *Michko*.[7]

This is almost the description of the effects of Post-Traumatic Stress Disorder (PTSD) in the DSM-III, except that we are dealing here with a PTSD *without* trauma, a "*Susto* without *Susto*." As to the causes alleged by the Quechua Indians for genuine *Susto*, they are not the same: in lieu of accidents, earthquakes, terrorist attacks, or torture, we find snakes, bulls, thunder, and Inca ruins. Of course, one might say that this difference of etiology is negligible, the important thing being the fright provoked by all these evil encounters: *we* know full well that Inca ruins are not at all traumatic (American tourists do not usually suffer from PTSD after visiting Machu Picchu), but the Quechua Indians, for their part, would be terrified if one were to drag them there. But the argument is reversible, for it is not just any fright that provokes the symptoms of *Susto*. A Quechua Indian is not going to become ill with *Susto* after escaping from a terrorist (and thus terrorizing) attack perpetrated by the Shining Path, for such an event is not part of the list of events-likely-to-provoke-*Susto*.[8] Imagine, on the other hand, that a bus full of American tourists were seized by the Peruvian Maoists: there is a very strong possibility that some of the survivors would then develop symptoms characteristic of PTSD. In other words, a given event will have traumatic effects only because one considers it capable of causing effects of that type.

This example illustrates the difficulty of applying a mechanical category like causality to human behavior in general, and to psychological disorders (or "maladies of the soul") in particular. My purpose here is not to defend Human Freedom against the assaults of Determinism, but simply to recall that human affairs are subject to all kinds of interactions and feedbacks that go far beyond the simple relation of linear causality. Above 100 degrees Celsius, water always reacts in the same way: it starts to boil. But the reactions of humans to events that happen to them are much less predictable, if only because they usually have all sorts of expectations about the effects these events will have, and those expectations affect in turn the way they react. To return to our example, an American tourist and a Quechua Indian will not react in the same way to a visit to Machu Picchu. Whereas the first will become ecstatic and take pictures, the second will most likely fall into a state of depression. Why? *Because he and his entourage expect that such an event will cause depression.* In other words, his depression is caused not by the so-called "traumatic" event, but by the theory professed by the Quechua on the effects caused by such an event. Indeed, that theory will not only influence his way of reacting to the event (he will be afraid, he will dread falling ill), it will also dictate the behavior of his entourage toward him (they will commiserate with him and advise him to see a healer, a *cur-andera*). Even if we suppose that his own apprehensions would not be sufficient to provoke the dreaded symptoms, the attitude of his entourage will soon lock him into a circle: the more he claims *not* to be irritable and depressed, the more his protests will be interpreted as confirmations of the diagnosis (as manifest-ations of bad temper), the more the gap will widen between him and his entourage, and the more he will, by that very fact, become irritable and depressed.

Isn't that exactly what happened in Vince's case? There was no predis-position for Vince to become a murderer before his fateful accident. Never-theless, that unpredictable and senseless event was immediately deciphered by his entourage – and thus by him – in terms of a theory about the *predictable* psychological effects of accidents of that type. His panic (quite justifiable at first) brought on a diagnosis of traumatic neurosis, which made him adopt the behavior expected in such cases, which in turn, provoked, on the part of his entourage, reactions of rejection that reinforced his behavior, and so on, to the final escalation.

Vince was out of luck. When his brother Ernest had been anxious, Parker had wisely given him a placebo. Vince, on the other hand, was the victim of a *nocebo* diagnosis that only added to his anxiety: "He saw several general practitioners, hospital doctors, neurologists, other specialist physicians and psychiatrists, but all gave the same opinion: he was suffering from a severe neurotic illness triggered off by the accident."[9] Obviously, we may punctuate that sequence differently and think that it was the specialists' *diagnosis* that triggered Vince's neurosis. Would he have sunk into depression if that symptom had not been predicted – and thus *produced* – by their theory? Just like the Indian theory of *Susto*, the theory of traumatic neurosis acted as a self-fulfilling prophecy. A modern-day Oedipus, Vince most certainly would not have killed his wife and daughter if his path had not crossed that of a drunken driver. But that event would not have had such tragic consequences if our modern psychiatric mythology had not transformed the stupid accident into destiny.

Here we have a good example of the way the theories we elaborate on the subject of human behavior affect us in turn. Those theories are not separate from the "human reality" they claim to describe. On the contrary, they are an integral part of it, and thus they influence it, which explains why these theories (even the most ludicrous) are so often self-confirming. Indeed, those to whom they apply are not at all indifferent to them: either they reject those theories right from the start; or they accept them and tend to conform to them, thus lending them a credibility that will steadily increase to the point where they become the object of a general social consensus (or collapse under the weight of their own implausibility).

The history of psychiatry abounds in looping effects of this type, just as might be expected from a discipline that deals with a reality as imponderable as illnesses of the "soul" or "psyche": diagnostic fashions, psychic epidemics, effects of suggestion, the rise and fall of clinical entities. This lability of illnesses is a clear indication that they are not independent of the theories of which they are the object. In fact, psychiatric theories are never simply external to the psychopathology that they are concerned with. Quite the contrary, they constantly interact with them: the physicians' expectations influence the patients' behavior, and the latter in turn influences the theories that are formed about it. For the most part, the history of psychiatry is nothing other than the history of these interactions and complex negotiations from which emerge in a more or less random fashion new syndromes, new "realities" shared by the patients, the physicians, and the society that surrounds them.

Take the notion of "psychic trauma." On June 28, 1975, when Vince had his first accident, that notion had long since acquired its title of "reality" (in quotation marks), and by that very fact its impact on Vince's life was all the more real (without quotation marks). But how, precisely, had the idea of psychic trauma become a reality? As I indicated above, it is a long story, too long for me to retrace here. I will therefore confine myself to a single chapter, but one that is particularly illustrative of the looping and amplification effects that I have just mentioned: the chapter stretching from Charcot's postulation of "traumatic hysteria" to the beginning of psychoanalysis.[10]

Charcot's 1885 experiments in the artificial production of post-traumatic hysterical paralyses under hypnosis have often been described as the inaugural moment of the discovery of the role played by psychic traumas in the formation of neurotic symptoms. This is only very partially true. In reality, Charcot's theory of "traumatic hysteria" (or "hystero-traumatism") is preceded, historically, by all sorts of implicit or explicit theories on the role of violent emotions in the triggering of psychological or psychosomatic disorders. In a way, the idea that one can become insane or ill because of a violent shock, sorrow, or remorse plunges into the night of time and one could find countless illustrations of it in universal literature.[11] But even without emphasizing these ageless beliefs, we can note more precisely with the historian Edward Shorter that paralyses, contractures, and motor symptoms – by far the most common psychosomatic illnesses in the nineteenth century – were frequently triggered by "shocks" of all sorts, both psychical and physical. Shorter thus cites pre-Charcotian cases of paralysis provoked by the announcement of bad news, by a violent emotion (seeing one's mother decapitated by a canon ball), by falling on the floor, by a surgical operation.[12] Paralysis could also be provoked by a work-related accident, that etiology being particularly widespread among men (this was the manly way to become hysterical).[13] Other beliefs, relayed this time by explicitly medical theories, concerned paralyses and other symptoms without apparent organic foundation (fatigue, nightmares, anxiety, etc.) observed in certain victims of railway accidents. In 1866, John Erichsen stated that these symptoms were due to microscopic spinal lesions ("railway spine") provoked by the intensity of the mechanical shock.[14] Herbert Page and other Anglo-Saxon authors,[15] continuing the work of Benjamin Brodie, Sir Russell Reynolds, and Sir James Paget on paralyses "by idea,"[16] proposed on the contrary that these symptoms were the result of a purely functional lesion of the nervous system ("railway brain," "nervous shock") due to the intense *fright* caused by the accident: "The incidents of every railway collision are quite sufficient – even if no bodily injury is inflicted – to produce a very serious effect upon the mind, and to be the means of bringing about a state of collapse from fright and fright only."[17]

Charcot was therefore not the first, nor the only one, to insist on the potentially neurogenic effect of certain psychic shocks. That idea was already in the air, as much with the theorists of hysteria as, in a more diffuse fashion, with the patients themselves. If Charcot's experiments with the artificial production of hysterical paralyses are nonetheless historically important, it is because they launched on the market of psychosomatic symptoms a completely new expectation, that of post-traumatic *amnesia*. Before Charcot's experiments, the patients remembered quite clearly the psychic or mechanical shock that had triggered their hysterical paralyses and attacks. After, they would tend not to know the cause of their symptoms any longer:[18] the era of "dissociation of consciousness" and of "repression" had begun. That expectation, so important to the evolution of modern psychotherapy, was not originally part of the definition of trauma, and, in fact, it has since had its ups and downs. Note for example that, in mid-1970s Australia, Vince and his doctors did not share it. Of course, one might think it was simply because they were not aware of the abundant North American literature on Post-Traumatic Stress Disorder and Multiple Personality Disorder that was, at about that time, making a remarkable return to the theory proposed by Charcot and his immediate successors.

Charcot exposed this theory for the first time in a series of five lessons given from March to May of 1885, devoted to seven cases of male hysteria.[19] He returned to the subject the following year, in relation to an eighth case (patient Joseph Le Logeais),[20] studied from March to November 1886.[21] However, for reasons that will soon become evident, I will limit myself to the seven initial cases, especially cases 6 and 7, Pinaud and Porczenska, on which Charcot first tested his theory.

Charcot's initial objective in these lessons was to establish the reality of male hysteria by comparing a sample of hysterical men with the clinical picture of female "grand hysteria," which Charcot had patiently constructed during the 1870s. For Charcot, hysteria was a neurological disorder due to a "functional" or "dynamic" lesion of the nervous system and, as such, not specific to the female sex (or the uterus).[22] As Charcot mentioned in his introduction, this was also the implication of the recent work by Page, Putnam, and Walton on so-called "railway spine": the victims of this strange disease were affected by "hysteria, nothing but hysteria,"[23] but they were men as well as women. Nonetheless, the sample that Charcot had at his disposal contained no cases of railway spine in the strict sense.[24] These men had developed their symptoms in a more classical fashion, following work accidents or violent emotions. One was almost crushed by a large barrel of wine (case 1), others had been more or less violently assaulted (cases 2, 4, and 5),[25] and others had taken a fall (cases 3, 6, and 7). As to their initial symptoms, they, too, were all typical of "popular" hysteria, as much male as female: some had suffered attacks (cases 1, 2, 3, 4, and 5), the others, paralyses (cases 6 and 7).

It should be noted that none of them initially presented the spectacular symptoms of female "grand hysteria" observed by Charcot at the Salpêtrière. Nevertheless, as soon as they had been admitted to the hospital, they were submitted to intensive tests, and Charcot could report to his satisfaction that this had led to the discovery of hemianesthesias, hysterogenic zones, and diminutions of the field of vision in all respects identical to those noted in cases of female hysteria. Similarly, the attacks, "not . . . clearly characterized" at the beginning,[26] quickly came to take the same form as the hystero-epileptic "grand attack" then being observed by Charcot among his female patients, with its four successive, well-defined phases (epileptoid phase, phase of "large movements," phase of "passionate attitudes," terminal phase). In some instances the number of attacks had increased spectacularly, as with case 5, who had no less than five the very day he was admitted, whereas till then he had had only one. Four days after his admission to the Salpêtrière, the patient Pinaud, who had previously spent nine months in another hospital, developed his very first attack: "On insisting a little more . . . we witnessed *the first attack of hystero-epilepsy* which the patient ever experienced. This attack was absolutely classic."[27]

For Charcot, all these symptoms were part of the clinical picture of hysteria (male and female) and there was no doubt in his mind that they existed in a "latent" state before their detection.[28] Nevertheless, there is every reason to believe that it was the systematic research on them by Charcot's assistants that created them, by indicating to the patients what was expected of them. Without even making a case of the "downright coaching" (*véritable dressage*)[29] of the patients later evoked by some of Charcot's former assistants, it is clear that his expectations, reinforced by the institutional ambiance, were quite sufficient to produce what the tests were supposed to discover. From this point of view, the fact that the men's ward (the *Service des hommes*) was separated from the women's cannot be invoked, as Charcot did, to exclude "the influence of contagious imitation."[30] As Bernheim and Delbœuf soon remarked,[31] it was Charcot's own theories that contaminated the patients, both male and female.

Nevertheless, this cannot hold for the various "traumatic" events that triggered the hysteria of the seven men. Obviously, Charcot could in no way be held responsible for these events, and his patients had no need of him to know that events of this type could provoke – or better yet, *authorized* – attacks and paralyses. This knowledge, in other words, predated Charcot's theories. It should also be noted that this knowledge was fully conscious: all seven patients remembered the triggering incident and attributed their symptoms to it. How, then, did Charcot come to propose the – unheard of – idea of a hysterical post-traumatic amnesia?

We recall that Charcot and his assistants had succeeded in provoking in Pinaud (case 6) his very first hystero-epileptic "grand attack" by pressing insistently on one of the hysterogenic zones they had detected. Pinaud developed other attacks (these ones "spontaneous")[32] in the following days, and he took this opportunity to regain the use of the left arm, which had previously been paralyzed. This unexpected cure disappointed Charcot somewhat, for it deprived him of a good subject of experimentation: "The idea, therefore, occurred to me that, perhaps by acting on the mind of the patient, by *means of suggestion*, even in the waking state – we had learned previously that the subject was not hypnotizable – we might reproduce the paralysis."[33]

Charcot hastened to add that there was nothing to fear from such a production of symptoms by verbal suggestion, "for I know from long experience, that *what one has done, one can undo*."[34] The experiment was indeed crowned with success, however shortlived.[35] Charcot had succeeded in *artificially* reproducing, by simple verbal suggestion, a paralysis that had previously appeared "*spontaneously*" following an accident (Pinaud had fallen from a scaffolding six feet high).

From there to the idea that the mechanism of "spontaneous" post-traumatic paralysis was the same as that of the artificial paralysis was only a small step. Two lessons further on, after studying the case of Porczenska, who had developed a post-traumatic paralysis of the arm similar to that of Pinaud, Charcot set out to hypnotize the female patient Greuzard and produce in her a paralysis identical in all points to that of the two men, first by verbal suggestion, and then by *indirect* suggestion, by giving her a slight tap on the shoulder. Charcot's provisional conclusion: in the hypnotic state, a simple sensation (of numbness, for example) can "suggest" an anesthesia or paralysis, even without the intervention of a hypnotist (by mere "autosuggestion," as he was to put it a year later).[36] And here comes the speculative hypothesis:

> In this respect it may be inquired whether the mental condition occasioned by the emotion, by the Nervous Shock experienced at the moment of the accident . . . is not the equivalent in a certain measure, in subjects predisposed as Porcz– and Pin– were, to the cerebral condition which is determined in "hysterics" by hypnotism.[37]

In both cases, argues Charcot, there is a veritable "annihilation of the ego,"[38] a "dissociation [of the mental unity] of the ego."[39] The sensation or "traumatic suggestion"[40] then takes advantage of this to install itself in the psyche as a "foreign body"[41] or a "fixed idea"[42] separated from the other groups of associations, and to realize itself according to the reflex automatism proper to the "unconscious or sub-conscious cerebration":[43] "That idea, once installed in the brain, takes sole possession and acquires sufficient domination to realize itself objectively in the form of a paralysis."[44] In other words: hysterical symptoms are due to a traumatic "shock" that provokes a dissociation of consciousness and the memory of which remains, by that very fact, unconscious or subconscious. Here, already, we have all the elements of the new traumatico-dissociative theory of neuroses that was to be taken up and developed by Janet, Breuer, and Freud, and, closer to us, by present-day advocates of Recovered Memory Therapy.[45]

It is a fascinating and, indeed, *suggestive* theory. But is it valid? With the benefit of hindsight, we can see all too well its many grave flaws, methodological as well as clinical. It is clear, for example, that Charcot's hypnotic experiments did not prove anything at all, given the seemingly limitless compliance of his subjects. Charcot's success in artificially reproducing paralyses that originally appeared spontaneously after a trauma proves only that his patients bent themselves to his suggestions, not that the spontaneous paralyses were due to a "dissociation of the ego" identical to that provoked under hypnosis. Supposing (a hardly fantastic hypothesis) that Charcot had a theory that attributed post-traumatic hysterical paralyses to the hidden influence of magnets, he could most certainly have artificially reproduced those paralyses by applying magnets to his patients.[46] Would this have proved that the spontaneous post-traumatic paralyses were *caused by magnets*?

Besides, Charcot's theory was flagrantly contradicted by the clinical material it was supposed to explain. Out of the seven cases analyzed by Charcot, five did not develop paralyses, but attacks (cases 1, 2, 3, 4, and 5). But nowhere does Charcot give us the slightest indication of the "traumatic suggestion" that would have been operative in those cases. Additionally, the new theory had it that a traumatic event provokes, at least in "predisposed" persons, a state of dissociation or hypnoid trance, accompanied by an "annihilation of the ego." Now, if we examine the sample of Charcot's male hysterics, we find that for five of them (cases 1, 2, 3, 4, and 6) the traumatic incident had provoked a more or less prolonged loss of consciousness – that is, according to Charcot's ad hoc and highly speculative interpretation, "the condition of psychical obnubilation suitable for the efficacy of suggestions."[47] Two of them, on the other hand, had not had the least loss of consciousness, especially Porczenska. He had fallen from the cab he was driving and, as Charcot himself writes, "there was *no loss of consciousness, no intense emotion*. Porcz– was able to regain his feet, go to the chemist's, and mount the box."[48]

This absence of a hypnoid state is all the more remarkable in that Porczenska, with Pinaud, was one of the *two* cases of post-traumatic paralysis with which Charcot had illustrated his theory. Which means that, unless I have miscalculated, Pinaud was the *only* case that fitted the new theory! It is easy to see why Charcot felt constrained to add an embarrassed footnote to align the case of Porczenska with that of Pinaud:

> So far as concerns the sensations produced by the shock, our two male patients are unable to enlighten us. The one, Pin–, in falling instantly lost consciousness; the other, Porcz–, asserts that he was conscious. Neither the one nor the other knows exactly how the affected member felt at the moment of the accident, nor for some days afterwards. *We know that on being awakened, no matter how slight the hypnotism may have been, hypnotized subjects retain no consciousness of what took place during that state.*[49]

Ergo, Porczenska really was hypnotized, despite all appearances to the contrary.

The argument is hardly convincing: not remembering physical sensations felt during an accident can hardly pass as proof of amnesia, even less as a case of post-hypnotic amnesia (if that were the case, we would all be in a perpetual state of hypnosis, since we do not consciously notice most of the sensations that constantly assail us). Charcot's footnote is obviously an ad hoc argument designed to compensate for the absence of a hypnoid state in Porczenska, for there was in fact no other justification for his introduction of the theme of post-traumatic amnesia. Neither Porczenska nor Pinaud nor *any* of the patients in Charcot's sample suffered from amnesia regarding the events that triggered their hysteria (apart, of course, from those that occurred during their eventual loss of consciousness).

It is therefore all the more remarkable to note the speed with which that ad hoc hypothesis crystallized into a dogma, thus creating a new expectation shared by the doctors and their patients. Less than a year after the experiments conducted on Pinaud and Porczenska, Charcot acquired a third case of post-traumatic hysterical paralysis at the Salpêtrière, Le Logeais. This patient had lost consciousness for six days after being hit by a van "driven ... at railway speed"[50] and had no remembrance of the exact circumstances of the accident (he had elaborated instead a "false memory" that was supposed to explain the hysterical paraplegia that he had developed at the hospital). Charcot recognized that this amnesia was probably due to the "intense cerebral commotion"[51] suffered by Le Logeais, but he did not let that stop him from comparing the patient's comatose state to hypnosis and seeing it as a new confirmation of his theory.[52]

Two years later, Charcot presented his auditors with a case of hystero-neurasthenia sustained following a train wreck by a railway employee. The subject had immediately lost consciousness at the moment of the accident and therefore no longer remembered very well what had happened. Charcot took this opportunity "to emphasize this amnesia relative to the circumstances of the accident. *This is almost always the rule* in grand nervous shocks."[53] Is it? A quick review of the cases of traumatic hysteria or neurasthenia that Charcot had presented up till then during his Tuesday Lectures reveals that even if some of them lost consciousness at the moment of the shock, not one presented a true amnesia of the accident (obviously, the patients did not keep abreast of the latest developments of science).[54] Once again, therefore, Charcot unduly generalized his theory to the detriment of his clinical material. After telling the story of a woman who had been knocked down by his coach and who, under the shock, had responded incoherently to his questions, Charcot continued:

> This will show you, my good sirs, that *you should never believe without reservations the stories that your patients volunteer* when you question them on the circumstances of the accident of which they were victims. In general, they know of them only by having heard the story narrated by onlookers, and I will add that often there is a sort of legend created in their mind concerning the incident, to which they readily give the most absolute credence and which they become used to telling naively, sincerely, as if it represented reality.[55]

We witness here the birth of a true psychiatric myth, fated to a grand future: *the patient is entirely ignorant of the trauma that caused his symptoms.* We must therefore distrust his memory, force it in order to recover the subconscious "fixed idea" (Janet), the unconscious "reminiscence" (Breuer and Freud). How so? Thanks to the use of hypnosis or some other related technique (automatic writing or speech, wakeful dreaming, crystal gazing,[56] later "free association"). Indeed, Charcot taught that it was possible, under hypnosis, to desuggest the "traumatic suggestion" in the same way that one could "deparalyze"[57] an artificial paralysis, and some of his followers did not take long to exploit these indications for therapeutic ends, hypnotizing their patients in order to find and desuggest their *forgotten* traumatic memories. As Janet later wrote, summarizing his research of the time:

> I soon became convinced that many of the most important traumatic memories might be imperfectly known by the subject, who was unable to give a clear account of the matter even when he tried to do so. It was necessary, therefore, to institute a search for hidden memories which the patient preserved in his mind without being aware of them.[58]

In other words, there can be traumatic neuroses without manifest trauma. Here we are in precisely the situation of the Peruvian "*Susto* without *Susto*": any symptom could henceforth be attributed to a hidden trauma. The boundless extension of the model of Charcot's "traumatic hysteria" to the whole of psychopathology had begun.[59]

Indeed, we learn without surprise that the patients, under hypnosis, strove to recall all sorts of traumas of which they had no knowledge during their waking life. In his 1889 philosophical dissertation, Janet had already described two cases of this type, "Lucie" and "Marie." The first suffered from attacks of fright without apparent reason, and Janet was able, thanks to automatic writing, to find the memory of an episode from her childhood in which she had been frightened by two men hidden behind a curtain: "This is because the unconscious (*l'inconscient*) has its dream: it sees the men behind the curtain and puts the body into an attitude of terror."[60] As for "Marie," she was cured of her symptoms after Janet recovered and desuggested, under hypnosis, various traumatic memories from her childhood.[61]

The same scene was reproduced shortly thereafter in Vienna, where Sigmund Freud had in all likelihood just read Janet's thesis.[62] Having decided during the year 1889 to apply Janet's method (which he preferred to call "the Breuer method")[63] to two of his patients, he obtained from them a veritable avalanche of forgotten traumatic memories. In the space of nine days, May 8–17, 1889, "Emmy von N." (Fanny Moser) reported nearly forty, ranging from the dramatic (witnessing the sudden death of her husband) to the downright trivial (being frightened by a toad). Similarly, "Cäcilie M." (Anna von Lieben) suddenly recovered for the first time an "old memory" (although she had been in treatment with Freud for more than a year):[64]

> For nearly three years after this she once again lived through all the traumas of her life – long-forgotten, as they seemed to her and, some, indeed, never remembered at all – accompanied by the acutest suffering and by the return of all the symptoms she ever had.[65]

There are manifestly two ways to interpret this sudden deluge of traumatic memories. One might – and this is the first, most common way of looking at this – see it as a striking *confirmation* of Charcot's theory of traumatic hysteria: the forgotten memories of "Lucie" and the others were there, in their "subconscious" or "unconscious," waiting to be discovered by Janet and Freud. But one might also think, conversely, that these astonishing reminiscences were the *effect* of the theory advanced by Charcot: the more his followers searched for forgotten traumatic memories, the more they found. This does not necessarily mean that these memories were suggested by the therapist, or invented by the patients. Some of them were, obviously,[66] but others were real enough (like the death of the husband of Fanny Moser–"Emmy von N.," for example). What matters here is that the patients would not have mentioned these memories if their therapists had not requested it. Even if they were real, these memories were dictated by the theory, preselected by it from the vast domain of "reality." Who has not at one time in his life felt terror or a strong emotion? It is only because Janet or Freud had a theory concerning the neurogenic character of shocks and violent emotions that these events were actively sought out and retroactively elevated to the grand status of traumas, of "etiologies."

Similarly, the patients would not have remembered *forgotten* traumatic events if their therapists had not had a theory insisting that they lift a pathogenic amnesia. Charcot's first patients, in conformity with the popular theory of the time, attributed their symptoms to an accident of which they retained a very vivid memory. Janet and Freud's patients quickly learned that what was expected of them was forgotten traumas. In that regard, we do not even need to assume that they were feigning or simulating their amnesia, all the better to remove it for the therapist's benefit, even though that obviously occurred in many cases.[67] The therapists' expectations, their leading questions, their hypnotic rituals were quite sufficient to persuade their patients to search always further in their memory for the cause of their illness. Far from being spontaneous phenomena discovered by the therapists, these amnesias, these "forgettings," these "repressions" were created, *produced* by the feverish quest for unconscious memories. Charcot's theory had introduced new expectations, which in turn created new symptomatic behaviors, new therapeutic rituals, new ways of interpreting reality.

The rest is history: the birth of psychoanalysis and the "whole climate of opinion" celebrated by Auden. What began as mere speculation by Charcot in a footnote became, from doctor to patient and patient to doctor, an irresistible, self-propagating machine and a powerful cultural myth. That is to say, a new reality. That is to say, for many, a destiny.

Translated by DOUGLAS BRICK

Notes

1 Fischer-Homberger 1975. On the history of the concept of traumatic neurosis, see also Schivelbusch 1979, chs. 7 to 9; Micale 1994; Hacking 1995; Young 1995; Antze and Lambek 1996; Micale and Lerner 2001.

2 Laplanche and Pontalis 1971, p. 286.

3 Parker 1980.

4 Parker 1980, p. 408.

5 Parker 1980, p. 408.

6 On this subject, see W. B. Cannon's classic article, "'Voodoo' death" (Cannon 1942); Jeanne Favret-Saada cites similar examples in her book on sorcery in present-day French rural Mayenne (Favret-Saada 1980).

7 Ellenberger 1970, p. 8. Ellenberger summarizes Sal y Rosas 1957. On the *Susto* illness in South America, see Gillin 1948. *Susto* is compared to Post-Traumatic Stress Disorder in Kenny 1995, pp. 450–452.

8 At least, it was not in 1957, when Sal y Rosas published his study. I do not exclude the possibility that such terrorist attacks have now been integrated in the Quechua etiology under the combined influence of the Shining Path and North-American-inspired psychiatry. These types of etiology change constantly, which is precisely what I want to emphasize.

9 Parker 1980, p. 407.

10 Marcel Gauchet's excellent study, "Les chemins imprévus de l'inconscient" (in Gauchet and Swain 1997), covers in great detail the same episode.

11 Gladys Swain, in her essay "De la marque de l'événement à la rencontre intérieure" (Swain 1994), cites Balzac's short story *Adieu* and Eugène Sue's *Les mystères de Paris*, but one could obviously find many other examples before the nineteenth century.

12 Shorter 1992, p. 112–115.

13 Shorter 1986, p. 567.

14 Erichsen 1866.

15 Page 1883; Putnam 1883; Walton (1883; 1884).

16 Reynolds 1869; Brodie 1873; Paget 1873. Charcot frequently cites Brodie's "admirable little book" (Charcot 1878, p. 335), which was published in French by *Progrès Médical* in 1880.

17 Page 1883, p. 147.

18 I do not exclude that there had been, before Charcot, cases of amnesia or memory disorders following psychic shocks. Hacking (1995, pp. 188–189) cites four cases of this type, dating from the Franco-Prussian war of 1870, reported by Lunier 1874. However,

even without going into the difficulty of making retrospective diagnoses of this type, it should be noted that these were only four out of the 386 cases of people suffering from "commotion" listed by Lunier. Hacking cites them from the 1885 medical dissertation of a certain A.-M.-P. Rouillard, who saw them as examples of amnesia caused by a "moral trauma" (Rouillard 1885, p. 87). Now, 1885 is precisely the year when Charcot began to propose his theses on post-traumatic hysteria. Could it be that the dissertation candidate redescribed Lunier's cases in terms of the new theory?

19 Lessons 18 to 22 in Charcot (1991 [1887]), pp. 220–316. This third volume of the *Clinical Lectures on Diseases of the Nervous System* appeared in December 1886. Lessons 18, 19, and 21 were prepublished in *Progrès Médical*, for May 2, 1885, August 8, 1885, and September 12, 1885.

20 Following Marcel Gauchet, I restore here the patients' names, which are usually abbreviated for confidentiality in Charcot's *Lectures*.

21 The case is the object of Appendix 1 in Charcot 1991, pp. 374–389. This appendix was not included in Freud's German translation, which appeared five months before the French edition of the *Lectures* (noted by Chertok and Saussure 1973, p. 98 n. 2).

22 On this question, see Micale 1990.

23 Charcot 1991, p. 221.

24 Charcot had several cases of "railway injuries" (*accidentés du chemin de fer*) later on (Charcot 1888; 1890, pp. 131–139 and 527–535).

25 Case 5 had been affected by shaking after somebody had thrown a stone in his direction.

26 Charcot 1991, p. 238 (in relation to case 3).

27 Charcot 1991, p. 257; Charcot's emphasis.

28 Thus, in relation to Pinaud's attacks: "The disease has since become, as it were complete, for at the present time, the attacks do exist. But during a long period of eleven months it was a latent case" (Charcot 1991, p. 251).

29 Marie 1925, p. 691 (quoted by Shorter 1992, p. 182). See as well what Janet wrote regarding the diagnosis of hysterical paralyses of the hand, as it was practiced at the Salpêtrière: "How could it be that, in a ward where that is spoken of all day, with patients who live in that ward for years, those patients do not know that the three positions of the hand are determined by such and such a nerve? They could find it out as well as the students of the ward, and very easily" (Janet 1929a, p. 467).

30 Charcot 1991, p. 243.

31 Delbœuf 1886; Bernheim 1891.

32 Charcot 1991, p. 258: "During the following days the attacks recurred *spontaneously* many times, always presenting the same character as the *provoked* attack"; emphasis added. Note Charcot's constant use of the formula "spontaneous or provoked" to categorize the attacks in his patients (1991, pp. 230, 234, 239, 246).

33 Charcot 1991, p. 258.

34 Charcot 1991, p. 259. This paradoxical law of hypnosis, which justified the most extravagant experiments at the Salpêtrière, had its origin in Victor Burq's "metalloscopic" research and Charcot's observation that one could just as easily *create* a hysterical anesthesia as suppress it, by the application of metallic plates on the zone concerned. On this point, see Harrington 1988, pp. 229–230. On the use of hypnosis at the Salpêtrière, see Barrucand 1967; Gauchet and Swain 1997.

35 Charcot 1991, p. 259: "Unfortunately this did not persist for more than twenty-four hours. The following day a new attack supervened, in consequence of which the voluntary movements became definitely re-established." Pinaud was removed from the hospital for insubordination in January of 1886.

36 Charcot 1991, p. 384.

37 Charcot 1991, p. 305.

38 Charcot 1991, p. 305.

39 Charcot 1991, pp. 383, 387 n. 1. This "dissociation" is what Janet, a few years later, was to call "psychological disaggregation" (Janet 1989, pp. 294–302). Janet later readopted

the term "dissociation," notably in his lectures given in English at Harvard in 1907 (Janet 1929b, pp. 331–332; see also Janet 1904). It is ironic to note that the term "dissociation," now unanimously attributed to Janet by the leading (English-speaking) theorists of "recovered memory therapy" and of "dissociative disorders" (Hart and Horst 1989; Putnam 1989b), is actually Charcot's (who himself inherited it from Taine and Ribot, as Malcolm Macmillan has pointed out to me; see for instance Ribot 1884, p. 79).

40 Charcot 1991, p. 307.

41 Charcot 1892, p. 98. This term appears again (but without quotation marks) in Josef Breuer and Sigmund Freud's 1893 "Preliminary Communication": "We must presume rather that the psychical trauma – or more precisely the memory of the trauma – acts like a foreign body which long after its entry must continue to be regarded as an agent that is still at work" (Breuer and Freud 1895, p. 6). The metaphor of the foreign body seems to come from Ribot 1884, p. 116 (Malcolm Macmillan, personal communication).

42 Charcot 1991, p. 310. See also Charcot 1892, p. 281: "There are fixed ideas, so fixed that it is impossible to escape the obsession with which they pursue you." We know what Janet would do with this notion of "fixed idea."

43 Charcot 1991, p. 387. The expression "unconscious cerebration" comes from William Carpenter and, more generally, refers to the Anglo-Saxon "physiology of the mind" of the time (Maudsley, Bain, Spencer). The term "subconscious," fated to its well-known brilliant career, seems to come from Lewes (1877) via Ribot (1884, pp. 109, 123), which gives the lie for once to the erudition of Henri Ellenberger, who attributes its invention to Janet (Ellenberger 1970, p. 413 n. 82). My thanks to Sonu Shamdasani and Malcolm Macmillan for helping me to clarify this point.

44 Charcot 1991, p. 305.

45 See for example Putnam 1989a, in particular ch. 1; Herman 1992.

46 It was common at the Salpêtrière to "transfer" hemianesthesias from one side of the body to the other by applying magnets or metal (Babinski even managed to transfer them from one patient to another; see Babinski 1886). Bourru and Burot used magnets to provoke in their patient Louis Vivet different personalities, each accompanied by specific paralyses and contractions corresponding to such and such a period of the subject's life; see Bourru and Burot 1888, as well as Ian Hacking's summary in Hacking 1995, ch. 12.

47 Charcot 1991, p. 383. Here Charcot is speaking of Le Logeais, who was not part of the original sample.

48 Charcot 1991, p. 263; emphasis added.

49 Charcot 1991, pp. 305–306 n. 2; emphasis added. Post-hypnotic amnesia, which Charcot made one of the obligatory traits of the "grand hypnotism," is a belief that goes back to the phenomenon of demonic possession. Bernheim, as Freud recalls in *Studies on Hysteria*, soon demonstrated its artificial character (Breuer and Freud 1895, pp. 109–110).

50 Charcot 1991, p. 375.

51 Charcot 1991, p. 375. This suggestion of Charcot's has recently been revived by Richard Webster, who emphasizes with some reason that Le Logeais's initial symptoms accord well with a diagnosis of closed brain injury (Webster 1995, pp. 74–77 and 568 n. 6–569). However, to be entirely convincing, this retrospective diagnosis would have to take into account the fact that Le Logeais was not gradually cured toward the end of 1886, contrary to what Webster seems to believe. Webster attributes this fact to a hypothetical "fall in intracranial pressure" (1995, p. 569). In fact, two years later, Le Logeais was still at the Salpêtrière, afflicted with a typical hysterical contracture of the tongue, which Charcot, he admits, had originally "taken . . . for a paralysis of the lower face" (Charcot 1892, p. 214).

52 Elsewhere it is the states of anger, drunkenness, and even "profound demoralization" that Charcot compares with hypnosis, see Charcot 1892, pp. 98, 279; 1890, p. 353. One sees that Charcot did not wait for Frank Putnam's Dissociative Experiences Scale (DES) to

extend the notion of dissociation to all sorts of states far removed from hypnosis proper (on DES and the "dissociative continuum," see Putnam 1989b, pp. 9–11).

53 Charcot 1890, p. 133; emphasis added.

54 See Charcot 1892, pp. 95–102, 214–215, 278–291, 367–374, 442–446; 1890, pp. 28–30. The only ambiguous case is that of a female patient who had developed a paralysis of the arm after being bitten by a dog and had been, "understandably, so moved, so terrified even, that she no longer remembers very much" (Charcot 1892, p. 224). On the other hand, a patient struck by lightning whom Charcot studied a bit later remembered quite well all the circumstances of the incident (Charcot 1890, pp. 438–442).

55 Charcot 1890, p. 134; emphasis added. Charcot then made reference to the case of Le Logeais (studied in Appendix 1 of Charcot 1991).

56 These techniques are summarized in Janet 1901, pp. 280–281.

57 Charcot 1892, p. 282.

58 Janet 1919, vol. 2, p. 282.

59 One finds it already in Charcot himself: "Neurasthenia is not, far from it, the only form of neuropathology that can be produced under the action of the fortuitous causes of which we have been speaking: trauma or nervous shock. On the contrary, one might say that not a single one of the species composing the grand family of neuroses has not shown itself in the etiological conditions here in question. Such are the insanities (*vésanies*) of all kinds, spastic paralysis, epilepsy, chorea, etc., etc., and above all, hysteria, yes, hysteria, and especially male hysteria" (Charcot 1890, p. 30). Of the 591 cases reported by Janet between 1889 and 1903, 257 were attributed by him to one form or another of "trauma" or "moral shock," and they included hysterias as well as anxiety neuroses, phobias, obsessions, or "psychasthenias" (on this subject, see Crocq and Verbizier 1989, pp. 483–484). There is a similar generalization of the traumatic model in the Freud of the years 1895–97 (and beyond).

60 Janet 1989, p. 409. Janet had already published this case in 1886 (Janet 1886).

61 Janet 1989, pp. 410–413. Three years later Janet could report to his satisfaction that "Lucie" and "Marie" had since had no recurrences, cf. Janet 1891, p. 405 n. 1.

62 On Janet's influence on the beginnings of the cathartic method, see Macmillan 1979, pp. 299–309; 1997, pp. 75–81. Macmillan establishes that the publication of Janet's thesis took place between December 1888 and April or early May 1889, which happens to be the date of the beginning of Freud's treatment of "Emmy von N." The coincidence is obviously quite striking, although one cannot rule out that Freud arrived independently at the same method as Janet.

63 On the fallacious use of the "Anna O." case to claim Breuer's priority over Charcot and Janet, see Borch-Jacobsen 1996, ch. 5.

64 See Swales (1986a), pp. 26, 33.

65 Breuer and Freud 1895, p. 70.

66 "Marie" thus dated her blindness in the left eye and her facial anesthesia on the same side to the age of 6, when she had been forced to sleep with a child who had impetigo on the left side of its face. Oddly enough, however, none of her entourage had noticed these easily detectable symptoms: "No one noticed that from that moment on, *she was anesthetic on the left side of her face and blind in her left eye*" (Janet 1989, p. 413; Janet's emphasis). Likewise, when Freud, a year after his first treatment of "Emmy von N.," evoked the toads that had figured in some of her alleged traumatic reminiscences, "she threw a reproachful glance at me, though unaccompanied by signs of horror; she amplified this a moment later with the words 'but the ones here are *real*'" (Breuer and Freud 1895, p. 84).

67 For those who know how to read between the lines, it is easy to find all sorts of indications that Janet and Freud knew quite well what was going on with the post-somnambulistic "amnesias" of some of their patients. Thus Janet's "Marcelle," when coming out of her "crises of clouds" (*crises de nuages*), "could no longer, despite her

efforts, recall the memories to describe them to us. But we know that nothing in the human mind is lost and that there are persistent traces after the crises, after dreams, as after somnambulisms. In reality, the phenomena that arose during the cloud have an extremely significant influence, *even on intervals of lucid thought*" (Janet 1891, p. 280; emphasis added). And Freud, in regard to "Emmy von N.": "Her behaviour in waking life is directed by the experiences she has had during her somnambulism, in spite of her believing, while she is awake, that she knows nothing about them" (Breuer and Freud 1895, p. 56).

2 Neurotica: Freud and the seduction theory

Etymologically, the infant is an animal without language: *infans*, it does not speak. Or, if it speaks, it babbles, making up stories, speaking illogically and irrationally. How then could a child be taken as a qualified witness? How could we believe, for example, if he told us he had witnessed a crime or had been molested? But, on the other hand, how can we prove that he is not telling the truth? Old debate, quite insoluble. The child, like the feeble-minded or the hypnotized person, is the unreliable witness *par excellence*; not because he always lies (if only!), but because, without external corroboration, it is as impossible to prove he is telling the truth as it is to prove the contrary. And yet, as soon as he speaks, his speech must be judged. True or false? Since there is no real basis for a decision, the decision is bound to be a matter of belief and interpretation, and, as such, perfectly arbitrary and unjustifiable. How many juries have thus been accused of letting criminals off the hook or, on the contrary, of condemning innocents? Some in the USA are outraged by the acquittal of the teachers at the McMartin Preschool, who were accused of sexually abusing the children in their care. Others, in Great Britain, are indignant about the Cleveland case, in which pediatricians and social workers took 121 children away from their parents on mere suspicion of sexual abuse.

We are told that this is the sort of situation that confronted Sigmund Freud in his elaboration and abandonment of the so-called seduction theory. Having begun by believing his hysterics, who told him that they had been raped or "seduced" during their early infancy, he finally decided, in September 1897, that these stories arose from the realm of fantasy, that they were part of the properly *fantastic* speech of the child within. Here is what he himself had to say about this in 1933:

> In the period in which the main interest was directed to discovering infantile sexual traumas, almost all my women patients told me (*erzählten*) that they had been seduced by their father. I was driven to recognize in the end that these reports (*Berichte*) were untrue and so came to understand that hysterical symptoms are derived from phantasies and not from real occurrences.[1]

Yes, but is there any proof that this really was the case? After all, the feminists and child abuse specialists object, isn't it possible that these women were telling the truth, the gruesome truth of the patriarchal family? Shouldn't

we trust their word rather than Freud's? To which the psychoanalysts (especially the Lacanians and Narrativists) respond that you cannot prove the truth of
speech, which has nothing to do with reality. All you can do is listen and accept
it in its fictive, narrative dimension. How then can we settle the matter, since
here again we have nothing but the word of the patient's "inner child"? In this
trial concerning the seduction theory, are we not once again faced with one of
those irritating cases of having to judge without proof, of decision in
uncertainty?

I would like to argue that, despite appearances, this is not the case. Psychoanalysts and proponents of real seduction oppose one another concerning the
truth value of Freud's patients' narratives, but they never question the narratives
themselves. Yet we can legitimately ask whether there ever were such narratives, if these "narratives" were really *narratives*, and whether these narratives
were really *spontaneous*. I propose to examine the following hypothesis: these
stories were less the patients' than the doctor's; they were less confessions than
suggestions. If Freud must be criticized, it is not because he refused to trust his
patients' word, but because he extorted confessions from them that corresponded
to his expectations and refused to acknowledge this when he realized it. What
proofs do I have? Though they are not absolute, at least they have the advantage
of being on the record, unlike speculations concerning the fantastic or real nature
of the seduction scenes, and they are available to anyone who takes the time to
read Freud without preconceived notions. At any rate, they seem to be numerous
and convergent enough to justify a reopening of the case. I submit them here in
the hopes of finally unveiling the artificial nature of the debate. I also intend to
call several witnesses whose testimony has been barely taken into account till
now: Freud's colleagues.

This debate over the seduction theory was begun by the publication in 1984
of Jeffrey Masson's *The Assault on Truth*.[2] An ex-professor of Sanskrit,
ex-psychoanalyst, and ex-projects-director at the Sigmund Freud Archives,
Inc., Masson claimed in this book that Freud abandoned his seduction theory
"not for theoretical or clinical reasons, but because of lack of courage."[3] In
itself, this thesis was hardly new: Florence Rush, Judith Herman, and other
feminist critics of psychoanalysis had no need of Masson in order to see
Freud's abrupt about-face as an expression of his masculine prejudices and a
violence done to the words of his female patients.[4] The new element was that
the critique came this time from an insider. Because of his privileged position
in the Freud Archives, Masson had had access to documents that were
inaccessible to the public and that supposedly proved the extent of Freud's
denial of the reality of sexual abuse. The *New York Times Review of Books* did
not hesitate to speak of a "Watergate of the psyche": Freud had been the
accomplice of the perverse papas, and there really had been, as the feminists
had long suspected, a cover-up and a conspiracy of silence. As further proof,
Masson himself was immediately sacked by Kurt R. Eissler, the well-named

"Secretary" of the Freud Archives, as soon as the latter got wind of Masson's heretical views. Would such violence have been necessary, argue Masson's defenders, if there was nothing to hide?

Who are we to believe? Masson or the psychoanalysts? The question is a hot one, given the importance of the stakes, but it is not certain that it is well formed. Something does seem to have been hidden by Freud and his successors, but was it necessarily what Masson claimed? Conversely, if Masson and his feminist allies are wrong about the reality of the scenes of seduction alleged by Freud's patients, does that mean that Freud was right to see them as fantasies and that we should follow the same course a hundred years later? Here is an alternative solution, one that is as disastrous for Masson as it is for the psychoanalysts: what Freud and his followers hid so carefully, or at least denied, is the *suggested* nature of those famous "scenes." There was a cover-up, yes, but not the one that people think.

This hypothesis not only is plausible in light of the current debate concerning the iatrogenesis of "memories" of sexual abuse recovered in therapy, it also conforms to Freud's *initial* debate with his colleagues, which revolved around precisely that question. In this respect, it is notable that Masson's interpretation completely ignores the discussion that was going on at the time about suggestion in general and its role in Freud's theory of hysteria in particular (the term "suggestion" is not even listed in Masson's index). As a matter of fact, Masson attributes the abandonment of the seduction theory to two convergent facts: (1) Freud's desire to minimize Fliess's role in the bleeding of his patient Emma Eckstein, by attributing it to wishes and fantasies rather than to the disastrous surgical intervention of his friend;[5] and (2) Freud's no less pressing desire to reconcile himself with his male colleagues, who were scandalized by his allegations of incest and pedophilia.

The first reason invoked by Masson, which elaborates the classic explanation by the transference on Fliess,[6] is not at all decisive, for Freud's remarks on Emma Eckstein's "fantasies" actually could be easily reconciled with Freud's seduction theory. The notion of fantasy is in fact a first attempt at *rationalizing* the seduction theory, a way for Freud to account for the manifestly fantasist nature of certain scenes, while allowing him to continue believing in the reality of the initial scene. At the time he was proposing his remarks on Emma's fantasies (notably in his January 17, 1897 letter to Fliess, in which he reports Emma's satanic scenes), Freud was convinced that the fantasies were "protective fictions," intended to hide or "sublimate" the memory of the *real* trauma.[7] So it is hard to see why Freud would have felt compelled to sacrifice his seduction theory on the altar of his friendship for Fliess, since in his mind the theory already sufficiently exonerated the latter.

As to Masson's second reason, which interests us more at this point, it would be plausible only if Freud's colleagues were actually repulsed by the idea of real incest and sexual perversion. But this is far from being the case: on this point, Masson is the victim (a quite willing one, to be sure) of the hardy legend of the hero forged by Freud and his biographers in regard to that episode. Not only did Freud not "suffer . . . intellectual isolation" during that period, as Masson claims,[8] but he was not the first nor the only one interested in sexuality, including perverse sexuality. As Frank Sulloway has expertly shown,[9] Freud had been preceded along that path by the sexologists of the 1880s, notably Albert von Schrenck-Notzing, Richard von Krafft-Ebing, Leopold Löwenfeld, and Albert Moll. These had therefore no a priori reason to be scandalized by the sexual theory of hysteria proposed by their young colleague. Krafft-Ebing, in particular, had himself mentioned numerous cases of child sexual abuse, including incest, in his *Psychopathia Sexualis* (1886),[10] and his famous remark about Freud's lecture on "The aetiology of hysteria" – "It sounds like a scientific fairy-tale"[11] – could not possibly have the significance of offended indignation that Masson claims for it. In reality, the objections of Freud's colleagues to his new theory of hysteria had to do not with the content of the seduction scenes alleged by Freud, but rather with the way that he obtained them from his patients.

Indeed, we tend to forget that these sexologists, like Freud himself, were theorists and practitioners of hypnosis.[12] As a result, they were very sensitive to the role of suggestion in the treatment of hysteria, since they had all observed the collapse of Charcot's theory of *grande hystérie* under the criticism of Bernheim and the Nancy School. In all likelihood, this is what Krafft-Ebing meant when he spoke of a "scientific fairy-tale": he knew the tendency of hysterics to make up stories in the sexual domain, but most especially, like everybody at the time, he tied that *pseudologia phantastica* to hysterical "suggestibility." In other words, the seduction theory was a "fairy-tale," a hysterical lie, but above all it was a "scientific" fairy-tale, a fairy-tale *suggested* by Dr. Freud. The German neurologist Robert Gaupp said it quite clearly in his review of Freud's essay on "Screen memories" (1899):

> Anyone who can give his questions a suggestive twist, whether done consciously or unconsciously, can obtain from susceptible patients any answer which fits into his system. That may be the reason why Freud's psychoanalyses abound in material which other researchers seek in vain.[13]

Albert Moll – a man whom Freud called "a petty, malicious, narrow-minded individual"[14] and "a brute"[15] – put it no less bluntly in 1909 in regard to Freud's case histories, and there is every reason to believe that his words reflect an opinion he had already formed in 1896:

> These clinical histories . . . rather produce the impression that much of the alleged histories has been introduced by the suggestive questioning of the examiner, or that sufficient care has not been taken to guard against illusions of memory. The impression produced in my mind is that the theory of Freud . . . suffices to account for the clinical histories, not that the clinical histories suffice to prove the truth of the theory.[16]

The most striking document, however, comes from the person whom Freud, in 1900, called "the stupid Löwenfeld."[17] What was Löwenfeld's crime? In

1899 Leopold Löwenfeld, who had already criticized the Freudian notion of "anxiety neurosis,"[18] and who would somewhat later question the therapeutic value of the "Breuer–Freud method,"[19] published a commentary on the seduction theory, in which he had this to say – among other things:

> By chance, one of the patients on whom Freud used the analytic method came under my observation. The patient told me with certainty that the infantile sexual scene which analysis had apparently uncovered was pure fantasy and had never really happened to him.[20]

It is easy to see why Freud was furious: Löwenfeld had said out loud what he himself had been quietly thinking for the last two years, though carefully refraining from announcing publicly. Masson quotes this document in his edition of the Letters to Fliess,[21] as well as in the preface to the third edition of his *Assault on Truth*, where he adds the following commentary:

> This account no doubt distressed Freud. Here was a well-known German psychiatrist saying that Freud's patients were merely engaged in fantasies, that they were not remembering, and for proof he had a retraction from one of these very patients whom Freud had relied on to devise his original theory.[22]

Clearly Masson would like us to conclude that Löwenfeld, on the basis of a single "retraction," pushed Freud to see his patients' stories as mere fantasies. He neglects, however, to quote the beginning of the passage, in which Löwenfeld spelled out what he meant by "fantasy." After quoting a passage from "The aetiology of hysteria," where Freud explained that even under steady pressure his patients generally refused to consider the scenes as genuine memories, Löwenfeld continued (I quote here the English translation of Han Israëls and Morton Schatzman, who correctly restore the passage in a recent article):[23]

> These remarks [by Freud] show two things: 1. The patients were subjected to a suggestive influence coming from the person who analyzed them, by which the rise of the mentioned scenes was brought quite close to their imagination. 2. These fantasy pictures that had arisen under the influence of the analysis were definitively denied recognition as memories of real events. I also have a direct experience to support this second conclusion.

Obviously, Löwenfeld's "fantasy" is neither the mere hysterical confabulation that Masson intends, nor Freud's later "wish-fantasy": it is the hypnagogic imagery solicited in the patient by the suggestive pressure of the psychoanalyst. In fact, "stupid" Löwenfeld had a hypnotic, interpersonal theory of fantasy, for which Freud's theory of hysteria looked like a pure suggestive illusion. (Those interested in conspiracy theories will be happy to learn that the passage from Löwenfeld, even in the truncated version given by Masson, has inexplicably disappeared from the German edition of the complete letters to Fliess.)[24]

Unlike Masson, Freud knew these objections quite well, for they were the very ones raised by Bleuler, Strümpell, Michell Clarcke, and others at the publication of *Studies on Hysteria*.[25] Indeed, he knew them so well that he continually anticipates them in his writings from this period, starting with the *Studies*:

> We are not in a position to force anything on the patient about the things of which he is ostensibly ignorant or to influence the products of the analysis by arousing an expectation. I have never once succeeded, by foretelling something, in altering or falsifying the reproductions of memories or the connection of events.[26]

Of course, we might well wonder how Freud could be so certain. Breuer, in a public statement of 1895, advanced the following line of defense:

> If Freud's theories at first give the impression of being ingenious psychological theorems, linked to the facts, but essentially aprioristically constructed, then the speaker can insist that it is actually a matter of facts and interpretations that have grown out of observations. As against the suspicion that the recollections of patients might be artificial products suggested by the physician, Breuer can assert from his own observations that it is enormously and especially difficult to force something upon, or put something over on, this sort of patient.[27]

Freud seems to have particularly liked this argument, which one might call "the argument by resistance," for he takes it up in 1896 in "Heredity and the aetiology of the neuroses,"[28] and again in "The aetiology of hysteria":

> The behaviour of the patients while they are reproducing these infantile experiences is in every respect incompatible with the assumption that the scenes [of seduction] are anything else than a reality that is being felt with distress and reproduced with the greatest reluctance. Before they come for analysis the patients know nothing about these scenes. Only the strongest compulsion (*Zwang*) of the treatment can induce them to embark on a reproduction of them ... It is less easy to refute the idea that the doctor forces reminiscences of this sort on the patient, that he influences him by suggestion to imagine and to reproduce them. Nevertheless, it appears to me equally untenable. I have never yet succeeded in forcing on a patient a scene I was expecting to find, in a way that he seemed to be living through it with all the appropriate feelings. Perhaps others may be more successful in this.[29]

We can see that if Freud did not manage to obtain perfect scenes, it was not for lack of trying. And we can well imagine that what he says in 1898 concerning his method for obtaining admissions of masturbation from his neurasthenics applies equally to the way he proceeded with his hysterical patients:

> Having diagnosed a case of neurasthenic neurosis ... we may then boldly demand confirmation of our suspicions from the patient. *We must not be led astray by initial denials*. If we keep firmly to what we have inferred, we shall in the end conquer every resistance by emphasizing the unshakeable nature of our convictions.[30]

This martial therapeutic voluntarism, which appears again in the writings of current "trauma work" experts,[31] in no way prevented Freud from concluding two sentences further along: "Moreover, the idea that one might, by one's insistence, cause a patient who is psychically normal to accuse himself falsely of sexual misdemeanours – such an idea may safely be disregarded as an imaginary danger."[32] We can rest assured.

This is no small matter. For, as Freud himself later rhetorically objected in reference to the transference, if the suggestion factor intervenes in analysis, "there is a risk that the influencing of our patients may make the objective certainty (*die Objectivität*) of our findings doubtful."[33] Freud always maintained that suggestion, despite appearances, did not enter into analytical constructions and interpretations, and he repeats it again in 1925 concerning his seduction theory: "I do not believe even now that I forced (*aufgedrängt*) the seduction-fantasies on my patients, that I "suggested" them."[34] This denial of the role of suggestion is constant in Freud, and it goes back to one of his most precocious and decisive theoretical choices. Indeed, behind all of it lies the quarrel between the Nancy and Salpêtrière schools concerning the suggested or non-suggested nature of Charcot's *grande hystérie*, in which Freud took the position of the latter. Even though he used and advocated Bernheim's suggestive method quite early – first in a direct form and later, under the name of the "Breuer method," to act on the traumatic memory as Janet and Delbœuf had done before him – Freud never sided with Bernheim against Charcot on the problem of the "objectivity" of the hypnotic and hysterical manifestations observed at the Salpêtrière. Charcot claimed he could describe fixed, non-simulated hysterical "stigmata," by using a hypnosis that was itself conceived as a specific and objectifiable "state," and Freud followed him on these two points. As he wrote in 1888-89 in his preface to the translation he had done of Bernheim's first book:

> we may accept the statement that in essentials [the symptomatology of hysteria] is of a real, objective nature and is not falsified by suggestion on the part of the observer. This does not imply any denial that the mechanism of hysterical manifestations is a psychical one; but it is not the mechanism of suggestion on the part of the physician.[35]

What Freud is alluding to here is Charcot's theory of traumatic hysteria, which made traumatic hysteria a phenomenon of *self*-hypnosis and *auto*-suggestion.[36] As we know, it was precisely this part of Charcot's theory that Breuer and Freud took it upon themselves to develop, following Janet, after the rest of the Salpêtrière edifice had collapsed under the heavy pounding of Bernheim and the Nancy School. In this regard, the theory of the "psychical mechanism of hysteria" set forth in the *Studies* remains typically Charcotian, in that it continues to insist that hysterical dissociation of consciousness is a spontaneous, and thus objective, phenomenon, uninfluenced by the observer. As for the hypnosis that serves to artificially reproduce that self-hypnosis for the purpose of reliving *in statu nascendi* the pathogenic trauma, Freud continues, here too, to think of it as a specific state, and not as one degree of suggestibility among others, as the Nancy School would have it. Hypnosis, he declares in a lecture from 1892, is not

> only an artificial product of medical technique, as Delbœuf claims. ... He [Freud] tends to think that we must hold firmly to the authenticity of hypnosis; he takes his arguments from observation of the hypnotic state in hysterics and thus, on this important point, agrees with the views of the Charcot School.[37]

This point is, indeed, extremely important, for it was this Charcotian – and, let us add, extremely naive – presupposition that allowed Freud to remain blind for so long to his own intervention in the phenomena that he observed in his patients. As long as hypnosis was identified with the hysterical state, itself understood as a modality of self-hypnosis, there was no reason to worry about the suggestive influence that Bernheim warned against, since the hypnotic treatment was supposed to do nothing more than bring an internal, autonomous psychical determinism to the surface. Such was Freud's confidence in this psychical determinism that he thought it capable of resisting every external influence, even the therapist's most persistent pressure. As he continued to say in 1910, at a meeting of the Vienna Psychoanalytical Society, "if one wants to come up with anything, one cannot avoid asking some leading questions. Besides, the patient can be influenced only in a direction *that suggests itself to him*."[38] Freud is often credited with liberating his patients from the "tyranny" of hypnotic suggestion and giving them back their status as speaking subjects. In reality, Freud's refusal to recognize the role of suggestion corresponds theoretically to a very profound *objectification* of the therapeutic relationship, as if his patients' speech was merely the reproduction of a psychical mechanism observable from the exterior. Even the fact, repeated over and over by Bernheim, Forel, and Delbœuf, that the hypnotized subject remains *aware* of the hypnotist's suggestions and *responds*, in every sense of the word, to them[39] does not seem to have made Freud reflect on his own role in the relation – witness this stupefying letter of May 28, 1888, to Fliess:

> I have at this moment a lady in hypnosis lying in front of me and therefore can go on writing in peace. [Two paragraphs later:] The time for the hypnosis is up. I greet you cordially. In all haste, your Dr. Freud.[40]

With methodological presuppositions of this sort it is a wonder that the disaster of the seduction theory did not blow up long before it did. For fellow travelers of the Nancy School such as Krafft-Ebing, Moll, and Löwenfeld, it must have been patently obvious that Freud was simply repeating the errors of his "Master" Charcot.

Objection: "But you are forgetting that at the time he was elaborating his seduction theory Freud had already given up using hypnosis. How, then, can you claim that he was suggesting the scenes reported by his patients?"

True, the dates seem to contradict my thesis. Beginning in the autumn of 1892, Freud gradually gave up hypnosis in favor of "concentration" in the waking state and the "pressure technique" (*Druckprozedur*), a method consisting in pressing with the hand on the patient's forehead and asking him to evoke some idea or image. This abandon of hypnosis corresponds, theoretically, with Freud's increasing emphasis on the role of repression in hysteria, to the detriment of the "hypnoid" mechanism of dissociation of consciousness. The final rupture with hypnosis seems to have been made in the early part of 1895,[41] precisely at the moment Freud began to formulate his theory of the etiology of hysteria. But simply because he was no longer practicing direct hypnosis and suggestion, does this mean that Freud did not "suggest" in the larger sense of the word? We must get rid of two false ideas here:

(1) Contrary to what Freud seems to imply most often by the term, hypnosis cannot in any way be reduced to somnambulism followed by amnesia. There are, as Bernheim had already asserted, many degrees of hypnosis, and it is impossible to rigorously quantify them. It is therefore difficult to say where hypnosis begins and where it ends, as Freud himself recognizes at several points in *Studies on Hysteria*: "I told the patients to lie down and deliberately close their eyes in order to 'concentrate' – all of which had at least some resemblance to hypnosis."[42] He also compares his "pressure technique" to a "momentarily intensified hypnosis" and to the well-known hypnotic technique of crystal gazing.[43] In *The Interpretation of Dreams*, Freud even goes so far as to say that his method of free association produces "a psychical state which ... bears some analogy to the state of falling asleep – and no doubt also to hypnosis."[44] Much later, the Wolf Man would still recall how Freud jokingly compared psycho-analytic transference to hypnosis:

> When I do what transference shows me, it is really like being hypnotized
> by someone. That's the influence. I can remember Freud saying,
> "Hypnosis, what do you mean, hypnosis, everything we do is hypnosis too."
> Then why did he discontinue hypnosis?[45]

Excellent question: where are we to place the famous Freudian "epistemic rupture" in such a continuum? If it is true, as Freud said in 1917, that "psychoanalysis proper began when I dispensed with the help of hypnosis,"[46] we might well wonder if such a pure psychoanalysis *ever* came into existence!

(2) Second false idea: the degree of suggestibility has nothing to do with the depth of the hypnotic trance. On the contrary, it often happens that suggestibility is more pronounced in the waking state than in a state of deep hypnosis: "Suggestibility can be very complete outside of artificial somnambulism; it can be totally lacking in a completely somnambulistic state."[47] This point had been forcefully made by Bernheim, who concluded quite logically in 1891 that "suggestive psychotherapy" would be just as effective, if not more effective, *without hypnosis proper*.[48] Freud, who translated Bernheim's second book in

1892,[49] was obviously aware of this, and we might well consider that Freud's (like others')[50] turning, in that very year, toward a less directly hypnotic technique was nothing more than a following of Bernheim's example. Be that as it may, it is clear enough that the absence of deep hypnosis cannot be equated with the absence of suggestibility on the part of the patient (and thus of suggestion on the part of the therapist). As Freud himself admitted quite bluntly to Fliess in 1901: "My clients are sick people, hence especially irrational and liable to persuasion (*bestimmbar*)."[51]

In short, just because at some point Freud stopped inducing somnambulistic trances and using direct suggestion, it does not mean that the new "psychoanalytic" treatment was *ipso facto* non-hypnotic and non-suggestive. In this regard, it is clear that the *Druckprozedur*, which Freud inherited from Bernheim[52] (and perhaps more directly from Berger and Heidenhain),[53] was a technique of the hypnotic type. Under Freud's insistent "pressure," his patients seem to have gone through an altered state of consciousness, characterized by visual scenes of a hallucinatory nature, a great emotional expressivity, and an increase in ideo-motor and ideo-sensorial activity. As Freud says in "The aetiology of hysteria," "While they are recalling these infantile experiences to consciousness, [the patients] suffer under the most violent sensations."[54]

It is no accident, then, that during this whole period, Freud speaks of "reproductions" of the infantile sexual scene, and not of memories or reminiscences. In accordance with the "trance logic" of hypnosis, these scenes were actually experienced, *acted* in the present, rather than being truly recalled as memories (they were *Wiederholungen*, not *Erinnerungen*, to use Freud's later terminology). As Jean Schimek judiciously notes: "The reproduction of the seduction scenes may have often been a kind of minor hysterical attack, with both verbal and non-verbal expression,"[55] which immediately brings them close to the "relivings" *in statu nascendi* previously obtained through the cathartic method. Read, for instance, the letter of January 24, 1897 to Fliess:

> I was able to trace back, with certainty, a hysteria . . . to an abuse (*Mißbrauch*), which occurred for the first time at 11 months and [I could] hear again the words that were exchanged between two adults at that time! It is as though it comes from a phonograph.[56]

Clearly the whole scene was being played (mimed) here for the benefit of the fascinated therapist (you could call it the "scene of His Master's Voice"). Or read the letter of December 22, 1897, apropos a patient who identified with her mother, anally penetrated by the father during a scene allegedly observed by the child at age 3:

> The mother *now* stands in the room and shouts: "Rotten criminal, what do you want from me? I will have no part of that. Just whom do you think you have in front of you?" Then she tears the clothes from her body with one hand, while with the other hand she presses them against it, which creates a

very peculiar impression. Then she stares at a certain point in the room, her face contorted by rage, covers her genitals with one hand and pushes something away with the other. Then she raises both hands, claws at the air and bites it. Shouting and cursing, she bends over far backward, again covers her genitals with her hand, whereupon she falls over forward, so that her head almost touches the floor; finally, she quietly falls over backward onto the floor. Afterwards she wrings her hands, sits down in a corner, and with her features distorted with pain she weeps.[57]

This preponderance of the mimetico-dramatic "now" over the diegetical-narrative past is a typically hypnotic trait and it conforms, it is worth noting, with the argument Freud advances in "The aetiology of hysteria" in order to convince us of the non-simulated nature of the scenes of seduction:

> Even after they have gone through [the infantile experiences] once more in such a convincing manner, [the patients] still attempt to withhold belief from them, by emphasizing the fact that, unlike what happens in the case of other forgotten material, they have no feeling of *remembering* the scenes.[58]

Freud interprets this as a resistance to remembering (and thus, in his usual style, as proof of the scene), but it is actually a pure and simple *absence* of any memories. There was no memory, no story, as Freud would have it (and as Masson faithfully repeats). What there was was something completely different: little mimetic dramas or acts, played out by the patients in a more-or-less light hypnotic state, during which their suggestibility was most likely very strongly increased.

In order to prevent a possible misunderstanding, I hasten to add that this hypnotic suggestibility is not the product of some mysterious power of the hypnotist, as Freud insisted too often in speaking of the "tyranny" of suggestion.[59] Good hypnotists have always known that initially suggestibility is nothing but the sheer accepting of the hypnotic contract: the subject must accept the hypnotic game, failing which the game cannot even begin. In this sense, suggestibility is always autosuggestion or, more precisely, a consensual suggestion, *negotiated* with the hypnotist. In fact, it starts the very instant that the patient decides to visit the medicine man, turning himself over to this man (or his theory), in order to make his ills disappear. This mechanism, which comes into play in all therapeutic relationships, is all the more pronounced in any therapy that uses techniques of the hypnotic type, and it is hard to see why the early psychoanalysis would have mysteriously escaped it. The psychiatrist Aschaffenburg – whom Freud called a "scoundrel"[60] – said it well in 1906: "Most of the patients who go to see Freud know already beforehand what he is getting at and this thought immediately evokes the complex of ideas pertaining to sexuality."[61] In this sense, suggestibility is not pure passivity or automatism (no more than hypnosis, of which suggestibility is one of the fundamental characteristics). On the contrary, it goes quite well with the inventiveness of the patients who play the hypnotic game with their therapist, sometimes even imposing new rules for it, as Bertha Pappenheim with Breuer or Fanny Moser and Anna von Lieben with Freud. Hypnosis is always a matter of interaction – a "joint endeavor," says Milton Erickson.[62] Thus, the history of psychoanalysis, insofar as it begins (and ends) with hypnosis, cannot be written solely from the point of view of Freud's theories, as if Freud simply discovered phenomena in his patients that had formerly been undetected. In reality, his patients did their best to confirm his theories, beyond his wildest expectations. Psychoanalysis is the product of this feedback, the magical fulfillment of its own prophecy.

Let's examine the seduction theory from this point of view. The seduction theory is a theory of the *sexual* etiology of hysteria and, more generally, of the "psycho-neuroses of defense." The idea that sexuality plays a role in neurosis has become so self-evident, so natural, that we never even ask how it came to Freud. After all, why did he come to view the trauma that he first evoked with Breuer as a specifically sexual trauma? Was this some stunning discovery made by the clinician Sigmund Freud? That is what he has always suggested, as much before as after abandoning the seduction theory, insisting that experience literally forced him into giving sexuality this role.[63] If we follow the chronology of the letters to Fliess attentively, however, it becomes obvious that this is nothing but a handy legend, designed to cover up what were originally highly speculative hypotheses.

As a matter of fact, it is very striking to see to what extent these hypotheses *precede* the clinical material that they are supposed to explain. As Malcolm Macmillan has shown,[64] the idea of a sexual etiology first came from the work of George Miller Beard, whose concept of "neurasthenia" seems to have furnished the original point of theoretical contact between Fliess and Freud. In his 1884 *Sexual Neurasthenia*, Beard evoked the expenditure of "nerve force" due to sexual problems as *one* of the causes of neurasthenia, and Freud, at the start of 1893, boldly radicalized this point of view:

> It may be taken as a recognized fact that neurasthenia is a frequent consequence of an abnormal sexual life. The assertion however, which I wish to make *and test by observation* [my emphasis, M.B.-J.], is that neurasthenia actually can *only* be a sexual neurosis [Freud's emphasis].[65]

We do not know what Freud's basis for this highly speculative hypothesis may have been, and the patients on whom he "tested" it seem to have been as surprised as we are. Letter of October 6, 1893: "The sexual story (*die sexuelle Geschichte*) attracts people who are all stunned and then go away won over after having exclaimed, 'No one has ever asked me about that before!' "[66] Would Freud have found sexuality in neurasthenia and the "actual neuroses" if he had not looked so actively for them? Letter of November 27, 1893: "The sexual business (*Sexualgeschäft*) is becoming more firmly consolidated, the contradictions are fading away ... When I take a case for thorough repair, everything is confirmed and sometimes the seeker finds more than he wishes."[67]

As for the hypothesis of a sexual etiology for hysteria and for the psycho-neuroses in general, it appears to have been introduced initially for the sake of symmetry, without any clinical basis whatsoever. On May 15 and again on September 29, 1893, Freud announced that he was *going* to attack the question of the sexual etiology of hysteria: "I happen to have very few new sexualia. I shall soon start tackling hysteria."[68] Then, for two years, there is hardly a mention of hysteria, except, once again, in a highly speculative vein.[69] It is not till October 8, 1895 that Freud finally formulates his seduction theory:

> I am on the scent of the following strict precondition of hysteria, namely, that a primary sexual experience (before puberty), accompanied by revulsion and fright, must have taken place; for obsessional neurosis, that it must have happened, accompanied by *pleasure*.[70]

Note the expression "must have taken place." This "strict precondition for hysteria" is once again nothing but pure intellectual speculation on the respective roles of unpleasure and pleasure in hysterical and obsessional neuroses. But only a month later, Freud finds the first clinical confirmation of his new theory. Letter of November 12, 1895: "Today I am able to add that one of the cases *gave me what I expected* (sexual shock – that is, infantile abuse in male hysteria!)"[71] What admirable foresight! As Freud would write later, "Most of my hunches *in neuroticis* [in regard to neuroses] subsequently turned out to be true."[72] They sure did. Three months after his first clinical confirmation, in his "Further remarks on the neuro-psychoses of defense" (February 1896), Freud was already publicly announcing no less than thirteen cases confirming his new etiology. His lecture on "The aetiology of hysteria," delivered in April, puts the number at eighteen. (This did not prevent Freud from bragging in that same article that his results were "based on a laborious individual examination of patients which has in most cases taken up *a hundred or more hours of work*"[73] – an unlikely figure if we consider the short time-span between Freud's initial hunch and its first "confirmations.")

Freud adds another hypothesis the following month: the "pre-sexual sexual" scene, whose "posthumous" return provokes the "pathological defense," took place in the case of hysteria *before the person was four years old*. Why is that? Because the major symptom of hysteria is somatic conversion, so it must be imagined that the traumatic memory dates from a time when it could not be "translated into verbal images."[74] A logical consequence of this speculative time-regression is that the sexual assault must have been particularly perverse, and perpetrated, in all likelihood, by a person in the immediate family. Here again it is a matter of pure hypothesis, which Freud himself admits "still awaits confirmation from individual analyses."[75] Freud's patients hurried to supply it. As Freud wrote on November 22, "My work on hysteria is progressing nicely"[76] – and for good reason: when you look for memories that go back to such a precocious age, you will necessarily find what you are looking for, especially if you operate using a technique of the hypnotic type. Indeed, where could the patient find any way to refute the scenes that he or she hallucinates under the analyst's persistent "pressure," since they go back to a time prior to any memory – or at least any reliable memory? In the absence of any objective verification, the hallucinatory intensity of the scenes provoked by the *Druck-prozedur* must have been very convincing. Take the letter of December 17, 1896: "Will you believe that the reluctance to drink beer and to shave was elucidated by a scene in which a nurse sits down *podice nudo* [with bare buttocks] in a shallow shaving bowl filled with beer in order to let herself be licked, and so on?"[77] Letter of January 3, 1897: Freud succeeds in tying one of his patient's various oral symptoms to the act of sucking the paternal penis. Letter of January 12: one of Freud's patients has convulsive attacks because his nurse gave him a "*lictus* [licking] . . . in the anus," and another because he had been similarly *gamahuché*, as the Marquis de Sade would say, by his father before he was one year old.[78]

But there is still better to come, which eerily anticipates the current reports of Satanic Ritual Abuse (SRA) by American psychotherapists. In the last weeks of 1896, Freud is reading Krafft-Ebing's *Psychopathia Sexualis*, and certain passages in it renew his interest in the witch-hunts of the Middle Ages, a subject that had already been the object of contradictory discussions by Charcot and Bernheim.[79] Freud suddenly realizes that the stories of diabolic debauchery extorted by the Inquisitors bear a remarkable resemblance to the stories of his patients,[80] and so, by analogy, he deduces that the satanic cults and abuses evoked under torture must also be *real* (and not suggested, as Bernheim had claimed):[81]

> I am beginning to grasp an idea: it is as though in the perversions, of which hysteria is the negative, we have before us a remnant of a primeval sexual cult (*Sexualkultus*) which once was – perhaps still is – a religion in the Semitic East (Moloch, Astarte) . . . I dream, therefore, of a primeval devil religion whose rites are carried on (*deren Ritus sich . . . fortsezt*) secretly, and understand the harsh therapy of the witches' judges. Connecting links abound.[82]

As more recent SRA experts would put it, there is a "transgenerational" transmission of the abuse, each generation of "cult survivors" exercising the same perverse violence that programmed it upon the following generation. The faithful Emma Eckstein, at any rate, immediately got the message. Letter of January 17: "Eckstein has a scene [here Masson feels the need to add in brackets: 'that is, remembers'] where the diabolus sticks needles into her fingers and then places a candy on each drop of blood. As far as blood is concerned, you are completely without blame!"[83] One week later, letter of January 24: "Imagine, I obtained a scene about the circumcision of a girl. The cutting off of a piece of the labium minor (which is even shorter today),[84] sucking up the blood, after which the child was given a piece of the skin to eat."[85] If it is true that Freud "[was] read[ing] his own thoughts into other people,"[86] as Fliess later accused, here we have perhaps a nearly literal illustration of it. In the same letter of January 24, 1897: "I *read* one day that the gold the devil gives his victims regularly turns into excrement; and *the next day* Mr. E, who reports that his nurse had money deliria, suddenly told me ... that Louise's money always was excrement."[87] This is mind reading in real time!

Summarizing the seduction theory, Judith Herman writes: "What he [Freud] heard was appalling. Repeatedly his patients told him of sexual assault, abuse, and incest."[88] Not so. It was *Freud* who began speaking of sexual abuse, incest, and satanic cults, not his patients. Just like Masson, the feminist critics of psychoanalysis are victims of the ex post facto myth forged by Freud himself, claiming that he was fooled at first by the fantasy stories *of his patients*. In reality, there is every reason to doubt that these stories were spontaneous or that they even had the consistence of true stories. Paul Chodoff and Alexander Schusdek,[89] in the 1960s, were the first to emphasize this point:

> [I]n the 1896 paper, "The aetiology of hysteria," Freud describes how immensely difficult it is to wrest the memories of seductions from his patients, how they protest and deny, and how they insist that they have no feeling of recollecting the traumatic scenes ... It is legitimate to suspect that the uniformity of the memories produced under such conditions, which Freud adduced as proof of their universality in hysteria, was a product, rather, of the uniformity of Freud's "convictions."[90]

This has since been amply confirmed by the meticulous revisionist studies of Frank Cioffi, Peter Swales, Jean Schimek, Anthony Stadlen, Allen Esterson, Max Scharnberg, Han Israëls, and Morton Schatzman:[91] Freud literally *imposed* his arbitrary constructions on his patients, piecing them together like a "puzzle"[92] from doubtful, fragmentary material.

Does this mean that Freud was guilty of bad faith when in 1914 he claimed to have been led astray by "the statements (*Berichte*) made by patients in which they ascribed their symptoms to passive sexual experiences in the first years of childhood"?[93] This is what some of the authors I have just cited affirm (notably Israëls–Schatzman and Esterson), but it seems to me that on precisely this point their demystifying zeal (with which I sympathize) misses its target. Crazy as it may sound, Freud's patients – or at least some of them – really did "spontaneously" tell him everything that he wanted him to say. Even though it is often hard to separate Freud's constructions from the authentic stories of his patients, the letters to Fliess generally leave no doubt on the subject. Rather than accuse Freud of retroactively inventing stories that did not exist, it seems more plausible to me to admit that his patients actively responded to his suggestions, "reproducing" all the scenes that he expected of them.

This hypothesis, proposed a while ago by Malcolm Macmillan,[94] would explain certain anomalies noted by more recent commentators. Indeed, in his "Further remarks on the neuro-psychoses of defense" (as well as in "Heredity and the aetiology of the neuroses"), Freud says that he "completed" an analysis of *thirteen* cases of hysteria.[95] Of these thirteen cases, he says, *seven* had been the object of sexual assaults by other children, and *six* by nearby adults, like nurses; Freud does not mention parents. Four months later, however, Freud claims *eighteen* cases (that is, the initial thirteen, plus *five* new ones), and he says that this group is divided into three subgroups, this time without giving precise figures: children abused by another child, children abused by strangers, and children abused by a nearby adult, "unhappily all too often, a close relative." And he adds that the last-mentioned subgroup "consists of the much more numerous cases,"[96] which is odd if one goes strictly by the figures. In fact, even if we suppose that the subgroup of children abused by unknown adults only has two members, there cannot, unless I am wrong in my calculations, be more than *nine* children abused by a nearby adult or parent: $18 - (7 + 2) = 9$. It seems fairly clear that some of the cases initially abused by another child got implicitly recycled into victims of an intra-familial assault.

But that is not all. A little more than a year later, in his famous letter of recantation of September 21, 1897, Freud states that "in all cases" *the father* was designated as the guilty party – a fact that he did not mention in a single one of his articles (and which he took more than a quarter of century to reveal publicly in his *Autobiographical Study*).[97] We must therefore admit that in slightly less than two years, a relatively stable sampling of patients[98] were abused *mostly* by other children, then *mostly* by nearby adults or parents, and finally *always* by the father! How can this strangely elastic statistic be explained? Three hypotheses present themselves. The feminist hypothesis of Judith Herman: Freud knew from the very start that the father was guilty, but preferred to hide this fact in his published accounts.[99] The revisionist hypothesis of Allen Esterson and Frederick Crews: Freud said whatever he felt like and put words that were never spoken into the mouths of his patients.[100] The hypnotic hypothesis of Freud's colleagues: Freud said whatever he felt like, *and his patients faithfully repeated after him.* In other words, the same patients successively claimed that they had been abused by children, by nurses, and by the father, all in accordance with the preferred theory of the moment (and they stopped – how strange – after Freud definitively abandoned his theory . . .).

I tend to believe that this last hypothesis is the correct one, for it alone agrees with the chronology of the letters to Fliess, in which Freud's patients do mention "paternal" scenes (contrary to what Crews says),[101] but only *after* the publication of "The aetiology of hysteria" (contrary to what Herman suspects).[102] And I believe that it was also the implicit hypothesis of Freud himself when he abandoned (or began to abandon) his cherished "*neurotica.*" Indeed, why did Freud abandon his seduction theory? Innumerable explanations have been offered for that mysterious episode, but at least one thing is sure: Freud did not change his mind for lack of clinical "evidence." Quite the contrary, he had plenty of it, and it is simply not true that Freud was "not hearing enough seduction stories from his patients, and that the stories he heard did not fit the pattern the theory required."[103] The reasons he advances in his letter of

September 21, 1897 are merely reasons, themselves speculative, for *doubting* the authenticity of the alleged confirmations that he had obtained. I list them here in no particular order: an absence of infantile scenes in the psychoses, where they should have appeared spontaneously because of the lack of defense; a total absence of conclusive therapeutic results (whereas Freud had publicly claimed to have "completed" the analyses of eighteen cases!);[104] the impossibility of distinguishing between "truth and fiction that has been connected with affect";[105] and finally, the statistical improbability of the "paternal etiology." But all of these reasons had been available to Freud before. So, if he decided to take them seriously at this point, it is likely that this was because the influencing machine that he had put in motion was working *all too* well, so well that he could no longer believe in the stories he had extorted from his patients. As he wrote in 1914: "This aetiology broke down under the weight of its own improbability."[106]

All this was bound to make Freud wonder about the way he had obtained these pseudo-memories of sexual abuse. If the scenes were not real, where did they come from? Freud would say later (much later) that they came from the Oedipal fantasies of his female patients (note the feminine, as if he did not have male patients too . . .). But in 1897, Freud had not yet come up with this handy excuse; so the only thing it could have been was this: the scenes *came from him* – which is precisely what his colleagues had objected all along. That this is what Freud himself thought is indicated by a passage from the letter where, after having admitted the failure of his cures, he evokes "the possibility of explaining to myself the partial successes in other ways, *in the usual fashion* (*auf die gewöhnliche Art*)."[107] In the context of the time this is a clear allusion to the elimination of the symptoms by suggestion and/or autosuggestion. Freud is here admitting that his new "psychoanalytic" treatment is finally nothing but suggestive psychotherapy *à la* Bernheim. Twenty years later, in *An Autobiographical Study*, Freud would be even more explicit:

> Under the influence (*unter dem Drängen*) of the technical procedure which
> *I used at the time*, the majority of my patients reproduced from their childhood
> scenes in which they were sexually seduced by a grown-up person.[108]

So, after all, it was not the patients' Oedipal unconscious that had forged these aberrant stories, but the *Druckprozedur* of Dr. Freud. It is true that this admission in the *Autobiographical Study* is followed by the usual denial: "I do not believe even now that I forced the seduction-fantasies on my patients, that I "suggested" them."[109] But this denial must finally be exposed for what it really is: an evasion, the *proton pseudos* of psychoanalysis. Indeed, it is clearly refuted by a letter that Freud addressed to Max Eitingon in August 1933, shortly after Ferenczi's death. In this letter, which Jeffrey Masson exhumed from the Jones Archives, where it had carefully been hidden from public curiosity, Freud denounces the technical innovations proposed by Ferenczi toward the end of his life and compares them explicitly to his own seduction theory:

> His source is what the patients tell him when he manages to put them into what he himself calls *a state similar to hypnosis*. He then takes what he hears as revelations, but what one really gets are the phantasies of patients about their childhood, and not the real story. *My first great etiological error also arose in this very way. The patients suggest something to him, and he then reverses it.*[110]

Clearly Freud knew very well that the scenes of seduction had been the direct result of the hypnotic-suggestive aspects of his psychoanalytic method and the veritable *folie à deux* that it unleashed between him and his patients. The trouble is *he never admitted this in public*, neither at the time nor afterward. Masson claims that "the letter [of September 21, 1897] symbolizes the beginning of an internal reconciliation with his colleagues."[111] Not so. Freud, on the contrary, carefully hid from his colleagues the fact that he had renounced his theory, and he did such a good job of it that Löwenfeld – the "stupid" Löwenfeld – was still asking in 1904 "to what extent he [Freud] still holds to his views published in 1896."[112] In the *Three Essays on the Theory of Sexuality* of 1905, referring to the reality of the seduction scenes, Freud still insists: "I cannot admit that in my paper on the 'Aetiology of hysteria' I exaggerated the frequency or importance of that influence."[113] And a year later: "I . . . over-estimated the frequency of such events (*though in other respects they were not open to doubt*)."[114] As Jean Schimeck has shown, it was not till 1914 that Freud began to publicly admit the fantasmatic nature of these scenes, and it was not till 1925 that he mentioned his patients' accusations against their fathers – and not till 1933 did he pull from his hat the "seductive" *mother* (who, for the record, appears nowhere in the letters to Fliess).[115]

"I shall not tell it in Dan, nor speak of it in Askelon, in the land of the Philistines":[116] Freud never admitted the real reason for his abandoning the seduction theory, for that would have been an admission, not only of the defeat, but of the dangers of his psychoanalytic method. On the contrary, he continued to publicly support his theory and even, for a certain time, to cynically apply it in his practice,[117] all the while searching for a way to get himself out of the cul-de-sac he had gotten himself into. The rest is well known: the birth of "psychoanalysis proper." In the weeks that followed, Freud suddenly found in his self-analysis that he had been in love with his mother and jealous of his father, and then concluded, based on an analysis of Sophocles' *Oedipus Rex*, that this is a "universal event in childhood . . . Everyone was once a budding Oedipus in fantasy."[118] Was this the dazzling "discovery" of the Oedipus complex? Not at all: the universality of the Oedipus complex is affirmed in a perfectly arbitrary fashion, with no supporting clinical material whatsoever (except for the particularly suspect self-analysis), in order to find an ad hoc explanation for his patients' constant stories of paternal seduction. The same goes for the Fliessian idea of infantile sexuality, to which Freud gradually gravitated in the months that followed:[119] if the Freudian child is "polymorphously perverse," it is because Freud had to find an explanation for his patients' torrid stories of sodomy and fellatio, not at all because he had any empirical evidence of it.

In clear: the Oedipus complex, infantile sexuality, the wish-fantasies, all of Freud's self-proclaimed discoveries are arbitrary constructions designed to explain away his patients' stories of incest and perversion while simultaneously excusing the method that had provoked them. Freud never abandoned his seduction theory, nor hypnosis, nor suggestion. He simply denied them, attributing them to his patients' stories, to *their* unconscious wishes, and attributing the hypnotic-suggestive elements of the analytic cure to *their* transference love. Masson, feminists, and child abuse activists tell us that Freud covered up the despicable actions of pedophile fathers. Not so. He covered up the hypnosis that allowed him to obtain the stories, while leaving the astonished world with an Oedipal unconscious. The Oedipus complex is a hypnotic myth, superimposed on the no less hypnotic myth of infantile seduction, and it serves no purpose whatsoever to oppose the one myth to the other, for they are intrinsically bound together. True, we are all obsessed with incest, but do we know that it is because we are living in a world fashioned by the hypnotic pact between Dr. Freud and his patients?

Translated by DOUGLAS BRICK

Postscript

Did Freud lie when he wrote in 1914 that at the time when he still believed in the seduction theory, he "was readily inclined to accept as true and aetiologically significant the statements made by patients in which they ascribed their symptoms to passive sexual experiences in the first years of childhood – to put it bluntly, to seduction"?[120] Or did the patients indeed volunteer such scenes in order to match Freud's theoretical expectations, as I argue above? Han Israëls, Allen Esterson, and Frederick Crews, whom I take to task on this point, have each graced me privately with eloquent and precise rebuttals, which have led me to qualify somewhat some of my statements.

I will summarize here my critics' objections:

1. Contrary to what I claim, Freud's patients did not "*tell* him everything that he wanted them to say." As Han Israëls rightly points out in a letter to me, most of the time "they 'reproduced' certain 'scenes' ... performed certain *acts*, including, maybe, screaming, or protesting," which were then interpreted by Freud as signs of sexual molestation. In other words, what we are dealing with are not verbal accounts made by the patients themselves, but highly interpretive translations of dramatic acting-outs into narratives of abuse.

2. Far from consisting of complete memories of sexual scenes, the material obtained from the patients was usually in the form of disconnected

fragments of ideas, images, or sensations from which *Freud* – not the patients – "re"-constructed the alleged sexual seduction. As Freud wrote himself in "Heredity and the aetiology of the neuroses": "The memory must be extracted from [the patient] piece by piece."[121]

3. Far from volunteering confirmatory-looking memories, the patients more often than not resisted vehemently Freud's reconstructions of the supposed sexual event: "Nor do they ever in the course of a treatment suddenly present the physician with a complete recollection of a scene of this kind. One only succeeds in awakening the psychical trace of a precocious sexual event under the most energetic pressure of the analytic procedure, and against an enormous resistance."[122] In 1913, in an article in which he is clearly referring to the seduction theory period, Freud even goes as far as to write that "telling and describing [the patient's] repressed trauma to him did not even result in any recollection of it coming into his mind"[123] – which flatly contradicts what he writes one year later in the "History of the psycho-analytic movement."

4. Even the passages that seem to refer to actual recollections on the part of the patients are highly ambiguous. When Freud writes to Fliess, for example, "Eckstein has a scene where the diabolus sticks needles into her fingers,"[124] or "Imagine, I obtained a scene about the circumcision of a girl,"[125] how can we be sure that Freud is not referring in fact to a scene analytically reconstructed by himself? Given Freud's life-long confidence in his own reconstructions and interpretations (even the most far-fetched), this kind of statement can hardly be taken as evidence that the scenes were reported by the patients themselves.

All these points are well taken, and I do actually make some of them myself. Concerning the first three, my critics are right to point out that, in many instances, Freud simply foisted his analytical reconstructions on his patients without getting the slightest corroboration from them (see for instance the exemplary case of G. de B. in the letters to Fliess: "She is now in the throes of the most vehement resistance . . . I have threatened to send her away and in the process convinced myself that she has already gained a good deal of certainty which she is reluctant to acknowledge").[126] I must therefore recognize that I got carried away by my own rhetoric when I wrote that "Freud's patients – or at least some of them – really did 'spontaneously' tell him everything that he wanted them to say," or again, that "Freud said whatever he felt like, and his patients faithfully repeated after him." I will allow that in many cases they did not, and that when they did, the confirmations that Freud extracted from them were in fact much more ambiguous than he would have it.

This does not mean, however, that Freud did not get *any* scenes from his patients. The fact that these scenes had to be "extracted . . . piece by piece" and "against an enormous resistance" does not preclude that the patients – or their memory – eventually gave in to Freud's relentless suggestions, especially as Freud was still using at the time a technique of the hypnotic type (a point that has not been taken into account by previous reconstructions of the whole episode). The full-blown "reproduction" of the infantile scene that I quote above is a good example of this. However fragmentary and ambiguous some of the scenes mentioned in the Fliess letters may have been, it cannot be doubted on the whole that many patients eventually did provide Freud with what he was looking for, and that this fueled his confidence in his investigative technique. The patient quoted by Löwenfeld, for example, denied having ever believed in the reality of the scenes elicited by Freud, not that he had had these scenes. Given Freud's methodological recklessness, that was enough to get him going. Besides, that Freud's patients must have come up with confirmatory scenes (full-blown or fragmentary) is indirectly corroborated by the letter of recantation of September 21, 1897, for Freud does not list there the absence of confirmations among the reasons for his abandoning his theory. Quite the contrary, he mentions the fact that such scenes never surface *in the psychoses*, implying by the same token that they do *in the neuroses*. See also his statement to the effect that "there are no indications of reality in the unconscious, so that one cannot distinguish between truth and fiction that has been cathected with affect": what Freud is saying here is that he doubts the reality of scenes *that he did obtain*.

As I see it, it is probably a chicken-and-egg problem to try to determine whether Freud's statements regarding his patients' scenes refer to actual "reproductions" *or* to speculative interpretations and reconstructions on his part. Both processes were at work simultaneously: Freud's constructions prompted "confirmations" from the patients which prompted other constructions, and so forth. The limited, historical point that I am trying to make here is that however arbitrary Freud's interpretations and reconstructions may have been, his patients (at least those who did not slam the door after a while) must have participated to some extent in his theoretical delusions, otherwise his speculations would quickly have come to a halt for lack of evidence. My larger claim is that this is the only kind of "evidence" that one is likely to get in psychoanalysis and, more generally, in any kind of clinical or psychological encounter. Freud's seduction theory was clearly a *folie à deux*, or rather a *folie à plusieurs*, but so too is orthodox psychoanalysis, Jungian analytical psychology, Adlerian individual psychology, cognitive-behavioral therapy, and even the most rigorous experimental psychology. Each of these disciplines *produces* the evidence on which it rests, which means that it is pointless to try to disconfirm them.

Here resides my disagreement with my fellow Freud critics: whereas they think that psychoanalysis should be criticized for its lack of evidence, or for its manufacturing of evidence, I tend to think that the problem with psychoanalysis is rather its overabundance of evidence. It is not that psychoanalysis is false, speculative, or fabricated that should concern us most, but rather that it always becomes true for those who submit to it. Debunking psychoanalysis's false claims is not enough. What we need to understand is how it creates the reality it purports to describe.

Notes

1 Freud 1933, p. 120.
2 Masson 1992.
3 Masson 1992, p. 190.
4 Rush 1977, pp. 31–45; Herman 1981, pp. 9–10.
5 At Freud's request, Fliess had operated on Emma Eckstein's nose to cure her of a "nasal reflex neurosis" and forgot to remove a mass of surgical gauze. The patient almost died from profuse bleeding when the gauze was finally removed and was left permanently disfigured.
6 Despite his assurances to the contrary (Masson 1992, pp. 213–214, n. 4), Masson draws heavily on Schur (1966, p. 83): "It would . . . seem that Emma was one of the first patients who offered Freud a clue to the crucial realization that what his patients had described to him as actual episodes were fantasies." See also Schur 1972.
7 Freud 1985, p. 239. This idea had already been expressed in a footnote to Freud's "Further remarks on the neuro-psychoses of defence" (February 1896): "I myself am inclined to think that the stories of being assaulted which hysterics so frequently invent may be obsessional fictions which arise from the memory-trace of a childhood trauma" (Freud 1896b, p. 164). Contrary to what Masson seems to think, fantasy is an integral part of the seduction theory, insofar as it is conceived of by Freud as a formation that is *added* to the memory of the real "scene." On this point see Laplanche and Pontalis 1964, pp. 1847–1848; Schimek 1987, p. 239; and especially Swales 1982a, pp. 11–14.
8 Masson 1992, p. 134. For a more sober assessment of what Freud called his "splendid isolation" during that time, see Ellenberger 1970, pp. 448, 455, 468; Borch-Jacobsen and Shamdasani 2006, pp. 148–153.
9 Sulloway 1992, ch. 8; see also Foucault 1978; Makari 1997.
10 See the edition available to Freud in 1896–97: Krafft-Ebing 1894, ch. 6, par. 1, "Offense against morality in the form of exhibition," Cases 108 and 199; par. 2, "Rape and Murder," pp. 361–362: "Today, rape on children is remarkably frequent. Hofmann (*Ger. Med.*, i, p. 155) and Tardieu (*Attentats*) report horrible cases. The latter establishes the fact that, from 1851 to 1875 inclusive, 22,017 cases of rape came before the courts in France, and of these, 17,657 were committed on children"; par. 6, "Violation of individuals under the age of fourteen," p. 375: "The manner in which acts of immorality are committed on children differs widely . . . They consist chiefly in libidinous manipulations of the female genitals, active manustrupation (using the child's hand for onanism), flagellation, etc. Less frequent is cunnilingus, *irrumare* in boys or girls, pederasty of girls, coitus between the thighs, exhibition"; par. 9 on "Incest," pp. 412–414; etc. See also Krafft-Ebing 1895, reissued and expanded in 1898 in Krafft-Ebing 1897–99, Heft IV, pp. 91–127.
11 Freud 1985, p. 184.
12 Schrenck-Notzing 1892; Moll 1889; Löwenfeld 1901; Krafft-Ebing 1893; 1891; 1896. Krafft-Ebing founded a private clinic in 1886 where "psychical treatment" – in other words, Bernheim's method of suggestion – was used intensively; see Shorter 1992, p. 154. Among others who divided their interests between hypnotism and the "sexual theory" were August Forel, Paul Möbius, and Max Dessoir.
13 Gaupp 1900, p. 234 (also in Kiell 1988, p. 38).
14 Nunberg and Federn 1967, p. 49.
15 Freud and Jung 1974, p. 223.
16 Moll 1913, p. 190.
17 Freud 1985, p. 412.
18 Löwenfeld 1895. See also Freud 1985, p. 141.
19 Löwenfeld 1901, p. 358.
20 Löwenfeld 1899, p. 195.

21 Freud 1985, p. 413 n. 3.

22 Masson 1992, p. xxii.

23 Israëls and Schatzman 1993, pp. 43–44.

24 Noted by Israëls and Schatzman 1993, p. 44 n. 5.

25 See Bleuler 1896, p. 525: "we cannot be at all sure that the 'state of concentration' is not quite simply a particular form of hypnosis. It is also quite possible that the therapeutic successes of the 'cathartic method' are based quite simply on suggestion rather than on abreaction of the suppressed affect" (also in Kiell 1988, p. 74). See also Strümpell 1896, p. 161: "I wonder about the quality of materials mined from a patient under hypnotic influence. I am afraid that many hysterical women will be encouraged to give free rein to their fantasies and inventiveness. The attending physician can easily be put into a very slippery position" (also in Kiell 1988, p. 68). See also Clarcke 1896, p. 414: "The necessity of bearing in mind, in studying hysterical patients, the great readiness with which they respond to suggestions, may be reiterated, as the weak point in the method of investigation may perhaps be found here. The danger being that in such confessions the patients would be liable to make statements in accordance with the slightest suggestion given to them, it might be quite unconsciously given to them, by the investigator" (also in Kiell 1988, p. 82). Somewhat later, Oskar Vogt attributed the therapeutic results alleged by Breuer and Freud to autosuggestion (Vogt 1899, p. 74).

26 Breuer and Freud 1895, p. 295.

27 Original account of the discussion of November 4, 1895 that followed the three lectures "On hysteria," given by Freud before the Vienna College of Physicians, October 14, 21 and 28, 1895, in Freud 1895b, pp. 1717–1718.

28 Freud 1896a, p. 153.

29 Freud 1896c, p. 204–205.

30 Freud 1898, p. 269; emphasis added.

31 Compare with what Judith Herman, one of the most forceful advocates of "recovered memory therapy," says about the preliminary work with "incest survivors": "The patient may not have full recall of the traumatic history and may initially deny such a history, even with careful, direct questioning" (Herman 1992, p. 157).

32 Freud 1898, p. 269.

33 Freud (1916–17), p. 452.

34 Freud 1925, p. 35.

35 Freud (1888–89), p. 79.

36 On this question, see Borch-Jacobsen, Koeppel, and Scherrer 1984, pp. 49–51; Makari 1992, pp. 415–432.

37 Original account of the lecture "On hypnosis and suggestion" given by Freud before the Medical Club of Vienna, April 27 and May 4, 1892 (Freud 1992, p. 175). Freud returns to this point in *Group Psychology and the Analysis of the Ego*, a sign of his long-lasting attachment to Charcot's theories: "It seems to me worth emphasizing the fact that the discussion in this section [ch. 10 of *Group Psychology*] has induced us to give up Bernheim's conception of hypnosis and go back to the *naif* earlier one [clearly an allusion to Charcot]. According to Bernheim all hypnotic phenomena are to be traced to the factor of suggestion, which is not itself capable of further explanation. We have come to the conclusion that suggestion is a partial manifestation of the *state* [emphasis added] of hypnosis, and that hypnosis is solidly founded upon a predisposition which has survived in the unconscious from the early history of the human family" (Freud 1921, p. 128).

38 Nunberg and Federn 1967, vol. 2, p. 453; emphasis added.

39 See what Freud himself wrote in "Psychical (or mental) treatment" 1890, a defense of Bernheim's suggestive psychotherapy: "But hypnosis is in no sense a sleep like our nocturnal sleep or like the sleep produced by drugs … While the subject behaves to the rest of the external world as though he were asleep, that is, as though all his senses were diverted from it, he is *awake* in his relation to the person who hypnotized him; he hears

and sees him alone, and him he understands and answers" (Freud 1890, p. 295; Freud's emphasis).

40 Freud 1985, pp. 21–22.

41 At least officially: we know now that as late as 1919, Freud continued to recommend the use of hypnosis in some cases; see the letters to Paul Federn mentioned in Fichtner and Hirschmüller 1988, p. 412; and in Chertok, Stengers, and Gille 1990, p. 265. Intriguingly, the Hungarian stage hypnotist Franz J. Polgar published in 1951 an autobiography in which he claimed to have been introduced to Freud by Ferenczi and to have acted as his "medical hypnotist" for a period of six months in 1924: Polgar 1951; see also Schneck 1976; Gravitz and Gerton 1981. However, one finds no trace of Polgar in the Freud–Ferenczi correspondence.

42 Breuer and Freud 1895, p. 268. In Draft H, which dates from January 1895, Freud even speaks of "concentration hypnosis" (Freud 1985, p. 109).

43 Breuer and Freud 1895, p. 271.

44 Freud 1900, p. 102.

45 Obholzer 1982, p. 38.

46 Freud 1916–17, p. 292. On this question of psychoanalysis's alleged break with hypnosis, see Borch-Jacobsen 1988, ch. 3; and "Hypnosis in psychoanalysis," in Borch-Jacobsen 1992.

47 Janet 1989, pp. 174–175.

48 Bernheim 1891. A similar point has been made more recently by Milton Erickson, for whom there can well be "hypnosis" without hypnotic ritual. See Erickson 1967, pp. 8, 18, 31, etc.; Haley 1973, pp. 20, 193.

49 Bernheim 1892.

50 See for instance Benedikt 1892; Strümpell 1892.

51 Freud 1985, p. 446; modified translation. The context of this admission is not insignificant, since it is to be found in a letter in which Freud tries to defend himself against Fliess's accusation of "read[ing] his own thoughts into other people" (1985, p. 447).

52 Breuer and Freud 1895, pp. 109–110.

53 See Heidenhain 1888, p. 62: "At a sitting of the medical section on the 13th of February, 1880, Professor Berger [a neurologist from Breslau] made a communication to the effect that a lady he had for months been treating for cataleptic symptoms, during one of her fits obeyed the order to perform certain actions, as soon as he lightly laid his hand on the crown of her head, and he also stated that the same observation had been made on an artificially hypnotized individual." As a footnote to the next page makes clear, this new hypnotic technique belonged in fact to the old paraphernalia of magnetic "passes": "When the above-described researches were discussed, we were told from all sides that [the Danish stage hypnotist Carl] Hansen, when he wished to make his media perform certain actions, kept one hand on their heads or moved it from side to side." Freud quotes Heidenhain alongside Charcot in his 1889 preface to Bernheim's *Suggestion* (Freud 1888–89, p. 76).

54 Freud 1896c, p. 204.

55 Schimek 1987, p. 944. It is worth noting that Schimek, after having thus emphasized the hypnotic nature of Freud's pressure technique, promptly shies away from drawing the obvious consequence of his analysis: "But my emphasis is not primarily on the role of suggestion in the contents of the patients' material" (1987, p. 944). Why not?

56 Freud 1985, p. 226; modified translation.

57 Freud 1985, p. 288; Freud's emphasis.

58 Freud 1896c, p. 204; emphasis added.

59 Freud 1921, p. 89.

60 Freud and Jung 1974, p. 88.

61 Aschaffenburg 1906, p. 1796.

62 Erickson 1967, p. 19.

63 Among so many other similar passages, see Freud 1896c, p. 199: "the singling out of the sexual factor in the aetiology of hysteria springs at least from no preconceived opinion on my part. The two investigators as whose pupil I began my studies of hysteria, Charcot and Breuer, were far from having any such presupposition; in fact they had a personal disinclination to it which I originally shared. Only the most laborious and detailed investigations have converted me, and that slowly enough, to the view I hold to-day." See also Freud 1910, p. 40.

64 Macmillan 1997, ch. 5.

65 Freud 1985, p. 39.

66 Freud 1985, p. 57; modified translation.

67 Freud 1985, p. 61.

68 Freud 1985, pp. 48 and 56.

69 Freud 1985, pp. 74, 76–77, 82, 111–112.

70 Freud 1985, p. 141; Freud's emphasis.

71 Freud 1985, p. 149; emphasis added.

72 Freud 1985, p. 226.

73 Freud 1896c, p. 220; emphasis added.

74 Freud 1985, p. 188.

75 Freud 1985, p. 187.

76 Freud 1985, p. 204.

77 Freud 1985, p. 218.

78 Freud 1985, pp. 223–224.

79 Freud 1985, p. 219. On this subject, see Swales 1982a; 1983.

80 Freud 1985, p. 224.

81 Bernheim 1891, pp. 12–13: "all these stories of Sabbath, of succubi, of incubi, all these diabolic scenes were nothing other than suggested hallucinatory phenomena; all these scenes, all these turpitudes can be artificially produced by hypnotic suggestion, either as dreams that are actually experienced, or as retroactive memory-illusions that leave in the mind of those subjected to the suggestion an impression of absolute truth. The bewitched were reporting all this as if it had actually taken place, and the sorcerers themselves were confessing to it"; quoted in Swales 1988, pp. 154–155 nn. 46 and 47. Bernheim's remarks were implicitly directed against Charcot and Richer 1887, who equated the various *stigmata diaboli* of the possessed with the specific (that is to say non-suggested) "stigmata" of *grande hystérie*. Bernheim's interest in the legal implications of suggestion had been piqued initially by a murder case in Eastern Europe, in which a rabbi's son had testified that he had seen his father ritually murder a Christian child; see Bernheim 1891, pp. 245–248.

82 Freud 1985, p. 227. One will note the parallel drawn by Freud between the Inquisitors' "therapy" and his own.

83 Freud 1985, pp. 224–225. This last sentence is an allusion to the near fatal bleeding caused by Fliess's botched nasal operation (see note 5 above).

84 Did Freud check this interesting detail himself?

85 Freud 1985, p. 227.

86 Freud 1985, p. 447.

87 Freud 1985, p. 227; emphasis added.

88 Herman 1992, p. 13.

89 Chodoff 1966; Schusdek 1966.

90 Chodoff 1966, pp. 508–509.

91 Cioffi 1998, pp. 199–204, 205–210; Swales 1982; 1983; Schimek 1987; Stadlen (unpublished lectures); Esterson 1993; Scharnberg 1993; Israëls and Schatzman 1993.

92 Freud 1896c, p. 205: "It is exactly like putting together a child's picture-puzzle: after many attempts, we become absolutely certain in the end which piece belongs in the empty gap ... In the same way, the contents of the infantile scenes turn out to be indispensable supplements to the associative and logical framework of the neurosis,

whose insertion makes its course of development for the first time evident, or even, as we might often say, self-evident."

93 Freud 1914a, p. 17.

94 Macmillan 1991, ch. 8.

95 Freud 1896a, p. 152; 1896b, p. 163.

96 Freud 1896c, p. 208.

97 See Jean Schimek's excellent chronological reconstruction in Schimek 1987, pp. 955–960.

98 See letter of May 4, 1896, in Freud 1985, p. 185: "this year for the first time my consulting room is empty ... for weeks on end I see no new faces, cannot begin any new treatment, and ... none of the old ones is completed."

99 Herman 1981, p. 9: "Recognizing the implicit challenge to patriarchal values, Freud refused to identify fathers publicly as sexual aggressors. Though in his private correspondence he cited 'seduction by the father' as the 'essential point' in hysteria, he was never able to bring himself to make his statement in public. Scrupulously honest and courageous in other respects, Freud falsified his incest cases."

100 Esterson 1993, p. 29: "Freud's early patients did *not* recount stories of infantile seductions, these stories were actually analytic reconstructions which he foisted on them." Crews 1995, pp. 60–61: "In 1896 the alleged seducers of infants were said to have been governesses, teachers, servants, strangers, and siblings, but in later descriptions Freud retrospectively changed most of them to *fathers* so that a properly oedipal spin could be placed on the recycled material."

101 I agree on this point with James Hopkins's contention that "Freud's [unpublished] writings of 1897 ... make clear that during 1897 he held a theory of paternal abuse" (Crews has since granted this point). However, I would certainly be loath to jump with Hopkins to the conclusion that the scenes of paternal abuse "were liable to arise without suggestion" (Crews 1995, p. 81). The paternal etiology appears for the first time in a letter to Fliess of December 6, 1896 and clearly occupies Freud's mind until at least April 1898 (see letters of January 24, 1897; February 8, 1897; April 28, 1897; May 2 and 31, 1897; July 7, 1897; September 21, 1897; October 3, 1897; December 12, 1897; April 27, 1898).

102 Besides, Herman's cover-up hypothesis does not tally with the abstract of "The aetiology of hysteria" included in the very official bibliography of his scientific writings that Freud submitted in May 1897 when he applied for the position of "Professor extraordinarius" (Krafft-Ebing being his referee): "In their content [the infantile sexual experiences] must be described as 'perversions,' and those responsible *are as a rule to be looked for among the patient's nearest relatives*" (Freud 1897, p. 254; emphasis added). Since Freud is even more explicit here than he had been the year before, it seems fairly obvious that he was quite prepared to go public with his incest theory.

103 Klein and Tribich 1982, p. 18. As Frank Cioffi has cogently argued against Grünbaum 1984, the abandonment of the seduction theory is *not* a case of Popperian falsification (Cioffi 1998, p. 240–264). See also Borch-Jacobsen 2006.

104 No later than two weeks after his lecture on "The aetiology of hysteria," Freud was already confessing to Fliess that "none of the old [cases] are completed" (Freud 1985, p. 185).

105 Freud 1985, p. 264.

106 Freud 1914a, p. 17.

107 Freud 1985, p. 265; emphasis added.

108 Freud 1925, p. 33; emphasis added.

109 Freud 1925, p. 35.

110 Quoted in Masson 1992, p. 182; emphasis added. The true significance of this letter clearly escapes Masson, who is content with repeating the usual Freudian mantra: "What Freud states here explicitly is that memories of seduction (and, by extension, of real traumas) are not memories at all, but fantasies." In reality, what Freud states here

(and states nowhere else so explicitly) is that these fantasies of seduction were fantasies *elicited under hypnosis*, hence liable to be cases of suggestion and/or autosuggestion.

111 Masson 1992, p. 110.
112 Löwenfeld 1904, p. 296; quoted in Masson 1992, p. 121. Löwenfeld, who had been in correspondence with Freud, mentioned that, according to the latter, obsessional symptoms did not stem "directly from real sexual experiences, but from fantasies which attach themselves to these experiences." But, as Löwenfeld judiciously added: "This modification does not change the basic tenets of the theory." One finds a similar summary of Freud's theory in Moll 1909, p. 190.
113 Freud 1905a, p. 190.
114 Freud 1906, p. 274; emphasis added.
115 Freud 1933, pp. 232 and 238: "girls regularly accuse their mother of seducing them."
116 Letter to Fliess of September 21, 1897, in Freud 1985, p. 265. Masson rightly restores Freud's slip – "Dan," instead of "Gath" – which the editors of Freud 1954 had piously (and silently) corrected. 2 Samuel 1:20 reads: "Tell it not in Gath, publish it not in the streets of Askelon; lest the daughters of the Philistines rejoice, lest the daughters of the uncircumcised triumph" (King James Bible).
117 Freud's analysis of one of his dreams of that period reveals his feelings of guilt in this respect: "The whole dream was full of the most mortifying allusions to my present impotence as a therapist ... The dream could be summed up as 'bad treatment.' Just as the old woman got money from me for her bad treatment, so today I get money for the bad treatment of my patients" (Freud 1985, p. 269).
118 Freud 1985, p. 272.
119 Freud 1985, p. 279: "We must assume that in infancy the release of sexuality is not yet so much localized as it is later, so that the zones which are later abandoned (and perhaps the whole surface of the body as well) also instigates something that is analogous to the later release of sexuality." On this question, see Sulloway 1992, ch. 6.
120 Freud 1914a, p. 17.
121 Freud 1896a, p. 153.
122 Freud 1896a, p. 153.
123 Freud 1896b, p. 141.
124 Freud 1985, pp. 224–225.
125 Freud 1985, p. 227.
126 Freud 1985, pp. 220–221.

3   A black box named "Sybil"

Since the mid-1970s, a strange ailment has spread across the North American continent. All over (notably in therapy), men and women (especially women)[1] have discovered that they are not one, but multiple. The insignificant person that they thought they were up until then was nothing but a mask, they say. Behind this misleading façade hid a host of personalities that the ostensible personality knew nothing about. This orderly bureaucrat was harboring a wild biker who would tour the bars while he, the bureaucrat, was sound asleep. This soccer mom had no idea that she was a stripper in the evening. This dutiful student couldn't understand why she kept receiving bad grades: it was *the other*, the party girl, who took the tests in her place!

The people afflicted with this peculiar ailment, which psychiatrists call Multiple Personality Disorder, or MPD, will tell you that these personalities are as real as you and me. They each have their own distinct character, their own diction, handwriting, name, history, and personal memories. One can call them, talk to them, even shake their hand. One day, you marry personality A, and the next you find yourself with personality B. You go to bed with personality C, and personality D hauls you into court for rape. A person suffering from MPD, writes the psychiatrist Bennett G. Braun, is

> one human being demonstrating two or more personalities with identifiable, distinctive, and consistently ongoing characteristics, each of which has a relatively separate memory of its life history ... There must also be a demonstration of the transfer of executive control of the body from one personality to another (switching). However, the total individual is never out of touch with reality. The host personality (the one who has executive control of the body the greatest percentage of the time during a given time) often experiences periods of amnesia, time loss, or blackouts. Other personalities may or may not experience this.[2]

How are we to explain this sudden multiplication of souls? Only forty years ago, multiple personality was considered an extremely rare psychiatric condition. In a very thorough historical survey published in 1944, the psychiatrists Taylor and Martin listed only seventy-six cases over a period of 128 years; by the time of their study the syndrome had all but disappeared from the psychiatric map.[3] In 1980, however, Georges Greaves, one of the first psychiatrists to specialize in the treatment of multiple personality in the 1970s, reported no less than thirty-seven cases since 1971, six of whom came from the clientele of his colleague Ralph B. Allison.[4] That same year, Eugene Bliss, another pioneer, mentioned that he had personally observed fourteen cases.[5] Two years later, Myron Boor and Richard Kluft counted, respectively, 79 and 130 cases (of which 70 were treated by Kluft himself).[6] Boor already spoke of an "epidemic," even though at this stage the epidemic seems to have raged mainly in the offices of a few select specialists. In 1984 there were 1,000 cases in treatment, and 4,000 in 1989.[7] The movement continued the following decade. Specialists mentioned a total of 30,000 and even 50,000 cases. Others, boldly extrapolating, claimed that 2 or 3 percent of the US population probably suffered from this disorder without knowing it.[8] Clearly, these fanciful projections have more to do with psychiatric marketing than with statistical science, but the scale of the phenomenon cannot be doubted. From the beginning of the 1990s onwards, "multiples" were everywhere – in therapy, in psychiatric hospitals, on television, and in the courts.

It is not only the number of people afflicted with MPD that has increased, it is also the number of personalities. The classical descriptions given near the end of the nineteenth century by Azam, Janet, Breuer, William James, or Morton Prince mention a limited number of personalities.[9] In the most typical scenario, that of the dual personality, the patient would oscillate between a depressed, anxious, puritan host-personality afflicted with various psychosomatic symptoms and lapses of memory, and a seductive, uninhibited, teasing personality full of contempt for the host-personality. Sometimes, a third persona joined in the game, but the list of players seldom grew longer than this. Of the seventy-six cases counted by Taylor and Martin, forty-eight presented two personalities, twelve presented three, and only one presented more than eight. On this point as well, the "multiples" of the 1980s–1990s broke new ground. In 1979, the average number of personalities per patient was slightly below ten. In 1989, it was thirteen, and the following year it jumped to twenty-five personalities.[10] Since then, it has become customary to hear about patients presenting several dozen, even several hundred personalities. In order to keep track of them, therapists draft complicated tables with arrows tracing the genealogy of the various personalities (often therapists use computers to compile these genealogical tables).

Most of the personalities – or "alters," as MPD experts call them – conform to specific types, indeed caricatures. First of all, there is the unflagging host-personality, a poor sap whose ignorance of the other personalities exposes her to all sorts of snubs and mix-ups. In her wardrobe, she finds clothes that she never bought. Strangers greet her on the street, claiming to have known her for a long time. She is asked to pay the mortgage on a house that she is told she purchased recently. Some alters, called "internal persecutors," seem to have no other purpose in life than to hurt her, sabotaging her treatment or romantic relationships. Often these hostilities lead to physical aggression and homicide attempts – what uninformed people interpret, inevitably, as self-mutilation and attempted suicide.

Fortunately, there are also "protector personalities" who keep a look-out and intervene to thwart the machinations of the internal persecutors. Without them, "multiples" would perish in droves, for it is they who call the doctor when the host-personality takes too strong a dose of barbiturates or slits her wrists.

Then, there are the child personalities – "the little ones," as they are fondly called – who curl up in your arms, demand the breast or the bottle, swamp you with touching drawings. Add to this list as well:

personalities of loose morals (often prostitutes), who indulge in debaucheries that would horrify the host-personality

personalities of the opposite sex and gay personalities, who occasion various titillating, erotic schemes

administrators and obsessive-compulsive personalities, who help the host-personality make a living

anesthetic personalities, capable of withstanding pain and physical or sexual violence

"Special Purpose Fragments," sub-personalities that correspond to extremely specific tasks, like "driving the car into the garage" or "preparing dinner for a guest"

substance abusers, addicted to alcohol or to drugs

animal personalities (spider, starfish, turtle, and so on), resistant to therapy

demons

spirits

extra-terrestrials

imitators and imposters, who play all kinds of outrageous tricks on the host-personality and the therapist (they simulate the other personalities, so that one can never know for sure with whom one is dealing)[11].

The relations between these various personalities are complex, as one might expect. Some hold a comprehensive view of the whole system of alters; others have only a partial understanding of it; and others still believe they are alone in the world. When two or more personalities know each other, one speaks of "co-consciousness," a term taken from Morton Prince's analysis of the famous "Sally Beauchamp" case. Indeed, this is the goal of treatment: to break the "amnesic barriers" between the personalities in order to encourage an increasing co-consciousness and, through this process, a "fusion" or "integration" of the alters into a single personality. Like diplomats engaged in difficult, multilateral negotiations, therapists shuttle between the various personalities, relaying the messages of one party to another, dealing with personalities delegated by other personalities, passing "contracts" with the different sides in the hopes of creating irreversible situations on the ground. For instance, one asks this or that internal persecutor not to hurt the host-personality during a set period of time, while another personality is asked not to "come out" during a given situation in daily life. Yet there are always new personalities who do not consider themselves bound to these contracts. Or else the delegates with whom one had dealt are disowned by those on whose behalf they were speaking, or they turn out to be imposters, and the whole process starts all over again. The integration of personalities is a constant struggle, indeed an interminable one.

Another aspect of the treatment, the "abreactive work," consists of putting patients under hypnosis or in some other altered state of consciousness and making them relive the traumas that are supposed to have caused their condition. This is the most bizarre thing: almost all of them, once in therapy, declare they have been subjected to physical and sexual abuse during their childhood. In their trance, the personalities relive the scenes of incest or rape that the host-personality had until then preferred to forget, exactly like when Freud exhumed "seduction scene" after "seduction scene" from his hysterical patients. But Freud, as we know, quickly came to see these scenes as fantasies expressing Oedipal desires, rather than memories of real, traumatic events. MPD experts on the other hand, encouraged by the writings of renegade psychoanalyst Jeffrey Masson,[12] are convinced that Freud was wrong to abandon his seduction theory. Statistics in hand, they assure us that child abuse and incest are much more widespread than was ever imagined in Freud's time and that their patients are in no way fantasizing.

One recognizes here a new version of the traumatic-dissociative theory of hysteria proposed more than a century ago by Freud and his colleague and rival Pierre Janet. MPD is due, present-day experts claim, to severe traumas suffered during childhood, or, to be more exact, to the "dissociations" caused by these traumas. Helpless, paralyzed by pain and shame, the child had no other recourse, they say, than to dissociate the traumatic event from the rest of her psyche. She put herself into a kind of hypnotic trance, acting as if nothing had happened – as if the unbearable occurrence had happened not to her, but to *someone else*. Like the lizard who separates from its tail in a dangerous situation, she cleaved, divided, multiplied herself to avoid being totally annihilated. And of course, the more severe and repetitive the trauma, the more fragmented the psyche will be, the more the subject will get used to dissociating in situations that remind her of the trauma in one way or another. The slightest emotion or annoyance acts upon "multiples" like a trigger that sets in motion the coping mechanism that had previously enabled them to escape the reality of the original trauma.

Faced with a person presenting dozens of personalities, one can be sure, the theory predicts, that he or she has survived terrible abuse, much like the survivors of the Holocaust or of totalitarian regimes. Under these circumstances, one is not surprised to find that the increase in the number of personalities has been matched by an increase in the severity of the traumas alleged by the patients and their therapists. From the beginning of the 1980s onward, the memories of the "multiples" became ever more macabre. People spoke of extreme perversities, of sadistic torture, and even of ritual abuse perpetrated on children by a secret satanic cult, with blood sacrifices, necrophagy, and gang rapes. (One is reminded again of the memories of satanic torture that Freud obtained from his patients during his hunt for seduction scenes.) According to this satanic rumor, multiple personality was not a spontaneous dissociative disorder, but a deliberate creation of satanists using hypnosis on their victims in order to conceal their crimes. Concerned about respectability, the most political amongst MPD theorists did their best to minimize the rumor, but there was, in fact, no way they could possibly resist it. Why refuse to believe accounts of satanic ritual abuse when one has already taken at face value accounts of sexual and physical abuse? Rejecting the satanic etiology would have called into question the traumatic etiology itself, as well as the techniques of soul probing thanks to which the first memories of sexual abuse had been obtained.

In the absence of any corrective mechanism, the rumor continued to spread. According to the chronology established by the anthropologist Sherrill Mulhern,[13] there were two papers devoted to the satanic etiology of MPD at the annual conference of the International Society for the Study of Multiple Personality and Dissociation (or ISSMPD) in 1984; two years later, there were three; in 1987, eleven; in 1989, twenty, plus a plenary session and a day-long seminar with seven speakers. In 1991, a survey of members of the American Psychological Association revealed that 30 percent of them had had at least one "cult survivor" in treatment; according to another survey of social workers in California, almost half of them believed in the existence of "the Cult."[14] During the course of fieldwork conducted at the beginning of the 1990s in Seattle, I had an opportunity to sit in on consultation groups in which the main topic of discussion between therapists was the imminence of winter solstice, that portentous day of the satanic calendar: the persecutor personalities, programmed by the Cult, were probably about to go into action . . . No need to be a historian of religion to realize that the spread of the MPD diagnosis, introduced in 1980 in the psychiatric nomenclature of the DSM-III, has amounted to a veritable epidemic of demonic possession, comparable to those of Loudun or of Morzine in the seventeenth and nineteenth centuries.

When one speaks of demons, it does not take long for the witch hunt to start. Once it was agreed that "multiples" suffered from the psychological aftermath of real abuse, the implication was inescapable: those responsible had to be found and punished. At the beginning of the 1980s, dozens of parents, daycare workers, and ministers were put on trial for sexual or satanic abuse and condemned to stiff sentences on the basis of memories recovered in therapy or during questioning by psychiatric experts and psychologists. Timeless mechanisms were put back in place, legitimized by the brand new science of trauma and dissociative disorders. The most spectacular case is that of Paul Ingram, deputy sheriff of Olympia in the state of Washington, who was accused by his own daughters of having raped them with two of his colleagues.[15] Diagnosed as suffering from MPD by two psychologists collaborating with the police investigation,[16] he submitted to exhaustive interrogations during which, put into a trance state, he recalled all the crimes that he was accused of, adding for good measure his participation in a satanic network that was responsible for twenty-five child sacrifices. In spite of having subsequently retracted his confession, he was sentenced in 1990 to twenty years in prison and served his term under number T0261446 in Building D-West A-6 of the Delaware Correctional Center, Smyrna. Indicted in similar cases, other defendants were given life sentences.

Enough was enough. Journalists and academics started to denounce the miscarriages of justice caused by advocates of MPD and recovered memory therapy (RMT).[17] Psychologists such as Elizabeth Loftus pointed out the fragility of memory, as well as the ease with which one can suggest false memories, with or without the aid of hypnosis.[18] Influential psychiatrists questioned the very reality of MPD, reproaching their colleagues for having iatrogenically created it themselves.[19] But above all, parents accused of sexually abusing their children fought back by creating an advocacy group, the False Memory Foundation, with the goal of assisting the victims of the rumor, of informing the public, and of mounting a legal counter-offensive.

In a surprising reversal, MPD experts and RMT therapists soon found themselves hauled into court for professional misconduct and were summoned to justify their allegations in front of tenacious lawyers and counter-experts armed with hard science and statistics. As it turned out, they couldn't, and the house of cards collapsed. One after another, patients turned against their ex-therapists and reproached them for having destroyed them psychically with as much vehemence as when they had implicated their parents in imaginary fornications. Advocacy groups for victims of therapeutic abuse were set up that gradually supplanted the support groups for MPD sufferers and incest survivors. As for the media, burning what they had previously adored, they now denounce the MPD humbuggery, the implantation of false memories, the pseudo-science of traumatologists, and the myth of Freudian repression.

Faced with very real legal consequences, MPD advocates were forced to downgrade their claims. Most of them now make their patients sign a release form that informs them of the potential dangers of hypnosis, and of the eventual creation of false memories and artificial "personalities" during the course of treatment. Even the term Multiple Personality Disorder is now avoided like the plague. Conforming to the new terminology introduced in 1994 in the DSM-IV, people speak instead of Dissociative Identity Disorder (DID). In actual practice, most therapists have silently opted for the less controversial diagnosis of Post-Traumatic Stress Disorder (PTSD), which has the advantage of being covered by most insurance companies. Under these circumstances, one should not be surprised that "multiples" have dwindled to the point of becoming an endangered psychiatric species. The International Society for the Study of Multiple Personality Disorder and Dissociation, which claimed at one point several thousand members, is at present anemic and was forced, in 1998, to dismiss its permanent staff. Even if a few therapists persist in producing "multiples" behind the padded doors of their offices, it is clear that MPD is no longer profitable and that it will soon be erased from the North American psychiatric landscape.

Multiple Personality Disorder is a striking example of what Ian Hacking calls a "transient mental illness," meaning by that a psychiatric syndrome that arises, evolves, and disappears according to very specific historical and local conditions.[20] Burton's "melancholy" thrived in seventeenth-century England, the "vapors" of ladies of Parisian high society in the eighteenth century, *grande hystérie* at Charcot's Salpêtrière, Beard's "neurasthenia" in late nineteenth-century, industrialized America, and "shell shock" in the muddy trenches of the First World War. MPD, likewise, has an exact date and locality: it appeared in the USA at the beginning of the 1970s; it spread over a period of twenty-five years throughout the Anglo-Saxon world and in Holland, but not elsewhere;[21] and it is now fading away, for want of what Hacking calls an "ecological niche" that would allow it to continue to develop. Critics of MPD see this as proof that we are not dealing here with a real mental condition. MPD, they say, is an iatrogenic fiction, a blend of credulity or simulation on the side of patients and of a more or less unwitting suggestion on the side of therapists – in brief, a mere illusion destined to evaporate with time. "In but a few years," predicts the psychiatrist Paul McHugh, "we will look back at the events described in this book and be dumbfounded by the gullibility of the public in the late twentieth century and by the power of psychiatric assertions to dissolve common sense."[22]

This debunking of MPD is undoubtedly useful and even absolutely necessary in court, when what matters is defending an innocent against the accusations of inquisitors disguised as psychiatric experts. It is however inadequate when it is a question of accounting for a transient illness such as MPD. To call on the good sense of the *future*, when reason and psychiatric science will have finally dissipated this groundless belief, will never allow us to explain why the American good sense of *today* (or of a little while ago) considers it a very real phenomenon. How can we hope to understand a phenomenon that we simultaneously reduce to nonexistence? And why should we reduce transience to illusion, as if only the ahistorical (nature, substance, permanence) could lay claim to reality? It is not because a phenomenon is historical and cultural that it is unreal or false, for in that case we would have to admit that the major part of our existence (including what pertains to the eminently historical accomplishments of science)[23] unfolds in a dream. To say that a mental illness is historical does not mean that it is imaginary, but only that it is created, fabricated, constructed, and that it exists as long as one *makes* it exist, exactly like any other fact (*factum* means "made").

MPD lasted as long as the consensus of psychiatrists, hypnotic practice, the concept of repression, insurance companies, judges, the campaigns for the prevention of child abuse, the feminist movement, the media, and *x* number of other elements conjoined to make it last, to support its existence in the manner of a "continued creation." When some of these elements came undone, the reality of MPD was undone at the same time. Does this mean that MPD never existed, that it was nothing but an inconsistent mirage? No, only that it does not exist anymore (at the moment),[24] now that some of the elements that had once made it possible no longer exist. It is making bad history (and bad episte-mology) to measure a historical phenomenon against some intemporal truth ("science," "common sense"), as if we did not know that such "truths" are more often than not the expression of a very temporal and continually revised con-sensus. The question to ask about a historical reality like MPD is not the critical and disqualifying one of the philosopher-judge: "Is it true or false? Real or imaginary?" It is the technical and pragmatic one of the artisan or the engineer: "How is it made? Out of what elements? How does it work? What purpose does it serve?" The historian has no need of philosophical tribunals, no use for "epistemic breaks" and "demarcations" between science and pseudo-science, science and ideology. He only wants to know how MPD was constructed, how it held together and why, after a while, it was de-constructed.

This question cannot be reduced, however, to that of the "social construction" of MPD, even if the professional interests of some psychiatrists, their networking, their political lobbying, their institutional strategies, their scientific rhetoric, and their tactics of intellectual intimidation have obviously contributed in creating a consensus around this diagnosis.[25] All too often, the notion of social construction implies the idea of a quasi-demiurgic creation, as if social actors manufactured facts, behaviors, or emotions out of a fundamentally passive material. This unilateral approach has been rightly critiqued from within "science studies" for its refusal to take into account the role played by non-human "actants,"[26] and such a critique applies all the more to the eminently human and social science that is psychiatry. Humans, even when afflicted with psychiatric disorders, are fully qualified actors and the ecological niches in which mental illnesses develop are also constructed, in part, by the patients themselves. They cooperate with doctors, theories, and institutions to keep the syndrome they suffer from alive. Far from passively submitting to the diagnosis that was given to them, the "multiples" of the 1980s–1990s thus collaborated in the definition of their con-dition, participating in the annual meetings of the ISSMPD, being active in grassroots organizations, sharing their experience with support groups,[27] on bulletin boards and in chat rooms on the Internet, or making the rounds of TV and radio talk shows. For many of them, multiplicity was not even an illness to cure, but a way of life that was to be cultivated, preserved, and spread.

Psychiatric syndromes such as MPD are always negotiated between several actors. More precisely, they are constantly *re*-negotiated on the basis of expectations, theories, and practices that precede the actors and which the latter remodel, modify, and transform in turn. Thus, it is clear that MPD is rooted in a long tradition that dates back to demonic possession[28] and continues through eighteenth-century somnambulism,[29] Mesmeric "dual consciousness,"[30] the American revivalist movements,[31] spirit mediums,[32] and *fin-de-siècle* multiple personalities produced under hypnosis by Janet, Morton Prince, and their col-leagues. On the other hand, however, the MPD of baby boomers was also decidedly innovative, introducing or amplifying traits that were previously either absent or barely outlined, such as the number of alters, the presence of infantile and transexual personalities, or the recollection of child sexual abuse.

So where did these innovations and inventions come from? Usually, it is difficult to trace with precision the emergence and genealogy of a psychiatric syndrome. Fortunately for the historian, MPD is different. Both its critics and its advocates agree: MPD took front stage – and with what a splash! – in 1973, with the publication of Flora Rheta Schreiber's book *Sybil*, subtitled "The True and Extraordinary Story of a Woman Possessed by Sixteen Separate Personalities." In his textbook on MPD, Frank Putnam, one of its main theorists and advocates, is thus at pains to distinguish the case of "Sybil" from that of the famous "Eve," which had drawn quite a lot of attention in the 1950s:

> [The book] *The Three Faces of Eve,*[33] while well known, gives a
> misleading picture of MPD and ironically may have helped to obscure the
> clinical features of the disorder. The book *Sybil*, with its graphic treatment of the
> amnesias, fugue episodes, child abuse, and conflicts among alters, served as a
> template against which other patients could be compared and understood.[34]

Before *Sybil*, the new brand of multiple personality was unknown by psychiatrists. Afterwards, it literally exploded. This book – or rather the case whose history it narrates – thus provides a good means of studying in detail the formation and launching of a transient mental illness, before its standardization and serial production.

Flora Rheta Schreiber, an academic and a journalist, described in her book the strange case of "Sybil Dorsett," the pseudonym given to an artist who developed sixteen different personalities after having been subjected to severe physical and sexual abuse during her childhood. Born in 1923 in a small Midwestern town (all place names and people were carefully disguised by Schreiber in the book), Sybil had been raised in a Christian fundamentalist and puritan atmosphere where it was forbidden to go to the movies and even to read novels. However, in blatant contradiction to her rigid education, she had been forced to witness her parents' lovemaking from her bed (Schreiber called this the "primal scene," echoing Freud's case of the Wolf Man). Sybil's mother, a serious schizophrenic who suffered from frequent bouts of catatonia that terrorized the young girl, prevented her from playing with other children and inflicted upon her all sorts of bizarre and perverse ill-treatments. She made Sybil watch while she masturbated other children under her care, indulged in homosexual orgies with young teenage girls or defecated in her neighbors' yards. She would tie Sybil to the piano and strike chords for hours on end. She forced odd objects into her vagina, suspended her by a cord from the ceiling, gave her constant enemas of ice water that left her undernourished, manhandled her to the point of dislocating her shoulder, and locked her up in a wheat-crib where she nearly suffocated in the grain. Sybil's father, a weak man, pretended to see nothing, just like the town doctor and the staff of the neighboring hospital.

Abandoned by all, Sybil had no other alternative than to "dissociate" during each important trauma, splitting into several divergent, even antagonistic, personalities. "Vicky," the first of these, appeared in September 1926, when the young Sybil had been brought to the Mayo Clinic in Rochester in a state of advanced malnutrition and the doctor had not been able to figure out what was going on. "Peggy" appeared during the burial of Sybil's grandmother and replaced Sybil for nearly two years. Peggy, during this period, witnessed with horror the tragic death of one of her playmates, Tommy Ewald, who accidentally killed himself with a gun while they played together in a hayloft. When Sybil, the "host personality," eventually came to, she found herself in seventh grade, not knowing her multiplication tables since she had never learned them in the first place. Terrified, her memory riddled with holes, confronted by inconsistencies for which she had no explanation, Sybil continued to lead a chaotic life until she ended up, at the age of 22, in the office of the psychiatrist Cornelia Wilbur at the hospital in Omaha, Nebraska. According to Schreiber, Peggy came out during one of the sessions with Wilbur, but the doctor, at the time, did not notice anything. Nevertheless, before leaving Omaha to enter a psychoanalytic training program in New York, Wilbur recommended that Sybil leave her parents and go to Chicago to undergo analysis. But Sybil was prevented from doing this by her parents, for whom analysis was an invention of the Devil, and she thus returned to her erratic, "multiple" life, all the while nourishing the hope of one day seeing the good doctor again. Nine years later, summoning up her courage, she finally decided to go to New York in order to study art at Columbia University and begin an analysis with Wilbur. According to the chronology established by Schreiber, the treatment began on October 18, 1954, and by December 21 Peggy had already made her appearance in Wilbur's office, soon followed by Vicky, Mary, Marcia, Mike, Sid, and the others. Wilbur, using injections of pentothal and later hypnosis, undertook to make Sybil – or rather, her personalities – relive the diverse traumas that haunted her (them). On September 2, 1965, after eleven years, 2,354 analytic sessions and 436 pages of intense psychological suspense, Wilbur could finally write in her journal: "All personalities one."[35] The "first psychoanalysis of a multiple personality,"[36] as Schreiber called it, had ended and the "new Sybil," freed from her demons, left New York shortly thereafter to take a position as an art therapist in a psychiatric hospital, and then, two years later, an art professorship in a university. The last words in Schreiber's book were: "happy ending."

Although the action had been dramatized and most of the protagonists' names had been modified, Schreiber insisted that her narrative was based on meticulous research and first-hand documents such as Wilbur's analysis notes, taped recordings from analytic sessions, Sybil's diaries and correspondence, and family archives, as well as medical files obtained from the hospital where Sybil had been admitted several times during her childhood and her studies. *Sybil* was a true story, not a novel. Launched with an impressive publicity budget (60,000 dollars at the time),[37] the book became an instant best-seller worldwide (11 million copies sold in seventeen different languages) and was no less instantly made into a TV movie, with Sally Field in the role of Sybil and Joanne Woodward in that of Cornelia Wilbur (the contract for the film adaptation had been signed, it is worth noting, before the book had even been published).[38]

According to Ian Hacking, observability is one of the four indispensable "vectors" in the dissemination of a transient mental illness: the illness must be visible, recognizable as such, and known by all. The visibility of the "Sybil" phenomenon was huge and it was the result of a marketing campaign in due form. MPD is, with depression,[39] the first psychiatric syndrome to have been launched onto the market with the aid of advertising techniques – it is, one might say, mental illness in the age of media reproduction.

Soon after the book came out, Schreiber was deluged by letters from readers thanking her for having enabled them finally to put a name to the condition they suffered from. By February 1974, Schreiber had already counted six self-diagnosed cases.[40] "I have just finished reading your publication of *Sybil*," one of them wrote to her, "and I now realize that I suffer the same illness as she had. I had never heard of it (Multiple Personalities) before I read *Sybil*, but this book has helped me open my eyes ... Right now I am in prison serving time for a crime I don't remember doing."[41] "You see," asserted another reader, "I too am a multiple personality ... I felt as though I was reading my life while reading *Sybil* ... I have 8 people dictating this letter."[42] Another Sybil emulator requested that Schreiber write her sad story: "At the age of 12 [my father] sexually molested me with a live snake in a strange ceremony to make me a woman."[43] Another wrote in the first person plural: "We have read your book *Sybil* with great interest and gave a copy to our doctor ... June 11, 1974 at Peninsula, psychiatric ward in Burlingham, Calif., we were diagnosed (finally) as a multiple personality ... This Body is 43 years old; it has three verified personalities: Elizabeth (43), Liz (43) and me (Mary, 16 yrs old) ... Elizabeth ... suffered a traumatic event at 12 yrs of age and dissassociated ... she would like to tell her story so others might see themselves and not commit suicide."[44] The vogue for "multobiographies," as Hacking calls them, was launched. *The Five of Me* came out in 1977, soon followed by *Tell Me Who I Am Before I Die* (1978), *Michelle Remembers* (1980), *The Minds of Billy Milligan* (1981), and many others. These books did not reflect a pre-existing condition; rather, they were the reason why people became ill in the first place. As we will see, this is exactly what happened with the arch-"multiple" Sybil herself.

Who was Sybil? In spite of her celebrity, nobody knew. As happens so often in the field of psychoanalysis and of dynamic psychiatry, the true identity of the founding case remained stubbornly hidden. "Sybil," wrote Schreiber in her preface, "wants to maintain anonymity"[45] and everything had indeed been done to preserve it. As a result, Schreiber's and Wilbur's accounts were impossible to verify. How could one know whether Schreiber had not omitted or embellished this or that detail as needed for her "non-fiction novel"? What guarantee did one have that the "facts" uncovered by Wilbur during Sybil's analysis were not colored by interpretation? How could one be sure that Sybil's memories were indeed reliable? Schreiber claimed that they were, but after all one had only her word for it. *Sybil*, much like Freud's case histories, functioned like a "black box,"[46] all the more foundational as it was impossible to open. One could know what came out of it, but not how this information had been processed, produced, engineered.

One had therefore to identify the real Sybil if one wanted to have some chance of penetrating the manufacture of MPD, even if this meant breaking the sacrosanct principle of medical confidentiality. Far too often, in the domain of dynamic psychiatry, medical confidentiality is invoked for no other reason than to prevent researchers from reopening the black boxes that are the founding cases of the discipline.[47] The politics of withholding of the Sigmund Freud Archives is the most famous example of this epistemic control, but the situation was not much different as far as Sybil and MPD were concerned. Schreiber and Wilbur passed away, respectively, in 1988 and in 1992, and both left behind instructions to prevent any indiscretion. Cornelia Wilbur's will stipulated that the portion of her personal archives concerning Sybil should remain "strictly confidential until seven years after the death of the person known as 'Sybil'." Since no one knew the true identity of this person, this provision effectively amounted to sealing these archives indefinitely. As for Schreiber, she bequeathed her own archives to the library of the John Jay College of Criminal Justice in New York, but all the documents that would have revealed "Sybil"'s identity were placed in a "confidential" collection that could not be consulted except with the permission of Flora Rheta Schreiber's executor. This executor gave this authorization only once, making the researcher promise not to publicly reveal Sybil's identity.[48]

In 1995, the psychiatrist Herbert Spiegel, who had known Sybil in the early 1960s and had seen her in therapy during Wilbur's absences, agreed to share his memories with me[49] and thus to open, ever so slightly, the black box. Sybil, he claimed, was a highly suggestible hysteric, a virtuoso of hypnosis, and her "personalities," far from being spontaneous manifestations, were in reality artifacts of Wilbur's hypnotic treatment. This is what he had explained to Schreiber and to Wilbur when the two had wanted to secure his collaboration with the book they were preparing, to which Schreiber had apparently replied: "But if we don't call it a multiple personality, we don't have a book! The publishers want it to be that, otherwise it won't sell!"[50] As a result, Spiegel did not participate in the book, and he was glad he hadn't, for *Sybil* had started, he said, "a whole new cult, a whole new wave of hysteria" that would go down in history as an "embarrassing phase of American psychiatry."[51] For reasons of medical ethics, Spiegel nevertheless declined to reveal Sybil's real name, the result being that his testimony was as unverifiable as that of Schreiber and Wilbur.

Upon reading Spiegel's interview in the *New York Review of Books*, the psychologist Robert Rieber, an ex-colleague of Schreiber's at John Jay College,

suddenly remembered tapes that she had given him in 1972. At the time Rieber
was studying the language of the mentally ill and Schreiber had asked him to
examine the recordings of analytic sessions with a patient of Wilbur's – obviously, the famous Sybil. Rieber had not followed up on this and had since let the
tapes lie in a drawer, using them on occasion to make other recordings. To his
great dismay, Rieber found that only one taped conversation between Schreiber
and Wilbur on the subject of Sybil had survived. Rieber nevertheless made it the
base of a sensational paper at the annual meeting of the American Psychological
Association (August 1998), in which he claimed that the recording in his possession proved that Wilbur had suggested Sybil's personalities and that she and
Schreiber "were not totally unaware" of it.[52] Nothing like tapes to suggest a
Watergate of the psyche: the media immediately amplified Rieber's declarations
about the "the fraudulent construction of a multiple personality,"[53] as well as the
furious controversy it elicited. The commentators of the other side objected, with
some reason, that the "evidence" invoked by Rieber was, to say the least,
ambiguous and proved nothing at all. To top it all, Sybil in person stepped into
the debate through the mouth of the psychiatrist Leah Dickstein, of the University
of Louisville, Kentucky. Dickstein claimed that "she was in touch with Sybil for
several years after Wilbur's death" and she told the media that Sybil had asked
her (but when was this?) to "tell people every word in the book is true."[54] How
could one doubt the words of the victim herself?

It was not until autumn 1998 that Peter J. Swales, in collaboration with
myself, managed to identify, from clues gleaned from the non-confidential
portion of Schreiber's archive,[55] the true "Sybil Dorsett," who had died a few
months before. From there, it was relatively easy to collect the testimony of
relatives and friends who had known her, and to gather the significant *Nachlass*
that she had left behind her – correspondence, writings, paintings, drawings,
photographs. Moreover, because the extensive media coverage of the discovery
of the real Sybil made the secrecy surrounding her identity pointless, the John
Jay College decided, despite the expressed opposition of Schreiber's estate, to
de-restrict the archives in its possession and to grant access to the famous
documents and tapes on which Schreiber claimed that she had based her story.
The black box named Sybil could finally be opened.

Sybil's true name was Shirley Ardell Mason and she was born on January 25,
1923 in Dodge Center, a small rural town in eastern Minnesota. Her parents
belonged to the Seventh-Day Adventist Church, a millenarian denomination
founded in the nineteenth century by the prophetess Ellen G. White (whose
illnesses and trances intimate, incidentally, some aspects of Shirley Mason's
psychiatric career).[56] Nevertheless, contrary to what Schreiber wrote, the
Masons were not at all fanatics. The mother, originally a Methodist, did not
hesitate to break the Adventist rules when it suited her and it is simply not true
that movies and novels were forbidden for the young Shirley (according to her
own testimony, her parents "read a lot"[57] and her father took her to see the

movies of her namesake Shirley Temple).[58] Likewise, it is not true that her mother in any way prevented her daughter from playing with children her own age. All the testimonies of her playmates at the time agree: it was Shirley herself who preferred to remain alone with her dolls, to the great despair of her mother who always urged her to go play with the other kids. Far from being mistreated, Shirley, the only daughter of aging parents, seems to have been fairly spoiled and egocentric (some of her ex-playmates still reproach her to this day for never having let them touch the near fifty dolls she possessed, a huge luxury in that period of economic depression). In family photos, Shirley looks slight and skinny (as she would remain the rest of her life), but people who knew her in Dodge Center deny that she was ever malnourished.

They also deny that Shirley's mother, Martha Atkinson, was ever schizophrenic. "Mattie," as she was called in the town, was notoriously whimsical and she had a strange laugh, but that is all. Her only known psychiatric episode seems to have been a bout of depression resulting from a miscarriage in 1927 (it is probably on this temporary depressive state that Wilbur based her rash diagnosis of schizophrenic catatonia). As for the physical and sexual abuse that Mattie had allegedly inflicted upon her daughter and other children, the witnesses are divided. Some, under what seems to be the influence of Schreiber's book, do not exclude the possibility (after all, Mattie was weird. . .). But Dessie Blood Engbard, a friend of the family who had lived at the Masons' and corresponded regularly with Shirley until the publication of the book, registered her total disbelief in 1975: "I just can't believe all that stuff about her. No sir, it just doesn't sound possible. That was a fine family."[59] The two daughters of doctor Otoniel Flores, the Dodge Center doctor at the time, were as adamant about this when Peter Swales and I interviewed them in Nacogdoches, Texas, in 1998: it is unthinkable, they said, that such atrocities could have taken place without the family doctor and the other members of this small rural community noticing it.[60] The same applies to the black-out periods during which Shirley is supposed to have been replaced by her other personalities: no one in Dodge Center had noticed anything of the kind. Shirley, judging by her school reports, was a normal child in all regards, and her seventh grade maths grades do not reflect in any way a sudden inability to multiply beyond three, as Schreiber claims in her book (from 7th to 9th grade, her grade was "B"). Asked about this in 1975, her 5th-grade teacher at the time could not hide her irritation: "That stuff about her forgetting her multiplication tables is nonsense!"[61] Dodge Center people note as well that there was no wheat-crib on the Masons property in which Shirley could have nearly suffocated in the grain.[62] Even the episode of the accidental death of her playmate "Tommy Ewald" proves to be fictional: it is true that a teenage boy named Johnny Greenwald died in this way, but this happened in 1940, when Shirley was 17 years old, and the local papers at the time do not mention her presence at the scene of the accident.[63]

In fact, Shirley Mason's psychological problems seem to have begun at the end of high school, with an episode that is in no way mentioned in Schreiber's book and about which one wonders if Shirley ever told it to Wilbur. According to doctor Flores's eldest daughter, a retired psychologist, Mattie had brought Shirley to the doctor for consultation because she spent her days shut up in her room, masturbating with a hairbrush. The doctor told his daughter about this in confidence, asking her to pay a visit to her friend Shirley once a week to talk to her and encourage her to leave her room. Virginia Flores thus became, unwittingly, Shirley Mason's first therapist.

Shirley's symptoms got worse once she left her family home to study at the Teachers College in Mankato, Minnesota, in order to become an art teacher. Confronted by many significant changes, notably the move into adulthood and to a city-life in which her religion seemed archaic, Shirley began to have anxiety attacks that sometimes caused her to faint in class. However, it is worth noting that her classmates at the time noticed nothing that might resemble personality changes.[64] Shirley was placed under the care of the school nurse, de facto her second therapist, who awakened her interest in psychiatry and Freud's theories while ascribing the origin of her problems to her family and religious upbringing. God or Freud? Salvation in the beyond or therapy in this life? For the first time, Shirley was confronted with the conflict between psychiatry and religion, which was to play such an important role in her analysis with Wilbur: how was she to heal, if this meant repudiating her faith, her parents, her roots?

After many visits with the school's doctors and a consultation with the head of the psychiatry section of the famous Mayo Clinic in Rochester, who diagnosed a "hysterical neurosis,"[65] Shirley was treated with Luminal (phenobarbital), a barbiturate commonly used in the 1940s–50s to calm anxious and neurotic conditions. It also seems, judging by an elliptical passage in her diary,[66] that she was put in a prolonged barbiturate-induced narcosis (this technique, devised in the 1920s by the Swiss psychiatrist Jakob Klaesi, was used notably for mood disorders of a psychotic nature). Nevertheless, Shirley's condition worsened and in 1944 she was asked to leave the school pending her recovery.

A partial improvement followed, notably under the influence of Albert Leiske, an Adventist pastor and friend of the family, who found her work and odd jobs within the congregation.[67] (This is a constant in Shirley Mason's biography: each time she took a break from therapy and went back to her family and religious environment, she got better.) In 1945, she consulted a doctor in Omaha, Nebraska, to get a medical certificate that would allow her to return to the Teachers College and continue her studies. The doctor, however, diagnosed once again a hysteria and referred her to the psychiatrist Cornelia B. Wilbur. Wilbur was working at the time with Abram E. Bennett, one of the pioneers of electroshock therapy (he is noted for having introduced the use of curare for limiting patients' convulsions).[68] Wilbur and Bennet had just produced together a documentary film on the applications of narcosynthesis (or narcoanalysis), a technique which consisted in administering barbiturates by injection and which had been used with some success during the war to lift the amnesia of soldiers suffering from traumatic neurosis.[69] The film was made up of four case studies, and the last, quite sensational, showed how Wilbur had cured a young, 11-year-old girl of her hysterical convulsions by injecting her with pentothal and making her relive "numerous traumatic experiences at the hands of a drunken father."[70] This shows that Wilbur, in the mid-1940s, already had a ready-made theory of infantile trauma that combined the work done by army doctors on the war neuroses with certain elements from the Freudian Vulgate.

Shirley seems to have been instantly dazzled by Wilbur, who embodied all that she herself wanted to become. As she would write later in a diary that she kept for her analyst: "When I was in Omaha, I had a crush on you like I had on other women in other places."[71] As early as the second session with Wilbur, Shirley had a spectacular fit of convulsions (it was then, according to Schreiber's book, that "Peggy" made her clandestine appearance). Wilbur, who was about to leave Omaha for New York, saw Shirley no more than six times and was content with prescribing her "pills"[72] (probably sedatives).

Shirley, during the following years, followed her family and pastor Leiske to various places in the central United States, all the while sporadically continuing her studies. According to various testimonies, she continued to have ill-defined psychological problems, but these did not prevent her from obtaining a double degree in English and art, and from taking charge of the occupational therapy department at a large Adventist hospital in Denver, the Porter Hospital and Sanitarium, where she had an average of thirty patients in treatment. At the beginning of the 1950s, she took a position as a school teacher in Michigan and her correspondence of this period shows her to be without psychological problems, well integrated into her social and professional environment, exhibiting her paintings in art galleries and getting recognition for her works, and even being courted by a young man whom she would gladly have married had he only been Adventist (unfortunately, he was Jewish).

In September 1954, Shirley moved to New York to get a master's degree in art at Columbia University, with the intention of then studying psychology at the graduate level to become an art therapist. She was doing fine. In a letter to her father, Walter Mason, she described her new life in the big city:

> I eat & sleep well & really feel tops nearly all the time ... I have never been this well before ... She [a friend] says I am good for her when she gets blue – everyone around here gets blue but me – I'm having a fun time![73]

In another letter, Shirley writes again: "I feel so well here that I just am not EVER sick so far anyway."[74] In this same letter, she announces that she "very accidentally discovered" that Cornelia Wilbur taught at Columbia and that she went by her office to say hello and see if she remembered her: "In fact I did not know she was in New York – thought she had gone to Chicago when she left Omaha" (this contradicts Schreiber's teleologically oriented account, according to which Sybil had gone to New York *in order* to find her dear doctor Wilbur). Wilbur had been glad to see her again. She was now practicing as a psychoanalyst and was "doing some kind of research in the use of certain drugs and their effect on certain types of mental illnesses." She got very interested when Shirley told her of her plans to become an art therapist and immediately proposed to introduce her to psychiatric institutions likely to hire her.

It so happens that there is at this point a hiatus in Shirley's correspondence with her father and his second wife, due to the loss of a packet of letters dating from this period. When the correspondence resumes in 1959, one is struck by the contrast: Shirley, unemployed, depressed and constantly sedated, lived now prostrated in a tiny apartment that she would leave only to walk Dr. Wilbur's poodles, all the while nourishing the illusion of one day starting to study medicine. So what had happened in the meantime?

Based on various documents, notably a very interesting analytic diary that Shirley kept for Wilbur, here is what one can piece together. For reasons that are not indicated, Shirley began an analysis with Wilbur at the end of 1954 or the beginning of 1955. The first personalities must have appeared shortly thereafter, for we know from Shirley's analytic diary that as early as 1955 "Peggy" had made a fugue to Philadelphia where she sent a letter wrongly dated 1945 to Wilbur's old medical office in Omaha, which was then forwarded to Wilbur in New York. It seems that it was this antedated letter that served as the basis of Schreiber's and Wilbur's contention in their book that Peggy, in 1945, had *really* made an appearance in Wilbur's office without her having noticed (the idea being that Peggy, in Philadelphia, had regressed to an event that had actually taken place). But in fact, before Shirley started her analysis with Wilbur in New York, no one had ever noted the slightest shift in personality – neither her family, nor her playmates, nor her shoolmates, nor her doctors, *nor even Shirley herself*. Wilbur made this very clear in a letter sent in 1971 to Schreiber:

> [Shirley] *never* had any perception of any other personality ... Until treatment she had *no* knowledge of her own re[garding] what she did in the black-outs. She was told and she sometimes retold this as if it were her knowledge but it wasn't ... she was as astonished when she found out that she was multiples of multiples as anyone.'[75]

Unless we hypothesize, with Wilbur and Schreiber, an absolutely massive and universal denial on the part of her entourage, one is drawn to the conclusion that Shirley's multiple personality, far from being a spontaneous condition predating the treatment, was in reality an artifact of the latter. This is confirmed moreover by the fact that Shirley's personalities were confined to the space of therapy: the only people for whom they ever showed themselves were, as if by chance, Wilbur; a patient of hers with whom Shirley shared an apartment, Willie P.; and Flora Rheta Schreiber. As Wilbur was to confess to Schreiber, who asked her for some examples of the misfortunes that had befallen Shirley in her real life: "You know, it's funny. She very seldom had a bad experience in the outside world."[76] (The book nonetheless abounds in episodes of this kind.)

Was it Shirley who introduced the theme of multiple personality into her treatment or her analyst? We might as well ask which came first, the chicken or the egg. Shirley's multiple personality appeared *between* the patient and the therapist, and it is futile to try to know "which came first." It is more worthwhile to note that multiple personality had just made a come-back that exact same year, 1954, in the form of an article published by the psychiatrists Thigpen and Cleckley on the case of their multiple personality patient "Eve."[77] This article, which would later be expanded in the book and then the movie *The Three Faces of Eve*, built upon a presentation given in May 1953 at the annual conference of the American Psychiatric Association, which Wilbur, the ultimate professional, would not have missed. Be that as it may, we know from Thigpen and Cleckley that "accounts of this report were carried by the Associated Press and appeared in many newspapers . . . Comments on the case in the lay press apparently attracted widespread attention."[78]

Schreiber states in her book that Wilbur had heard about Thigpen and Cleckley's article from her colleagues, but did not read it at the time because the issue of the journal in which it was published was not available at the library when she wanted to check it out.[79] Even supposing this to be true, it is worth noting, still according to Schreiber, that Wilbur on the other hand knew very well Morton Prince's tome *The Dissociation of a Personality*, published in 1905.[80] In December 1955, in a taped conversation with Wilbur, Shirley asked her analyst: "Do you mind if I do some research on multiple personalities? Read Morton Prince, etc., last winter." Shirley continued:

> I was just wanting to know how it was for others. Looked up references in psychological abstracts. Not much material written on the subject . . . Read about one boy who had three. Most of those listed were developed medically, I mean, induced by drugs[81]

We know also that two years later Shirley went to the opening of the movie *The Three Faces of Eve* with her friend Willie P.[82] The next morning she wrote in her analytic diary:

> something just made a chain of connections . . . . . . was thinking about the movie . . . . . . Eve's grandmother . . . . . . my grandma.[83]

Both the patient and her analyst had thus ample opportunity to familiarize themselves with the great classics, before elaborating in turn on the old scenarios. Besides, one need only read *Sybil* to realize that it is, in terms of both content and form, an imitation of Prince's and Thigpen and Cleckley's books. It does not therefore come as a surprise to learn that Schreiber, during the preparation of her own book, had also studied Prince's very closely: "I am now reading Morton Prince's book with great thoroughness," she wrote Wilbur in 1970.[84] Shirley Mason's multiple personality was through and through bookish, literary.[85]

That's not all. Also in December 1955, Shirley mentioned in her analytic diary that Wilbur had proposed that she collaborate with her on a book about her case: "I would like to have you collaborate with me on something. I want to write a book about your difficulties, and I would like you to help with it."[86] From the very beginning, the patient thus participated in the treatment as a co-author, very literally so. The deal was that Wilbur would analyze Shirley for free and that the latter would reimburse her once the book (and/or the treatment) had ended – which she did: in 1973, having received a third of the royalties from the book, Shirley used the money to finish paying her analysis debt, which totaled $37,854 (a significant amount at the time).[87] Wilbur considered Shirley a "research project,"[88] as she wrote Schreiber, and she did not hesitate to assist her financially by paying her rent, providing for her needs or giving her, in exchange for payment, odd jobs to do around the house or at her office. Indeed, Shirley had dropped out of school and no longer worked, Wilbur having apparently put into her head the idea of beginning analytic training with her colleague (and probably also training analyst), the psychoanalyst William Silverberg.[89] This meant studying first medicine and psychiatry (at the time only MDs could set up shop as psychoanalysts) – and this in turn required that Shirley first recover, that all her personalities fuse into one. The treatment therefore became for Shirley a full-time job upon which depended both her emotional and material well-being, her professional future, and her hope to one day repay her debt for the treatment itself. Rarely has Karl Kraus's quip been more appropriate: "Psychoanalysis is the very malady of the mind for which it claims to be the remedy." Shirley developed as many personalities as needed for Wilbur to be able to write a book about her recovery; she made herself as ill as possible to better become a doctor in turn, like her beloved analyst.

But here comes the most troubling aspect. The 1950s mark the beginning of the psychopharmacological revolution in psychiatry, and Wilbur, like many other American psychiatrist-psychoanalysts at the time, had no qualms about combining analysis and the use of psychotropic drugs or physiotherapies such as electroshock.[90] It is impossible to know whether medications played a role in the emergence of Shirley's very first personalities, for we have precious little information about the first months of her treatment. Shirley's rather odd mention of older cases of alternate personalities "induced by drugs" would seem to point in that direction. What is certain is that in December 1955 or in January 1956,[91] Wilbur started to administer pentothal by injection to Shirley – or rather, to "Peggy" – in order to make her recover and abreact the memory of what had taken place during her fugue to Philadelphia,[92] using the technique she had already used in Omaha with the young hysterical girl in the film *Narcosynthesis*. Pentothal (sodium thiopental), commonly known as "truth serum," is a barbiturate that elicits a stuporous state during which the patient's resistance and amnesic barriers are supposed to be lifted. Shirley's resistance, as a matter of fact, begged to be lifted. Very soon, the traumatic memories began to flow, from the (very Kleinian) aggression of the "hard nipple" to the bad mother's "vaginal attacks,"[93] and the rest:

> Somewhere along in my analysis when I was able to face the existence of more personalities than just Peggy, Vicky, we began, *at your instigation*, to consider – try to find the time when first split occurred ... we found (*or rather you did*) one partial or faint, or something one, when I was eighteen months. I think that is how it was. We discussed my doing the first due to Mother's unbearableness – I believe that did precipitate it –- and no doubt the earlier one also – maybe even sooner a trace of one (*supposition only*) when someone [i.e., one of the personalities] under pentothal mentioned hating the hard nipple.[94]

In our day and age, female "multiples" typically accuse their *fathers* of having sexually abused them, their mothers more often playing the role of a passive accomplice. With Shirley, it was the opposite. At the beginning of the 1950s, the theory had it that psychoses were caused by "schizophrenogenic mothers," as Frieda Fromm-Reichmann called them.[95] Wilbur went one step further: she made Shirley's mother a schizophrenic (a diagnosis, it should be noted, that she and Schreiber tried in vain to corroborate when scouring for documents to buttress their book's narrrative).[96] Shirley's "dissociations" and psychotic "splits" were due, in her view, to the insane cruelties of her schizophrenic mother. Ian Hacking, in his book on multiple personality, suggests that the link established between MPD and child abuse corresponds to the emergence, during the 1960s, of the notion of "battered child syndrome"[97] and he certainly has a point. Here is what Schreiber wrote Wilbur in 1965:

> What do we say, by way of selling the idea, that establishes uniqueness, that makes a publisher feel that this is sufficiently different from Eve to justify his interest?
> ... One [factor] I can think of, of course, is the linkage with the battered child syndrome.[98]

This, nevertheless, does not apply to the founding case itself. Shirley's "memories" of maternal abuse predated the publication in 1962 of Henry Kempe's article on the "battered child syndrome,"[99] and they emerged within the context of the psychoanalytic theory of psychosis at the time. These were not the memories of a battered child, but of the daughter of a psychotoxic mother.

Pentothal is a drug to be handled with care. As Wilbur well knew, and it bothered her, it can cause lethal thromboses and create a state of physiological addiction. Schreiber, in her book, quickly passes over the use of pentothal in Sybil's treatment and claims that Wilbur decided very early on to do without it because the patient had developed a "psychological addiction" to it.[100] Actually, Wilbur's use of pentothal lasted for almost four years, until the end of 1959, and for good reason: Shirley was "hooked" on pentothal, like others are on heroin, and Wilbur was not able to wean her. Each time she tried, one of the personalities would have a crisis or attempt suicide and Wilbur had to rush over, often in the middle of the night, to inject the needle into the swollen arm of the host-personality. Shirley's analytic diary from this period broods obsessively on this and it is clear that her so-called "transference" onto Wilbur had become a relationship of abject physical dependence, of the kind that exists between the junkie and his pusher: "Begged, please, for pentothal for relief."[101] In October 1959, when Wilbur seems finally to have been able to wean her, Shirley described her periods of withdrawal:

> I no longer expect you to come here and/or give me the pentothal, so I do not spend endless (and useless) hours waiting for you ... that waiting was awful .... listening for the steps and then hearing them go past and on upstairs ...... I could not accept it at first ... I was certain you would come again and then I would be so disappointed ......[102]

Wilbur, in addition, would give Shirley electroshocks at home with a portable machine. She also prescribed all kinds of other barbiturates, sedatives, and psychotropic drugs – phenobarbital, Dexamyl (dextroamphetamine and amobarbital), Dartal (thiopropazate), Seconal (secobarbital), Demerol (meperidine), Equanil[103] and Deprol (mepromabate), as well as Serpasil (reserpine)[104] and Thorazine (chlorpromazine), two of the very first antipsychotics to be put on the market. Clearly, Wilbur used her "research project" to test dosages, combinations, and possible applications of new medications. The entries in Shirley's analytic diary (the lab log, we might just as well call it) give an idea of these experiments:

> January 27, 1956: "She came at 4 o'clock. Pentothal ...
> Treatment electric first, must have been shock. Saturday – pentothal"
> February 5, 1956: "Asked for pentothal instead of electric treatment."
> February 9, 1956: "Barbiturate, intravenous, also pentothal. Very nauseated. Same arm, very dizzy, couldn't walk to bathroom alone. Willie carried me. [Wilbur] Came two or three times a day. Talked about mother."
> February 10,1956: "[Wilbur] Came three times. Gave pentothal and shock. Sustained release spansuals of phenobarbitol. Began to menstruate."
> February 16, 1956: "[Wilbur] Gave equinol and dexamyl. Should be all right in 30 minutes or so."[105]

Not surprisingly, Shirley's health deteriorated in a spectacular fashion during this whole period. It is now known (and it was known in part at the time) that the substances administered by Wilbur all have serious side-effects: reserpine induces depression, chlorpromazine stupefies, mepromabate and barbiturates are addictive. Shirley, in this regard, literally accumulated addictions. She self-medicated wildly, mixed medications, and regularly took more than the prescribed dose because each personality would try to outdo the others. Thus Peggy, in 1962, mentioned certain "red pellets": "She [Shirley] takes 5, but I take 6 or 7."[106] As to Shirley, the host-personality, she constantly flirted with overdose – witness this "suicide note" written in the early 1960s:

> My Doctor dearest, 11:45, I am sorry – but I took a lot of several kinds of [follows a series of drug acronyms] to make sure ... You trusted me with medication and I let you down – I am sorry ... 2 a.m. I *do love you* ... Forget me, please, I am not worth it.[107]

Elsewhere: "It is such a temptation to take more seconal and just keep on sleeping. I have had so much stuff I can't quite see straight this morning . . ."[108] Or again: "Saturday night I decided to add thorazine to the two seconal I was taking nightly . . . . slept very well for eight hours." Two days later: "I took extra dexamyl [A little further on:] Took more dexamyl," etc. [109] Shirley slept thirteen to sixteen hours a day [110] and, according to the testimony of one of her friends, seemed drugged when speaking on the telephone.[111] In a letter to her stepmother, she described herself as a "walking drugstore."[112]

It was during this long "trip" under medication that most of Shirley Mason's personalities appeared and that she remembered the gruesome abuses to which she had been subjected. It is obvious enough that these memories had been suggested by Wilbur in the course of an intensely "transferential" relationship, but this psychological explanation does not tell the whole story. Shirley's "traumas" were also, in large part, hallucinated in a drug-induced state. This point is not insignificant, insofar as "Sybil" is today high up amongst the heroines of psychotherapy, next to her no less pseudonymous sisters "Anna O." and "Dora." Even, some critics often praise the MPD movement for having at least resisted the biomedical wave in American psychiatry. But this is not accurate, at least historically: MPD, in fact, is the incestuous child of psychoanalysis and psychotropic drugs. As Peter Swales rightly suggests, the history of psychoanalysis and of modern psychotherapy owes much more to the use of psychotropic substances than is generally admitted.[113] Shirley, just like Breuer's Anna O. or Freud's Cäcilie M.,[114] was a "woman under the influence."

Near the end of 1959, Wilbur finally managed to wean Shirley from pentothal by substituting hypnosis. To this end, Wilbur had referred Shirley to Herbert Spiegel, an eminent hypnosis specialist, for she herself had no experience in this technique. Spiegel immediately noticed Shirley's unusual hypnotic capacities and proposed to study them free, at the rate of three sessions per week. He also used her as a demonstration subject for experiments in hypnotic age regression that he carried out in front of large student audiences at Columbia University.[115] Once again, Shirley became a "research project" for a psychiatrist.

Shirley loved hypnosis, as well as the attention she received: "I get a lot of information, insight and meet some very nice doctors."[116] As for Wilbur, she was learning her trade by assisting Spiegel with the hypnotic age regression sessions. The quest for traumas thus continued with this less addictive, if not more reliable, technique.[117] Some recordings of the hypnosis sessions with Wilbur have survived and it is patently obvious that it was Wilbur who reconstructed the sexual scenes, à la Freud, while Shirley and her personalities were most of the time content with acquiescing. Here, for example, is how Shirley recovered the "memory" of the famous "primal scene":

> Peggy (*under hypnosis, regressed to childhood*): When Mommy and Daddy, they slept in a big bed, and I had a little bed, myself, and I used to get awful mad at them.

Wilbur (*speaking as to a child*): Because they had intercourse, and you could hear them … Why did you get mad at them for having intercourse? Because it made you feel lonely, or it stimulated you sexually, or both? Why do you think I ask you questions like that, sweetie?

Peggy: I am trying to think of my answer. I think I didn't know what they were doing, but if I didn't know, then why would I get mad?

Wilbur: Well, maybe you got mad because they made such a fuss about these things, they wouldn't explain about them and talk about them, and yet they did them, and they acted like they didn't do things like that, or think about things like that, and yet they made them, and it made them seem like they weren't fair, and they were cheating. Could that be?

Peggy: That sounds like it … That's it, they weren't honest.[118]

At the same time, all the while continuing with Seconal, Dexamyl, and Thorazine, Shirley now took Compazine (prochlorperazine), an antipsychotic, Spartase, an anti-fatigue medication, and Librium (benzodiazepine), the first anxiolytic put on the market in 1960. As a matter of fact, Shirley seems to have taken Librium in phenomenal doses: 600 mg a day by injection over a period of several months,[119] while the normal prescription for treating anxiety was 20 to 30 mg a day taken orally.[120] (Librium by injection was used at the beginning of the 1960s for resuscitation in the treatment of tetanus and some epilepsies. The maximum dosage in a given 24 hours was 150 mg. One could give up to 400 mg in the treatment of acute alcoholism – sometimes beyond, for a few days, in cases of great agitation.[121] None of this applied to Shirley, obviously.) Shirley also took Librium orally and Wilbur gave her a refill prescription,[122] which was at the very least unwise given the well-known addictive properties of this product[123] and Shirley's track record in this regard. Add to this the fact that Librium, even taken orally in small doses, often causes fatigue, drowsiness, muscle weakness, and dysarthry (a neurological speech disorder),[124] and one would think that Shirley's general state could not have improved much under the influence of this new medication cocktail.

In 1963, Wilbur, who had been interviewed by Schreiber for an article on homosexuality in *Cosmopolitan Magazine*,[125] managed to interest her in her book project. She organized a dinner for three in a "swanky place"[126] on Madison Avenue and Shirley wrote to her father the following day: "The 3 of us are beginning now to write that book about me … 'Twill put me through med. school."[127] Schreiber also met the other personalities during a hypnosis session and discussed the contract with them.[128] It was agreed that the three women would share the royalties, but that Shirley would remain anonymous. Schreiber, nevertheless, made it clear that she could not commit herself firmly as long as the treatment was not finished:[129] this story had to have a happy ending. In the summer of 1965, for reasons that are not very clear but which seem to have been related to Wilbur's plans to leave New York, Shirley went through an acute crisis during which she developed all sorts of psychosomatic symptoms, as well as a new and last personality, "The Blonde." A new, unidentified medication was tried on this occasion,[130] but it does not seem to have been more effective than the earlier ones. To Schreiber, who worried about these developments ("Does the emergence of a new personality at this stage indicate a setback ...?"),[131] Wilbur wrote in assurance that: "This last episode is a break in the case. This came with the decision to stop medication, which has been done; this for both physical and psychological reasons precipitated a response of symptomatology."[132] One week later, Wilbur announced the near completion of the treatment: "I am sure she will be well within the year, maybe sooner."[133]

The prediction did not take long to come true. According to a treatment calendar kept by Wilbur, the last analysis session with Shirley Mason took place two months later – not September 2, as claimed by Schreiber, but October 8, 1965. The dates matter. In her book Schreiber decribes how Sybil, cured at last, had left New York on October 15, 1965 to begin a new life. What she does not say is that the very next day, October 16, Wilbur took up her new position as superintendant of the Weston State Hospital, a psychiatric hospital in Weston, West Virginia.[134] The end of the treatment and Shirley's spectacular recovery – good and real, this time – thus coincided neatly with Wilbur's move and her separation from her second husband, the lawyer Keith Brown. Far from leaving Wilbur to lead an autonomous life, Shirley in fact *followed her*, taking a position as occupational therapist at the psychiatric hospital in Lakin, located a few hours by road from Weston. This obviously gives quite a different twist to Schreiber's *happy ending*, as well as to the so-called "end of analysis."

Shirley spent all her weekends and vacations with her ex-analyst, whom she now called "Connie" and the two soon formed a pair, if not a couple. Shirley was well appreciated by her colleagues at the Lakin hospital, who still remember her "creative" methods with patients.[135] In 1967, Wilbur took a professorship in psychiatry at the University of Lexington, in Kentucky, and the following year Shirley was named Assistant Professor of Art at the University of Rio Grande, in Ohio. Shirley continued nevertheless to go back and forth during the weekends and vacations. In 1973, soon after the publication of *Sybil*, she left her position at the university to live off her royalties in Lexington, in a house a few blocks away from her dear Connie. Practically nobody knew who she was, for she had abruptly cut off all contact with her stepmother and her relations in Dodge Center, who could have contradicted the facts alleged in *Sybil* (her stepmother, in particular, had been profoundly shocked when she had come across the book in 1975).[136] The "new Shirley" was without past, without family, without ties. Famous and anonymous at the same time, she painted, took care of the poodles that she shared with Connie and led a quiet life. In 1977, she briefly thought of publishing (anonymously) a volume entitled *Sybil's Paintings*, with theoretical commentaries of her own "regarding understanding and interpretation of creative activity."[137] The project never saw the light of day.

Wilbur, on the other hand, led a very active life, giving lectures and interviews, publishing theoretical articles on multiple personality and sexual abuse, and participating in the launching of the MPD movement and the International Society for the Study of Multiple Personality and Dissociation. Within the MPD movement, people talked about the "Wilburian paradigm."[138] In 1982, Wilbur proposed that Schreiber write a book about her career, *Sybil's Doctor*. Schreiber politely declined.[139] The relationship between the two women, which had never been simple, had turned definitely sour since the publication of *Sybil*. Schreiber, who had hoped to receive the Nobel Prize for literature for her book,[140] was irritated that Wilbur presented herself as the author of *Sybil* in public and she even thought at one point of suing the "obnoxious lady."[141] In Schreiber's papers, however, we find this Christmas card sent by Wilbur in the 1980s:

> Dear Flora – I think of you often too. The whole development of MPD (which is stupendous) hinges on what we did – and I think I benefited the most – would like sometime to share the outcomes (for example the establishment of the International Society – last meeting 650 therapists) with you, Love, Connie.[142]

Wilbur died in 1992 and left Shirley part of her estate, as well as her portion of the rights to the book. Shirley, who never recanted her faith in spite of her analyst's exhortations, became (once again) very religious late in life.[143] She died on February 26, 1998 and left all of her estate to an Adventist TV network. As is only fair, her fellow Adventists now hold the majority of the rights of the book for which Shirley Ardell Mason let herself for a time be possessed by the demons of psychiatry. *Happy ending*.

Edifying moral aside, what lessons can we draw from this fable? First of all, that it is a fable – more precisely, a legend. The life of Shirley Mason was *to be read* (*legenda*), as were, during the Middle Ages, the lives of the saints that were recited during matins. It was a life offered for imitation, emulation, replication – and God knows that it got cited and recited! But it was also, and more profoundly, a life *in view of* this recitation, *in view of* this reading. The book *Sybil* did not come to reflect, after the fact, Shirley's life; it was, on the contrary, for this book that she lived from a certain point onward. This life is therefore to be read from the end, from the *happy ending* backwards, not the other way round. Schreiber retained from Shirley's life only what conformed to the already well-established genre of the "life-of-a-multiple-personality," and Wilbur and Shirley made sure that this life conformed to the legend that was expected of them.

This did not go without a lot of editing. Shirley selected from her past the memories liable to be included in the story to come, inventing some when needed, and neglecting others that would have disrupted the narrative progression. As for Wilbur, she suggested corrections or improvements, filled up blanks with interpretive constructions, decided where to put the period, and more generally enforced the narrative order when Shirley was tempted to stray from the scenario. On two occasions, Shirley had wanted to take back what she had told Wilbur and Wilbur had had to intervene to put things back in order. The first time, in May 1958, Shirley wrote her analyst a long letter (partially quoted by Schreiber)[144] in which she admitted to having faked her different personalities:

> I do not have any multiple personalities .... I do not even have a "double" to help me out ...... I am all of them. I have essentially been lying in my pretense of them, I know.[145]

Shirley also stated that the abuses she had attributed to her mother were all figments of her imagination:

> The things I told you about her (the extreme things, that is) were not true ..... I did not exactly "make them up" ahead of time nor plan to say them...they just sort of rolled out from somewhere and once I had started and found you were interested, I continued .... under pentothal I am much more original than otherwise, so I said more .... it made a good story and it accounted for some of the fake symptoms I displayed.[146]

Such an admission of malingering was of course unacceptable. Wilbur, in pure Freudian style, interpreted this confession as a "major defensive man-euver"[147] against Shirley's unconscious hate for her mother, and Shirley, firmly put back on the narrative track, soon attributed her letter of recantation to an "intruder" who had impersonated her.[148]

However, Shirley seems to have relapsed at least one other time. In March 1972, Schreiber wrote Wilbur a somewhat alarmed letter:

> I find one point in the tape you sent extremely disquieting. S's denial of what some of the other personalities and she herself said in the analysis about the primal scene – and I have a transcription of the actual language[149] – is disturbing. I have already written the primal scene. It is on its way – and was before I heard the tape. To revise its essential meaning would distort the truth. I could tell that you are as dismayed as I.
> At any rate, I'd be interested in your reaction to the primal scene I sent you. It is important to keep moving forward because of the possibility of book clubs that Mr. Abel raised. I should try to revise chapter 11 as I go, without forfeiting the forward movement.[150]

In other words, changing the scenario was out of the question. Wilbur fully agreed:

> I was surprised too, but we can fight that out with S. when the final script is ready. I think we have the original scene on tape and that the present statement is a reworking of many times. Don't worry about the primal scene. I didn't want to differ with S. at the time we were making this last tape because I wanted to get it off to you.[151]

Advice to young psychoanalyst-writers: when patients object to your case histories, hush them up.

As for Schreiber, she edited out the episodes deemed too risqué or too unbelievable, such as an alleged fugue to Amsterdam during the Second World War,[152] animated the characters, and put dialogues into their mouths. Spontaneously, the journalist rediscovered and amplified the stylistic trick used by Freud in his case histories: the narrative transmutation of interpretations into real facts – what one might call the analytic *interprefaction*.[153] Personalities that nobody had ever met outside of the office of Wilbur were described as if they *really* walked down the street, *truly* talked among themselves, and had *real* physical characteristics (Marcia's grey eyes, Sid's blue eyes, etc.). Purely hypothetical events were narrated in great detail, clues became proof, suppositions became irrefutable "documents." Thus, while working on the book, Schreiber insisted that Wilbur get hold of medical files liable to corroborate her retrospective diagnoses. In particular, she was interested in the hospitalization for malnutrition during which Shirley had supposedly dissociated for the first time:

> As for [Shirley] – my greatest concern is her visit on September 5, 1926 when she was $3\frac{1}{2}$. That is the pivot of the book – of the multiplicity ... We simply must document the diagnosis we think was made.[154]

But when it turned out that the hospital doctor had diagnosed nothing but a banal follicular tonsilitis,[155] Schreiber nonetheless maintained Wilbur's supposition and put the character Vicky in charge of vouching for it in the book:

> The doctor made the diagnosis, follicular tonsilitis, but that wasn't all. He couldn't understand why we [the personalities] were malnourished – coming from a good family as we did ... But you and I know that it was the enemas and the laxatives after meals that caused the malnutrition.[156]

The legend does not bother with hypotheses. It requires facts, events, and "primal scenes," otherwise there is nothing to tell.

Should we speak of lies, mystification, and fraud then? It is of course very tempting, insofar as Schreiber and Wilbur presented as established facts interpretations which they knew were not supported by the documents they had in their possession. This is a hardly excusable narrative abuse of confidence and their 11 million readers are perfectly entitled to feel cheated – not to mention the thousands of "multiples" who modeled their life on the martyrdom of St. Sybil. Let me therefore be crystal clear: all of this was, yes, fabricated, and for the vilest and most cynical motives. But fabricated does not mean false or unreal. Wilbur and Schreiber's lies and tampering with documents notwithstanding, it remains that Shirley, out of naïveté or calculation, actively went along and that this simulation was as real as it gets. Shirley was not solely a passive object of Wilbur's analytic interpretations and of Schreiber's creative writing, she actively anticipated and *verified* these interpretations and this writing by becoming Sybil, and Vicky, and Peggy, and Sid, and Marcia. The fact that such a transformation took place, for the most part, in the "un-real" space of Wilbur's office does not change anything: Shirley became her own legend, she made it real in making herself ill. Who could deny the seriousness of this drama (*drama* means "action"), even if from the outside it gives the impression of a buffoonish comedy? One cannot be content in denouncing the deceptive character or fictionality of the legend, since the actress Shirley embodied it, quite literally, and since life, here, imitated art. In Shirley's own words: "Every word in the book is true."

One might object, of course, that such a statement only goes to show her incredible gullibility or, if one prefers, her pathological "suggestibility." "Poor Shirley *believed* in the nonsense that her analyst put into her head, just like children believe in Santa Claus, or savages believe in their myths and their amulets. Is this any reason to grant any reality to this nonsense (or to Santa Claus)?" – "Well, no, since you just dissipated this reality with your very question!" Belief is claimed only from the point of view of the *un*believer, of he who makes fun of another who, inexplicably, does not see that he is in the wrong. There would be no point in speaking of belief from the point of view of he who makes the legend or the myth alive. Every "Credo" is a "Fiat," in the sense that it is a decision of living according to the legend and hence of performing it, of carrying out its promise.[157] Shirley "believed" in her multiple personality and in her traumas no more than children "believe" in Santa Claus or the Greeks "believed" in their gods[158] – and not only because she happened to recant them from time to time. She *made them be*, which is a different matter entirely. She played with them, she explored their possibilities, she invented all sorts of stories and rituals that supported their existence, she shared these stories and rituals with her analyst, then with her friend Willie P., then with Schreiber, and finally, little by little, with 11 million readers, thousands of "multiples," the American Psychiatric Association, judges, social workers, politicians, journalists, writers, Hollywood ... A whole world, a whole society coalesced around the initial "Credo", retroactively confirming it. Speaking of belief with respect to such an effective performance is obviously insufficient, for what was unreal before it, was not afterwards (do we say that a marriage is fake because it did not exist before the bride and groom's "I do"?). Shirley's illness was certainly legendary, but this is not to say that it was simply fictional or fake: it was the becoming-real of this fiction (its *Verwerklichung*, in Hegelian parlance).

Every transient mental illness has a legendary structure of this kind, in the sense that it conforms to some narrative or theory, to expectations that precede and inform it. The illness, here, is not something that this narrative or this theory comes to reflect after the fact. Quite the opposite, it is the illness that reflects the narrative and the theory, in that the patient adopts the therapist's or the culture's idiom in order to make herself heard, or "read." What we call "illness" here is nothing but this legendary idiom, before which there is nothing – nothing, in any case, which would be truer or more real.

One might protest, again, that Shirley was well and truly ill *before* starting her analysis with Wilbur and reading the accounts of the case of "Eve." "Didn't she already have panic attacks and convulsions at the Teachers College in Mankato? Didn't the doctors diagnose her with hysteria?" – Yes, but Shirley was playing at the time a different game and performing a different legend. Having not heard yet of multiple personality, she adopted the traditional idiom of female hysteria – the attacks, the faintings, the ceaseless demands for care and medication. Different times, different doctors, a different neurosis.

"Now, this is sheer sophistry! Do you deny that Shirley was ill?" – No, quite the contrary. But it all depends on when and from what. Shirley Mason was not born ill. She was not potentially ill either. Even if we might be tempted to see in her behavior as an introverted and dreamy child a forerunner of her illness to come, nothing allows us to state that this was her unavoidable fate. Shirley *was* not ill, she *became* ill: the first time between 1940–41 and *c.* 1950 , when she suffered from hysteria; a second time between the end of 1954 and October 8, 1965, when she suffered from multiple personality. The rest of the time, she was not sick at all.

"Listening to you, it is as if Shirley switched illnesses as easily as she switched personalities! Would you go so far as to claim that she made herself ill?" – Why not? Even though it is clear that many of her symptoms were artificially created by the psychotropic drugs administered to her by Wilbur, one can hardly describe Shirley as an innocent victim of medical *hubris*. For one thing, Shirley wanted to be sick, she wanted to enter psychiatric legend – and this as early as her time at Mankato, well before meeting Wilbur. It is not being cynical to observe that illness was for her, very literally, a full-time career in which she put all her hopes and ambitions. One cannot, therefore, place all the blame on Wilbur, as if she, and she alone, was responsible for Shirley's illness. Shirley was more than happy to let herself go, to let herself *be* drugged, hypnotized, dissociated, influenced, manipulated: anything was fine, so long as she was not responsible for it happening to her! Here as always, the concepts of "suggestion," "influence," and "transference" conceal the patient's profound demand for irresponsibility, sustaining the illusion that she plays no role in her illness. Shirley decided to be ill, she decided to no longer have any control over her decisions, just like she decided, later, to no longer be ill. Indeed, how can one not be struck by her sudden recovery? In August 1965, she was going through an acute crisis, afflicted with a host of psychosomatic symptoms and panicked to the point of creating a new personality. But on October 8, when she moved away with Wilbur, her sixteen personalities miraculously fused together, instantaneously and permanently. Was it because her desire to get well was stronger than her illness? Or, more prosaically, was it because this desire to get well was only the other side of her desire to be ill? That which desire made, desire can undo as well.

"Even supposing that you are correct and Shirley Mason wanted everything that happened to her, should this prevent us from searching for the deeper causes of this wanting-to-be-sick?" – But what causes? Organic, biological causes? One may of course speculate about some biochemical imbalance or a genetic predisposition, but the fact is that nothing in Shirley Mason's biography points to an organic pathology. Should we look for psychological causes? Certainly not, at least if we mean by this unconscious causes: it should be obvious by now that Shirley's "unconscious" was a mere construction of the analysis and served essentially as a convenient megaphone for Wilbur. As for the conflicts with her mother during Shirley's adolescence, her anguish regarding sex, her difficulty adapting to adulthood, her desire to be always the center of attention, all of this clearly played a role in her "flight into illness." But does this explain anything? We should not confuse context with explanation. Countless teenagers suffer through the same growing pangs as Shirley without falling ill.

Sociological causes, then? In one of the best books written on the subject, the sociologist Michael Kenny[159] proposes that we recognize in the North American brand of multiple personality a secularization of the old themes of puritan Protestantism – the dualism of Good and Evil, the rejection and surrender of the old self, its rebirth and resurrection following a painful conversion mimicking the Passion of Christ. All these themes do indeed pertain quite well to Shirley Mason, torn as she was between her Adventist religious beliefs and psychoanalytic atheism, her parents and her transference-love for Wilbur, the country and the big city. But does this explain her decision to make herself ill? Many other Americans of her generation went through the same conflicts without developing a multiple personality, and moreover Shirley herself had opted first for a banal hysteria. That she eventually found in multiple personality a language particularly well suited to encode her problems does not imply that she was predestined by her place in society and culture to adopt this "idiom of distress"[160] rather than another. Placed in different situations and confronted with different doctors, she might just as well have become anxious, depressed, neurasthenic, anorexic, bulimic, or a borderline personality. In a way, anything might have done the trick, as long as it allowed her to be ill. Her illness did not "reflect" or "express" society in any way, and society does not explain it. At best, it supplied the disparate elements with which Shirley and Wilbur fashioned their micro-society, before extending it by recruiting an ever-growing number of patients and therapists.

"You have still not explained why Shirley Mason became ill in this manner, nor why so many others followed her example. Are you saying that all this was just a matter of chance?" – Why do you always want to find explanations, causes, reasons? Does chance frighten you that much? Nowhere was it written that Shirley Ardell Mason would fall ill, nor that she was going to meet Cornelia Wilbur and Flora Rheta Schreiber, nor that together they would come to be at the origin of one of the most bizarre social phenomena of the twentieth century. It just happened that way and not otherwise, that's all. All that we can do now is describe how this chance event created its own necessity, its own rules of the game and its own players – until the next throw of the dice.

Translated by GRANT MANDARINO

Notes

1 About 90 percent, according to statistics quoted by Hacking 1995, ch. 5; see also Putnam 1989a, pp. 55–56.
2 Braun 1979.
3 Taylor and Martin 1944; see also Thigpen and Cleckley 1984 and Merskey 1992.
4 Greaves 1980; Hilgard 1986, pp. 300–301.
5 Bliss 1980.

6 Boor 1982; Kluft 1982.
7 Humphrey and Dennett 1989.
8 Ross 1989, pp. 90–91; Loewenstein, in Flammer 1994. Ross and Loewenstein are both former presidents of the International Society for the Study of Multiple Personality and Dissociation.
9 Azam 1887; Breuer and Freud 1895; Prince 1905; James 1984; Janet 1989.
10 North, Ryall, and Wetzel 1993, quoted in Spanos 1996, p. 232.
11 On the thorny question of simulators, see Putnam 1989a, p. 113, and Braude 1991, p. 55.
12 Masson 1992.
13 Mulhern 1991.
14 Wright 1993, May 17, p. 79.
15 The affair is outlined in detail in Ofshe 1992; Wright 1993; Ofshe and Watters 1994.
16 Ofshe 1992, pp. 149–150.
17 See especially Crews 1995 and 1997, as well as Pendergrast 1996.
18 Loftus and Ketcham 1994; Ofshe and Watters 1994; Spanos 1996.
19 McHugh 1993.
20 Hacking 1998.
21 On the epidemiology of MPD, see Spanos 1996, pp. 234–235.
22 McHugh 1997, p. x.
23 On the historicity of scientific facts, see Latour 1999, ch. 5.
24 In many respects, MPD is a return to the "multiple personality" of the end of the nineteenth century and nothing precludes, circumstances provided, that it will resurface in a slightly different guise in the future. One could say about multiple personality and MPD what Pierre Janet said about hypnotism: "Hypnotism is well and truly dead... until it comes back to life" (Janet 1919, vol. 1, p. 187).
25 On the history of the MPD "movement," see Hacking 1995 and Acocella 1999.
26 See for example Callon and Latour 1992 and Pickering 1995, ch. 1, who prefers to speak of "material agency."
27 See the ethnographic investigation conducted by Antze on one of these groups in Toronto, Antze, and Lambek 1996, pp. 3–23.
28 Crabtree 1985.
29 Carlson 1981.
30 Crabtree 1993, ch. 14.
31 Fuller 1982; Kenny 1986.
32 Shamdasani 1994.
33 Thigpen and Cleckley 1957.
34 Putnam 1989a, p. 35. Putnam adds: "Schreiber's (1972) account is both detailed and accurate enough to serve as mandatory clinical reading for students of MPD." See as well Hacking 1995, pp. 40–41.
35 Schreiber 1974, p. 436.
36 Schreiber 1974, p. 13. Schreiber forgot about Breuer's "Anna O.," who was a classic case of dual personality.
37 Letter from Schreiber to Wilbur dated April 30, 1973, Flora Rheta Schreiber Papers (subsequently referred to as "SP" followed by file number), Lloyd Sealy Library, John Jay College of Criminal Justice, New York, no. 315.
38 Letter from Patricia Schartle to Schreiber dated January 16, 1970, SP no. 1104.
39 See Healy 1997, pp. 75–76.
40 See Wilbur's letter to Schreiber from February 1974, SP no. 315: "I am amused that you have had letters from 6 persons who described themselves as MPs, because if they know about themselves and have no amnesia, they are not MPs."
41 Reader's mail dated October 3, 1975, SP no. 304. In a letter dated May 28, 1973, another prisoner described how he had been tortured sexually by his parents and proposed that Schreiber write a book about him, suggesting that the title be "The Making of a

Criminal." Schreiber (1983) would later publish a book about the serial killer Joseph Kallinger, a victim, according to her, of sexual abuse during his childhood.

42 Reader's mail dated February 14, 1974, SP no. 301.

43 Reader's mail dated April 20, 1975, SP no. 304.

44 Reader's mail dated July 14, 1974, SP no. 302. In postscript, Mary adds: "I am 'out' and going to mail this before Liz and Elizabeth wake up and keep me from it."

45 Schreiber 1974, p. 13.

46 On this concept taken from cybernetics, see Latour 1987.

47 This attitude contrasts singularly with that in force in other disciplines, as is testified by the good will shown by scientists toward anthropologists and historians of science who come to nose around their laboratories and archives; see, for example, Latour and Woolgar 1979, Pickering 1995, and Knorr Cetina 1999, p. 21: "Openness seems to be characteristic of researchers who are both confident of the positive knowledge in their fields and aware of the essential fragility and contestability of this knowledge, which they do not attempt to hide." Compare this with the answer given by the psychoanalyst Hermann Nunberg to Paul Roazen, who wanted to interview him about Freud and his patients: "You are not going to get our secrets!" (Roazen 1975, p. xxxiii).

48 Telephone interview with the executor of Flora Rheta Schreiber's will, November 18, 1998.

49 Borch-Jacobsen 1997.

50 Borch-Jacobsen 1997, p. 63.

51 Borch-Jacobsen 1997, p. 63.

52 Associated Press 1998.

53 Reuters, unpublished press release, August 17, 1998.

54 Associated Press 1998.

55 The decisive clue was provided by a letter sent to Schreiber by a childhood friend of Sybil, in which her name had apparently escaped the attention of the archivist in charge of tracking down the "compromised" correspondence (letter from Anita Bird to Schreiber dated August 20, 1975, SP no. 315). Another clue was found in a letter from Schreiber to her literary agent, which mentioned a trip to Dodge Center and Mankato, respectively the true Sybil's birthplace and the town where she later studied (letter from Schreiber to Gladys Carr dated May 7, 1970, SP no. 1103). For a more picturesque account of our discovery, see Boynton 1998–99.

56 On Ellen G. White, the Adventist movement, and the dietetic inventions of doctor John H. Kellogg, see the excellent study by Numbers 1976, as well as Numbers 2003.

57 Transcript of taped interview between Shirley, Wilbur, and Schreiber, August 9, 1970, SP no. 1095.

58 Summary by Schreiber of an analysis session recording, dating from 1962, SP no. 1093.

59 Dessie Blood Engbard, quoted in the *Minneapolis Star and Tribune* in its August 27, 1975 edition (Johnson and Norris 1975). Oddly enough, this newspaper article that established Sybil's identity as early as 1975 has remained completely ignored by researchers for a quarter century, while being well known by the people in Dodge Center (it is proudly reproduced in a history of Dodge County edited by the Dodge County Century and Quarter Club).

60 Interview with Virginia Cravens and Graciela Watson (both née Flores), Nacogdoches, Texas, December 6, 1998.

61 Pearl Peterson Lohrbach, quoted in Johnson and Norris 1975.

62 V. Cravens and G. Watson, cited interview.

63 "John Greenwald dies from gun accident," *Dodge County Republican*, August 29, 1940 (article tracked down by Peter J. Swales with the help of the Dodge County Historical Society).

64 Responses to a questionnaire sent to Shirley's classmates in 1999 by Dan Houlihan, professor of psychology at Minnesota State University in Mankato; Dan Houlihan archives.

65 Report of doctor Henry W. Woltman to his colleague Henry B. Troost dated April 1, 1942, SP no. 1103.

66 On April 15, 1942, Shirley notes that she went to the clinic to receive some "injections" (diary 1940–42, SP no. 1080). Later, she would recall that strong doses of Luminal were administered to her by injection: "They gave me three shots and it still didn't knock me out" (transcript of taped interview between Shirley, Wilbur, and Schreiber, August 13, 1970, SP no. 1096).

67 On the picaresque career of "Bishop" Leiske, itinerant preacher, businessman, and TV host, see Shaw 1981.

68 Bennett 1940. Wilbur would publish three articles on electroshock therapy, one of them in collaboration with Bennett: Bennett and Wilbur 1944b; Wilbur, Michaels, and Becker 1947; Wilbur 1947.

69 See Wilbur 1944.

70 Bennett and Wilbur 1944a.

71 Shirley Mason, analytic diary, *c.* 1957, SP no. 1083.

72 Transcript of taped interview between Shirley, Wilbur, and Schreiber, August 13, 1970, SP no. 1096.

73 Letter from Shirley Mason to Walter Mason dated October 6, 1954; David Eichman papers (subsequently referred to as "EP").

74 Undated letter from Shirley Mason to Walter Mason, *c.* September–October 1954, EP.

75 Letter from Wilbur to Schreiber dated March 1, 1971, SP no. 1102. See also the letter from Shirley to Wilbur dated May 2, 1958, SP no. 1085, in which Shirley admits to having simulated her personalities: "You might ask me … why I ever began… and worse yet, continued such a sham with you…I say with you because I did not do it before I came to New York… I did not do it in Omaha."

76 Wilbur, transcript of taped interview between Wilbur and Schreiber, August 7, 1970, SP no. 1095.

77 Thigpen and Cleckley 1954. The article was followed in October 1954 by an analysis of the semantic productions of Eve's personalities by Osgood and Luria 1954.

78 Thigpen and Cleckley 1957, p. 6.

79 Schreiber 1974, p. 108. The writer Schreiber seems to have opportunely mixed here the character of Wilbur with the true-life Shirley, who wrote in her analytic diary on July 18, 1957, SP no. 1084: "I meant to read the *Three Faces of Eve* (curiosity!) but the librarian said someone had stolen the book thirty minutes after he had put it on the shelf."

80 Schreiber 1974, p. 108.

81 December 15, 1955, excerpts transcribed by Schreiber, SP no. 1081.

82 Shirley Mason, analytic diary, December 11, 1957, SP no. 1083. See as well Schreiber 1974, p. 381, where "Teddy" (a.k.a. Willie P.) reports to Wilbur that "the movie was exactly like Sybil" – or was it the reverse?

83 Shirley Mason, analytic diary, December 11, 1956 (the punctuation is reproduced as it appears in the diary), SP no. 1083. Eve had been traumatized from having seen the body of her dead grandmother. Sybil, similarly, dissociated during her grandmother's burial.

84 Letter from Schreiber to Wilbur dated May 14, 1970, SP no. 1102 .

85 On the exchanges between multiple personality and literature in general, see Carroy 1993 and Borch-Jacobsen 1994b.

86 Shirley Mason, analytic diary, December 15, 1955, SP no. 1081.

87 Figure cited by Wilbur in a document titled "Economics," SP no. 1098. From 1965 to 1973, Shirley made payments of 100 dollars per month (letter from Shirley Mason to Florence Mason dated May 9, 1973, EP).

88 Letter from Wilbur to Schreiber dated July 26, 1965, SP no. 1102. In April 1959, Wilbur presented a paper titled "Transference phenomenon as illustrated by a multiple personality" at the conference of the Academy of Psychoanalysis; a heavily annotated copy of the manuscript is among the Schreiber papers at the John Jay College.

89 Shirley Mason quotes Wilbur in her analytic diary dated January 12, 1956, SP no. 1081: "Dr. Silver[berg] for your training analysis." Silverberg, a founding member of the Academy of Psychoanalysis (with, among others, Franz Alexander, Erich Fromm, and Herbert Spiegel), had sponsored the request for membership to this group by his "student" Wilbur (letter of recommendation from Silverberg to Frances S. Arkin dated August 20, 1956; Peter J. Swales papers). He also moderated the session at the annual meeting of the Academy of Psychoanalysis during which Wilbur presented her "preliminary communication" on Shirley's case (the fact is mentioned in the margin of the manuscript).

90 On this therapeutical eclecticism, see Stepansky 1999.

91 In an undated entry in her analytic diary, Shirley mentions that she had taken penthotal for the first time on "95th St." (SP no. 1083). We know from a letter addressed by Schreiber on August 9, 1973 to her lawyers regarding Willie P. that Shirley had lived briefly at this address from mid-December 1955 to January 1956.

92 Shirley Mason, analytic diary, November 15, 1956, SP no. 1083.

93 Wilbur, cited by Shirley Mason in her analytic diary, March 14, 1956, SP no. 1081.

94 Shirley Mason, analytic diary, March 20, 1961, SP no. 1806; emphasis added.

95 Fromm-Reichman 1948. On the mother as scapegoat in the works of Bruno Bettelheim and his psychoanalytic colleagues after the war, see Pollack 1997, especially pp. 160–161.

96 See the letter from Schreiber to Wilbur dated October 27, 1970, SP no. 1102, in regard to Wilbur's fruitless efforts to find any trace of the "suspected" diagnosis at the Mayo Clinic in Rochester: "It is very important, I think, to get some records of Hattie's [=Mattie's] schizophrenia . . . Tell him [Dr. Howard P. Rome, senior psychiatrist at the Mayo Clinic] frankly about *your diagnosis after the fact* of schizophrenia (the catatonic mutism and excitement on the farm, etc.) of the *suspected* visit to Mayo, etc. Try to get confirmation in writing"; emphasis added.

97 Hacking 1995, ch. 4.

98 Letter from Schreiber to Wilbur dated July 25, 1965, SP no. 1102.

99 Kempe *et al*. 1962.

100 Schreiber 1974, p. 363.

101 Shirley Mason, analytic diary, April 2, 1956, SP no. 1082.

102 Shirley Mason, analytic diary, October 11, 1959, SP no. 1086.

103 Uncertain: in her analytic diary, Shirley speaks of "equinol" and of "equinal."

104 Uncertain: Shirley speaks sometimes of "serapilin," sometimes of "serpatilin."

105 Shirley Mason, analytic diary, SP no. 1081.

106 Transcript of a taped analysis session from 1962, SP no. 1093.

107 Transcript of a suicide note addressed to Wilbur, *c*. 1961–63, SP no. 1101; Shirley Mason's emphasis.

108 Shirley Mason, analytic diary, June 12, 1957, SP no. 1084.

109 Shirley Mason, analytic diary, January 25 and 27, 1957, SP no. 1084.

110 Letter from Shirley to Walter and Florence Mason dated February 1, 1962, EP: "I need from 13 to 16 hours sleep almost every night. That will clear up with time she [Wilbur] says."

111 Interview with Jean L. conducted by Peter J. Swales, New York, March 3, 1999; Peter J. Swales papers.

112 Letter from Shirley Mason to Florence Mason dated April 1, 1962, EP: " . . . there are so many new medications on the market available. I should know, I have taken enough over a long enough period of time to be a walking drugstore."

113 Swales 1989. Swales notes that Freud, at the beginning of his career, administered to his patients chloral, sulfonal, opium, and, under Fliess's influence, cocaine. His own use of cocaine (as is now known from Freud 1985), lasted, with some interruptions, for a period of approximately fifteen years.

114 On the morphinomania of Anna O. (Bertha Pappenheim), see Hirschmüller 1989; on that of Cäcilie M. (Anna von Lieben), see Swales 1986a.

115 To get an idea of the hypnotic age regression technique used by Spiegel, see Spiegel, Shor, and Fishman 1945. According to Spiegel, Shirley had been filmed during one of these hypnotic experiments, but unfortunately this film could not be found in Columbia University's archives.

116 Letter from Shirley to Walter and Florence Mason dated January 25, 1962, EP.

117 See Wilbur 1960. It is interesting to note that Shirley is described (anonymously) in this article as suffering from psychosomatic troubles – dysmenorrhaea, chronic constipation, nausea, vomiting, extreme fatigue, etc – without any mention of her personalities: "All of her symptoms are now under control and the majority of them have been resolved" (p. 526).

118 Tape recording of the analysis session of February 8, 1960, SP no. 1090.

119 See the letter from Shirley to her stepmother Florence Mason dated June 23, 1962, EP, regarding the Librium that Florence started taking after the death of Walter Mason: "It is not like a lot of medications – hard to leave alone afterward – *that* is only when you've had 600 or so mgs. a day by injection for several months – you only have about 30 mgs. a day, don't you?"

120 Dosage indicated in 1965 in Goodman and Gilman's pharmacological textbook (1965, p. 189).

121 Information kindly provided by Dr. Henri Grivois.

122 Letter from Shirley to Florence Mason dated June 23, 1962, EP.

123 These were almost immediately recognized, see Hollister *et al*. 1961; Goodman and Gilman 1965, p. 189.

124 Goodman and Gilman 1965, p. 188.

125 Schreiber 1963. Wilbur wrote extensively on homosexuality, notably female: Bieber, Wilbur *et al*. (1962; Wilbur 1964; 1965; 1970; Wilbur *et al*. 1967.

126 Letter from Shirley Mason to Walter Mason dated May 4, 1963, EP.

127 Letter from Shirley Mason to Walter Mason dated May 4, 1963, EP.

128 Transcript of taped interview between Schreiber and Mr. and Mrs. Winsey, July 4, 1970, SP no. 1094: "FRS: I met them all under hypnosis, and they were distinctly different people, with different voice qualities, different vocabularies, even their appearances, the look in the eye, the facial expression ... it was done for my sake, and it was to secure their cooperation."

129 Schreiber 1974, p. 13.

130 Letter from Shirley to Schreiber dated May 20, 1965, SP no. 1100.

131 Letter from Schreiber to Wilbur dated July 23, 1965, SP no. 1102.

132 Letter from Wilbur to Schreiber dated July 26, 1965, SP no. 1102.

133 Letter from Wilbur to Schreiber dated August 4, 1965, SP no. 1102.

134 Wilbur's curriculum vitae, 1970, SP no. 1103.

135 Telephone interview with Dr. Mildred Bateman, June 26, 1999.

136 Interview with Harold and Cleo Eichman (son and stepdaughter of Florence Mason), Roseburg, Oregon, January 15, 1999.

137 Letters from Shirley to Schreiber dated February 22 and April 23, 1977, SP no. 1100.

138 Acocella 1999, p. 6.

139 Letter from Schreiber to Wilbur dated July 7, 1982, SP no. 315.

140 See letter from Schreiber to Dominick A. Barbara dated September 18, 1974 and January 8, 1975, SP no. 317. Schreiber had asked Barbara to nominate her for the Nobel Prize and had prepared for him a document titled "Why I consider *Sybil* a candidate for the Nobel Prize in literature," in which one can read: "*Sybil* is a monumental achievement not only for its psychiatric content, the culmination of ten years of research, but also as a literary and dramaturgical expression ... On the scientific level, this book represents a pioneering effort, a spectacular breakthrough in the study and presentation of the unconscious."

141 See letters from Schreiber to Patricia Myrer dated November 2, 1977 and January 31, 1981, SP no. 315.

142 Undated postcard from Wilbur to Schreiber, SP no. 315.

143 Interview with Jim and Naomi Rhode conducted by Peter J. Swales, New York, November 30, 1998; Peter J. Swales papers.

144 Schreiber 1974, p. 374.

145 Letter from Shirley to Wilbur dated May 2, 1958, SP no. 1085; quoted in Schreiber 1974, p. 374.

146 Letter from Shirley to Wilbur dated May 2, 1958, SP no. 1085; not quoted in Schreiber 1974, p. 374.

147 Wilbur quoted by Schreiber in a transcript of undated tape recording, SP no. 1089. Compare with Breuer's very similar attitude vis-à-vis Anna O.'s admission of simulation in Breuer and Freud 1895, p. 46; see Borch-Jacobsen 1996, ch. 8.

148 Shirley Mason, analytic diary, July 7, 1958, SP no. 1085: "One Friday, 'someone' stalked into your office, imitated me, had a paper written about how she had now become well and was confessing (or something to that effect, I believe) that it had all been put on anyway. Well, you knew better."

149 This transcript is not extant in SP.

150 Letter from Schreiber to Wilbur dated March 24, 1972, SP no. 1102.

151 Letter from Wilbur to Schreiber dated March 27, 1972, SP no. 1102.

152 Peggy supposedly flew to Amsterdam, then occupied by the Nazis, and back on April 9–13, 1942. See taped interview between Shirley and Schreiber, August 1970, SP no. 1095; see also Wilbur's letter to Schreiber dated August 30, 1970, SP no. 1102: "Woman saw her [Peggy] in the P.[ost] O.[ffice]. Asked if she was a student and would she like to make $100. To Minneapolis and by air, over water for a long time, landed, Nazi soldiers with Swastikas, walked th[r]ough, got on plane, slept, Minneapolis and to 'Kato [Mankato] on bus." Wilbur and Schreiber went to great lengths to try to corroborate this "Amsterdam episode," see Schreiber's letter to Wilbur dated June 22, 1970, SP no. 1102: "Let's bring it as close to the occupation as possible. Who were the uniformed men? Soldiers? Airport personnel? Or something else?" Schreiber seems to have quietly dropped the matter after her friend Aubrey Winsey pointed out to her that the US were at war with Germany at the time: "1942? But wasn't Holland at that time occupied by Germany? Weren't we at war with Germany? We were at war from Dec. of 1941"; transcript of taped interview between Schreiber and Mrs. and Mr. Winsey, July 4, 1970, SP no. 1094.

153 See Borch-Jacobsen and Shamdasani 2006, chs. 2 and 3.

154 Letter from Schreiber to Wilbur dated October 27, 1970, SP no. 1102.

155 Letters from Doctor Howard P. Rome to Wilbur dated August 31 and November 13, 1970, SP no. 1102. The medical file quoted by Rome in the second letter contains only this: "Temp. down. Abd. soft. No tend. whatever. Bowels did not move, throat only slightly reddened. P. M., want to go home. Dismissed."

156 Schreiber 1974, p. 337.

157 See François Roustang's related remarks on the subject of the placebo effect and the sacrament in the Christian tradition (Roustang 2000, pp. 206–207).

158 Veyne 1983. For a critique of the concept of belief, see Good 1994 and Latour 1996.

159 Kenny 1986.

160 Kleinman 1980.

PART II

Fragments of a theory of generalized artifact

4   What made Albert run?

You wake up one morning, the whole world is gray, you have had enough of your cold, colorless life. You want to drop everything, escape, far away, where life is real. Who has not had this dream from time to time? Nothing could be more normal. The desire to escape, to travel, is deeply rooted in the heart of man, from the young runaway to the tourist, from the beatnik to the Sunday hiker. But suppose now that this desire to flee becomes an obsession, a truly irresistible compulsion. Suppose further that it all happens in a state of absence and you cannot remember any of it: you arrive somewhere, dazed, without the slightest idea of what happened in the interval. Obviously, you have become a *pathological* runaway, a *mad* traveler, fit for the asylum and therapy.

So how do you get from normal escapist desire to travel madness? What is the difference between these two, almost identical, impulses? How did you become mentally ill? Besides, are you *really* ill? Ian Hacking has written a wonderful philosophical fable about these and several other equally fascinating questions.[1] Its moral is simple, if somewhat untimely: what we call "mental illness" is not a permanent, intangible reality. For it to develop, it needs a hospitable environment, what Hacking compares to an ecological niche. Without a facilitating environment, mental illness languishes, wastes away, disappears, or emigrates somewhere more propitious. You who dream of dropping everything, for example, there is almost no chance of your becoming a pathological *fugueur* (the French word for "runaway"). Our modern psychiatric bibles (DSM-IV, ICD-10) may still make room for the diagnosis of "dissociative fugue," but there is no longer, in early twenty-first-century Europe, any environment on which that illness could truly thrive. A century ago it was different. Hacking is more precise (or peremptory): fugue, he claims, became an illness in 1887 with the publication of Philippe Tissié's medical thesis *Les aliénés voyageurs* (*Insane Travelers*),[2] and it began to wane after the 1909 Congress of alienists and neurologists in Nantes.

Hacking even gives us the name of the first pathological *fugueur*: Jean-Albert Dadas, an employee in a gas equipment company in the Bordeaux region. Tissié spotted him in 1886 at the Hôpital Saint-André in Bordeaux:

> He had just come from a long journey on foot and was exhausted, but that was not the cause of his tears. He wept because he could not prevent himself from departing on a trip when the need took him; he deserted family, work, and daily life to walk as fast as he could, straight ahead, sometimes

doing 70 kilometers a day on foot, until in the end he would be arrested for vagrancy and thrown in prison.[3]

This strange compulsion had seized him for the first time when he was twelve. He had suddenly disappeared from the gas factory where he was an apprentice, and when his brother found him in a nearby town he had seemed to awaken from a dream, astonished to find himself there. As a rule, his attacks were preceded by migraines, insomnia, and sessions of intense masturbation. Then Dadas would take to the road and walk, walk, till he found himself in some spot that he had heard about – Paris, Marseilles, Algiers, Frankfurt, Vienna, Moscow, Constantinople (Hacking provides us with a map of his impressive peregrinations across Europe). Dadas never remembered much, but Tissié quickly realized – this was 1886, the golden age of hypnotism à la Charcot–Bernheim – that you only needed to put him under hypnosis to have him recollect the sometimes picaresque details of his travels. Tissié also had photographs taken of Dadas, in which we see him in his different states: normal (perky, smiling at us); at the end of an attack (groggy, stupid); under hypnosis (asleep, eyes closed).

Tissié diagnosed a form of hysteria. Dadas, he noted, had all the typical "stigmata" of hysteria listed by Charcot: anesthesias, hyperesthesias, narrowing of the field of vision, and the like. Charcot himself was of a different opinion. The following year, in the course of his famous "Tuesday Lectures" at the Salpêtrière, he presented a second *fugueur* and advanced a diagnosis of "ambulatory automatism," a latent form of epilepsy. With the authority of the Master, the fugue was launched. In the following months and years the literature presented an avalanche of similar cases, some described as "ambulatory automatism" (or "delirium"), others as "hysterical (or psychasthenic) fugues." New names were invented for the phenomenon: *dromomanie*, poriomania, *determinismo ambulatorio* (in Italy), *Wandertrieb* (in Germany, some ten years later). In 1893, Henri Meige published *The Wandering Jew at the Salpêtrière*, a study of a sample of Jewish "neuropathic travelers." Then, as time went by, the fugue waned. Hysteria was "dismembered" by Babinski, and the diagnosis of "dementia praecox," imported from Germany, got the upper hand. The matter was settled at the Congress of Nantes in 1909: fugue, dispersed amongst all sorts of other diagnoses, had ceased to be an independent, discernible illness.

Why bother about this minor chapter in the history of psychiatry? Because it illustrates, in a striking way, a much broader phenomenon: mental illnesses change from one place and time to another, undergo mutations, disappear and reappear. As the medical historian Edward Shorter has shown,[4] a "neurotic" person was likely to have fainting spells and convulsive crises in the eighteenth century, or some kind of paralysis or contracture in the nineteenth, and now would be likely to suffer from depression, fatigue, or an eating disorder. As for what we call "psychoses," it has long been commonplace in ethnopsychiatry and the sociology of mental illnesses to emphasize their cultural relativity: our pathetic paranoiacs and schizophrenics would elsewhere have been sacred or accursed beings - people possessed by the devil, prophets, shamans, "holy fools." Each age, each society, produces its own type of madness, of malady of the soul, and it is pointless to try to translate one into another or make of this one the truth of another, for the cultural paradigms that give birth to them are incommensurable.

That is why, rather than speak of neurosis, psychosis, or psychosomatic ill-nesses – all categories proper to our own era and psychiatric culture – Hacking prefers to speak of "transient mental illnesses" (which I will henceforth abbre-viate as TMI, to give them their proper seriousness and technicality). What matters is not whether an illness is mental (imaginary, arising from fantasy or subjective delirium) or physical (thus real, we would say, because arising from an objective causality); the real dividing line is between illnesses that vary and those that do not. Very few mental illnesses can be confidently called fixed or ahistoric (the fact that they react to this or that medication is obviously not decisive). Hacking thinks, with some reason, that schizophrenia is one of the latter, but he himself recognizes that this may simply be "hope" on his part. Others will say that this hope is in vain and that schizophrenia too is due to disappear some day.

If the illnesses we used to call "mental" are so variable and historical, it must be because they depend on the surroundings in which they are born, grow, and wither. It is a profound mistake to look for the reasons of unreason in an isolated psyche or body, or even in some "social construction" of the illness, as if it did not react to expert knowledge. In reality, a transient illness cooperates and interacts with what surrounds it. To use Hacking's metaphor, it adapts to an "ecological niche," just as a living organism adapts to a particular climate, a particular flora, a particular altitude. We should not, therefore, try to isolate one parameter of the niche to the detriment of the others, making it the central or determinant element: *all* the parameters – or "vectors," as Hacking puts it – act in concert and any local modification immediately impels a modification of the whole.

Hacking lists four vectors that appear to him essential to the viability of a TMI.

1. The illness must be detectable as deviant behavior. In a country obsessed with identity checks (*contrôles d'identité*) like late nineteenth century France, Dadas and his colleagues were immediately spotted, put in jail for vagrancy, taken to hospital for observation. According to Hacking, one reason pathogenic fugue never caught on in Anglo-Saxon countries is that they did not have the same system of identity checks. Go West, young man: fugue was, literally, invisible.

2. The deviant behavior must fit into a pre-existent taxonomy that allows it to be situated and recognized as an illness. Fugue, for example, fell neatly between hysteria and epilepsy, two illnesses that at the time were the focus of a lot of attention on the part of alienists and neurologists.

3. The illness must fit somewhere inside a cultural polarity that singles out certain behaviors as positive – "virtuous," Hacking says – and others as

negative or vicious. Dadas"'s fugues oscillated between the new popular tourism (strongly valorized) and vagrancy (strongly devalorized). As Hacking presents it, this vector may seem somewhat arbitrary and far-fetched, but it touches upon a profound truth. Far from being something submitted to passively, the pathological behavior is actively chosen by troubled people to communicate both their distress and their desire to return to society. A TMI is always, in this respect, a mix of negative and positive, of abjection and possible redemption.

4. The illness must provide some release - what one could call, quoting (and correcting) Freud, the "primary gain from illness." Dadas escaped his work and the overwhelming boredom of Bordeaux, just as the soldiers afflicted with shell shock escaped the trenches, and Breuer and Freud's hysterical patients their stifling families.

As a good pragmatist, Hacking does not exclude the possibility of other vectors. As I see it, there is a very important one that he mentions only in passing:

5. There must be a clause of irresponsibility that allows the ill person to lay the "fault" for his behavior on something else – genes, a biochemical imbalance, trauma, the unconscious, the devil, the horrible-neighbor-who-cast-a-spell-on-me, or whatever. Why did Dadas run away? *He couldn"t help himself.* You may say that this clause of irresponsibility falls under Hacking's second rubric, which it obviously does. But it also explains why a TMI needs to be diagnosed in order to develop. Indeed, it is only when it has been declared a true illness that it provides the sufferer with the benefits of irresponsibility. How many soldiers in the Great War would have been treated as fakers were it not for the diagnosis of shell shock? It is only because British military doctors considered the soldiers' paralyses as symptoms of a real (though psychical) disease that they escaped the firing squad – and, consequently, shell shock spread like wildfire.

Does this mean that TMIs are false, factitious, or simulated illnesses? Here we arrive at the central question of Hacking's book: "Is it real?" Hacking asked himself the same question in his previous book about multiple personality, only to add immediately: "I am not going to answer that question. I hope that no one who reads this book will end up wanting to ask exactly that question."[5] Great books of philosophy teach us to stop posing certain types of questions, or to pose them differently, and it may be that Hacking's *Mad Travelers* is one of these. Indeed, Hacking provides us with all the elements we need in order to understand that the question "Is it real?", is pointless when applied to TMIs. The real is in a constant state of change (admittedly at different paces), and it does not follow from the fact that "mental" illnesses are transient that they are any less real than, say, an infectious or neurological disease. Do we ask if dinosaurs are real, just because they have disappeared from the surface of the earth? Or smallpox, because the last strains that existed in laboratories have finally been destroyed by man? No, it is just that the ecological niche that allowed them to be real at a given moment no longer exists.

Why would it be otherwise with TMIs? Because they are a human product, an artifact of psychiatry, of culture? But who says that an artificial product – the computer on which I write this article, for example, or a laser beam – is not real? Dadas's travels, his migraines, his masturbation, his trances, his dreams (to which Tissié dedicated another book), all of that was perfectly real, even if it was the transient product of all sorts of contingent factors – *even if it was artificial, suggested, and simulated through and through*. To ask if TMIs are real makes no sense, unless we suppose that only the uncreated, that which exists in and for itself and remains identical under all its accidents (the eternal "substance" of the Scholastics), is really real.

So why does Hacking insist on trying to answer that poisoned question? "Was hysterical fugue a real mental illness?" he asks at one point. And his answer is, "No." Why not? Hacking invokes Charles S. Peirce's cautious definition of the real: "The opinion which is fated to be ultimately agreed to by all who investigate, is what we mean by the truth, and the object represented in this opinion is the real."[6] There is no longer any consensus on fugue among "all who investigate": hysterical fugue died in 1909 at the Congress of Nantes. We understand, of course, why Hacking insists on this strict (and slightly provocative) nominalism: TMIs exist only in ecological niches, and they depend therefore, at least in part, on the discourse concerning them. But why draw the conclusion that hysterical fugue or any other TMI is not real? It can only be because Hacking, more or less implicitly, supposes – or "hopes," *à la* Peirce – that there are other mental illnesses that are real and non-transient, on the subject of which there could be a permanent consensus among experts. But, as he says himself, citing Peirce once again, such a hope is more an act of faith than anything else. So why not admit, once and for all, that the very distinction between the permanent–substantial and the transient–accidental, the real and the artificial, the natural–objective and the social–constructed, no longer works? Otherwise, how will we ever be able to understand that some people *really* do suffer from *factitious* illnesses?

It is indeed toward this conclusion that Hacking seems to be leaning in his "Supplement 1", which was obviously written after the four main chapters. This time he asks himself: "What ailed Albert?" Discarding the hypothesis that Dadas's fugues were objectively caused by a concussion he suffered at the age of 8, Hacking lists all the reasons we have for thinking that his symptoms, his dreams, and the memories of his journeys were (at least from the time of his encounter with Tissié) the result of the latter's expectations, which Dadas was only too happy to fulfill. Was Tissié interested in dreams? Dadas produced an abundance. Was Tissié interested in cycling (the object of his second book, *L"hygiène du vélocipédiste*)? During one of his dreams, Dadas, who had never traveled other than on foot, began to move his legs vigorously as if pedaling a bicycle. It seems fairly clear that if there was wish fulfillment in this dream, it was first and foremost Tissié's.

Having come this far, Hacking could have denounced the suggestive, iatrogenic, and consequently fictitious nature of Dadas's symptoms. Generalizing, he could have ridiculed TMIs in their totality: from the vapors of eighteenth-century ladies to our modern multiple personalities and incest survivors, from neurasthenia to anorexia, from astasia–abasia to Post-Traumatic Stress Disorder (PTSD), Attention Deficit Hyperactivity Disorder (ADHD), Chronic Fatigue Syndrome (CFS), and the rest. But this is precisely what Hacking refuses to do, and quite rightly so:

> Clinician and patient, experimenter and subject, are so much part of each other that the question of what "really" ailed Albert Dadas late in his interactions with Philippe Tissié becomes idle, a free wheel that ceases to mesh with the course of events. I must repeat that I do not accuse Dadas or Tissié of falsifying or faking anything. Perhaps the best word for two people in a hypnotic relationship, the hypnotizer and the hypnotized, is that the two are extremely accommodating to each other's needs and expectations.[7]

There is no better way to say that the question, "Is it real?" when applied to TMIs, is hopelessly off the mark. What Hacking says here of the mutual accommodation of the hypnotizer and the hypnotized applies equally to all the other elements of the ecological niche. Reality is not all on one side, fiction on the other. There is – always different and changing – a reality constructed by two, by several, by many. Tissié accommodates his theory to Dadas's odd behavior. Dadas accommodates his behavior to Tissié's theory. Patients, psychiatrists, institutions, the culture, all accommodate each other to create a TMI, just as the elements of an ecosystem accommodate each other to create a particular plant, animal, or virus. Faced with such entities, the question is no longer whether it is real, but only whether it propagates or not, and how. And to what extent our own discourse – Hacking's, mine, yours – contributes to this process.

Translated by JENNIFER CHURCH

Notes

1 Hacking 1998.
2 Tissié 1887.
3 Tissié 1887, p. 3.
4 Shorter 1992.
5 Hacking 1995, p. 16.
6 "How to make our ideas clear," Peirce 1986, vol. 3, p. 273.
7 Hacking 1998, p. 111.

5 The Bernheim effect

I define suggestion in the broadest sense: *the act by which an idea is introduced into the brain and accepted by it.*[1]

***

Here is the paradox of suggestion: how can you induce someone to become passive (suggestible) if this passivity requires his prior acceptance? If he accepts, it is because he was already willing. But if he was willing, can we say that he passively executed a suggestion?

Another way of formulating the problem: is suggestion the act of *le suggestionneur* ("the act by which an idea is introduced into the brain . . ."), or that of *le suggestionné* (". . . and accepted by it")? Hippolyte Bernheim, in his writings on hypnosis, never manages to fully answer this crucial question. Very often he decides in favor of *le suggestionneur*, investing him with an exorbitant power of psychic manipulation. According to this conception, eagerly spread by the popular press of the time,[2] *le suggestionneur* (the hypnotist) literally takes over the other's mind; he penetrates into it (rapes it) and manipulates its machinery as if it were an automaton: "Sleep!" "Wake up!" "Hallucinate!" "Become anesthetic!" "Be cured!" "Forget!" "Remember!" Incapable of resisting, *le suggestionné* (the suggestioned, hypnotized person) obeys blindly, without even knowing that he is obeying. Each time, Bernheim explains, the suggested idea becomes a sensation, image, movement (or an absence of sensation, image, movement), thus illustrating the fundamental law of ideo-dynamism:

> *Every suggested and accepted idea tends to become an action . . . Every cerebral cell activated by an idea activates the neural fibers necessary to realize that idea.*[3]

Bernheim's guiding model here is obviously that of the reflex. Just as a reflex movement short-circuits the brain, a suggestion is acted upon without the subject's knowledge, outside of consciousness and of will: "A decapitated frog continues to execute with its four legs and trunk adaptive, appropriate, defensive movements."[4] This comparison of the *suggestionné* and the decerebralized frog should not come as a surprise. After all, Bernheim was a professor of internal medicine, and his "psychology" is the "physiology of mind" (Maudsley) of his time, which can be characterized in short as an extension of the reflex schema to cerebral activity. In this perspective, the higher psychic activity arises from a basis of automatism that it dominates and integrates by inhibiting it:

> The higher level of the brain (this is what I schematically call the part of the brain dedicated to the control functions) has a moderating action upon the lower level (this is what I call the part of the brain dedicated to the faculties of imagination, to cerebral automatism), just as the brain has a moderating influence on the spinal automatism.[5]

And elsewhere:

> The state of consciousness intervenes to moderate or neutralize the automatic action, to correct or destroy the false impressions insinuated into the nerve centers.[6]

Suppress the inhibiting function of consciousness and will, and what you get is the original automaton, the *suggestionné* that we all are before the time of reflection (Hughlings Jackson's notion of "dissolution" is not far off). Suggestion, in this sense, is nothing other than the normal mode of functioning, even if normally inhibited, of our "cerebral unconscious."[7] Compare Charcot's description of the cataleptic stage of the *grand hypnotisme* observed at the Salpêtrière hospital:

> The suggested idea or group of ideas will be isolated, outside the control of that vast collection of personal ideas, accumulated and organized long ago, which constitutes consciousness properly so called, the *ego*. That is why the movements that translate these acts of unconscious cerebration to the exterior are distinguished by their automatic, purely mechanical character. This is truly, in all its simplicity, the *machine man* dreamt of by De la Mettrie that we have then before our eyes.[8]

The contrast between the somatic theory of hypnosis advocated by the Salpêtrière School and the psychological theory of the Nancy School is actually much less than it appears, for they are both rooted in one and the same psycho-*physiology*. What difference between Charcot's machine man and Bernheim's decerebralized frog, between the theatrical hysteric of the Salpêtrière and the "suggestioned criminal" of Nancy? All are pure psychic things in the hands of the scientist who dissects them, psychological automatons whose fascinating (and disquieting) mechanism one tirelessly assembles and disassembles in the laboratory.

***

From all the preceding, I conclude that an honest man can, by suggestion, commit a crime.[9]

All consciousness has disappeared in the hypnotized individual that one pushes to a criminal act; he is, therefore, irresponsible and should be acquitted. Only the one who made the suggestion is guilty . . . The somnambulist is for the hypnotist a simple instrument, like the pistol that contains the bullet.[10]

***

Let us now ask ourselves how one provokes this state of self-absence. The theory of suggestion presents no problem as long as one is talking of a subject who is *already* regressed, *already* plunged into some hypnoid state (day-dreaming, state of "nervous shock," hysterical attack). Since consciousness in this case is no longer playing its role of inhibition, any idea introduced into the brain will immediately be acted out. But what if the subject is awake, lucid, in full possession of her faculties of inhibition? How is it possible to suggest to this person . . . not to resist suggestion? Will it do to say: "Sleep, for I will it"? Just try this with the first passer-by in the street and see what happens!

Clearly, the success of suggestion presupposes an already established suggestibility, or else "the idea introduced into the brain" will not be "accepted by it." One cannot, therefore, invoke the operator's suggestion to explain the patient's suggestibility. And yet, this is what Bernheim does very often, especially when he has to explain the principles of hypnotic or suggestive psychotherapy. Indeed, how does psychotherapy work? It relies, says Bernheim, on an artificial increase of that suggestibility or "credivity" that has always been the basis of miracle cures as well as of cures due to "medicinal suggestion"[11] (to the placebo effect, we would say nowadays). So, how does one provoke this credivity? By way of hypnosis, Bernheim begins by responding:

> Credivity is moderated by the higher faculties of understanding. Hypnosis, like natural sleep, exhalts the imagination and makes the brain more accessible to suggestion . . . *To provoke this special psychic state by hypnotism and to exploit, with the purpose of cure or relief, the suggestion thus artificially enhanced, such is the role of hypnotic psycho-therapy.*[12]

But how does one provoke hypnosis? By way of suggestion, once again:

> What one calls hypnotism is nothing but the activation of a normal property of the brain, *suggestibility*, that is, the aptitude to be influenced by an accepted idea and to seek its realization.[13]

But was it not precisely this "activation" of suggestibility that was to be explained? A burst of laughter from the Salpêtrière, for if "everything is in suggestion,"[14] then nothing is, especially not the hypnosis that was supposed to be accounted for. Alfred Binet:

> What dominates this book [Bernheim's *De la suggestion*] is a theory of suggestion that is pushed so far that it ends up destroying itself. Indeed, if it is true that everything in hypnotism is suggestion, this state possesses no characteristic other than the suggested ones; in other words, it presents nothing of interest beyond the very fact of the patients' suggestibility.[15]

Pierre Janet: "I am not ready to believe that suggestion explains everything, and in particular that it can explain itself."[16] Thirty years later, reopening the dispute in *Group Psychology and the Analysis of Ego*, Freud would spontaneously rediscover this argument from his Charcotian youth (even though he conveniently forgot that he owed it to his old rival Janet):

Later on my resistance [against the "tyranny of suggestion"] took the direction of protesting against the view that suggestion, which explained everything, was itself to be exempt from explanation. Thinking of it, I repeated the old conundrum:

> Christopher bore Christ,
> Christ bore the whole world,
> Say, where did Christopher
> Then put his foot?[17]

***

The remark is cruel, but it falls short of the mark insofar as it targets Bernheim only as the *ideologue* (in the sense of Destutt de Tracy) of suggestion, the one for whom suggestion is reduced to a mere mechanism of the mind activated by *le suggestionneur*. Indeed, it is time to note that Bernheim, simultaneously and contradictorily, lays great stress on *le suggestionné*'s active participation in the success of the suggestion. In particular, Bernheim knows very well that the suggestion must be "accepted" by the subject before being executed, as can be seen from the fact that certain subjects stubbornly resist suggestion. These people "do not know how to put themselves into the psychic state necessary to realize the suggestion"; they "give themselves a sort of counter-suggestion."[18] So it is not *le suggestionneur* who provokes the receptivity to suggestions; it is the *suggestionné* himself who disinhibits himself, who lets himself go, who makes himself passive.

Suddenly, it is the aporia denounced by the Salpêtrière that appears hopelessly abstract and artificial. Just as Zeno's reasoning will never prevent Achilles from catching the tortoise, so Binet's, Janet's, and Freud's arguments will never prevent the subject from allowing himself to be "suggestioned" *if he is willing*. The mystery of hypnotic induction disappears as soon as one understands that suggestibility is not an automatism and that submission to suggestion is in fact a very voluntary servitude, revocable at any moment. In the end, there is no hypnosis, only a self-hypnosis, or a consent to hypnosis. As Joseph Delbœuf, Bernheim's colleague, noted, *le suggestionneur* proposes, the *suggestionné* disposes: "There is no power either mysterious or dangerous, and hence no one is endowed with it. All hypnotic manifestations are due to the subject and to no one but the subject."[19] (So where is the "tyranny," the totalitarian "authoritarianism" that one so often contrasts with the Freudian respect for the subject's resistances?[20] Where is the fascist "barbary" denounced by the historian Elisabeth Roudinesco?)[21]

***

With the idea of perfecting my hypnotic technique, I made a journey to Nancy in the summer of 1889 and spent several weeks there ... I was a spectator of Bernheim's astonishing experiments upon his hospital patients, and I received the profoundest impression of the possibility that there could be powerful mental processes which nevertheless remained hidden from the consciousness of men.[22]

Even before the time of psycho-analysis, hypnotic experiments, and especially post-hypnotic suggestion, had tangibly demonstrated the existence and mode of operation of the mental unconscious.[23]

***

Bernheim and Delbœuf never tire of repeating that the unconsciousness of the *suggestionné* is an illusion:

> This false idea of unconsciousness . . . has been the source of all the errors that have been made. The subject is conscious: he/she is so at all periods, at all degrees of hypnosis; he/she hears what I say; his/her attention can be directed toward any object in the exterior world. Hypnotic unconsciousness, hypnotic coma do not exist.[24]

Bernheim the clinician flatly contradicts here the theorist of ideo-dynamism: far from being a spinal automaton, the *suggestionné* observes the scene that one has him play, he reflects upon his state, "he forces himself not to laugh."[25] It is a mistake to think that the *suggestionné* is in a state of sleep (that is why one should not speak of "hypnosis"). Quite the opposite, he is alert, hyper-attentive, a little like an athlete attempting to anticipate his opponent's move: "Many somnambulists have a very strong finesse of perception; the least indication serves to guide them. Knowing that they are supposed to realize the hypnotist's thoughts, they do their best to read them."[26] Delbœuf: "The subjects ask themselves what one wants of them, they guess and give it a try."[27]

The "riddle of suggestion,"[28] from this point of view, all but evaporates. If the *suggestionné* does everything *le suggestionneur* suggests to him (or nearly), it is simply because he has been asked to. There is nothing here any more astonishing than if I ask X, "Could you please open the door for me?" and he accedes to my request, of his own accord and fully aware of what he is doing. This everyday interaction becomes mysterious, strictly speaking inexplicable, only if one supposes that X *does not know* that he has been asked to open the door, and that he complies unconsciously, without being able to resist. All the classical rituals of hypnosis thus involve tasks that the subject is supposed to execute unwittingly or involuntarily. For example, if X, once he is "awakened," feels an irresistible urge to open the door to *le suggestionneur*, without being able to recall that the latter had suggested it to him while he was "asleep," one sees in this a sign that X was truly in a state of profound hypnosis (and one will use tests of this sort to measure the degree of suggestibility of the subject). But if we follow Bernheim and Delbœuf, this is merely an illusion induced by the paradoxical character of the hypnotic request. The subject is content with responding to the request, except that here it is a request for *irresponsibility*: "Be unconscious"; that is to say: "Do not be aware of the current request," "Respond against your will," "Open the door without knowing it." Placed before such an incongruous request (before such a double bind),[29] the subject actually has only the choice of two possible responses. Either he resists and flatly refuses to lend himself to the game of irresponsibility, which then cannot even begin. Or, good sport (good actor), he accedes to the paradoxical request and hence adopts *consciously* the role of the *unconscious* automaton:

> I have never seen a somnambulist bump, spontaneously, into objects that he supposedly does not see. But if I tell him that he will bump into them without seeing them, he will enter, I think, into the spirit of his role enough to really

bump into them. Is this due to illusion or complaisance on his part? I lean toward complaisance.[30]

The illusion, then, is not on the part of the *suggestionné* but on the part of *le suggestionneur*, of the one who naively imagines that he has succeeded in illusioning the other: the illusionist illusioned.

Quietly, Bernheim and Delbœuf debunk here a great myth, that of the psychic unconscious. It is well known that the idea of a psychic activity independent of consciousness owes everything, historically speaking, to the somnambulists and hypnotized subjects of the nineteenth century (on this, see Henri Ellenberger's marvelous book on *The Discovery of the Unconscious*).[31] That I am ignorant of what happens in me, that I am the plaything of thoughts and memories of which I am unaware, is an observation that Freud, like so many others at the time, made at first on subjects under hypnosis, before hypostasizing it in a grandiose topography of consciousness and the unconscious, of repression and the repressed. But what if the splitting of hypnotized subjects was factitious? What if their "dissociation of consciousness" was in fact a product of the request for hypnosis – of the *request for the unconscious*? No matter how much distance Freud later tried to place between himself and hypnosis, his "unconscious," just as Janet's "subconscious," was originally nothing else than an artifact of hypnotic procedures, a mirage of the same kind as the colourful multiple personalities produced by Janet, Binet, or Bourru and Burot. Consider for example post-hypnotic suggestion, so often invoked by Freud to prove the existence of the unconscious:

> The idea of the action ordered in hypnosis ... was translated into action as soon as consciousness became aware of its presence. The real stimulus to the action being the order of the physician, it is hard not to concede that the idea of the physician's order became active too. Yet this last idea did not reveal itself to consciousness, as did its outcome, the idea of the action; it remained unconscious, and so it was *active and unconscious* at the same time.[32]

All very well, Bernheim and Delbœuf might object at this point, but how does Dr. Freud know that the post-hypnotic subject does not remember the order that she is supposed to have forgotten? (One imagines here said subject trying very hard to keep a straight face ...)

***

I have at this moment a lady in hypnosis lying in front of me and therefore can go on writing in peace. [Two paragraphs later:] The time for the hypnosis is up. I greet you cordially. In all haste,

Your Dr. Freud.[33]

***

The subject remains conscious, even though she gives all the signs of being asleep. Does that mean she *feigns* unconsciousness, irresponsibility? All

theorists of hypnotism are haunted by the specter of simulation, and it is easy to
see why: if the subject is simulating hypnosis, then there is no hypnosis and
their theory has quite simply no object. So one should not be surprised to see
Braid, Richet, Heidenhain, Charcot, and Janet constantly anticipating the
objection, either by stressing the moral integrity of their subjects or by submitting them to physiological tests intended to rule out the possibility of a
simulation. Bernheim and Delbœuf are no exception, even as they are des-
troying the myth of the hypnotic unconscious: if the *suggestionné* complies with
the suggestion out of complaisance, how does he differ from the actor who
follows the indications of the director? Delbœuf, always more radical than
Bernheim, does not shy away from stressing this theatrical aspect: "The somnambulists are excellent actors, and they quickly enter into the spirit of their
role. Nevertheless, even in this regard, a certain education seems indispensable
to me. It is sometimes necessary to guide them, to train them" – witness a
certain somnambulist who, regressed to the age of 6, did her best to write
poorly, but forgot that she "was not supposed to know how to spell."[34]

And yet, neither Bernheim nor even Delbœuf is quite ready to dilute the
scene of suggestion into pure role-playing (as do, closer to us, social psychologists such as Sarbin and Spanos):[35]

> If many know how to resist unpleasant suggestions, if others accomplish the
> suggested act like actors playing their role, there are those who have no power
> of resistance, there are those who identify with their role. The false
> consciousness dominates in them and annihilates the true consciousness.[36]

Note how Bernheim hesitates at the moment of drawing the implications of
his remarks on the consciousness of the *suggestionné* and falls back momentarily on a theory of ideo-dynamism and hypnotic obnubilation. Elsewhere, in a
more subtle way, he concedes that the subject "sometimes has the impression
that he is simulating or that he is complaisant: when the doctor has left, he
boasts in good faith that he didn't sleep, that he pretended to sleep." But
Bernheim hastens to add that this is an illusion: "He doesn't always know that
he cannot not simulate, that his complacency (*complaisance*) *is forced*."[37]
Delbœuf's variation:

> When one puts the subject's arm in catalepsy and orders him to lower it, he
> does not at all make the appropriate efforts. Quite the opposite, he activates
> antagonistic muscles, and thus pretends not to be able to lower the arm. It is a
> simulated catalepsy, and he is the dupe of his own simulation. It is in this sense
> that I say he complacently countenances the game of catalepsy. This
> *complaisance* is unconscious; it is he who, without knowing it, wants what is
> demanded of him.[38]

Without knowing it? How can Delbœuf and Bernheim be so certain that the
subject is ignorant of his simulation, or of being forced to simulate? Everything
they say elsewhere about the vigilance of the *suggestionné* supports on the
contrary the idea of a deliberate, hyper-attentive behavior: you have to want very
badly not to move to hold your arm in catalepsy; you have to concentrate very

hard not to feel the pin going through your finger. How, then, does this differ from simulation? The actor plays his role before spectators who know that he is playing, whereas the hypnotized person (or the hysteric) plays hers before spectators who think that she does not know that she is playing. The rules of the game are different, but it is a game all the same: "Play me the grand game of the unconscious, pretend not to know that you are pretending."

Under these circumstances, it should not come as a surprise if the *suggestionné* does everything to persuade himself that he does not feel the pain that nevertheless he *does* feel, that he does not see the chair that nevertheless he *does* see. If he confesses to simulation, he will be told that he is wrong, that in reality he cannot prevent himself from doing what he is doing (and how could he gainsay this, since he *has* indeed simulated the anesthesia, the negative hallucination?). Or again, the experiment will be repeated until he finally agrees to play the game of the unconscious (and why not, after all, since it is nothing but a game?).

> Simulation is possible, it is easy; it is even easier to believe in simulation when it does not exist... This happens to me every day before my students; but I show them that the subject is not deceiving and that I am not deceived myself either. For I put the subject back in a hypnotic state and I provoke a catalepsy or a contracture which I defy him of escaping, *inviting him not to be at all complaisant.*[39]

Recipe to produce the unconscious: refuse to believe the subjects when they say they are playing.

Take for example amaurotic patients, who claim not to see with their left eye. Bernheim, with his assistant, submits them to a device "designed to smoke out simulation." It does not take long to establish that "they *see with the left eye without knowing it ... The amaurosis, due to hysteria or to suggestion, is purely psychic.*"[40] But Bernheim's assistant "was tempted to believe in simulation. So I explained to him that the amaurosis, being purely psychic, that is, imaginary, cannot obey the laws of optics."[41] (One recognizes here Charcot's and Freud's argument regarding hysterical paralyses that do not follow the laws of anatomy.) But why conclude that the amaurotic patients are not, therefore, simulating blindness? Why say that they see "without knowing it," when, clearly, *they see*? The blind spot, in this case, is on the side of Bernheim, who does not want to see the game that his patients are playing with him, for him, because of him. Does anyone care to ask if the movements of the tennis player are real or imaginary? He returns the ball, that's all...

***

With regard to the Suggestion book you know the story. I undertook the work very reluctantly, and only to have a hand in a matter that surely will deeply influence the practice of nerve specialists in the next years. I do not share Bernheim's views, which seem to me one-sided, and I have tried to defend Charcot's point of view in the preface – I do not know how skillfully, but I do know for sure, unsuccessfully. The suggestive (that is, Bernheim's iatro-suggestive theory) acts

*like a commonplace charm on German physicians who need to make no great
leap to get from the simulation theory where they stand now to the suggestion
theory.*[42]

*[Anna O.] brought up . . . the idea that she had not been ill at all and that the
whole business had been simulated. Similar observations, as we know, have
frequently been made.*

*Once a disorder of this kind has cleared up and the two states of con-
sciousness have once more become merged into one, the patients, looking back
at the past, see themselves as the single undivided personality which was aware
of all the nonsense; they think they could have prevented it if they had wanted
to, and thus they feel as though they had done all the mischief deliberately.*[43]

***

Here is another hypnotic myth: the subject, once awakened, no longer
remembers what happened during her sleep (whereas she remembers very well
once she is put back to sleep). Braid, Richet, Charcot, Binet, and Féré, all the
theorists of hypnotism rediscover this ancient trait of animal magnetism and
demoniacal possession, which one also finds in most trance rituals. It is the
game of irresponsibility, once again: "How can I remember what I did, since I
wasn't myself, since I was an *other*?" But here comes Bernheim, who shows
with simplicity that you just have to ask:

> When the memories of the somnambulistic state seem completely effaced
> and the subject can no longer spontaneously find them, one just needs to say
> to him: "You will remember everything that happened." If the subject does
> not remember immediately, I put my hand on his forehead and say: "You
> will remember." After a while, the subject, having concentrated, remembers
> everything and recalls with perfect precision everything, absolutely
> everything, that happened. Proof that consciousness was not abolished, that
> the somnambulist never acts as an unconscious automaton, that he sees, that
> he hears, that he knows what he is doing . . . It is not an unconsciousness; it
> is another state of consciousness.[44]

Which is what Bernheim repeats in regard to hysterical attacks, debunking by
the same token one of the dogmas of Charcot's Salpêtrière:

> I put my hand on the forehead of our patient and I stated that she would
> remember everything that happened during the attack. She concentrated for
> a few minutes and, little by little, the memory came back of all the details
> of her crisis.[45]

As is well known, it was these experiments that led Freud to forgo (in 1892,
the very year that he translated this particular book by Bernheim) classical
hypnosis in favor of the more supple method of pressure on the forehead
(*Druckprozedur*)[46] accompanied by "concentration hypnosis."[47] However, he
does not seem to have drawn the properly theoretical implications of
Bernheim's remarks, for the *Druckprozedur* remains for him a method aiming
at recovering "reminiscences" from which the conscious ego is separated by a

post-traumatic – that is, as Charcot taught, post-hypnotic – amnesia. Even if Freud, at that time, was already beginning to substitute the model of repression for that of post-hypnotic amnesia dear to Charcot, Janet, and Breuer, he nonetheless remained convinced that something had been forgotten by the hysterical subject and that this was the source of the symptoms. Now, it was precisely this postulate of amnesia, on which hinges the theory of repression, that Bernheim's experiments called radically in question. If the subject does not remember, it is simply because one implicitly demands it of him: *"He no longer remembers that he remembers."*[48] Forgetfulness, just like the unconscious, is an artifact of the hypnotic setup.

It is to Delbœuf, more than to Bernheim, that the merit of having drawn this sobering conclusion belongs. Bernheim was content with showing that post-hypnotic amnesia could be lifted. Delbœuf, more rigorous, shows that the amnesia, far from being spontaneous, is itself the result of the expectations of *le suggestionneur*:

> Magnetizers and magnetized, building on the preconceived idea that the memory will be abolished, unconsciously did their best to abolish it ... I repeat, the subject can be trained to remember just as he can be to not remember, and the training can be done in a conscious or an unconscious manner.[49]

Take a new subject, that is to say (but is this at all possible?) one having no preconceived idea regarding hypnosis, and you will obtain from her a perfect recollection if you do not believe in post-hypnotic amnesia, and a total amnesia if you believe in it:

> My first two subjects, who were new, displayed the phenomenon of amnesia. But I myself was persuaded at that point that amnesia was the typical phenomenon, and my experiments had no other point – feel free to reread them[50] – than to show the possibility of and to provide the technique for an artificial recall.[51]

Admirable self-reflexiveness. Delbœuf does not say, as does Bernheim, that he is in possession of the right theory of the relation between hypnosis and memory. He says, which is quite different, that the theorized phenomenon varies in accord with the theory, and that there are therefore, strictly speaking, no "new", good, uncontaminated subjects in whom we would be able at last to read the truth of hypnosis and memory. Charcot will have hypnotized subjects who remember nothing, Bernheim will have *suggestionnés* who remember after having forgotten, Delbœuf will have subjects who remember from the start – and Freud, let us add, will have patients who "resist" rememoration during years of analysis. In other words, there is no essence of the phenomenon, only accidents: "Memory and the absence of memory are only accidents, without any characteristic value."[52]

One wishes Freud had been so lucid, so sophisticated. We might have been spared psychoanalysis.

***

The ultimate question is this: is there an essence of hypnosis, beyond its accidents? Is there even such a thing as hypnosis?

Charcot had no doubt about it, no more than he had doubts about the reality of the hysteria that he observed in his hospital. He and his assistants never tired of provoking the three states of *grand hypnotisme*, supposed to be proper to hysteria. Press on the subject's eyelids, she falls into a lethargy and remains inert, all the while manifesting a "neuro-muscular hyper-excitability" (the slightest contact provokes a contracture). Reopen her eyes (or sound a gong), and you will get catalepsy, during which the subject holds whatever pose you give her and "transfers" at will the contractures on the side of the body where you apply a magnet. (A variation noted by Delbœuf during his visit to the Salpêtrière:[53] open only one eye and you obtain a hemicatalepsy, the other half of the body remaining in lethargy.) Now rub the top of the skull, you get somnambulism, during which the subject speaks to you and moves normally. If you want to obtain hemisomnambulism, press on the right or left side of the skull. Total amnesia upon reawakening.

To which Bernheim and Delbœuf retort that one can equally well, if one wishes, artificially provoke these phenomena in non-hysterical patients, or again, provoke in hysterical patients phenomena completely different from those observed at Charcot's Salpêtrière. All one has to do is to announce or suggest that there will be recollection upon awakening, that the magnet will have no effect (or that a false magnet will produce one), that pressure applied to the third frontal circonvolution on the right (or left) will trigger somnambulism, etc. In other words, there is no specificity of the *grand hypnotisme*, nor even of the hysteria that supposedly forms its substratum (one can, Bernheim thus shows, vary at will the alleged symptoms of *grande hystérie* with appropriate suggestions). These morbid states that Charcot claimed to study objectively were in the end nothing but the product of his own suggestions, a "cultured" hypnosis and hysteria:[54]

> The operator will regard as essential completely individual, if not accidental, characteristics, presented by his first subject. Unconsciously using suggestion, he will change them into typical signs; he will strive, still unwittingly, to obtain them in other subjects who will produce them by imitation, and thus the master and the students, reciprocally influencing each other, will continue to feed their error.[55]

What Bernheim and Delbœuf highlight here, with a prescience remarkable for the time, is what present-day experimental psychology has rediscovered, with much uneasiness, under the name of "experimenter expectancy effect."[56] One can never be sure, Robert Rosenthal demonstrates, that the results are not falsified by the experimental setup, for the subjects tend to conform to the expectations unintentionally communicated by the experimenter. Administer, for example, a Rohrschach test: the subject will choose the responses that you unintentionally indicate.[57] Compare with Delbœuf's observations:

> J. recognized more and more quickly, depending on the quality of the maneuver, what I wanted, if it was a paralysis, a contracture, or a mere

> figure ... If, therefore, J. seems to have an inkling of my wishes, it is because, simply by the way I grasp her arm, I already manifest to her what I want from her. This may explain the illusion – if illusion there is – of those who believe that somnambulists divine their hypnotist's desire.[58]

Similarly, Martin Orne has shown in classic experiments that the "demand characteristics of the experiment"[59] inevitably skew the results, for the subjects do not behave in the same way in the artificial situation of the laboratory as they would in a real situation. But here again, this is exactly what Delbœuf wrote seventy years earlier with respect to the "crimes" suggested in the laboratory by his friend Jules Liégeois:

> This hypnotized lady, so full of *good sense*, doesn't she have the good sense to know that she is hypnotized, that she is being used in an experiment, that one is going to play a scene, and that Monsieur Liégeois, whom she knows, would not give her a loaded pistol to shoot at her mother?[60]

So one does not experiment *on* subjects; one plays a game *with* them, the experimental game: tell me what you're looking for, and I'll help you prove it. What Bernheim and Delbœuf observed in the enlarging mirror of hypnosis and hysteria is a looping effect that can be observed in any experimental or clinical situation, no matter how controlled it may be. Where Charcot and so many others saw the promise of a scientific psycho(patho)logy, they already foresaw the endless and uncontrollable proliferation of artifacts: the end of psychology.

And the end of hypnosis also. Indeed, if all of the supposedly objective characteristics of Charcot's *grand hypnotisme* turn out to be artifacts, doesn't the same apply to Nancean hypnosis? That was Binet's objection: "When Monsieur Bernheim tells us that the sleeper is in rapport only with the operator, one could ironically object that it is by suggestion that one has persuaded the sleeper to respond solely to that person."[61] But unlike most present-day experimental psychologists, who are preoccupied with the experimenter's effect only to better try to control it, Bernheim and Delbœuf know full well that they themselves cannot avoid being subject to the same criticism that they level against the Salpêtrière: there is no escape from the interaction between the *le suggestionneur* and *le suggestionné*, no meta-level allowing one to extract oneself from the experimental or clinical game. Delbœuf, in particular, never tires of stressing that the characteristics of Nancean hypnosis (elective rapport with *suggestionneur*, amnesia that can be lifted, etc.) are themselves products of suggestion. But then, what remains of hypnosis once all these artifacts are removed – lethargy, catalepsy, somnambulism, amnesia, rapport, unconsciousness, sleep, and so forth? Nothing. Hypnosis is not "some thing" that would persist beneath the various theories that attempt to account for it, for it is nothing but their artifact or effect (as when one speaks, for example, of the "Larsen effect"). We have thus the Mesmer effect, the Puységur effect, the Braid effect, the Charcot effect, the Pavlov effect, the Erickson effect. And the Bernheim effect: stop assuming that there is something-called-hypnosis, and hypnosis will evaporate. Which is what Berheim, literally, performs:

> The best thing, in my view, would be to do completely without the word hypnotism and replace it with *state of suggestion*. The so-called hypnotic procedures can be reduced to demonstrating or exhalting various suggestibilities... There is no hypnotism... there are only more or less suggestible subjects.[62]

"So there is no such thing as hypnotism," Delbœuf repeats in a famous article.[63] Why then seek to produce a hypnotic state that does not exist (or that exists only because one makes it exist)? Since we inevitably create artifacts, we might as well do it openly: from the beginning of the 1890s, Bernheim and Delbœuf abandoned hypnosis, deliberately restricting themselves to suggestion in the awakened state. These authors who are so often described as naive hypnotists are in reality the first to stop believing in hypnosis and to undertake its dismemberment (just as Babinski, their former Salpêtrière foe, would undertake that of Charcot's hysteria). Having set out to theorize hypnosis, they ended up with a theory and a practice of generalized artifact from which we have still a lot to learn: let's stop believing that there is such a thing as a psychic reality that we could study from the outside; let's understand instead that we are always already manipulating it (manipulators–manipulateds) and *that there is nothing wrong with that*:

> The existence of many schools of hypnotism is therefore quite natural and easy to explain. They owe their birth to the reciprocal action of the hypnotized persons upon the hypnotists. But their rivalry has no reason for being: *they are all equally valid.*[64]

***

This is not the proper occasion for carrying out a detailed justification of the symptomatology of hysteria; but we may accept the statement that in essentials it is of a real, objective nature and is not falsified by suggestion on the part of the observer. This does not imply any denial that the mechanism of hysterical manifestations is a psychical one; but it is not the mechanism of suggestion on the part of the physician.[65]

Of the contents of the preface to the first edition the translator would only like to repeat one remark to which he adheres no less firmly to-day than he did then. What he entirely misses in Bernheim's exposition is the view that "suggestion" (or, rather, the accomplishment of a suggestion) is a pathological psychical phenomenon which calls for particular conditions before it can come about.[66]

***

One frequently gives Freud credit for having renounced hypnosis in favor of the method of free association: "I do not deny," Jacques Lacan writes,

> any more than Freud himself did, the psycho-physiological discontinuity manifested by states in which the hysterical symptoms appear, nor do I

> deny that the symptoms may be treated by methods – hypnosis or even narcosis – that reproduce the discontinuity of these states. I simply repudiate any reliance on these states – and as deliberately as Freud forbade himself recourse to them after a certain time – whether to explain the symptom or to cure it.[67]

Denial, repudiation, rupture: a beautiful legend, but one which has little to do with reality. It was not Freud but Bernheim and Delbœuf who first abandoned hypnosis in their psychotherapeutic practice. When Freud gradually abandoned hypnosis, starting in 1892, he was only jumping on Bernheim's bandwagon, like many others at the time. So it is not the abandonment of hypnosis as such that makes the difference between Freud and the Nancy School, it is the way in which he interpreted this change in technique.

Bernheim and Delbœuf, as we have seen, abandoned hypnosis because they diluted it in the broader concept of suggestion: why maintain the hypnotic ritual, when one can suggest as well in the awakened state? But Freud, in rejecting hypnosis, thought that he could *get rid* of suggestion. Just like his "Master" Charcot, Freud continued to view suggestibility as a characteristic trait of hypnosis, which he in turn assimilated to an objectifiable pathological state. As he explains when discussing Delbœuf's theses in a lecture given in 1892 to the Medical Club of Vienna:

> Hypnosis can easily be distinguished from other states of suggestibility, at least from the point of view of its definition. "Suggestion" means, in a general way, that one leads another person to accept an idea for psychological, rather than logical reasons. This definition applies word for word to the other types of suggestion, but in the case of hypnosis this does not take place because one provides the other with a psychological reason, but because one supresses the state of resistance to the new idea... This speaker tends to think that we need to hold firmly to the authenticity of hypnosis; he takes his arguments from the observation of the hypnotic state in hysterics and thus agrees, on this important point, with the views of Charcot's school.[68]

Likewise, in regard to the somnambulism into which Freud would put his patient "Emmy von N.": "I may well have *called up* the state by my suggestion but I did not *create* it."[69]

For Freud, therefore, the hypnotist (the doctor) is not at all responsible for the suggestibility of the hypnotized (of the hysteric). One sees here how the belief in the "authenticity" of hypnosis fits together with a denial of the intervention of the doctor in the phenomenon that he provokes. Charcot's theory of hypnosis amounted to an exorcism of the suggestive artifact, which was quite simply projected on to the patient. The rejection of hypnosis by Freud clearly follows the same sacrificial logic: let's expel hypnosis and we will purify our procedure of all suggestive contamination. The method of free association is thus supposed, according to Freud, to give us the same access to the unconscious as hypnosis, but without adulterating it. As to the various obstructions that hinder the free and spontaneous communication of the unconscious ideas (repression, resistance, transference, etc.), the idea is that the analyst will simply remove them. The analytic method, according to the famous analogy, operates *per via di levare*, not *per via di porre*.

But did the abandonment of hypnosis ever solve the question of suggestion? From Eugen Bleuler in 1896 to Adolf Grünbaum in 1984, all of Freud's critics have basically asked the same question: what guarantees that the analyst, under the cover of analytic neutrality and noninterventionism, does not surreptitiously suggest everything that he claims to be "listening to"?[70] James Jackson Putnam put it very well in 1906:

> When the physician is fully imbued with the belief in the sexual origins of the patient's illness he must, by virtue of the closeness of this relationship, be in a position to impress his views, unconsciously, upon his patients and might easily draw from them an acquiescence and endorsement which would not in reality be as spontaneous as it seemed.[71]

There is no spontaneity, no more in the analyst's office than in the laboratory of the experimental psychologist. The analyst might well remain silent as the grave, the experimenter might well communicate with his subjects through a pre-recorded tape, the Bernheim–Delbœuf effect will take place: "The subjects ask themselves what one wants of them, they guess and give it a try."

This is not hypnosis, even though it is an effect that Bernheim and Delbœuf first observed in hypnosis. Freud, obviously, did not understand, or did not want to understand, that hypnosis is only one example amongst others (even though it be a spectacular one) of a generalized and uncontrollable suggestion or artificiality. The abandonment of hypnosis, therefore, was no escape from suggestion; it only made it more subtle, more insidious, more interminable because of its denial:

> An analyst, indeed, who hears this reproach, will comfort himself by recalling how gradually the construction of this phantasy which he is supposed to have originated came about, and, when all is said and done, how independently of the physician's incentive many points in the development proceeded; how, after a certain phase of the treatment, everything seemed to converge upon it, and how later, in the synthesis, the most various and remarkable results radiated out from it; how not only the large problems but the smallest peculiarities in the history of the case were cleared up by this single assumption. And he will disclaim the possession of the amount of ingenuity necessary for the concoction of an occurrence which can fulfil all these demands.[72]

Earlier, the analyst had written:

> I determined . . . that the treatment must be brought to an end at a particular fixed date, no matter how far it had advanced . . . Under the inexorable pressure of this fixed limit his resistance and his fixation gave way, and now in a disproportionately short time the analysis produced all the material which made it possible to clear up his inhibitions and remove his symptoms. All the information, too, which enabled me to understand his infantile neurosis

is derived from this last period of the work, during which resistance temporarily disappeared and the patient gave an impression of lucidity which is usually attainable only in hypnosis.[73]

***

Buda Pest, 31 August 1891

Dear Friend,

As promised, I am sending you a note from Pest. We think we will be back in Vienna on Wednesday evening and will be there throughout the next day or part of it. If by chance you are back in Vienna by then, I would be happy to spend a few more hours with you; in that case, I will wait for you between 8 and 9 at the Hotel Munsch. But don't come back especially for me; it would pain me to disturb your vacation. Fondly, your friend,

Bernheim[74]

Translated by DOUGLAS BRICK

Notes

1 Bernheim 1995, p. 37.
2 Hillman 1965, p. 37; Laurence and Perry 1988, ch. 9.
3 Bernheim 1995, p. 45; Bernheim's emphasis.
4 Bernheim 1891, p. 181.
5 Bernheim 1995, p. 67.
6 Bernheim 1891, p. 194.
7 Gauchet 1992.
8 Charcot 1991, p. 290; modified translation.
9 Bernheim 1995 p. 186.
10 Liégeois 1889, p. 119.
11 Bernheim 1995, p. 71: "How many cures have been obtained thanks to pills made of bread crumbs or to hydrogen protoxide given to the patient under other names and with the assurance that this would have an effect!"
12 Bernheim 1891, p. 297; Bernheim's emphasis.
13 Bernheim 1995, p. 99; Bernheim's emphasis.
14 Bernheim 1995, p. 120.
15 Binet 1886, p. 558.
16 Janet 1989, p. 150.
17 Freud 1921 p. 89. This passage repeats almost word for word an objection that Freud had already raised in 1889 in his review of August Forel's *Hypnotism* (Freud 1889, p. 101).
18 Bernheim 1891, p. 7.
19 Delbœuf 1993, p. 407.
20 See for instance the discussion between Jacques Lacan, Jean Hyppolite, and the anonymous Z* in Lacan 1988, ch. 2.
21 Roudinesco 1986, pp. 214–215.
22 Freud 1925, p. 17.
23 Freud 1915a, pp. 168–169.
24 Bernheim 1995, p. 127.
25 Bernheim 1891, p. 19.
26 Bernheim 1891, p. 140.
27 Delbœuf 1993, p. 272.
28 Freud 1921, p. 89.

29 See Haley 1965, pp. 279–282.
30 Delbœuf 1993, p. 359.
31 Ellenberger 1970.
32 Freud 1912, p. 161; Freud's emphasis.
33 Letter to Wilhelm Fliess of May 28, 1888: Freud 1985, pp. 21–22.
34 Delbœuf 1993, p. 270.
35 See for example Sarbin 1950, pp. 255–270; Spanos 1986, pp. 489–502.
36 Bernheim 1995, p. 178.
37 Bernheim 1891, p. 19; Bernheim's emphasis.
38 Delbœuf 1993, p. 368.
39 Bernheim 1891, p. 18; emphasis added.
40 Bernheim 1891, p. 69; Bernheim's emphasis.
41 Bernheim 1891, p. 68.
42 Letter to Wilhelm Fliess of August 29, 1888: Freud 1985, p. 24.
43 Breuer and Freud 1895, p. 46.
44 Bernheim 1995, p. 165.
45 Bernheim 1995, p. 281.
46 Breuer and Freud 1895, pp. 109–111.
47 Freud 1985, p. 109.
48 Bernheim 1975, p. 93; Bernheim's emphasis.
49 Delbœuf 1993, pp. 342 and 345.
50 Delbœuf 1886a, pp. 441–472.
51 Delbœuf 1993, p. 345.
52 Delbœuf 1993, p. 342.
53 Delbœuf 1886b, pp. 146–147.
54 Bernheim 1995, p. 253.
55 Delbœuf 1993, p. 259.
56 Rosenthal 1966.
57 Masling 1960, pp. 65–85; Masling 1965, pp. 198–201.
58 Delbœuf 1886b, pp. 153–154.
59 Orne 1962.
60 Delbœuf 1993, p. 356; Delbœuf's emphasis.
61 Binet, review of Bernheim, *De la suggestion*, in Delbœuf 1993, pp. 558–559.
62 Bernheim 1995, pp. 97 and 99.
63 Delbœuf 1891–92, pp. 129–135.
64 Delbœuf 1886b, p. 169; emphasis added.
65 Preface to the translation of Bernheim's *De la suggestion*: Freud 1888–89, p. 79.
66 Preface to the second edition of the translation of Bernheim's *De la suggestion*: Freud 1888–89, p. 86.
67 Lacan 1977, pp. 48–49.
68 Freud 1987 [1892], p. 175.
69 Breuer and Freud 1895, p. 101.
70 On this question, see Borch-Jacobsen and Shamdasani 2006, ch. 2.
71 Putnam 1906, p. 40.
72 Freud 1918, p. 52.
73 Freud 1918, p. 11.
74 Hippolyte Bernheim, postcard sent to Sigmund Freud, Sigmund Freud Collection, Manuscript Division, Library of Congress, Washington, DC.

6   Simulating the unconscious

> I, realizing that the experiment performed on me will probably be published in
> a scientific journal, solemnly declare that I was not faking or imitating the
> hypnotic trance but that I was genuinely hypnotized and do not remember the
> events of the experimental periods.
>
>   Statement signed by Frank Pattie's experimental subjects[1]

> [She voiced the idea that] she had not been ill at all and that the whole business
> had been simulated. Similar observations, as we know, have frequently been
> made. When a disorder of this kind has cleared up and the two states of
> consciousness have once more become merged into one, the patients, looking
> back to the past, see themselves as the single undivided personality which was
> aware of all the nonsense; they think they could have prevented it if they had
> wanted to, and thus they feel as though they had done all the mischief
> deliberately.[2]

"You do see, my dear Mikkel, no one really understands anything about
hypnosis. Nor do I, in fact." I can still hear my friend's laugh at the other end of
the line. Léon Chertok, a psychiatrist who was France's most distinguished
specialist in hypnosis,[3] was waging war on behalf of an enigma, a phenomenon
without a theory. You need courage for that, certainly in a country like France,
where facts call for a theory in order to claim an existence. Anywhere else,
empiricism would have been altogether normal and acceptable; in Paris it was a
sign of an unforgivable lack of taste. "How can one be a hypnotist?" But
Chertok refused to be intimidated. He dragged his colleagues to his seminar and
showed them videos, insisted on confronting them with his unwashed, hardly
presentable phenomenon. "Watch this blistering under hypnotic suggestion," he
would say to them. "Look at this surgery performed under hypnosis. How can
you say hypnosis doesn't exist? How with all your theories do you explain
that?" His provocation was all the stronger (altogether unbearable for some),
because Chertok put his questions with a big laugh and without bothering to
give any answer.

   Chertok may not have propounded any theory, but he was nevertheless
convinced he was dealing with a specific phenomenon, a phenomenon which he
produced with a certain technique of induction and which he called "hypnosis."
Now, we may well ask ourselves if hypnosis is, indeed, a raw, atheoretical
phenomenon. Does it exist independently of any of the techniques which
produce it and of any of the theories, albeit implicit, which inform these
procedures? Chertok produced a particular kind of phenomenon which he

reproached his colleagues for neglecting or for failing to recognize under the form of, say, the analytic transference. But what prevented his Freudian colleagues from reproaching him in exactly the same way: "*Mon cher Toc*,[4] you neglect the subject's desire, his fantasies, his resistances. Your famous hypnosis is only unanalyzed, badly digested transference. Come to think of it, have you ever got resolved yours?"[5] Chertok was certainly right to refuse this asymmetrical reduction of hypnosis to transference as an insult to *his* phenomenon. But when he set out to see transference as a sweetened derivative of hypnosis, as I myself did for a time,[6] analysts were equally justified in defending the rights of *their* phenomenon. In the end, hypnosis is no more the asymmetrical truth of transference than transference is the asymmetrical truth of hypnosis. Why not simply admit that we are dealing with two different phenomena – different because they are *produced* differently, with the help of different procedures, different expectations, and different theories?

Chertok spoke of a "non-knowledge (*non-savoir*) of the shrinks,"[7] but it seems to me now that what hypnosis reveals is less a stubborn phenomenon which resists "psy" knowledge and would thus falsify it, in the Popperian sense, than it is the fact that the phenomenon varies with the theories and therapeutic or experimental procedures which take it on, without our ever being able to stabilize it or locate it with precision. Chertok, who wanted to prove the reality of the hypnotic phenomenon, produced incontrovertible analgesias, somatizations, blistering. Others, intent on de-dramatizing hypnotherapy, provoke mild trances, relaxed states, guided imagery. Others still, in the United States and Holland, fabricate dissociated states and multiple personalities. Let's go a step further: in the *belle époque* of medical and experimental hypnotism, Charcot and his colleagues created at will anesthesias, catalepsies, contractions, blindness, amnesias, post-hypnotic suggestions, while spiritualists provoked the spirit to write or speak and the members of the Society for Psychical Research communicated by telepathy. Before them, the magnetizers produced clairvoyance, visions, precognition, self-diagnoses.[8] Puységur elicited a state of lucid somnabulism in his subjects, Mesmer a "crisis" followed by fainting. Their predecessors, the exorcists, obtained convulsions and *stigmata diaboli* – anesthesias, glossolalias, etc. In other parts of the world, people go into trance on ritual occasions or to heal various illnesses, shamans travel with spirits, yogis practice meditation, whirling dervishes eat cut glass, pathological fuguers wake in strange cities, and I myself routinely dissociate while driving on the highway.

Should we say that all these phenomena are "hypnosis"? This would only be justified if we could establish a consensus as to what hypnotism *is* – a consensus which would allow us to distinguish once and for all what are authentic and inauthentic manifestations of this state. But this consensus is precisely what is lacking. Each school has its own definition of hypnosis (or trance, or altered states, or dissociation) and each can produce phenomena to buttress its theory. What are we to conclude? We could, of course, blame this "non-knowledge of the shrinks" on our present ignorance and call on a future Copernicus or Darwin

of hypnosis, whose theory would at last stabilize the situation. That was
Chertok's attitude and it allowed him efficiently to ridicule the pretensions of
the pseudo-Darwins of our own time, Freudians or not. But we could also think
that this "non-knowledge" is due to a far more fundamental inability of our
psycho-logies and psycho-therapies to objectify the phenomena they are concerned with. If hypnosis so constantly problematizes our sciences of the psyche,
it is not because this object eludes them, but because, like some distorting
mirror, it reveals that these sciences produce, fabricate, their objects and that
there are as many objects (or psychic states) as there are psychological, psychiatric, or psychotherapeutic theories. To put it briefly, the instability of
hypnosis translates the impossibility of reducing the "reactive"[9] or
"interactive"[10] beings that humans (and animals) are to an objective psyche – it
translates, in other words, the impossibility of psychology.

Indeed, we ought to realize that hypnosis is bound up, historically, with the
will to objectification which characterizes the new "scientific" psychology of
the second half of the nineteenth century, in its desire to emulate the
experimental sciences. While the magnetizers and spiritualists listened to the
somnambulists and mediums whose creativity and inventiveness they
encouraged, the hypnotists, on the other hand, conscientiously applied
themselves to the production of psychic *automata*, of *objects* for psychological investigation. In his wonderful book on the construction of the
experimental subject, Kurt Danziger has aptly shown how the study of hypnotic phenomena constituted one of the royal roads for the new scientific
psychology, especially in France.[11] While in Germany and America the
nascent psychology essentially took its inspiration from the experimental
physiology laboratory, in France it took a more clinical and medical form
centered on the investigation of supposedly pathological states like hysteria
and hypnosis. This difference in approach should not, however, hide the fact
that the psychology of the French doctors was no less "physiological" than
that of their German or Anglo-Saxon colleagues. In particular, if hypnosis
seemed so promising to them, it was because it was supposed to make the
subject regress to a psychic reflex activity ordinarily inhibited by the higher
mental functions, thus providing the researchers with a privileged instrument
for "psychological vivisection" (Charles Richet).[12] In this sense, experimental
hypnotism is inseparable from what Marcel Gauchet has called the "cerebral
unconscious,"[13] that is, the hypothesis of a psychic activity made up of
automatisms and mechanisms which escape the subject's conscious will. If the
hypnosis we have inherited from Charcot, Bernheim, Janet, and Binet is an
authoritarian hypnosis in which the subject responds passively and submits to
the imperious suggestions of the hypnotist, it is because the hypnotized was
initially considered as a "machine man,"[14] or again a "thinking machine,"[15]
moved by an "unconscious or subconscious cerebration."[16]

This identification of the hypnotic state with an unconscious state is
altogether essential to the concept of hypnosis, as we still employ it today. In

fact, we can only talk of an objective state, susceptible of being studied by the psychologist "in the third person," on condition that the subject does not know what he is doing while he is hypnotized. If, in contrast, the subject were conscious of obeying the suggestions of the hypnotist, the psychologist would see his object disappear before his very eyes: the so-called "hypnotized" would simply have acquiesced to the demands of the hypnotist, whether it be in the spirit of a game, in compliance, or out of simple politeness. There would then be nothing here of an extra-ordinary psychological state, but simply a banal social interaction, of the kind that exists when I ask my table companion to pass me the salt and he complies. Given the conventions which in these parts govern our table manners, there is nothing in the least surprising in such behavior. To pass the salt to your neighbor only becomes astonishing if one assumes that the person does not know that he has been asked, which is exactly the scenario of post-hypnotic suggestion. In that case, the subject carries out the suggestion of the hypnotist, while knowing nothing of it. As Freud wrote in his "A note on the unconscious in psycho-analysis" of 1912:

> the order [of the hypnotist] had been present in the mind of the person in a condition of latency, or had been present unconsciously, until the given moment came, and then had become conscious ... The real stimulus to the action being the order of the physician, it is hard not to concede that the idea of the physician's order became active too. Yet this last idea did not reveal itself to consciousness, as did its outcome, the idea of the action; it remained unconscious, and so it was *active and unconscious* at the same time.[17]

So it seems that to explain the actions of my table companion who passes me the salt, I now have to suppose that he has split, dissociated, divided himself into two people, one who knows what I have asked him and the other who does not, one who is unconscious and hypnotized, and the other conscious and alert! But what if my companion had never in fact stopped knowing what he was supposed to do? Now is the moment to bring out Occam's hoary old razor: in that case, there would be no more unconscious and, by the same token, no more hypnosis, no more objective phenomenon. I would have got only that which I had asked for and nothing else.

It follows that the objectivity of hypnotic phenomena is entirely based on the hypothesis of a psychic unconscious – the "unconscious cerebration" of Carpenter and Charcot, the "subconscious" of Ribot and Janet, the "subliminal consciousness" of Myers, the "unconscious" of Freud and so on – the list is long. This is the reason why the hypnotist's injunctions are so often demands for the unconscious, or at least for unconsciousness. "Sleep." "You won't remember a thing." "You won't feel pain." "You won't be able to stop yourself from lifting your arm." "You will no longer know why you're passing me the salt." In reality, this demand for unconsciousness hides a profound "anxiety" in Devereux's sense:[18] what if the phenomena observed under hypnosis were never anything but a complacent reflection of the hypnotist's hopes, expectations, and suggestions? The demand for unconsciousness, in this sense, is a demand for the recipient of the demand to be unaware of it; the subject has to give proof that he will agree to play the game as if it were not one, as if he did not know he was playing a game with the hypnotist. Either he accepts, and then there is no reason for the game not to go on. Or he refuses and the game stops without ever having started.

The same pact of ignorance reigns over psychoanalysis; for if the latter has abandoned hypnosis and its induction rituals, it still continues to ask of patients to be unaware why they say this or think that. The rules of the analytic game demand that patients should not know why they love their analyst, why they have Oedipal dreams or fantasies of castration. Without these, the purportedly spontaneous manifestations of the unconscious would risk being seen as a product of the inherent demands of the analytic protocol itself and psychoanalytic theory would, as a consequence, be no more than a banal exercise in suggestion. That is why it is so important, so imperative, that *there be the unconscious*: in order to protect the therapist or psychologist against the accusation of contaminating his data, to prevent these appearing as the result of an interaction between the subject and the experimenter, the patient and the therapist. In this sense, the unconscious is not something that was "discovered" one fine day by Freud or the hypnotists that preceded him. Rather it is an imperative, an imperious demand for objectification on the part of the scientific psychologist, without which his object would simply not exist. "Be unconscious."

This injunction, which defines hypnosis and its related practices, is evidently most paradoxical. For how can one obey it without disobeying it? How to obey the demand to be unconscious without being conscious of it? We find here, in another form, the objection Sartre once raised to the Freudian idea of repression: how to repress an idea or a desire without knowing what one is repressing?[19] For that, Sartre said, one needs a lot of "bad faith." One needs, in other words, to pretend one does not know, to simulate unconsciousness, to split oneself into an actor who knows and a role which does not. Well, what guarantees that it is not exactly the same in the case of the hypnotized? Could not their unconsciousness (their supposed state of hypnosis) be simulated in order to please the hypnotist or to make them interesting? Couldn't all this simply be theatre, *mimesis*?[20]

This possibility haunts hypnotism from its very beginnings and it is the occasion for an acute methodological anxiety, betrayed by all kinds of experiments destined to put to the test the subjects' good faith. Everything is measured: their resistance to muscular fatigue or pain, their blindness, their contracture – all physical manifestations which supposedly cannot lie. The theorists of *fin-de-siècle* hypnotism constantly raise the possibility of simulation, and all of them, without exception, end up dismissing it. But not without ambiguity. As Jacqueline Carroy has pointed out,[21] some of them did not hesitate to describe the hypnotized subject as an actor capable of playing all kinds of roles (what Richet called the "objectification of types"). Yet this was only to add immediately that the actor does not know he is acting. He is like Diderot's bad "natural" actor (*le comédien de nature*), who identifies himself completely with his role and, in contrast to the true actor, *is therefore no longer acting*. This is what happens, Bernheim explains, with certain subjects when they are subjected to "criminal suggestions":

> If many know how to resist disagreeable suggestions, if others accomplish their suggested task like actors playing a part, there are some who have no ability to resist, who are identified with their role. A false consciousness dominates them and annihilates true consciousness. These act with conviction; they cry real tears, their faces express a real emotion; they believe what has happened; they descend into crime.[22]

Likewise, Richet writes that the hypnotized is:

> an actor who, taken over by madness, would imagine that the drama he plays out is a reality, not a fiction, and that he has been transformed, body and soul, into the character he has been asked to play.[23]

In short, if the hypnotized subject is an actor, he is an actor *hypnotized* by his role. His simulation, Bergson adds, is unconscious, and thus it is not a simulation in the strict sense.[24] Here is a variant from Bernheim:

> He sometimes suffers from the sense that he is simulating or being complacent ... He does not always know that *he cannot not simulate*, that *his complacency (complaisance) is forced*.[25]

Even Delbœuf, so attentive to the effects of imitation and mirror play between hypnotist and hypnotized, assumes that this imitation is unconscious. The cataleptic simulates his catalepsy, he writes, but:

> he is himself the dupe of his own simulation. It is in this sense that I say he lends himself complacently to playing the catalepsy. This complacency (*complaisance*) is unconscious; it is he who, without knowing it, wants what is required of him.[26]

Summing up this dossier, Jacqueline Carroy suggests we see in "the idea of unconscious simulation ... an attempt at compromise and overcoming (*dépassement*) in relation to physiologism and 'consciousness-ism.'"[27] But why speak of "overcoming" here? It is plain that the theme of unconsciousness serves above all to *annul* that of simulation, in making it an automatic and involuntary activity. Far from calling into question the objectivity of hypnotic phenomena, on the contrary the idea of unconscious simulation protects it very efficaciously by preventing the scene of hypnosis from appearing as a simple response to the hypnotist's demands.

But after all, how could Delbœuf and his colleagues be so sure that the subject does not know that she is simulating? Is it not simply the case that she has complied with the demand for unconsciousness that has been addressed to her and plays the game right to the end? The psychologist Ernest Hilgard has shown, in a series of experiments on hypnotic analgesia, that one only needs to question the subject under hypnosis and she will report that there was throughout a "hidden observer" who participated in the theatre of the trance and felt the pain that she was not supposed to feel: "When I'm in hypnosis, I'm imagining, letting myself pretend, but somewhere the hidden observer knows what's really going on."[28]

In other words, one only needs to make another demand to elicit another response.[29] What matters is not to know whether the hypnotized subject has simulated consciously or unconsciously, since in both cases she has simulated. What matters is rather that on each occasion she has played the role she was asked to play. This is what Bernheim and above all Delbœuf would end up recognizing toward the end of the 1880s: the hypnotic subject does everything one demands of her (everything that one "suggests" to her), in such a way that one cannot determine any characteristic specific to hypnosis – *not even unconsciousness*. Now, without this specific characteristic, hypnosis purely and simply evaporates. "So there is no such thing as hypnotism," Delbœuf concluded in a well-known paper.[30] There are only, we would say today, artifacts of the experimental or clinical situation.

Does this mean that Bernheim and Delbœuf, repudiating what they had so celebrated, would have ended up seeing hypnosis as fiction, a straightforward and simple illusion? Absolutely not. (If such were the case, one would not be able to account for the fact that Bernheim continued to practice hypnotherapy, which he called "suggestive psychotherapy," to the end of his life.) Asserting that hypnosis does not exist was only their way of recognizing the impossibility of objectifying the so-called hypnotic "state" and of deriving all the practical, technical and therapeutic consequences from that: one can just as easily practice suggestion in the waking state. No doubt it was necessary to push to the limit the attempt to reduce the subject to a passive thing, as Bernheim had done, to realize the futility of this enterprise. Hypnosis is consensual, obedience is voluntary, suggestion is accepted – and so it is not a suggestion in the initial sense in which Bernheim intended it, that is to say an idea which is put into action involuntarily, unconsciously. It is a game played by a subject *with* his hypnotist-partner – it matters little whether this is experimental or therapeutic – in accordance with rules which vary and are in a constant flux of renegotiation. What Bernheim and Delbœuf proclaimed is not, then, the unreality of hypnosis or its fraudulent character, but its artificiality, which is completely different. What is at issue here, they underscored, is neither truth nor science, but rather fabrication, production, and technique. In brief, at the dawn of the century of psychotherapy and experimental psychology, they affirmed that these disciplines were dedicated to the production of artifacts *and that there was nothing wrong with that*.

This was what Freud did not understand, or did not want to understand, gripped as he was by what Isabelle Stengers has called his "will to make science."[31] Aware of the epistemic fragility of hypnosis, he decided to rid himself of it, thinking that he would by the same token rid himself of the irritating "suggestion" spotlighted by Bernheim and Delbœuf. This was a profoundly naive gesture, as many of his colleagues did not fail to point out at the time,[32] since it was not hypnosis as such that was responsible for the elements of suggestion in hypnotherapy. On the contrary, as Bernheim and Delbœuf relentlessly pointed out, hypnosis is itself only one amongst many artifacts of suggestion, so that nothing guaranteed a priori that the method of free association is less suggestive or artificial. Nothing, *except the hypothesis of the unconscious*, supposed to express itself freely through the detour of the patient's associations:

> it is not only in the saving of labour that the method of free association has an advantage over the earlier method. It exposes the patient to the least possible amount of compulsion (*Zwang*) . . . it guarantees to a great extent that no factor in the structure of the neurosis will be overlooked and *that nothing will be introduced into it by the expectations of the analyst.*[33]

In retaining the idea of unconscious psychic activity, even if in a profoundly reworked form, Freud retained the fundamental presupposition of hypnotism, that which had allowed Charcot and his colleagues to deny that they were themselves producing the phenomenon they were observing. Under the name "psychoanalysis" (a contraction, it should be said in passing, of Janet's "psychological analysis)," Freud finally proposed a hypnosis without hypnosis, neither more nor less suggestive than the latter and just as blind to its own artifacticity. Charcot and Janet credited the hypnotic phenomena they produced in their hysterics to a dissociated or subconscious psychical activity they claimed to describe from the outside, without affecting it. Freud, likewise, attributed the stories of incest and sodomy that he heard in his consulting room to repressed fantasies-of-desire, to unconscious transference-love, without ever taking seriously the possibility that he had himself produced these in his patients through his insistent questions and theoretical expectations: "I do not believe even now that I forced the seduction-phantasies on my patients, that I "suggested" them."[34]

We know the consequences: a psychotherapeutic practice all the more indoctrinating, hypnotizing, as it refused to see in patients real interlocutors, partners capable of forestalling the analyst's demand.

One finds exactly the same refusal of the artifactual in experimental psychology. In this respect, it is worth noting that one of the most striking consequences of Bernheim's and Delbœuf's experiments was the abandoning of hypnosis as a tool for psychological investigation, once it emerged how unreliable it was. From the end of the 1890s, hypnosis fell into almost total epistemic discredit, exactly as animal magnetism had done before it. And when it resurfaced at the end of the 1920s, in the behaviorist Clark Hull's laboratory, it was as an experimental *object* and not at all as an experimental technique. Since then, the whole problem of experimental psychology has been to determine *if there is* something like hypnosis, if it is possible to identify, with experiments conducted with control groups, a core of phenomena which is *not* reducible to a suggestive artifact. Now, what is striking is that the more psychologists have sought to purify the phenomenon of hypnosis, the more they have attempted to treat the artifact as an independent variable capable of being experimentally controlled and measured, the more their protocols have turned out to be themselves artifactual, to the point of bringing into question the experimental project as such.

Take Clark Hull. Hull compared the performances of groups of hypnotized students with those of unhypnotized control groups, concluding that hypnosis was fundamentally defined by an increase in suggestibility. Very quickly, however, the question was raised whether the results of Hull and his followers were not due to the fact that they were not treating the hypnotized and unhypnotized groups in the same way, thus eliciting different behavior. T. X. Barber showed that one can very easily elicit an increase in suggestibility in *un*hypnotized subjects, solely by explicitly motivating them to accomplish a specified task.[35] Barber thus highlighted what, in the 1950s, Martin Orne proposed calling "the demand characteristics of the experiment": the experimental protocol, however neutral it may be, inevitably influences the subjects' behavior, to the extent that the latter, far from being purely passive objects, are agents who are conscious of being observed, ask themselves what the experimenter is trying to prove, and apply themselves to validating his hypotheses, at least such as they perceive them. From this point of view, there is nothing surprising in the fact that Hull's hypnotized subjects displayed a greater suggestibility than their unhypnotized peers, since such was the demand implicitly made of them by the experimental protocol. How can one determine, then, what truly belongs to hypnosis and what stems from the demands of the experimental situation? How is one to separate, to employ Martin Orne's terms, the "essence" from the "artifact"?[36]

The classical technique of control groups being clearly inadequate, Orne sought to call upon *quasi-control* groups. The method is simple and in certain respects it resembles that employed in placebo-controlled clinical studies (an analogy explicitly drawn by Orne):[37] instead of simply comparing the performance of the hypnotized group with that of the unhypnotized group, one compares it with that of a group of *simulators* whom one asks to do their best to feign hypnosis and fool the hypnotist, by attempting to divine what he expects of his subjects. The hypnotist in turn is blind, not knowing who is hypnotized and who is not, with the aim of eliminating all experimenter's bias. If the unhypnotized simulators manage to feign successfully the actions of the hypnotized group, one may draw the conclusion that these actions have probably been contaminated by the demands of the experimental set-up and hence they cannot be considered as authentic hypnotic phenomena. Or at least, Orne specified, they cannot be considered so rigorously:

> Such data are not evidence that hypnosis consists only of a reaction to demand characteristics. It may well have special properties. But so long as a given form of behavior is displayed as readily by simulators as by "reals," our procedure has failed to demonstrate those properties ... However, only when we are able to demonstrate *differences* in behavior between real and simulating subjects do we feel that an experiment is persuasive in demonstrating that a given effect is likely to be due to the presence of hypnosis.[38]

Now the experiments conducted using this model made it clear that there is no classical hypnotic phenomenon which cannot be successfully faked by simulators, including resistance to pain and to muscular fatigue (in fact, under certain conditions, simulators even achieved results superior to "real" subjects!). The only difference Orne was able to detect between simulators and "real" subjects resided in the indifference of the latter to the principle of contradiction, what Orne proposed calling "trance logic": whereas a "real" subject asked to hallucinate a person seated in a chair before him will have no difficulty seeing the same person simultaneously in another corner of the room, the simulator will either refuse quite simply to see this person or will pretend not to recognize him. In a paper published in 1977, Orne concluded that:

> the hypnotized individual's behavior cannot be explained as a *conscious* effort to please the hypnotist or as some form of *conscious* role playing ...
> Regardless of how we describe hypnosis, it is real in the sense that the subject believes in his experience and is not merely acting as if he did.[39]

So we are back, through an astounding short cut, to Richet's good old "objectification of types"![40] What remains, once one has eliminated the simulators' false witnessing, is, once again, *unconscious* simulation. Was it really necessary to conduct so many experiments, engage in so many tricks, to arrive at such a predictable result? After all, what is so astonishing about simulators not going as far as their hypnotized peers, since they were explicitly asked to remain "awake," vigilant, in short, to *control* their trance? As Orne himself writes of one of the experiments with simulators: "During the subsequent postexperimental inquiry ... the simulating subjects quite cogently pointed out that having been instructed to fool the experimenter put them on their guard lest they themselves be fooled."[41]

Under the term "trance logic," Orne thought he had finally isolated the non-artifactual kernel of hypnosis, but the result of his experiments is not what he believed. There is no question that he established that one elicits different behavior when one is dealing with "real" subjects rather than simulators. However, did he succeed in isolating an authentic, because non-simulated, phenomenon? No, all he did was produce another artifact, with the help of another experimental demand. Just as the demand for simulation produces cunning subjects, calculating and hyper-conscious, the demand for hypnosis produces naive subjects who willingly let themselves be fooled, since they know that this is what the experimenter wishes. So what Orne's experiments actually demonstrate, contrary to his express intent, is that one *cannot* separate the experimental variable from the demands of the experimental set-up. As he himself explains it with great clarity: "demand characteristics cannot be eliminated from experiments; all experiments will have demand characteristics, and these will always have some effect."[42]

Now this, which is true of hypnotic experiments, is also true of any psychological experimentation. Indeed, if Orne, in the end, failed to establish a distinction between hypnotized and simulating subjects, this means that the obedience characteristic of hypnosis is only an instance of a much more pervasive compliance of experimental subjects in response to the demands, both explicit and implicit, which the experimenter makes on them. As Milton Erickson remarked about Milgram's famous experiments on obedient behavior: "the laboratory setting and the experimental situation alone, with no utilization of hypnosis whatsoever, may be so demanding as to elicit behavior contrary to the subject's wishes, background, training, better judgment, and even moral sense."[43]

And why not, indeed, since the experimental set-up, just like the therapeutic situation and so many others which are "episodic" in Garfinkel's sense,[44] is just a conventional game, cut off from everyday reality? What one elicits in experimental psychology, just as in hypnosis, is always a *response* to a given experimental set-up, a move in the game that the subject plays with the experimenter, and never the psychic thing itself. By the same token, it is the entire project of measuring and controlling the artifacts, to which experimental psychology devotes the best part of its time, which appears to be hopelessly vain and futile. This project only made sense if it were in principle possible to turn the artifact into a simple variable capable of being manipulated experimentally. If, on the contrary, it turns out that the control procedure itself generates artifacts, we have an infinite regress: the more one seeks to control the artifacts the more one produces them. The dream of objectification that psychology inherited from modern experimental science evaporates before our eyes: there is no "psychic reality" to discover or to describe *in* the subject, only realities to produce and to negotiate *with* him.

In this respect, it is certainly no accident if it was in the domain of hypnotic research that this problem of the artifact first appeared in experimental psychology, before spreading under a variety of names – "experimenter's effect," "expectancy effect," "evaluation anxiety," etc.[45] Hypnosis being nothing other than what one makes of it, it has held up to experimental psychology a sort of magnifying mirror in which its project of objectification is finally reflected back to it in the shape of a caricature. In the end, it is not by escaping from it that hypnosis has destabilized and disquietened psychology. Quite the contrary: it is by obeying it, beyond anything one might have expected of it, to the point of bringing into full daylight the production of the psyche that defines it. "Nobody understands anything about hypnosis," Chertok used to say. But in fact, there is nothing to understand, know, or interpret. All there is to do is to *do*, to fabricate, to make things happen.

Translated by LISA APPIGNANESI and JOHN FORRESTER

Notes

1 Pattie 1937, cited by Orne 1965, p. 103 n. 4.

2 Breuer and Freud 1895, p. 46.

3 He was also a hero of the Jewish resistance against the Nazis; see his wonderful *Memoirs of a Heretic*: Chertok, Stengers and Gille 1990.

4 This is how Lacan addressed his ex-analysand; see Roudinesco 1990, p. 644. Lacan's cruel pun on Chertok's name depends on the colloquial French terms "toc" (fake, cheap, rubbishy) and "toqué" (nutty, crazy).

5 See Roudinesco's "obituary" 1991, p. xxx: "[Léon Chertok's] cure [with Jacques Lacan] was a complete failure ... He then decided to devote his energy to a combat completely at cross-purposes with the history of the Freudian movement, of every stripe, which consisted in rehabilitating hypnotism."

6 Borch-Jacobsen 1987.

7 This was the title of the book in which Chertok laid out his *différend* with his fellow psychoanalysts (Chertok 1979).

8 On the incommensurability between animal magnetism and hypnotism, see the indispensable tomes of Gauld 1992 and Méheust 1999.

9 Webb, Campbell, Schwartz, and Sechrest 1966.

10 Hacking 1999.

11 Danziger 1990, pp. 52–54.

12 Richet 1884, p. 157.

13 Gauchet 1992.

14 Charcot 1991, p. 290; modified translation.

15 Bérillon 1886, cited in Chertok and Saussure 1973, p. 215.

16 Charcot 1991, p. 387.

17 Freud 1912, p. 261; Freud's emphasis.

18 Devereux 1967.

19 Sartre 1956, pp. 90–92.

20 Compare with Sartre's famed description of the behavior in bad faith (*conduite de mauvaise foi*) of the waiter in a Parisian café: "Let us consider this waiter in the café. His movement is quick and forward, a little too precise, a little too rapid ... All his behavior seems to us a game. He applies himself to chaining his movements as if they were mechanisms, the one regulating the other; his gestures and even his voice seem to be mechanisms; he gives himself the quickness and pitiless rapidity of things. He is playing, he is amusing himself. But what is he playing? We need not watch long before we can explain it: he is playing at being a waiter in a café ... In a parallel situation, from within, the waiter in the café cannot be immediately a café waiter in the sense that this inkwell is an inkwell, or the glass is a glass ... In vain do I fulfill the functions of a café waiter. I can be he only in the neutralized mode, as the actor is Hamlet, by mechanically making the *typical gestures* of my state and by aiming at myself as an imaginary café waiter through those gestures taken as an "analogue" ... Yet there is no doubt that I *am* in a sense a café waiter – otherwise could I not just as well call myself a diplomat or a reporter? But if I am one, this cannot be in the mode of being in-itself. I am a waiter in the mode of *being what I am not*" (Sartre 1956, pp. 101–103; Sartre's emphasis). One would be hard pressed to find a better description of the hypnotic "dissociation."

21 Carroy 1997b; 1993, pp. 121–123, 147–170.

22 Bernheim 1995, p. 178.

23 Richet 1884, p. 237, cited in Carroy 1997b. One finds the same idea under the pen of one of the leading theorists of modern-day multiple personality; see Ross 1989, pp. 109–10: "Multiple personality disorder is a complex pretending. The patient *pretends* to be more than one person, extremely convincingly. If fact, she believes it herself ... The patient

behaves *as if* she were more than one person, but this is not the case. This is different from Hollywood-style acting since the patient is so absorbed in her different roles that she really believes in them."

24 Bergson 1886.

25 Bernheim 1891, p. 19; Bernheim's emphasis.

26 Delbœuf 1993, p. 368.

27 Carroy 1997b, p. 507.

28 Hilgard 1977, p. 209.

29 I am aware that my interpretation differs significantly from that of Hilgard himself, for whom the phenomenon of the "hidden observer" witnesses to a real dissociation between "cognitive systems," one of which perceives the pain while the other does not. However, as several counter-experiments conducted by Nicholas Spanos and his colleagues have demonstrated, these different responses to pain are easily explained by the expectations communicated by Hilgard to his subjects; see Spanos and Hewitt 1980; Spanos, Gwynn, and Stam 1983.

30 Delbœuf 1891–92.

31 Stengers 1992; see also Chertok and Stengers 1992.

32 On this point, see Borch-Jacobsen and Shamdasani 2006, ch. 2.

33 Freud 1925, p. 41; emphasis added.

34 Freud 1925, p. 34.

35 Barber 1969.

36 Orne 1965.

37 Orne 1969, pp. 164–173.

38 Orne 1969, p. 159; emphasis added.

39 Orne 1977, p. 29; emphasis added. It is worth pointing out that exactly the same conclusion is arrived at by the leading advocate of the rival theory of hypnosis as "role-taking," Theodore Sarbin: "In order to establish a logical link between hypnosis and another form of social psychological conduct which is accepted without resorting to traditional formulations, we first indicated the similarity between role-taking in the drama and role-taking in hypnosis. We postulated that success in taking a dramatic role or hypnotic role depended upon favorable motivation, a perception of the role, and role-taking aptitude. The chief difference in the two forms of role-taking was the degree of participation of the self in the role (*levels of consciousness*)" (Sarbin 1965, p. 252; emphasis added).

40 This point is made by Sonu Shamdasani in an unpublished paper whose argument I agree with in several points: "Simulating science. Hypnosis as a scientific problem in psychology and psychiatry in the late nineteenth and twentieth century."

41 Orne 1969, p. 174.

42 Orne 1962, p. 779.

43 Erickson 1967, p. 129. See also remarks by Orne 1970, pp. 253–258, who quite rightly points out that the "criminal" obedience of Milgram's subjects can easily be explained by their awareness of participating in an experimental game, which makes them of course very much like those hypnotized subjects whom Bernheim and Delbœuf subjected to "criminal suggestions"; Orne's analysis has since been fully confirmed by Parker's subsequent investigation of Milgram's subjects and his archives (Parker 2000, especially pp. 118–119). I would like to thank Vinciane Despret for drawing this extremely informative article to my attention.

44 Garfinkel 1967.

45 The large literature on the artifact in experimental psychology is usefully covered in Rosenthal and Rosnow 1968; Barber 1976; Farr 1978; Suls and Rosnow 1988. It is obviously not a matter of indifference to discover the name of the eminent specialist in hypnosis T. X. Barber on the cover of a classic on the artifact in psychology.

PART III

The Freudian century

7 Is psychoanalysis a fairy-tale?

Here is a narrative:

> It was in the summer during a period of extreme heat, and the patient was suffering very badly from thirst; for, without being able to account for it in any way, she suddenly found it impossible to drink. She would take up a glass of water she longed for, but as soon as it touched her lips, she would push it away like someone suffering from hydrophobia ... This had lasted for some six weeks, when one day during hypnosis she grumbled about her English lady-companion whom she did not care for, and went on to describe, with every sign of disgust, how she had once gone into that lady's room and how her little dog – horrid creature! – had drunk out of a glass there. The patient said nothing, as she wanted to be polite. After giving further energetic expression to the anger she had held back, she asked for something to drink, drank a large quantity of water without any difficulty and woke from her hypnosis with the glass at her lips; and thereupon the disturbance vanished, never to return ... In this way her paralytic contractures and anaesthesias, disorders of vision and hearing of every sort, neuralgias, coughing, tremors, etc., and finally her disturbances of speech were "narrated away" (*wegerzählt*).[1]

We all know this narrative: it is the story the miraculous cure of "Fräulein Anna O.," as told by Josef Breuer at the dawn of psychoanalysis. It is a fabulous story, one that deals with the curative and redemptive power of stories and narratives: "Narrate, recount the past that haunts you, and you will be healed." Narration, so says this narrative, heals the wounds of memory. It restores the continuity of our life history. It gives meaning and coherence to what was formerly inexplicable and absurd: "The sense of neurotic symptoms," Freud writes in the seventeenth of his *Introductory Lectures on Psychoanalysis*, "was first discovered by Josef Breuer from his study and successful cure ... of a case of hysteria which has since become famous."[2] Here we have the arch-narrative of psychoanalysis, the "germ cell," as Breuer puts it,[3] which generated so many other patients' stories, so many other case histories.

It turns out that this narrative is a myth, like all founding narratives. Thanks to the research of Henri Ellenberger and Albrecht Hirschmüller, we now know that the narrative healing of Bertha Pappenheim – the real name of "Anna O." – was in fact a failure. Less than a month after her alleged cure, Bertha Pappenheim was placed by Breuer and her family in a private clinic where she continued to develop the same kind of hysterical symptoms. Breuer declined to continue treating her, and it was not till six years later, after three additional stays in private clinics, that she slowly began to recover. Clearly, this recovery owed nothing to Breuer's "talking cure." As for the spectacular, albeit transient, reliefs mentioned by Breuer in his case history, it was only during the last phase of the treatment that they were wrought, by narrating under hypnosis the traumatic events of the patient's history. At first, if we are to believe Breuer, it was the narration of fictional stories "in the style of Hans Christian Andersen's *Picture-Book Without Pictures*"[4] that provided the desired relief. Then it was the acting out – the "tragedizing,"[5] writes Breuer – of morbid hallucinations. There is therefore no reason to grant any therapeutic privilege to autobiographical narration, or even to diegesis in general: a little mimetic psychodrama would do just as well. In short, the story of "Anna O." was neither the story of a *cure*, nor that of a *narrative* cure. Breuer's case history, with its happy ending and its emphasis on the "reminiscences" of "Anna O.," is in fact a rewriting of that story, a very selective and self-interested reconstruction dictated, as can be precisely shown, by theoretical presuppositions stemming from Charcot and Janet.[6]

Up till now, I may have given the impression that I am setting the *true* story of Bertha Pappenheim against Breuer's tendentious case history. Not so. I do not claim to know the truth of this murky story – nor of any story for that matter. I only know that Breuer's narrative, subsequently rewritten and propagated by Freud and countless psychoanalysts, was doctored and, as far as the therapeutic outcome goes, even disingenuous. What matters to me is that it was *this* narrative, the doctored one, that triggered the avalanche of stories that we call psychoanalysis. Indeed, we know that Breuer told the story of Bertha Pappenheim to his young colleague Freud, making no attempt to conceal the disastrous outcome of the treatment. One would expect therefore that this would have dissuaded Freud from following the same dead end. But Freud was at the time keeping abreast of Charcot's, Janet's, and Delbœuf's research on the desuggestion under hypnosis of traumatic memories, and he was quick to reread (to rewrite) the story of "Anna O." in light of the theories of the Salpêtrière. In 1888, at a time when nothing allowed him to think that Bertha Pappenheim would get better and he himself had not yet applied the cathartic method to a single one of his patients, he wrote in his encyclopedia article on "Hysteria":

> It is even more effective if we adopt a method first practiced by Josef Breuer in Vienna and lead the patient under hypnosis back to the psychical prehistory of the ailment and compel him to acknowledge the psychical occasion on which the order in question originated. This method of treatment is new, but it produces curative successes which cannot otherwise be achieved.[7]

The following year, Freud tried to apply this largely imaginary method of treatment to two of his patients, "Emmy von N." (Fanny Moser) and "Cäcilie M." (Anna von Lieben). Results did not take long. Within the space of nine days, between May 8 and 17, 1889, "Emmy von N." told the story of forty or so traumatic memories, supposedly the origin of her symptoms. Likewise, "Cäcilie

M." suddenly remembered an old forgotten memory and "for nearly three years after this she once again lived through all the traumas of her life."[8] Little did it matter that these purgative narrations had, in fact, been of as little therapeutic value as those of "Anna O.":[9] Freud had managed to replicate them, which allowed him to convince Breuer to write his case history in light of these "confirmations."

Here we have a fine example of what Freud calls *Nachträglichkeit*, "aftermath effect," or what historians call "retrodiction":[10] an event *x* takes meaning only at time *t2*, after it has been repeated, re-cited, integrated into a narrative sequence. The assassination of Archduke Franz Ferdinand in Sarajevo becomes the "trigger cause of the war" only after the actual declaration of hostilities. The Great War (the one they called "The war to end all wars") becomes World War I only once World War II is declared. Similarly, the pathetic story of Bertha Pappenheim becomes the founding event of psycho-analysis only once it has been repeated and "confirmed" by those of "Emmy von N." and "Cäcilie M.," which in turn, and so on. At time *t1* there is a senseless fiasco. At time *t2*, we have the *beginning* of the long story of psy-choanalysis, the *model* of all analytic cures to come. Freud's replication of the story transmitted to him by Breuer was enough to set off the irresistible self-confirmatory machine of psychoanalysis, each new narrative on the couch retroactively reinforcing the paradigmatic nature of the First Story.

And yet, that First Story never happened until it was taken up by Freud, until he rewrote Breuer's story in the light of the theories of the Salpêtrière, and took this new narrative as a model and theoretical schema to produce other identical narratives. I say "produce," for it is obvious enough that "Emmy von N.," "Cäcilie M.," and the others would not have told of all these traumatic events, real or imaginary, if Freud had not asked them. And he would not have asked them if he did not have in mind the example – the revised and corrected example - of the story of "Anna O." Here we come across an essential feature of case histories in psychoanalysis (and more generally in what Ellenberger calls "dynamic psychiatry"), namely their pragmatic, or performative character. By that I mean that their function is not so much to report past events as to provide the therapist and his patients with a model, a script upon which they elaborate in turn. In this respect, it is no accident that Freud talks about his case histories in terms of a paradigm (*Paradigma*), a model (*Vorbild*), or a pattern (*Muster*): it is because their primary value for him is that of a prototype, something to be emulated, propagated. What matters is not that these stories account accurately for what happened, but rather that they be replicated, re-cited. Freud with "Emmy von N." *emulates* Breuer with "Anna O.," so that the case history of "Frau Emmy von N." is less an independent confirmation of the case history of "Fraülein Anna O." than it is its effect, less a recording of facts than a variation on a pre-established theme. Similarly for the case history of "Miss Lucy R.," and so on. This cumulative effect, often invoked by Freud to prove the objectivity of his psychoanalytic "discoveries," actually hides an endless process of self-replication and self-validation, each narrative generating another that confirms it in turn. This is what Karl Popper used to call, somewhat mischievously, the "Oedipus effect,"[11] reproaching the psychoanalysts for not having studied it sufficiently: the story of Oedipus confirms the oracle only insofar as it is its exact consequence. Psychoanalytic case histories, likewise, predict what they claim to describe, they perform what they claim to observe.

Freud would have vigorously objected. If we are to believe him, his case histories only compile "observations," *Beobachtungen*. They are descriptions of treatments in which the analyst's theoretical prejudices play no role. Indeed, in the official Freudian epistemology, it is not theory (what Freud calls meta-psychology) that comes first. On the contrary, the "fundamental concepts" (*Grundbegriffe*)[12] of psychoanalysis are nothing but "conventions,"[13] theoretical "fictions,"[14] "speculative superstructures"[15] built on clinical observation. Freud often recognizes, it is true, that "[e]ven at the stage of description it is not possible to avoid applying certain abstract ideas to the material in hand."[16] But he always adds that these ideas can be discarded if the clinical material requires it, for they "are not the foundation of science, upon which everything rests: that foundation is observation alone."[17]

It is this "observation," the ultimate epistemological foundation of the whole edifice, that case histories are supposed to represent in psychoanalytic theory. Indeed, at a time when hospital and laboratory-based medicine and psychiatry were increasingly moving toward the statistical analysis of experimental trials on large populations, Freud, like his colleagues Morton Prince and Théodore Flournoy, continued to rely on the detailed narrative exposition of a few individual cases. In his view, only highly intricate narratives such as these could give an idea of the complexity of the "observations" on which the analyst relies to elaborate his theories. As he wrote in 1934 to the psychologist Saul Rosenzweig, who claimed to have experimentally confirmed the theory of repression: "I cannot put much value on these confirmations because the wealth of reliable observations on which [psychoanalytic] assertions rest make them independent of experimental verification."[18]

Case histories are thus invested with an exorbitant epistemological role in psychoanalysis, since they, and they alone, are responsible for presenting the clinical "evidence" on which the whole edifice rests. For this evidence is not only removed from all experimental control, it is also shielded from independent observers because of medical confidentiality. We possess no verbatim transcripts of Freud's analyses, not even the clinical notes that he made the evening after his sessions (with the notable exception of those of the first four months of the treatment of the "Rat Man").[19] Whoever wants to check Freud's theories and find out how he obtained his results is therefore reduced to falling back on a handful of narratives, always the same: "Dora," "The Rat Man," "The Wolf Man," and a few others. As Michael Sherwood pertinently notes: "This situation is almost unique: in perhaps no other field has so great a body of theory been built upon such a small public record of raw data."[20]

Freud has often been praised for his ability to give coherent narrative form to the extraordinarily complex and overdetermined progression of his analyses. Much less frequently noted is the huge epistemological problem hidden behind that stylistic brilliance. Indeed, contrary to what Freud most often implies, case histories are anything but a simple "observation" of reality. As is well known by historians and literary critics, every narrative implies a retrodiction of the narrated content, a plotting that (re)organizes it and gives it sense and direction, based on the conclusion of the story. Whether he deals with fictional or real events, the narrator inevitably selects them in order to integrate them – to "configure" them, as the historian Louis O. Mink puts it[21] – into a meaningful whole. The narrated event is therefore anything but neutral or innocent. It is an event that is constructed, fabricated, and assembled by the narrator who reflects it and makes it speak from his chosen point of view.

Now this, which is true of any story, is even more true of psychoanalytic case histories, which in this regard present specific features. Indeed, Freud's narratives have less to do with events perceived or observed during the analysis than with psychic events *(re)constructed* by the analyst on the basis of the patient's dreams, symptoms, and associations: "Dora"'s supposed love for the odious Mr. K., Anna Freud's fantasy of being beaten by her father in the article "A child is being beaten," or again, the scene of the young "Wolf Man" triumphantly urinating upon seeing the protruding buttocks of the maid Grusha as she knelt on the floor. To speak of "observation" in this regard is a pleasant joke, for no one ever witnessed these so-called events. The patients themselves have no knowledge of them, since we are dealing here with memories or fantasies that are supposed to be unconscious. So it is not they who narrate these events, at least at the beginning.[22] We must rid ourselves of the idea that psychoanalytic case histories relate stories told spontaneously by the patients themselves. Quite the contrary, they relate how the analyst reconstructs the elements of a story that the patient, according to good Freudian doctrine, *cannot* tell. These narratives, in fact, narrate nothing that predates them. They narrate only the fabrication, the "construction" (*Konstruktion*) of the narrative that they are themselves. As Freud writes in "Constructions in analysis":

> The analyst has neither experienced nor repressed any of the material under consideration; his task cannot be to remember anything. What then *is* his task? His task is to make out what has been forgotten from the traces which it has left behind or, more correctly, to *construct* it.[23]

It is this construction – which has strictly nothing to do with observation but, on the contrary, everything to do with the "superstructures" of metapsychological speculation – that Freud's case histories tell. Pieced together from interpretations laid end to end on the basis of fragmentary material, these case histories are nothing but theory presented in narrative form, more often than not without any assent from the patients.

Take the famous episode of the young "Wolf Man" watching from his cradle the copulation *a tergo* of his parents and greeting it with celebratory defecation. Is this scene related by the patient himself? Not at all. It is the end result of a dizzying series of risky interpretations taking their cue from a dream and implying all sorts of psychoanalytic hypotheses on the castration complex and the anal-sadistic stage, or mechanisms like the reversal into the opposite (immobility = agitation) and the transformation of activity into passivity (being watched = watching). Freud, when he introduces it, does not hide the purely speculative nature of this "constructed primal scene":[24] "I have now reached," he writes, "the point at which I must abandon the support I have hitherto had from the course of the analysis."[25] But this does not stop him from asking the reader to join him "in adopting a *provisional* belief in the reality of the scene"[26] and to proceed from then on to speak of it as if it were an event, not a hypothesis. A little while later, we thus read that the "Wolf Man" "assumed . . . that the event of which he was a witness was an act of violence, but the expression of enjoyment which he saw (*sah*) on his mother's face did not fit in with this."[27] Or again: "The patient was longing for some one who should give him the last pieces of information that were still missing upon the riddle of sexual intercourse, just as his father had given him the first in the primal scene long before."[28]

Two chapters later, in connection with the scene with the maid Grusha (itself a highly speculative construction based on a vague memory of the patient):[29]

> When he saw (*sah*) the girl on the floor engaged in scrubbing it, and kneeling down, with her buttocks projecting and her back horizontal, he was faced once again with the posture which his mother had assumed in the copulation scene.[30]

At this point the reader has of course long forgotten that the scene of copulation *a tergo* was no less hypothetical in its time than is the one to which he is treated at present. In presenting his constructions in narrative form, Freud kills two birds with one stone: he disguises his interpretations as events; and by using free indirect style, he surreptitiously imputes his interpretations to the patient himself. Suddenly it is no longer *Freud* who speculates on what the "Wolf Man" saw or thought. It is the "*Wolf Man*"– or his unconscious, it is hard to tell – who sees the expression on his mother's face during orgasm, or who is aroused when he finds Grusha in the same posture as her. From this to the thought that the "Wolf Man" is relating all this to Freud and that Freud only narrates how he helped his patient to restore this underlying narrative is obviously only a small step. "The 'true' narrative," writes Peter Brooks in his commentary on the "Wolf Man" case, "lies in-between, in the process of exchange [between the patient and the analyst]; it is the product of *two* discourses playing against one another."[31]

Brooks is careful to put the adjective "true" in ironic quotes, for he intends to underscore, with good reason, the fictional nature of the narrative thus woven between Freud and his patient. In this light, he makes much of the two passages added in 1918 to the case history, in which Freud questions the reality of the primal scene and proposes the hypothesis that it might be a fantasy provoked in the "Wolf Man" by the observation of copulation between animals, and then retroactively projected onto his parents. "We have here," writes Brooks, "one of the most daring moments in Freud's thought, and one of his most heroic gestures as a writer," in that Freud breaks the coherence of the case history that he wrote in 1914–1915, and suggests "that all tales may lead not so much to events as to other tales, to man as a structure of the fictions *he* tells about himself."[32]

So busy is Brooks with praising Freud's deconstructive daring, he does not realize that he has been manipulated all along by the Freudian narrative. Indeed, this whole discussion about the real or imaginary nature of the primal scene – which Freud, incidentally, concludes with a *non liquet*[33]– is nothing but a straw man argument. What really matters is not whether this narrative is a fantasy or not, but whether the "Wolf Man" ever told it – in other words, whether it was *he* who related this fiction about himself, as Brooks believes, or whether it was not rather Freud who told it *about him*. As it happens, the real "Wolf Man," Sergius Pankejeff, held a strong view about this. In the interviews that he gave at the end of his life to the Austrian journalist Karin Obholzer, he explained that he had never believed in the primal scene that Freud wanted him to remember: "It's terribly farfetched ... That primal scene is no more than a construct ... I have never been able to remember anything of the sort ... He [Freud] maintains that I saw it, but who will guarantee that it is so? That it is not a fantasy of his?"[34]

One could hardly put it better: this fantasy, this narrative, was *Freud's*, not his patient's. Moreover, Sergius Pankejeff is not the only one who protested against this confusion. Each time the characters of Freud's narrative have had the opportunity to express themselves, other than through Freud's intervention, they have mutinied against their author. Later in life, Freud's "Elisabeth von R.," Ilona Weiss, would make fun of this "young bearded nerve specialist"[35] who had tried to persuade her that she secretly loved her brother-in-law. Bertha Pappenheim, having become a pioneer of social work in Germany, forbade her coworkers to use psychoanalysis.[36] As for "Dora" (Ida Bauer in real life), we know that she broke off treatment when Freud tried to make her admit that she loved Mr. K., thus slamming the door of the narrative in which her analyst tried to confine her. Roy Schafer, one of the promoters of the narrativist reading of Freud that underlies Peter Brooks's analysis, claims that:

> The analyst establishes new, though often contested or resisted, questions that amount to regulated narrative possibilities. The end product of this

interweaving of texts is a radically new, *jointly authored* work or way of working.[37]

But where is the joint authorship in the case of Sergius Pankejeff, of Ilona Weiss, of Ida Bauer? None of them countersigned the narratives Freud put in their mouths – not any more, if one thinks about it, than "Little Hans," President Schreber, Dostoevsky, Leonardo, Shakespeare, or Woodrow Wilson. As these examples clearly demonstrate, Freud's case studies are no more the dialectical product of a joint narration than they are the objective recording of an "observation." They are narratives fabricated and fictionalized – *erdichtet* – by Freud himself, with the help of a decoding method informed by his theories.

The relation between case histories and theory is therefore exactly the opposite of that alleged by Freud in his metapsychological writings. Far from the "speculative superstructures" of metapsychology reflecting an observation laid down in the case histories, the latter are artifacts of the former: first because they are theoretical fictions, theory turned into narrative on the basis of elements provided by the clinical material; and second because the assent given to them by the patients, when there is one, is itself the product of the very *suggestive* character of the analyst's theories. To claim, as Freud does, that metapsychological concepts were regularly replaced when the clinical material demanded it is a colossal bluff, given how doggedly he held fast to his narrative constructions despite the protests of his patients.[38]

Jürgen Habermas, one of the many victims of this bluff, writes that the analyst "makes interpretive suggestions for a story that the patient cannot tell. Yet they can be verified in fact only if the patient adopts them and tells his own story with their aid."[39] But that was never the ultimate criterion of validation used by Freud. Even though he never refrained from invoking the patient's assent when it suited him, Freud knew quite well that this criterion was likely to turn against him, insofar as nothing guaranteed that the patient's "Yes" was not an effect of suggestion.[40] Freud therefore preferred to invoke the internal coherence of his narrative constructions and their capacity to lend intelligibility to the data.[41] In the "Wolf Man" case, for instance, he defends himself against having arbitrarily foisted his reconstruction of the primal scene on the clinical data by recalling

> how, after a certain phase of the treatment, everything seemed to converge upon it, and how later, in the synthesis, the most various and remarkable results radiated from it; how not only the large problems but the smallest peculiarities in the history of the case were cleared up by this single assumption.[42]

The analyst's certainty, Freud also explains elsewhere, is a logical one:

> What makes [the analyst] certain in the end is precisely the complication of the problem before him, which is like the solution of a jig-saw puzzle ... If one succeeds in arranging the confused heap of fragments, each of which bears upon it an unintelligible piece of drawing, so that the picture acquires a

meaning, so that there is no gap anywhere in the design and so that the whole fits into the frame – if all these conditions are fulfilled, then one knows that one has solved the puzzle and that there is no alternative solution.[43]

A good analytic construction has thus all the characteristics of a good plot (*muthos*), in the Aristotelian sense. A plot, writes Aristotle in the *Poetics*, "being the imitation of an action, must present it as a unified whole; and its various incidents must be so arranged that if any one of them is differently placed or taken away the effect of wholeness will be seriously disrupted."[44] Similarly, the final criterion of analytical constructions is their narrative coherence, what Aristotle called the probable (*eikos*), the source of the persuasive (*pithanon*). Consequently, it remains for us to determine the exact status of that narrative coherence or probability. Is it that of the historical or forensic narrative, limited as it is by the documents, traces, and clues that it tries to piece together into a meaningful whole? Or is it the more "philosophical" one, as Aristotle would have said, of poetry? In other words, do psychoanalytical narratives have an anchorage in what Aristotle called "what has actually happened"[45] or are they the products of Freud's speculative imagination, the offspring of a sort of powerful theoretical *machine célibataire, à la* Duchamp? Is psychoanalysis, as Krafft-Ebing once commented, simply a "scientific fairy-tale"?[46]

Freud himself underscored the troubling proximity between his case histories and fiction. In an oft-cited passage in the *Studies on Hysteria*, he writes:

> [It] still strikes me myself as strange that the case histories I write should read like short stories and that, as one might say, they lack the serious stamp of science ... A detailed description of mental processes such as we are accustomed to find in the works of imaginative writers enables me, with the use of a few psychological formulas, to obtain at least some kind of insight into the course of [hysteria].[47]

But Freud immediately adds: "Case histories of this kind are intended to be judged like psychiatric ones."[48] As he writes elsewhere in response to Havelock Ellis, the idea that "the writings of the creator of analysis should be judged not as a piece of scientific work but as an artistic production" is nothing but a typical expression of resistance to analysis, and it must be met "with the most decided contradiction."[49]

In so distinguishing his case histories from fiction, Freud clearly defines the rules by which he pledges to play the narrative game. They are those of history, in the broadest sense of the word. I borrow its definition from the French historian Paul Veyne: "History is a narrative of true events."[50] To this seemingly Aristotelian definition should be added that the "true events" of history, precisely because they are narrated, are no less constructed and plotted than the imaginary events of fiction. [51] Nevertheless, however fabricated the historical narrative may be, it is still distinguished from fiction in that it claims to construct its plots on the basis of "what has actually happened," and that such is the contract it undertakes with its readers. Whereas the novelist and the story teller are free to invent and combine characters and situations as much as they like, the historian, the biographer, the detective, and the psychiatrist are held by convention to limit themselves to a finite number of elements which are temporally ordered, which they cannot modify, and which they are under the obligation to take into account: documents, archival material, testimonies, sources, observations, etc. From this point of view, a historian who forges documents to improve his narrative is not a historian anymore, he is a fraud and an impostor. The same holds for a detective who covers up testimony, or a psychiatrist who tampers with the data.

It is a narrative pact of this type that Freud makes with us, his readers, in demanding that we consider his stories as psychiatric observations. That is why we spontaneously give credence to the clinical data that he presents us with, even when we happen to remain skeptical about the complex narrative constructions by which he unites them. For instance, we do not doubt for a moment that wolves really did appear in the eponymous dream of the "Wolf Man," or that "Dora" really was fourteen when Mr. K. sexually assaulted her, or again, that Freud really did help "a certain young man of academic background"[52] to restore the associations that made him forget the word *aliquis* in a verse of Virgil. And we are all the more trusting as we have most of the time simply no way of checking Freud's account: how can we know what was said a century ago behind the closed doors of Freud's office? Because of medical confidentiality, which the Sigmund Freud Archives enforce to this day with absurd rigidity, we can do nothing but rely on Freud and his good faith. As Lacan clearly saw, the Freudian field is structured by a symbolic pact with the Founding Father, to the "word" and the "letter" of whom psychoanalysts are constantly forced to "return" as the only guarantee of their theory and practice.[53]

It turns out, however, that this confidence in the Arch-Narrator is badly placed. At a pace that has accelerated over the last few years, Freud scholars increasingly bring into question the reliability of Freud's case histories, as well as that of the official historiography built around them by "authorized" historians of Freudianism. The "Wolf Man," we now learn, always maintained that the famous "wolves" in his dream were not wolves at all, but white Spitz dogs,[54] which changes everything as far as Freud's interpretation is concerned. "Dora" was only thirteen when Mr. K. sexually forced himself on her, which makes even more untenable Freud's diagnosis of her reaction of disgust as a sign of hysteria.[55] The "young man" of the *aliquis* episode was none other than Sigmund Freud speaking of himself in the third person,[56] which of course relativizes considerably the latter's hermeneutic feat (what is the big deal if Freud was able to follow the thread of his *own* associations of ideas?).

The list goes on. In the Schreber case, Freud characterized Schreber's father as an "excellent father,"[57] whereas in his correspondence of the same time with Ferenczi, he did not hesitate to describe him as a "tyrant at home who shouted at his son."[58] In his study on Leonardo da Vinci, he stated that Leonardo spent part of his childhood alone with his mother Caterina, whereas he knew quite well that this was contradicted by at least one of the biographies that he had at his disposal.[59] Worse yet, Robert Wilcocks has shown that the interpretation of the famous "Irma dream" that opens *The Interpretation of Dreams*, dreamt and supposedly analyzed by Freud on July 24, 1895, refers to an event (his daughter Mathilde's diphtheria) that took place *two years later*, in March 1897:[60] Freud, it seems, added this element after the fact to embellish his narrative and make it more captivating. According to Peter J. Swales's meticulous research,[61] the same holds for Freud's analysis of the forgetting of the name "Signorelli" in the *Psychopathology of Everyday Life*, where Freud retroactively inserted the name of a painter – Boltraffio – whom he did not know at the time of the "Signorelli" episode.

Clearly, we are dealing here no longer with a more or less tendentious narratization of analytic interpretations, but with a true fictionalization of the clinical data. Freud, it seems, had no qualms about modifying, inventing, or suppressing details if that would allow him to improve the plot he was weaving, as would any novelist. We know that Freud much enjoyed the genre of historical novels brought back into vogue by his friends and correspondents Thomas Mann and Stefan Zweig, and that he originally intended to entitle his last book, *The Man Moses, A Historical Novel*.[62] This is no accident: all his case histories are historical novels or romanticized biographies of that sort, that is, fantasies liberally constructed around a few real events and characters. (The same could be said, *mutatis mutandis*, of the official Freud historiography, with its legends, its censorships, and its partisan rewritings of history.)

The difference, of course, is that neither Mann nor Zweig ever claimed to be a historian, whereas Freud misleads us when he presents his theoretical fictions as case histories. It is one thing to "compete with the birth register" in the fashion of the Balzacian novelist; it is another to forge fake IDs. Krafft-Ebing was right: psychoanalysis is a scientific fairy-tale, fiction masquerading as science and history. For my part, I would call it a theoretical novel. This theory is a novel because it creates its own evidence, exactly as a novelist creates, fabricates his stories. And this novel is theoretical, for the narrative coherence of its plots is nothing other than a coherence with the theory. Indeed, if we think the stories of the "Wolf Man" or the "Rat Man" are good stories (if they convince us, in other words), it is only because they agree with the theory which they supposedly illustrate and which in fact lends them meaning. Otherwise, why on earth would these implausible tales of castration, incest, and sodomy make any sense to us?

One last word, on the subject of narrative truth. Aware of the quandaries that I have just highlighted, a growing number of analysts are claiming today that they no longer believe in the "historical truth"[63] of the stories told in analysis.

All that matters to them, they say, is the "narrative truth" of these stories, that is, their capacity to lend meaning to the material presented by the patient. "Narrative truth," writes Donald Spence, "is what we have in mind when we say that such and such is a good story, that a given explanation carries conviction, that *one* solution to a mystery must be true."[64] And again: "Associations and interpretations, as they are inserted into the developing narrative, become true as they become familiar and lend meaning to otherwise disconnected pieces of the patient's life."[65] We recognize this "narrative truth": it is, once again, Aristotle's good old "probable," the *eikos* of poets and makers of tales. Unlike Freud, narrativist psychoanalysts no longer claim to represent "what has actually happened." Judge us not, they say, on the historical and constative value of our narratives. Judge us solely on their pragmatic, performative, esthetic value.[66]

Fine, but let us draw the consequences then. If the only thing that matters in analysis is the narrative coherence of the stories proposed by the analyst, it follows that any good story should do the trick: a Freudian-analytic one, but also a Jungian-analytic or Adlerian-analytic one, or even – why not? – a Christian, Marxist, or astrological one. Is that what the narrativists mean? Of course not. The story is a good story, for them, only if it is a Freudian one. Explanations in analysis are of the narrative type, Paul Ricoeur tells us, relying on the work of Michael Sherwood.[67] But this does not prevent him from adding in the same breath: "A good psychoanalytic explanation must be coherent with the theory, or if one prefers, it must conform to Freud's psychoanalytic system."[68] Likewise, Roy Schafer informs us that "[p]eople going through psychoanalysis – analysands – tell the analyst about themselves and others in the past and present. In making interpretations, the analyst retells these stories... *This retelling is done along psychoanalytic lines.*"[69] Just as in Freud's time, it is the analyst who writes the story, and he does so, inevitably, on the basis of psychoanalytical theory and the paradigmatic case histories in which it incarnates itself.

At no point, therefore, is Freudian theory truly called into question by the narrativists, despite their apparent revisionism. Quite the contrary, this theory continues to guide the interpretations and the narrative constructions of the analyst, without his ever asking himself in what way a Freudian story is better than another, or in what way the theory that underlies these stories is anything but that – a story, a theoretical novel. If the narrativists wanted to be consistent, it is not only the interpretations proposed by the analyst that they would have to describe in narrative terms, it is also the theory that authorizes and guarantees these interpretations. One doubts that they will ever go that far. After all, what would remain of psychoanalysis if analysts announced to their patients right from the start that repression, the unconscious, infantile sexuality, and the Oedipus complex are just tall tales, "Just So Stories"?[70] "Listen, I am going to tell you a fairy-tale, nothing more: 'It was in the summer during a period of extreme heat, and the patient was suffering very badly from thirst ...'"

Translated by DOUGLAS BRICK

Notes

1 Breuer and Freud 1895, pp. 34–35.
2 Freud 1916–17, p. 257.
3 Letter from Breuer to August Forel, dated November 21, 1907, cited in Forel 1968, p. 396.
4 Breuer and Freud 1895, p. 29.
5 Breuer and Freud 1895, p. 27; Strachey translates "sie durchlebend ... tragierte" as "she acted these things through as though she was experiencing them."
6 Borch-Jacobsen 1996, pp. 49–61.
7 Freud 1888, p. 56.
8 Breuer and Freud 1895, p. 70.
9 See the footnote to the case history of "Emmy von N." added by Freud in 1924 (Breuer and Freud 1895, p. 105); on "Cäcilie M.," see Swales 1986a.
10 See Veyne 1971, ch. 8; Danto 1965, ch. 8.
11 Popper 1963, p. 38.
12 Freud 1915b, p. 117.
13 Freud 1915b, p. 117.
14 Freud 1900, p. 598; 1926, p. 194.
15 Freud 1925, p. 32.
16 Freud 1915b, p. 117.
17 Freud 1914b, p. 77.
18 Cited in MacKinnon and Dukes 1976, p. 703.
19 Freud 1907–08.
20 Sherwood 1969, p. 70.
21 Mink 1965.
22 This last point is important as Freud's patients tended to adopt their analyst's narratives as their own.
23 Freud 1937, pp. 258–259.
24 Freud 1918, p. 39.
25 Freud 1918, p. 36.
26 Freud 1918, p. 39.
27 Freud 1918, p. 45.
28 Freud 1918, p. 70.
29 See Jacobsen and Steele 1979, pp. 357–358; Spence 1982, pp. 117–120; Esterson 1993, pp. 77–93.
30 Freud 1918, p. 92.
31 Brooks 1992, p. 283; emphasis added.
32 Brooks 1992., p. 277; emphasis added. "Man as a structure of the fictions he tells about himself" is a hidden reference to the Lacanian maxim that "truth has a structure of fiction." For critical commentaries on Brooks's analysis of the "Wolf Man" case, see Fish 1986; and Wilcocks 1994, pp. 296 ff.
33 Freud 1918, p. 60: "I intend on this occasion to close the discussion of the reality value (*Realwert*) of the primal scene with a *non liquet* ['it is not clear']"; translation slightly modified.
34 Obholzer 1982, pp. 35–36.
35 "Memorandum for the Sigmund Freud Archives," S. Freud Collection, Manuscript Division, Library of Congress, Washington, DC; cited in Gay 1988, p. 72.
36 Edinger 1968, p. 15.
37 Schafer 1980, p. 36; emphasis added.
38 As an example, Abram Kardiner reports that Freud terminated Clarence Oberndorf's training analysis because Oberndorf did not accept one of his interpretations (Kardiner 1977, p. 81).

39 Habermas 1971, p. 260. This hypothesis is central to Habermas's interpretation of psychoanalysis in terms of "self-reflection" (*Selbstreflexion*).

40 This point is discussed at length in Freud 1937, especially p. 265: "We may sum the matter up by asserting that there is no justification for the reproach that we neglect or underestimate the importance of the attitude taken up by those under analysis towards our constructions. We pay close attention to them and often derive valuable information from them. But these reactions on the part of the patient are rarely unambiguous and give no opportunity for a final judgement."

41 I do not examine here the argument from therapeutic success, also invoked sometimes by Freud. See Grünbaum 1984, pp. 127–172, and, for a different view, Cioffi 1986; Esterson 1996.

42 Freud 1918, p. 52.

43 Freud 1923, p. 116. Compare this with a similar passage in Freud 1896c, p. 205: "It is exactly like putting together a child's picture-puzzle: after many attempts, we become absolutely certain in the end which piece belongs in the empty gap; for only that one piece fills out the picture and at the same time allows its irregular edges to be fitted into the edges of the other pieces in such a manner as to leave no free space and to entail no overlapping. In the same way, the contents of the infantile scenes turn out to be indispensable supplements to the associative and logical framework of the neurosis, whose insertion makes its course of development for the first time evident, or even, as we might often say, self-evident."

44 Aristotle 1983, p. 43; translation slightly modified.

45 Aristotle 1983, pp. 43–44: "It will be clear from what I have said that it is not the poet's function to describe what has actually happened, but the kinds of things that might happen, that is, that could happen because they are, in the circumstances, either probable or necessary. The difference between the historian and the poet is not that the one writes in prose and the other in verse ... The difference is that the one tells of what has happened, the other of the kinds of things that might happen. For this reason poetry is something more philosophical and more worthy of serious attention than history; for while poetry is concerned with universal truths, history treats of particular facts."

46 Freud 1985, p. 184: "A lecture on the etiology of hysteria at the psychiatric society was given an icy reception by the asses and a strange evaluation by Krafft-Ebing: 'It sounds like a scientific fairy-tale.'"

47 Breuer and Freud 1895, pp. 160–161.

48 Breuer and Freud 1895, pp. 160–161.

49 Freud 1920, p. 263.

50 Veyne 1971, p. 22.

51 In addition to the works by Veyne, Danto, and Mink already cited, see White 1974 and Ricoeur 1983.

52 Freud 1901, pp. 8–9.

53 Lacan 1977, *passim*.

54 See the letter sent by the "Wolf Man" to Freud on June 6, 1926: "The wolves sitting on the tree were in fact not wolves at all but white Spitz dogs with pointed ears [in German, *spitzen Ohren*] and bushy tails": Pankejeff 1957, p. 449. Freud does indeed mention in the case history that the wolves "looked more like foxes or sheep dogs" (Freud 1918, p. 29; see also p. 44), but this does not keep him from describing them as wolves nonetheless.

55 See Mahony 1996, pp. 8–9; Anthony Stadlen cited by Macmillan 1997, p. 640.

56 This identification, proposed a while ago by Swales 1982b, has since been definitely confirmed by Skues 2001. As Bernfeld 1946 has shown, Freud had similarly misled his readers in his article on "Screen memories."

57 Freud 1911, p. 78: "It may be suspected, however, that what enabled Schreber to reconcile himself to his homosexual phantasy, and so made it possible for his illness to terminate in something approximating to a recovery, may have been the fact that his

father-complex was in the main positively toned and that in real life the later years of his relationship with an excellent father had probably been unclouded."

58 See Freud and Ferenczi 1993, letter of Freud to Ferenczi of October 6, 1910: "I have asked Stegmann to find out all kinds of personal things about old Schreber ... [He] was otherwise a tyrant at home who 'shouted' at his son and understood him as little as the 'lower God' understood our paranoiac." The discrepancy between Freud's published and private presentations of Schreber senior is noted in Lothane 1989, p. 215.

59 See the passage underlined by him on October 10, 1909 in his copy of Gabriel Séailles's biography of Leonardo: "Without doubt, at the urgency of his father, Ser Piero broke with Caterina, *took his son and the same year* [six words underlined in green] married ... An illegitimate son received by his father, Leonardo missed that maternal influence to which every great man who respects himself must submit [whole passage emphasized by a green line in the margin]" (noted by Spector 1972, p. 58). Freud's omission is evidently not innocent insofar as the father's absence is supposed to account, in his interpretation, for Leonardo's thirst for knowledge and for his sublimated homosexuality.

60 See Wilcocks 1994, ch. 7; Borch-Jacobsen 2005b, pp. 110–113.

61 Swales 2003.

62 Freud and Zweig 1970, p. 91.

63 Freud 1937, p. 267: "there is not only *method* in madness, as the poet has already perceived, but also a fragment of *historical truth*"; Freud's emphasis.

64 Spence 1982, p. 31.

65 Spence 1982, p. 280.

66 Spence 1982, ch. 9. It should be noted that this narrativist turn is precisely what Lacan had already advocated in the early 1950s under the name of "return to Freud"; see for example his discussion of analytic "historization" in Lacan 1977, pp. 46–53; as well as this passage in Lacan 1988, pp. 13–14: "the fact that the subject relives, comes to remember, in the intuitive sense of the word, the formative events of his existence, is not in itself so very important. What matters is what he reconstructs of it ... What is essential is reconstruction, the term he [Freud] employs right up until the end ... I would say – when all is said and done, it is less a matter of remembering than of rewriting history."

67 Sherwood 1969.

68 Ricoeur 1981, p. 271.

69 Schafer 1980, p. 35; emphasis added.

70 This is how the anthropologist R. R. Marett characterized the Freudian narrative of the killing of the primal father in *Totem and Taboo*; see Marett 1920, p. 206.

8 Interprefactions: Freud's legendary science

IN COLLABORATION WITH SONU SHAMDASANI

In the beginning was Man, center of God's creation and of the celestial spheres. Then came Copernicus, who dislodged him from his solar position in the midst of the universe. Then came Darwin, who let him know that he was just one beast among others. And then finally came Freud, who taught him that his ego was not even "master of his house." Three humiliations, Freud tells us, three blows inflicted by science on mankind's self-esteem, each time raising a storm of protest among those stripped of their cherished illusions: "Hence arises the general revolt against our science (*unsere Wissenschaft*), the disregard of all considerations of academic civility and the releasing of the opposition from every restraint of impartial logic."[1]

Copernicus, Darwin, Freud: this genealogy of the de-centered man of modernity is by now so familiar to us that we no longer note its very ego-centered, very Freudocentric immodesty. Indeed, it is Freud himself who recounts this lineage in his 1916–17 *Introductory Lectures*, and in his essay "A difficulty on the path of psycho-analysis"; it is he who informs us that psychoanalysis revolutionized psychology in the same way as Copernicus and Darwin revolutionized cosmology and biology. But after all, how do we know that this is actually the case?

Freud was not the only one at the time to claim the title of the Darwin (or the Galileo, or the Newton) of psychology – far from it. This was the declared ambition of psychology as a whole at the end of the nineteenth century, from Wundt to Brentano, from Ebbinghaus to William James: to create a scientific psychology, one that would extract itself from philosophy, literature, and other disciplines to surpass all previous forms of human self-understanding by extending the methodology of the natural sciences to all aspects of human life. From the very beginning, the "new psychology" presented itself as an "imitation" of the natural sciences (a sort of scientific version of the "imitation of the Ancients"). William James, in his *Text-Book of Psychology*, thus called for a "Galileo and Lavoisier of psychology,"[2] someone capable of pulling psychology out of its pre-scientific state. Elsewhere, in a letter to James Sully, he placed his hopes in a new Newton.[3] Likewise, Stanley Hall stated in 1909 that "the present psychological situation calls out for a new Darwin of the mind."[4] In 1912, Arnold Gesell proclaimed it was Hall himself who was the

"Darwin of psychology,"[5] which, Hall later recalled, "gave me more inner satisfaction than any compliment ever paid me by the most perfervid friend."[6] As for Théodore Flournoy, he announced in 1903 that this "Darwin of the mind" could well be Frederic Myers, one of the founders of psychical research. He republished this in his 1911 book *Esprits et médiums*, a copy of which is to be found, not insignificantly, in Freud's library:

> At present, nothing permits one to foresee the end that the future reserves to Myers' spiritist doctrine. If future discoveries happen to confirm his thesis of the empirically verified intervention of the discarnate in the physical or psychological frame of our phenomenal world, then his name will be inscribed in the golden book of the great initiators, and, added to those of Copernicus and Darwin, will complete the triad of geniuses having most profoundly revolutionized scientific thought in the cosmological, biological, psychological order.[7]

Others nominated Freud, whom Jung compared variously to Kepler, Galileo, and Newton.[8] Bleuler, in a 1910 letter,[9] compared him to Darwin, Copernicus, and Semmelweis. Still others protested vigorously, among them the German psychiatrist Alfred Hoche, who shot back in the same year:

> To top it all, the [Freudians'] dogmatic arrogance leads them to compare Freud's role with the historical position of Kepler, Copernicus and Semmelweis, which requires, according to a comical reasoning, seeking its proof in the fact that they all had to battle the resistance of their contemporaries.[10]

In 1923, the psychologist Adolf Wohlgemuth reiterated this point:

> Freud – Darwin! You may as well couple the name of Mr. Potts, of the *Eatonswill Gazette*, with that of Shakespear or Goethe ... Both Copernicus' and Darwin's work was violently attacked and herein may be some resemblance to Freud's, but yet what a sea of difference! Who were the attackers of Copernicus and Darwin? The Church, whose vested interests were endangered. Astronomers, as far as they dared in those dark days and were not Church dignitaries, or teachers at clerical universities, received the work of Copernicus and his successors with admiration. Biologists and geologists were almost unanimously enthusiastic about Darwin's work. The chief objectors ... to Freud's theories, I say, are psychologists *vom Fach*, that is exactly those people who stand to Freud's work in the same relation as the Astronomers to Copernicus, and the biologists and geologists to Darwin's work, and who hailed it with joy and admiration.[11]

So the question of who would be the founding genius of psychology was still a matter of intense debate when Freud nominated himself in his *Introductory Lectures*. But then, this self-coronation which today seems to us so obvious loses much of its authority and legitimacy. Indeed, why should we place our trust in Freud rather than in his rivals? Because Freud triumphed, because the "scientific revolution" carried out by this new Copernicus sent his competitors once and for all into the shadows of non-science? This would amount to begging the question, and conceding everything to the supposed victor, whereas we would like to know, precisely, how he won and why. Was it because Freud's competitors were finally forced to concede defeat? Because a consensus emerged around his theories, despite the "violent oppositions" and the "resistance to psychoanalysis" that he alleges? Or was it, quite simply, because he managed to make everyone forget the controversy itself, and even the existence of many of his rivals?

In this respect, it is striking that Freud, in his parable of the "three blows," presents the scientific revolution carried out by psychoanalysis as a *fait accompli*, given that the scientificity of psychoanalysis was still at the time the object of a controversy which was far from resolved. It is worth recalling that from around 1905 onwards Freud's theories had been at the center of a very intense international controversy whose participants included the era's biggest names in psychology and psychiatry – Pierre Janet, August Forel, Emil Kraepelin, Eugen Bleuler, Gustav Aschaffenburg, Alfred Hoche, William Stern, Morton Prince, to name only a few. This controversy ended in 1913 in a complete defeat for psychoanalysis at the Congress of the German Psychiatric Association held at Breslau, where one participant after another rose to condemn Freud's theories as therapeutically dangerous and scientifically unsound.[12] But Freud, in his parable, makes as if the controversy had been resolved once and for all in his favor. All that we learn of his critics' arguments is that they were motivated by an irrational resistance and that they had been definitively relegated to the dustbin of the history of science, exactly like those of Copernicus' and Darwin's detractors. By the same token, we learn little of the actual objections that were raised against psychoanalysis, nor how Freud supposedly succeeded in overcoming them. When one places the parable of the three blows in its historical context, one realizes that Freud's famed victory over his adversaries was entirely imaginary and that it rests, in fact, on a veritable negative hallucination about the criticisms that were leveled at psychoanalysis.

"Make the past into a tabula rasa,"[13] chanted the French revolutionaries. It is in the nature of revolutions to do away with opponents, whether it be with the swipe of the guillotine or with epistemic breaks, and to rewrite history from the moment of "year I" of the new scientific or political order. Freud's parable of the "three blows" provides a marvelous illustration of this purging of history, right down to its transcription. Indeed, this edifying story has its own interesting genealogy, which is conspicuously passed over in silence by Freud. As Paul-Laurent Assoun has shown in his *Introduction to Freudian Epistemology*,[14] the comparison of humiliations produced by the Copernican and Darwinian revolutions comes from the well-known Darwinian propagandist Ernst Haeckel, who popularized it in several of his works. This comparison was taken up again by, among others, Thomas Huxley and Emil Du Bois-Reymond, and it had already become a commonplace when Flournoy tacked onto it Myers's psychological revolution. But here again, Freud says nothing of either Haeckel or

Flournoy, even while he is evidently appropriating their genealogical scheme. To Karl Abraham, who had teased him about his "colleague Copernicus," he replied:

> You are right to point out that the enumeration in my last paper is bound to create the impression that I claim my place alongside Copernicus and Darwin. However, I did not want to relinquish an interesting idea just because of that semblance, and therefore at any rate put Schopenhauer in the foreground.[15]

Thus a topos shared by an entire generation of scientists and psychologists suddenly became an "interesting idea"which simply occurred to Freud ...

The fable of the three blows is a good example of what Freud historians Henri Ellenberger and Frank Sulloway have called the "Freud legend." This legend, embroidered by Freud himself in his various historical accounts of psycho-analysis, has two essential traits: the pre-emptory proclamation of the revolutionary nature of Freudian theory, and the simultaneous obliteration of rival theories, sent back without further ado to the "pre-history" of psychoanalytic science. Freud, this legend goes, was the first in the history of mankind to have lifted the age-old veil of repression that hung over the unconscious, infantile sexuality, the meaning of neurotic symptoms, dreams, and parapraxes. Better yet, he made his epochal discoveries in total intellectual isolation, thanks on the one hand to the unprejudiced observation of his patients and on the other hand to his heroic self-analysis, which allowed him to overcome his own resistances. No one had ever preceded him on this path. The few remarks that his predecessors Charcot, Breuer, and Chroback had dropped regarding the importance of sexuality denoted nothing more than "a piece of knowledge which, strictly speaking, they themselves did not possess."[16] And when Freud presented his views on the sexual etiology of the neuroses, his colleagues – including his old friend Breuer – unanimously rejected them. Their "resistances" were too strong; their scientific objectivity was thrown out the window. A gulf formed around Freud, his work was ignored or vilified, he had no disciples:

> My "splendid isolation" was not without its advantages and charms. I did not have to read any publications, nor listen to any ill-informed opponents; I was not subject to influence from any quarter; there was nothing to hustle me.[17]

Freud, the legend continues, had not read Nietzsche, nor had he read Schopenhauer, nor Scherner, nor Popper-Lynkeus, where he would later find so many striking anticipations and confirmations of his theories on repression and dreams. He simply owed nothing to anyone – an orphan, without a father, without history. As the philosopher Louis Althusser faithfully recounts:

> To my knowledge, in the course of the nineteenth century, two or three children were born who were unexpected: Marx, Nietzsche, Freud ... A child without a father, Western Reason makes him pay dearly for it. Marx,

Nietzsche, Freud had to pay the price, sometimes terrible, of survival: a price counted in exclusions, condemnations, insults, miseries, hungers and death, or madness ... I speak only of them, because they gave birth to sciences, or to a critique.

Let's consider simply Freud's solitude in his time. I do not speak of human solitude ... I speak of his *theoretical* solitude. For when he set out to think, that is to say express in the form of a rigorous system of abstract concepts the extraordinary discovery he returned to every day in his *practice*, it was in vain that he looked for theoretical precedents, for fathers in theory. He had to confront and manage the following theoretic situation: to be his own father, build with his own artisan hands the theoretical space in which to place his discoveries, weave with borrowed threads, taken right and left, blindly, the great interlacing net where he would catch, in the depths of blind experience, the redundant fish of the unconscious.[18]

Legenda is a story meant to be repeated mechanically, almost unknowingly, as the lives of the saints that were daily recited at matins in the convents of the Middle Ages. Just as the removal of these *legendae* from history facilitated their vast transcultural diffusion, so the legendary de-historicization of psychoanalysis has allowed it to adapt to all sorts of contexts which on the face of it ought to have been inhospitable to it, and to constantly reinvent itself in a brand-new guise. Althusser gave psychoanalysis a structural, epistemological reading, but there have been many others throughout the twentieth century – positivist, experimentalist, existentialist, hermeneutic, Freudo-Marxist, narrativist, cognitivist, deconstructivist, and now even neuroscientific. These versions are as different as can be, but they have this in common: they all celebrate the miraculous exception of psychoanalysis, removed from any context, any history.

The fact is that psychoanalysis managed to impose itself in significant sectors of twentieth-century society as the only psychological theory worthy of the name and the only psychotherapy capable of theorizing its own practice. In such locations, calling into question the unconscious, the Oedipus complex, or infantile sexuality could – and still can – provoke the same incredulous hilarity as do Kansas creationists or members of the "Flat Earth Society."[19] There, psychoanalysis has become indisputable, incontrovertible. It is "blackboxed," to use the jargon of sociologists of science, that is to say it is accepted as a given that it would be simply futile to question. The Freud legend and its widespread acceptance are the expression of this successful blackboxing, of this supposed victory of psychoanalysis over rival theories. Better yet, they are this blackboxing itself, that which protects psychoanalysis from independent inquiry. Indeed, why would one want to reopen this black box? Why would one want, for example, to stir up the old controversies that accompanied the elaboration of Freudian theory, if one accepts that it triumphed once and for all over the "resistances to psychoanalysis," just as Copernicus and Darwin won out over the irrational prejudices that prevented man from seeing the truth? If Freud won, is it not simply because his theory was true? How else explain its success?

We have here a typical example of what the sociologist of science David Bloor[20] calls an "asymmetrical" explanation, that is, one that argues from the victory in a scientific controversy to beat the vanquished hollow and refuse to listen to their arguments. It is very difficult to question such an explanation, because to do so requires swimming against the current and flouting the status quo. Who would be foolish enough to lend a "symmetrical" attention to points of view that are seemingly already condemned by the tribunal of History? This, however, is precisely what historians, critics, and scholars of psychoanalysis have been doing for several decades now. They have attempted to understand *how* psychoanalysis triumphed over its adversaries, *how* for many it succeeded in establishing itself as the science of the psyche, and this without supposing this title awarded in advance. While there is little consensus among Freud scholars, it is nevertheless fair to state that the cumulative effect of such work has been to reveal the imaginary character of Freud's victory over his rivals, and to reopen the Pandora's box of psychoanalysis, in spite of the systematic censure of documents and testimonials by the administrators of Freudian archives.[21]

Thanks to such figures as Henri Ellenberger, Frank Sulloway, Frank Cioffi, Ernst Falzeder, Peter Swales, Anthony Stadlen, Malcolm Macmillan, and many others, we have thus come to see that much of what Freud and his followers presented as the history of psychoanalysis, starting with his *History of the Psychoanalytic Movement*, actually represented an epistemological fantasy. Freud was *not* intellectually isolated. His colleagues were *not* hostile to him, at least not at the beginning. His work was well received overall. He had disciples quite early on. He was hardly the only one at the time to have an interest in sexuality, including infantile sexuality. Breuer in no way denied the role of sexuality in neuroses, nor did Janet, Forel, or many others. The criticism leveled at him regarding the sexual etiology of hysteria had to do with a theory (the "seduction theory") which he himself later abandoned. The idea of an unconscious psychic activity was commonplace in the nineteenth century. The concept of repression was prominent in the theories of Herbart and his teacher Meynert. Freud's dream theory had multiple predecessors. He had read Scherner, just as he had read Schopenhauer and Nietzsche. His famous self-analysis hardly lasted six weeks and he himself considered it a failure. And so on, and so forth.[22]

Far from being born, one fine day, from the fortuitous encounter between Freud and the unconscious, as legend would have us believe, psychoanalysis is profoundly rooted in the scientific and philosophical theories of its time: Darwinian biology; the sexology of Krafft-Ebing, Moll, and Havelock Ellis; German neurology and brain anatomy; English psychophysiology; the French "scientific psychology" of Taine and Ribot; the experimental and therapeutic hypnotism of Charcot, Janet, Bernheim, and Delbœuf; Hartmann's "philosophy of the unconscious"; the esthetics of Lipps and Fischer – the list is long. Few would deny, of course, that Freud came up with a highly original synthesis of the various theories from which he drew his inspiration. It remains that psychoanalysis, like any other theory, was not born by "immaculate conception" (to use Peter Swales's expression), and that the legend of the lone hero propagated by Freud is a myth, a "Robinsonnade" that does not hold up to historical inquiry. Far from extracting itself all at once, ready-made, from what Freud called its "prehistory," psychoanalysis is in numerous ways rooted in historical–theoretical contexts without which its emergence would remain inexplicable and miraculous.

In this respect to invoke the concept of "epistemic break," in order to dissociate psychoanalysis from its past, amounts, once again, to celebrating this miracle without accounting for it. This is clearly visible in the epistemological–structuralist version of the legend, which has enchanted so many since Althusser proposed it for the first time, with the blessing of Jacques Lacan, in the early 1960s. In this version, Freud's "resistances to psychoanalysis" become "epistemic obstacles" à la Bachelard, pre-scientific residues that prevent the new science from finally coming into its own. Freud, the story goes, not only had to fight the resistance of his colleagues and of his patients; he first had to fight his own concepts, which were not his own but were concepts inherited, "imported," from the biology and the energetics of his time. In other words, he had to fight his own history, in order to achieve the theoretical self-genesis characteristic of science. Indeed, for this neo-Kantian rationalist who is Althusser, science is not a matter of linear progression or of accumulation of knowledge, each theorist conceptualizing a reality a little better than his predecessors. Just like Thomas Kuhn (but that is where the analogy ends), Althusser believes that science moves forward by way of jumps, leaps, ruptures, theoretically "producing" its objects instead of reflecting them. Science "structures," "constructs" its objects a priori (the Copernican revolution is not far off), and it is all the more scientific for knowing that this is what it does, without losing itself in the false "evidences" of empiricism, of common sense or of ideology. Science, from this point of view, owes nothing to its history. It hardly matters, for example, that Marx borrowed the term "dialectic" from Hegel or that Freud owes that of "libido" to Moll and Krafft-Ebing. The only thing that matters is that Marx and Freud organized the terms within a new theoretical "problematic," which in one fell swoop changed these ideological "notions" into truly scientific – that is to say, truly a priori – "concepts":

> We can observe in the history of human culture phenomena of the same type [as the emergence of psychoanalysis] when a new scientific discipline appears, whether it be Greek mathematics, Galilean physics, Marx's theory of society, etc. To the extent that we have here an epistemic break, a rupture in continuity from what was there before, we have a phenomenon of rupture that contains within itself, as a real potentiality, an ability to drastically change the field out of which it arises.[23]

But how do we know that the concepts of Freud's theory are scientific, and those of Krafft-Ebing or Moll are not? It is one thing to say, in Kuhnian fashion, that a new problematic is incommensurable with the problematic that preceded it, because it inaugurates, by way of a break, a new and completely different a priori. It is quite another thing to claim, as does Althusser, that this break is "epistemic" and that it separates once and for all science from non-science, the a priori from the empirical, reason from opinion. After all, even from Althusser's own point of view, the problematic of Darwinian sexologists did not construct its object less than did Freud's theory of sexuality, even if they were unaware of it. So why would Freud's theory be scientific, but not Krafft-Ebing's and Moll's? The answer seems to be that Freudian psychoanalysis, unlike Darwinian sexology, knows that it constructs its object. And how does it know this? Because Althusser (or Lacan) sees to it that it knows it, extracting from it the kernel of an a priori which, even in Freud's own understanding, remained hidden under its empirico-biological shell (*guangue*). Ultimately, everything rests on the philosopher of science's decision to grant the monopoly of the a priori to one problematic and not to others: psychoanalysis is a science because Althusser says so. This affirmation in turn rests on nothing other than Freud's own assertions concerning the status of psychoanalysis.

The philosophy of science as practiced by Althusser is simply a rubber-stamping operation. When one examines his reading of psychoanalysis more closely, one quickly realizes that it does nothing but ratify the scientific pretensions of Freudian theory, without ever questioning their validity. For all his neo-Kantian language, Althusser simply repeats the orthodox Freud legend, as one finds it presented, for example, in Ernst Kris's introduction to the censured edition of Freud's letters to Wilhelm Fliess:

> some observers have gained the impression that the fundamental principles of psycho-analysis must be out-of-date because a good deal of its terminology derives from the scientific terminology of the eighties and nineties of last century ... But the terms thus taken over into psycho-analysis have acquired new meanings which very often have little to do with their original meanings ... The question of the origin of the terminology and fundamental assumptions of psycho-analysis is therefore of only historical interest; it has nothing whatever to do with the question of the value of those assumptions and that terminology for psycho-analysis as a science.[24]

Psychoanalysis is a science, ergo it escapes its own history and the latter's anecdotal vicissitudes. Whether in the orthodox Freudian version or its Althusserian–structuralist counterpart, the arbitrary proclamation of the scientific character of psychoanalysis corresponds to a no less arbitrary negation of its historicity, that is to say, of its relative, controversial, and hence disputable, nature. Such a faithful repetition of the Freudian legend in contemporary philosophical language is by no means restricted to Althusser, but is exemplary of a whole host of so-called "post-structuralist" or "post-modern" readings of Freud.

Once this conclusion is made, it remains for us to grasp the deeper significance of this legendary de-historicization of psychoanalysis. The history of science is replete with legends intended to autonomize this or that discipline from what Hans Reichenbach would call its "context of discovery," but few can compare with the Freudian one. So how are we to understand that a thinker of Freud's stature would fashion such a mythical account of history, in spite of easily verifiable facts and, above all, the perfectly legitimate protests from his colleagues? Is it simply because he sought to satisfy his ego, his "desire for grandeur," his narcissism? Because he wanted to strengthen his own power by creating a personality cult within the psychoanalytic movement? Because it was a way to promote the product "psychoanalysis" on the market and beat the competition? None of these psychological or sociological explanations is fully satisfying in the end, because they all fail to grasp the internal, intimate links between the legend and psychoanalytic theory as such.

The Freud legend is not simply a propaganda tool or an external rhetorical garment, as such irrelevant to the theory itself and its "rational kernel." In reality, the legend is an integral part of Freudian theory, in that it functions as an epistemic immunization absolutely essential to countering the criticisms that were leveled at it. If Freud devotes so many pages to establishing his theoretical originality and virginity, it is not, as one might believe, because he is obsessed with questions of intellectual priority; it is because he tries to fend off claims that he imposed preconceived ideas on his clinical material, rather than allow himself to be guided by it. In other words, the myth of the immaculate conception of psychoanalysis is intended to clear Freud of suspicions that he fitted clinical observation to ready-made theories and thus contaminated the neutral and impartial observation of what his patients told him.

This, we must remember, was the main criticism leveled at Freud by his adversaries, from Janet to Hoche to Aschaffenburg to Moll to Forel, and many others. Psychoanalysis, they all said, is an a priori system, it applies an arbitrary interpretive grid to the psychical facts it deals with. Or again, to use the positivist language that Freud shared with his detractors, it is a "speculation" without basis in experience. To this critique of psychoanalytic methodology was regularly added a caution against its "suggestive" aspects, as understood by Bernheim and the Nancy School. Freud, according to his peers, was not content to read his theories into his patients' minds, but unwittingly suggested to them the responses he needed to support his theories. His observations and interpretations had therefore no objective value and his patients' testimony could offer no support to his theories since the psychoanalytic method changed them into disciples, that is to say into active and partial protagonists of the controversy. Here, for example, is what Alfred Hoche wrote:

> The confirmation of their intuitions that the "discovery" of the unconscious complex provides the followers of the [Freudian] doctrine with is nothing

surprising. The doctor who has faith and the patient ... are equally under the suggestive influence of an identical circle of ideas. The patients already know very precisely what is expected of them.[25]

In a similar vein, the psychiatrist Gustav Aschaffenburg said in 1906:

[Freud] allows the person he is examining to associate freely and continuously, except that from time to time, when he believes he has discovered a precise clue, he draws the patients' attention to it and lets them further associate from this newly gained point of departure. But most of the patients who will go and see Freud already know in advance what he is getting at and this thought immediately evokes the complex of representations pertaining to sexual life.[26]

It is important to understand that by "suggestion" Freud's colleagues were not speaking of direct verbal suggestion, as Freud all too often pretended to believe. What they had in mind was the much more fundamental process, brought to the fore by Bernheim and even more by Delbœuf, whereby the subjects of psychological investigation tend to validate the investigator's theoretical expectations. In physics, in chemistry, in molecular biology, one can reasonably expect that an erroneous conjecture will eventually be corrected through experiment or calculation, because in these disciplines, as Andrew Pickering[27] cogently explains, the "material agency" *resists* the hypotheses made about it, thus obliging the investigator to rectify them accordingly (this is what Pickering calls the "dialectic of accommodation and resistance"). It is not the same in social psychology and psychopathology, where heuristic hypotheses are tested on "human agencies" that are inevitably interested in the theories of which they are the object. In this case, as Delbœuf showed in the late 1880s and as Martin Orne and Robert Rosenthal rediscovered in the 1950s–1960s, the subject tends to accommodate the therapist's or the experimenter's expectations, such that there is no longer any resistance that could guide the investigator to correct and calibrate (or "mangle," as Pickering puts it) his theoretical hypotheses. Quite the opposite, the theory will in all likelihood produce its object, not in the sense that it imposes a conceptual grid upon it (as Althusser would have it), but in the sense that the so-called "object" modifies itself and adapts to the theory in order to validate it. This is how Charcot, according to the Nancy School, produced all of the phenomena of "grand hysteria" and "grand hypnotism" observed at the Salpêtrière. And this is also, according to Freud's colleagues, how the latter's interpretations produced the "seduction scenes," the sexual-infantile fantasies, the Oedipal desires, and the "transferential resistances" alleged by psychoanalytic theory. These "facts" that Freud claimed to have observed were in fact products of his own interpretations – they were *interprefactions.*

Freud, it goes without saying, could only reject the idea that his theories created or modified the phenomena he described. Theory, in his mind, does not interfere with the reality that it accounts for. Epistemologically speaking, Freud is a classic positivist for whom the ultimate foundation of knowledge is observation (*Beobachtung*), that is to say, perception and the description of phenomena. And like any good positivist – like Ernst Mach for example, who is, as Paul-Laurent Assoun[28] has shown, Freud's main reference in matters of theory of knowledge – he firmly distinguishes between observation and theory. Positivists generally mistrust theory, which they see as bent on taking the idea for the thing and lapsing into metaphysical speculation. They know quite well, of course, that science is not merely a matter of inductive generalization from observation, and that it cannot do without heuristic hypotheses. But they insist that these hypotheses be seen as such, that is to say, as theory and nothing else. Paradoxically, but at the same time very logically, the emphasis placed by positivists on observation often leads to a conventionalism, and even an odd theoretical playfulness: let's speculate, imagine, toy with ideas, because we know that these are only ideas which will later be corrected by experience. These ideas are "provisional fictions," Mach said, which we make use of because we have to start somewhere, but which are bound to be discarded as soon as we come across better and more "economical" ones. The "fundamental concepts" of psychoanalytic metapsychology, Freud repeats in turn, are nothing but theoretical "fictions," "conventions," "mythological beings," "speculative superstructures," "scientific" or "auxiliary constructions (*Konstruktionen*)" destined to be replaced as soon as they enter into conflict with observation. Here is one quote among many others of the same type, taken from the essay on "Narcissism":

> these ideas [the ideas of psychoanalytic metapsychology] are not the foundation of science, upon which everything rests; that foundation is observation alone. They are are not the bottom but the top of the whole structure, and they can be replaced and discarded without damaging it.[29]

The Freudian motif of theoretical fiction, which today is so often set against "the positivism and the substantialization of metaphysical or metapsychological agencies" (to cite Jacques Derrida),[30] is in fact a typically positivist trait. Speculative fiction is all the more tolerated, even encouraged, by Freud, as it supposedly never affects nor infects the observation of positive facts. Observation, in Freud, continues to provide the ultimate foundation of science because of its alleged ability to resist speculative divagations and erroneous hypotheses. Facts are hard, stubborn, uncompromising, and only those theories survive which know how to adapt to them (what Mach, as a good Darwinian of science, called the "adaptation of thoughts to facts").[31]

Now, it is exactly this very same positivist reasoning that Freud puts forward in the twenty-eighth of the *Introductory Lectures to Psychoanalysis*, one of the rare passages where he directly confronts the objection made by his colleagues that he suggests the phenomena he claims to observe. There is nothing to fear in proposing hypothetical interpretations to the patient, he tells us, because:

> After all, his conflicts will only be successfully solved and his resistances overcome if the anticipatory ideas (*Erwartungsvorstellungen*) he is given tally

> with the reality (*Wirklichkeit*) in him. Whatever in the doctor's conjectures is inaccurate drops out in the course of the analysis; it has to be withdrawn and replaced by something more correct.[32]

This famous argument, which Adolf Grünbaum has dubbed the "Tally Argument" and which he makes the cornerstone of Freudian epistemology, thus postulates that "psychical reality" is an objective *Wirklichkeit*, as such indifferent to the psychologist's or psychoanalyst's hopes, expectations, and suppositions. The patient is only cured if the theory corresponds to this reality, which also means that the cure provides an infallible criterion for assessing the validity of the analyst's interpretations and constructions. The problem however, as critics such as Woodworth, Hart, and Wohlgemuth were quick to note, is that this argument presupposes the non-suggestibility that was to be proven.[33] Supposing that the analyst's interpretations really do produce a therapeutic effect, how can we be sure that this effect is not, once again, a product of suggestion, just like cures obtained with other methods? Hence the English psychiatrist Bernart Hart's stern conclusion in 1929, which ought to have prevented Grünbaum from singing the praises of Freud's methodological rigor: "We must ... conclude that the argument from therapeutic results cannot provide the independent confirmation of psychoanalytic validity of which we are in search."[34]

In order to counter the objection of suggestion, Freud, as many of his colleagues in experimental psychology invited him to do, might have attempted to quantify the therapeutic results he claimed to have obtained, and compared them with those from other psychotherapeutic methods; or again, he might have attempted to develop procedures for controlling and measuring the effects of suggestion in the therapeutic situation. Such experimental verifications would certainly not have solved the basic problem, that of the inevitable interaction between the observing subject and the observed subject, which to this day haunts the most rigorously "controlled" studies. But at least Freud would have been faithful to his professed positivism, by accepting to put his theories to the test and trying to separate in the most rigorous way possible fact from artifact. Instead, he resorted to circular logic, by refusing to take seriously the objection made to his theory and by appealing to "observations" and "facts" obtained thanks to a method whose dependability was precisely in question. His critics, who in other respects shared for the most part his positivist convictions, were thus perfectly entitled to reproach him for having betrayed his own principles and having surreptitiously crossed over into pseudo-science, that is to say, into an imaginary positivism.

It is in the context of this controversy that the legend of the immaculate conception of psychoanalysis must be understood. This legend is a direct response to the objections raised by critics of psychoanalysis, which it is intended to silence once and for all. Indeed, given that Freud was not ready to test the method that allowed him to obtain the facts that he invoked, he had to find another way to clear his results from the suspicion of having been influenced by his hypotheses and speculations (of being "theory-loaded," we would say today). Now, what better way than to deny outright having had any theoretical preconceptions whatsoever in his approach to the phenomena? In the *Auto-biographical Study* of 1925, Freud claimed:

> Apart from emotional resistances ... it seemed to me that the main obstacle to agreement lay in the fact that my opponents regarded psychoanalysis as a product of my speculative imagination (*ein Produkt meiner spekulativen Phantasie*) and were unwilling to believe in the long, patient and unbiased work (*voraussetzungslose Arbeit*) which had gone in its making.[35]

In other words, metapsychological speculation is one thing; something else entirely is pure observation with no a prioris, with no pre-concepts. It is this absence of "presupposition" that the legend is intended to substantiate: if Freud had to fight against the irrational prejudices of his teachers and colleagues, who refused to grant sexuality any importance in the neuroses, one could no longer accuse him of seeing sex everywhere under the influence of this or that pre-conceived "sexual theory." Likewise, if he had worked in total isolation, if he had not read what Schopenhauer or Nietzsche had written about repression and instinctual forces, one could no longer reproach him for having projected "anticipatory ideas" onto his clinical material. And finally, if he had not been inspired by the biology of his time, one could no longer claim that his ideas about instinctual drives, infantile sexuality, and bisexuality had preceded and thus influenced the impartial observation of psychoanalytic "data."

The myth of the immaculate conception of psychoanalysis thus corresponds quite rigorously to what one may term the myth of the immaculate induction of Freudian theory, which states: Freud was not influenced by anyone, therefore he influenced neither facts nor patients. The legendary rewriting of history trans-forms Freud's hypotheses and speculations into hard, positive, incontrovertible facts, and it thus lends them epistemic legitimacy by purely and simply short-circuiting the objection of suggestion. Thanks to this rewriting, what was subjective suddenly becomes objective. What was situated in history becomes atemporal. What was interpretation becomes "psychical reality." What was speculation becomes experience. What was *Konstruktion* becomes "historical truth," a black box to which only the analyst has the key. As August Forel wrote in 1911, summarizing an oft-expressed grievance of the time, Freud and his disciples "ignore in a quite methodic manner their predecessors and ... they present all sorts of hypothetical things as facts."[36] The psychologist Joseph Jastrow echoed this judgment in 1932:

> One ... fallacy permeates pages and volumes of psychoanalysis: the fallacy of attributism. It consists in accepting as a reality an abstract concept devised by the thinker for the convenience of his thinking ... The fallacy of attributism subtly, insidiously, comprehensively invades every phase and phrase of the

psychoanalyst's technique. He has forgotten the realities and put in their place a mythology of forces – Ucs. [Unconscious], Id, Ego, Super-ego, Oedipus, libido in many guises, and other animated concepts – which he then uses to account for the clinical data which suggested them. As a consequence the sense of hypothesis is lost, and the assurance of reality substituted; that is the essence of delusion.[37]

We propose the term *interprefaction* for this transmutation of interpretations and constructions into positive fact, which is so characteristic of psycho-analysis. Interprefaction is the main trope of Freud's positivist rhetoric and of the diverse historical legends he wove around his so-called "discoveries." Interprefaction makes things and events with words; it fabricates facts with ideas, hunches, conjectures, hypotheses. As such, it is indistinguishable from the mythical epistemology of psychoanalysis, in the sense that it gives a falsely positivist presentation of the production of psychoanalytic data by causing this very production to be forgotten.

In this respect, it is entirely legitimate to critique this unwarranted reification in drawing attention to the rhetorical, *suggested* character of so-called analytic "facts." As we have seen, this is precisely what most of Freud's critics did, and still do today: "Your facts aren't facts, they are artifacts which you have fabricated." However, in many respects, such critiques remain close to Freud's positivistic outlook, in suggesting that one can clearly separate out fact from artifact in the domain of psychology. Thus many of Freud's initial critics, such as Aschaffenburg, Kraepelin, Hoche, Janet, and Morton Prince were by no means free of such reification when they proposed their own rival theories: the divide between what was considered fact and what artifact was simply drawn up differently.

But one can also reproach Freud not so much for having created new facts, but for having denied that this was what he was doing. From this perspective, what is significant is that Freud's positivism was simply nominalistic and concealed his active role in bringing about the "facts" that he claimed to describe. This second criticism is no less critical than the first, but it operates in an inverse manner. Rather than viewing analytic interprefaction as having given rise to false facts, one can see it as having led to true artifacts presented as facts. Rather than viewing the Freudian legend as a pure and simple fiction, one can see it as a fabrication which denies that it is a fabrication. What is at issue here, then, is the dissimulation of the construction of analytic facts, rather than their construction per se.

The legendary interprefaction of psychoanalysis can always be read in these two senses, depending upon whether one underlines its fictive or its productive character. In the first, one takes issue with the voluntary or involuntary manipulation of facts. In the second, one takes issue with the forgetting of this manipulation – or its active concealment. In the first instance, one reproaches Freud for being insufficiently positivistic; in the second, for being excessively so. Quite clearly, these two approaches differ widely as regards their theoretical and practical implications. However, it is often difficult to distinguish them, as the point at issue is the same: that Freud presented his interpretations and constructions as indubitable facts.

The epistemology of psychoanalysis is legendary through and through. It is not only that Freud wrote fictionalized accounts of his "observations" and "discoveries" in order to immunize them against the objection that he projected his theories onto his clinical material. More fundamentally, he never "observed" the entities and processes which he postulated, for reasons of principle. This is clear if one considers the psychoanalytic unconscious, which by definition neither appears nor ever presents itself to consciousness. Such an unconscious is strictly unobservable and cannot, therefore, be separated from the theory that postulates it. Freud commenced his essay on "The unconscious" by asking: "How are we to arrive at a knowledge of the unconscious? It is of course only as something conscious that we know it, after it has undergone transformation or translation into something conscious."[38]

But how does this "translation" take place, which transforms the "thing in itself" of the unconscious into an observable phenomenon? How do we know, for example, that little boys renounce their mothers as love objects for fear of being castrated by their fathers, or that women want to have babies to make up for their lack of penis? How do we know that such and such a symptom, dream, or slip of the tongue hides a repressed-unconscious wish? Better yet, how do we know that such a Freudian unconscious even exists? This we know only thanks to the interpretations of the analyst, who, with the help of rules of transformation called displacement, condensation, projection, identification, reversal into the opposite, symbolism, etc., translates the symptom, the dream, or the slip of the tongue into some "unconscious thought" unknown to the subject itself:

> Psycho-analytic work shows us every day that translation of this kind is possible. In order that this should come about, the person under analysis must overcome certain resistances – the same resistances as those which, earlier, made the material concerned into something repressed by rejecting it from the conscious.[39]

Here is why Freudian epistemology is so deceptive: Freud never "observed" the unconscious or infantile sexuality, nor did he ever "discover" the Oedipus complex or the meaning of dreams. He only guessed, inferred, deduced them from what his patients told him. More precisely, he constructed them with the help of interpretations, hypotheses, and speculations that were suggested to his patients and in turn obligingly confirmed by some of them. His colleagues were thus entirely justified in asking him how he could validate these conjectures except by circularly adducing the testimony of patients turned disciples; how he could guarantee, for example, that the displacements and the projections he attributed to their unconscious were not simply the result of his own interpretive activity, hypostasized for the occasion into a fantastic psychical dynamic. Freud never fully replied to this. He simply presented his interpretations as psychical facts, as events unfolding on "another stage" to which only he (or authorized analysts) had access, or again as memories and fantasies actually confessed by his patients on the couch. In final analysis, there is no "discovery" of psychoanalysis that does not lead back to such an interprefaction. When we read phrases such as "Psychoanalysis has established that" or "The analytic experience teaches us that," we ought to understand "Freud thought this," "Freud suggested that." Psychoanalysis never had other evidence to invoke in support of its theses except what it fabricated.

This is not to say that such "evidence" was unreal. Rather, what Freud actually did – in a similar manner to other late nineteenth- and early twentieth-century psychotherapists – was to form a self-confirming apparatus which could produce, *suggest* evidence for whatever theory one liked. Hence the endless reinventions of psychoanalysis in the twentieth century. As Joseph Delbœuf noted in 1886 apropos the hypnotic schools, "They owe their birth to the reciprocal action of the hypnotized on the hypnotizers. Only their rivalry has no raison d'être: they are all in the right."[40]

Faced with self-validating systems of this type, the question is one not so much of knowing if it is true or false, real or invented, historical or legendary (as it is each of these in turn), but rather of comprehending how it functions, how it produces effects, and which ones – in other words, how it interprefies the world.

Translated by JENNIFER CHURCH

Notes

1 Freud 1916–17, pp. 284–285. The same idea is more fully developed in Freud 1917a, p. 140.
2 James 1892, p. 468.
3 James 1999, p. 53.
4 Hall 1909, cited in Shakow and Rappaport 1968, p. 62.
5 Gesell and Gesell 1912, p. 20.
6 Hall 1923, p. 360. Interestingly, the same year Hall wrote to Freud: "In fact history will show that you have done for us a service which you are not at all extravagant in comparing with that of Darwin for biology"; cited in Burnham 1960, p. 313.
7 Flournoy 1903; 1911, p. 266.
8 Jung 1906, p. 9; 1912, p. 102.
9 Freud Collection, Library of Congress, Washington, DC; quoted in Alexander and Selesnick 1965, p. 5.
10 Hoche 1910, p. 1009.
11 Wohlgemuth 1923, pp. 227–228.
12 We detail this forgotten episode of the first "Freud wars" in Borch-Jacobsen and Shamdasani 2006, pp. 131–139. No mention is made of the Breslau conference in Freud's 1914 *History of the Psychoanalytic Movement*, nor in his 1925 *Autobiographical Study*, nor in Ernest Jones's biography of Freud.
13 "Du passé faisons table rase" (Eugène Pottier, *L'Internationale*).
14 Assoun 1981, pp. 191 ff.
15 Freud and Abraham 2002, p. 346.
16 Freud 1914a, p. 13.

17 Freud 1914a, pp. 21–23.
18 Althusser 1964, pp. 26–28.
19 See for example the national uproar caused in France by the publication of *The Black Book of Psychoanalysis*; Meyer *et al.* 2005.
20 Bloor 1976.
21 For more on this censure, see Borch-Jacobsen and Shamdasani 2002.
22 We survey this revisionist scholarship in further detail in Borch-Jacobsen and Shamdasani 2006, pp. 146–163.
23 Althusser 1996 [1963–64], pp. 78–79.
24 Freud 1954, pp. 46–47.
25 Hoche 1910, p. 1008.
26 Aschaffenburg 1906, p. 1797.
27 Pickering 1995.
28 Assoun 1981, ch. 3.
29 Freud 1914b, p. 77.
30 Jacques Derrida, in Derrida and Roudinesco 2001, pp. 282–283: "Among the gestures of Freud that convinced me, seduced me actually, is the indispendable audacity of his thought, which I do not hesitate to call his courage: this consists here in writing, inscribing, signing, in the name of a knowledge without alibi (and thus the most 'positive'), theoretical 'fictions'. We thus recognize two things at once: *on the one hand*, the irreducible necessity of stratagem, transaction, negotiation ... in the *position* of truth ..., and, *on the other hand*, the debt of every theoretical *position* ... to a performative power structured by *fiction*, by a figural invention ... 'The friend of psychoanalyis' in me is suspicious, not of positive knowledge but of positivism and substantialization"; Derrida's emphasis. It seems that Derrida confounds the positivist critique of metaphysics with its Heideggerian deconstruction.
31 Mach 1905, p. 120: "The adaptation of thought to facts, as we should put it more accurately, we call observation; and mutual adaptation of thoughts, theory."
32 Freud 1916–17, p. 452; translation modified.
33 See Woodworth 1917, p. 194; Wohlgemuth 1923, pp. 162–163; Hart 1929, pp. 79–81.
34 Hart 1929, p. 81.
35 Freud 1925, pp. 49–50.
36 Forel 1919, p. 224.
37 Jastrow 1932, pp. 227 and 230.
38 Freud 1915a, p. 166.
39 Freud 1915a, p. 166.
40 Delbœuf 1886b, p. 169.

9 Portrait of the psychoanalyst as a chameleon

What is progress in psychoanalysis? One of the arguments most commonly used by advocates of psychoanalysis during the recent "Freud wars" has been to reproach their adversaries for holding fast to an outmoded version of their discipline. Psychoanalysis, they say, no longer bears much resemblance to what its founder had envisaged, so that criticism focusing on the historical Freud is hopelessly off the mark. Who among psychoanalysts still believes in the preposterous "penis envy," in the connection between masturbation and "actual neurosis," in the founding father's grandiose phylogenetic speculations? Today's practioners have long since relegated these antiquities to the attic, in favor of more up-to-date concepts. Upholders of "ego psychology" amend the doctrine to make it compatible with developmental psychology; "object relations" theorists reject the solipsism of Freud's theory of drives in favor of a "two-persons psychology"; partisans of a "hermeneutic" reform of psychoanalysis no longer wish to be associated with Freud's scientist positivism; adepts of Kohut's "self psychology" blithely disregard the rules of analytic neutrality and abstinence in favor of an "empathic understanding" of the patient; narrativists no longer concern themselves with the "historical truth" of what is said on the couch; Lacanians reformulate the theory in terms of language and the "signifier." The Freudian collar cannot be attached to any of these, for they did not wait for the Freud bashers before profoundly revising both their theory and their practice. (*They* are the true "revisionists"!) Freud may be dead, as regularly announced in newspapers and magazines, but who can deny that psychoanalysis itself is alive and well, changing, adapting, expanding – i.e. progressing?

The argument is clever, but it hides a fallacy. For who, except the psychoanalysts themselves, claims that what we are dealing with here is a *progress*, and a progress in *psychoanalysis*?[1] What, after all, remains of psychoanalysis when one has ditched most of Freud's theories? And why should abandoning them constitute progress rather than a critique of psychoanalysis? The fact that analysts, by and large, no longer try to persuade their female patients that they want to have babies in order to make up for their lack of a male organ is undeniably progress. But why should this be construed as progress in the very theory that has been tacitly buried to accommodate feminist protest? There is something mysterious about the way psychoanalysis perpetually raises itself from its ashes, always more powerful, always more imperial, always more Freudian. How do psychoanalysts manage to transmute their defeats into victories? How do they change while remaining the same?

Here is a new book of psychoanalytic theory: *Mad Men and Medusas: Reclaiming Hysteria and the Effects of Sibling Relationships on the Human Condition*.[2] It is written by Juliet Mitchell, a grande dame of Freudo-Lacanian feminism. Her first book, *Psychoanalysis and Feminism*,[3] played a critical role in the feminist rehabilitation of Freud. The present one deals with hysteria, a neurosis reputed to be essentially feminine and the historical starting point of psychoanalysis. Mitchell informs us, as early as page 6, that Freud got it all wrong, however:

> my investigation of the gendering of hysteria has led me to question some of the basic psychoanalytic theory that was itself built up from an understanding of hysteria. Thinking about hysteria has led me to a different reading of the Oedipus complex and the need to insert the experience of siblings and their lateral heirs in peer and affinal relationships into our understanding of the construction of mental life.[4]

So are we about to be treated to an all-out critique of psychoanalysis, to a new anti-Oedipus? The book jacket quickly disabuses us: "Juliet Mitchell is a psychoanalyst," and her book "develops a major new psychoanalytic theory that stresses lateral relationships over generational ones." Mitchell's clients can rest assured: what they go through on her couch is still "analysis." Except it is no longer clear what the term "psychoanalysis" means.

According to the theory advanced by Freud and Breuer in their *Studies on Hysteria*, the symptoms of this strange and multifarious neurosis are a symbolic representation of sexual "reminiscences" that have been repressed because they are irreconcilable with the conscious ego. At first, Freud thought that the memories that he extorted from his patients were of real events, specifically of incestuous "seductions" by adults during early childhood (what we would now call "child abuse"). Then, after the debacle of his seduction theory, he decided that these memories were mere fantasies expressing infantile sexual wishes, notably Oedipal ones: the hysteric *wants* to be seduced by the adult. Behind hysteria, as behind all other neuroses, Freud always finds love for the parent of the opposite sex whom the subject wants to "have" and an ambivalent identification with the same-sex rival who the subject wants to "be" and to dethrone (to which is added, in the so-called "complete" form of the Oedipus complex, homosexual love for the same-sex parent and hostile identification with the heterosexual rival). Thus, in classic Freudian theory everything turns on the Oedipal triangle conceived as a "nuclear complex of neuroses." In particular, the horizontal relationship to siblings is always considered from the perspective of the vertical relationship of the Oedipus complex: brother and sister are seen not as "primary" libidinal objects, but as rivals with respect to the father or (most often) the mother.

Mitchell reverses this schema. What is primary, she tells us, is not the libidinal bond to a parental object that one wants to "have," but the mimetic identification with the sibling one wants simultaneously to be and to kill. Like Freud, she conceives of the appearance of a little brother or sister as a profoundly traumatic event for the subject, except – and this changes everything – that she sees in it an essentially narcissistic catastrophe. Until then, "His Majesty the Baby" has been alone in the world, the unique object of his parents' attention, when along comes another such object who steals his place and reduces him to nothing: "Who am I, I who was everything?" That, according to Mitchell, is the hysteric's fundamental question. Dislodged from himself, the (non-)subject tries everything to recover his lost being by identifying with (and letting himself be possessed by) the other and by "killing" him (absorbing him) in the same gesture: the hysteric never lets go of a deeply mimetic ambivalence toward his horizontal alter egos – siblings, friends, colleagues, partners. Or again, he (Mitchell insists on using the masculine pronoun) regresses toward one parent or the other and identifies with that parent's desire, in order once again to become the center of the world. Oedipal love for the mother or father, which for Freud was the basis of hysteria and other neuroses, in reality hides the desire to be loved (what Lacan called the "demand for love"). The hysteric "wants his mother, or lots of new clothes, or too much of something to eat. This wanting to *have* the mother or father and their substitutes always dominates in pictures of hysteria; it obscures the desperate need to *be* someone" (p. 47). But how to be someone else, if not by imitation? Earlier in the book, Mitchell had warned us that:

> "Wanting" is central to a theory of hysteria. The age-old observation that the hysteric mimes or imitates is replaced in psychoanalytic theory by a specific understanding of mimesis in the context of "wanting": one wants what the other person wants and mimes a person's desires.[5]

Obviously, this theory of mimetic desire has nothing Freudian about it, if only because it completely de-sexualizes and de-objectifies the "wanting" and makes it into a desire to be subject (autonomous, self-satisfying, self-identical). As Mitchell must know, such a theory is a direct outgrowth of the work of René Girard and, more distantly, of Alexandre Kojève's interpretation of the desire for recognition and the "fight to the death for pure prestige" in Hegel's *Phenomenology of Spirit*.[6] It so happens, however, that this theory has led to an explicit critique of psychoanalysis: as René Girard and I myself have argued,[7] the refusal to consider the primarily mimetic character of desire is not only a constant with Freud, but is one of the most fundamental presuppositions of his theory. "Freud," Mitchell contends, "posits ... that hysterics mimic other people's desires."[8] In fact, Freud maintains exactly the opposite. As he explains in *The Interpretation of Dreams* (1900), and again in *Group Psychology and Analysis of the Ego* (1921), the hysterical identification is *not* "simple imitation": the hysteric identifies with another person based on a "common element which remains in the unconscious,"[9] identification thus serving as a screen for a sexual wish that predates it and which is not in itself mimetic.

Why, then, does Mitchell so generously attribute to Freud a theory of mimetic desire that she has evidently found in Girard (cited only once in passing) and other writers? The answer seems fairly obvious: because it is the only way to take into account a critique from outside psychoanalysis without admitting that is what she has done, or, by the same token, drawing out the consequences. This is how psychoanalysis "progresses": not by openly rectifying the doctrine, but by silently recuperating the criticisms directed at it and by having Freud endorse the most varied and contradictory theories, according to the fashions and necessities of the moment. "Return to Freud!" clamors the chorus of psychoanalysts and then see how Freud, before our wondering eyes, becomes successively a phenomenologist, an existentialist, a hermeneuticist, an experimental psychologist, a Marxist, a Hegelian, an anti-Hegelian, a structuralist, a Derridean, a post-modernist, a Wittgensteinian, a feminist, a cognitivist, a neuroscientist – or a Girardian. What is the use of trying to criticize such a "zero theory"? It is everywhere only because it is anything.

Mitchell not only modifies the Freudian theory of desire, she also turns on its head the entire theory of repression, which Freud called the "cornerstone on which the whole structure of psychoanalysis rests."[10] As Mitchell reminds us, psychoanalysis began with the idea that "hysterics suffer from reminiscences"; that is, from traumatic memories (real or imaginary, it hardly matters here) that hysterics are unable to recall because they repress them. But this misses the point, Mitchell tells us. Hysterics suffer not from reminiscences, but from revivifications; not from representations, but from presentations. If they do not recall the trauma, it is because the traumatic incident, when it occurred, quite literally reduced them to nothing. The psychic trauma of the sibling, like the physical shock of bombardment or torture, returns the subject to non-being, to the fundamental helplessness of premature birth (shades of Lacan). So how would such a non-subject ever be able to remember something that never happened to "him"? Overwhelmed by the trauma, he becomes that which invades him, identifies so completely with the "other" that this other can be neither represented nor remembered as other (another silent borrowing, this time from my past work on non-representational mimesis):[11] "If I am you or he is she, then you, she, "the other" cannot be recalled as there is insufficient distance between the two terms."[12] Such an identification cannot be represented, it can only be presented/repeated in the form of body memory, compulsion, hallucinatory perception, or flashback. The aim of an analysis, in this sense, is not to unearth a repressed memory, as Freud would have it; it is to repeat the non-memory in order to give it a context and gradually change it into memory – that is to say, into representation, history, and narrative: "For the trauma victim to recover ... absence and presence must become first loss and presentation in memories-in-the-body-ego, then representation and memory-in-the-mind."[13] Compare this to Judith Herman's description in *Trauma and*

Recovery of her work with "survivors" of physical or sexual abuse: "Out of the fragmented components of frozen imagery and sensation, patient and therapist slowly reassemble an organized, detailed, verbal account, oriented in time and context."[14]

Mitchell piles up references to the Freudian text ("primal repression," the rupture of the "protective shield," the "mystic writing-pad," etc.); yet it is clear that her traumatology comes not from psychoanalysis, but (with the exception of the theme of mimesis) from today's sinister "recovered memory therapy" (RMT) movement and from the theory of dissociation and "fixed ideas" of Freud's old rival, Pierre Janet. Indeed, it is not Freud but Herman and Janet who distinguish "normal memory," which consists in the "action of telling a story" and in representation, from "traumatic memory," which interrupts (dissociates) the continuity of the subjective narrative and persists in the form of an unassimilable, amnesiac "fixed idea."[15]

Mitchell fails to mention any of this. On the contrary, she reproaches RMT theorists with *ignoring* this distinction (between what she calls "memory" and "perception," or "trace") in favor of a crude notion of "memory as a repro- duction of a fixed event, true or untrue."[16] The same confusion, she adds, undermines the arguments of those who, like Frederick Crews,[17] simplistically identify the "memories" of incest unearthed by RMT therapists with the Oedipal "memories" obtained by psychoanalysts: "To do so ... is to misun- derstand the psychoanalytic explanation of memory."[18] By an admirable sleight of hand, a distinction originating with Janet and RMT theorists thus becomes the alpha and omega of psychoanalytic theory of memory. The irony, of course, is that the psychoanalyst Mitchell succeeds in officially distancing herself from the RMT witch-hunters only at the price of clandestinely surrendering to their theses, thus justifying Crews's worst suspicions about psychoanalysis.

Mitchell, it is true, takes care to inject sexuality into her mimetico-traumatic theory of hysteria, lest anyone mistake its authentic Freudian character. This might seem quite a formidable task, for what is sexual about being dislodged by a rival or subjected to a violent shock (an objection already raised by army psychiatrists with respect to "shell shocked" soldiers during the First World War)? But psychoanalysis has infinite metaphoric resources. In a passage worthy of Paracelsus, Mitchell writes:

> [T]rauma and sexuality are analogous experiences. The effraction of the subject's protective skin, which is an essential part of trauma (the breaking of the actual skin in the case of physical trauma, of an imaginary boundary in the case of psychic trauma), is comparable to the sense of a breaking open of the mind/body in sex.[19]

Swept down the slippery slope of analogy, we find ourselves ready to admit that all traumatic penetration is simultaneously sexual, sexualizing, and excit- ing. It is the libidinal excitement attendant on annihilation, we are told, that the hysteric endlessly repeats, beyond all satisfaction ("beyond the pleasure principle"), whether he is a Don Juan, a rapist, an abusive husband, a hateful and self-destructive lover, or a sadist. However, behind all these forms of hysterical sexuality, one finds hatred of the annihilating other, with whom the subject identifies all the more as he wants to annihilate him in return. Before love and sexuality there is mimetic hatred: "Freud claimed the hysteric loves where he hates; I would argue instead that he sexualizes where he hates."[20]

Why, then, did Freud see none of this? That is the question that all revisionist theories must address if they want to present themselves as psychoanalytic. Since Freudian revisionists cannot simply say that the founder of psychoanalysis was wrong, they must present the new theory as more embracing or "deeper" than the old one. That way, they leave classical theory untouched, while suggesting that its validity is only relative. Some of them propose that the Freudian Oedipus be reinterpreted as an echo of the birth trauma, others that it be re-evaluated from the perspective of the pre-Oedipal relation to the mother, others yet that it ought to be reframed within a theory of the paternal Law and of symbolic castration. Mitchell, for her part, tells us that the Oedipal theory is the product of Freud's repression of his own hysteria.

We know that in the mid-1890s Freud suffered from various somatic symptoms that were very likely due to cocaine use,[21] but which he himself attributed to a "hysteria." He recovered from this (hypothetical) hysteria, if one is to believe the psychoanalytic legend, after having "discovered" in the course of his self-analysis that he had harbored in his unconscious Oedipal desires vis-à-vis his father and mother. Mitchell does not question this sequence of events, nor "the existence and signification of Oedipal and castration fantasies";[22] but she considers them to be a screen hiding the lateral relationships of mimetic rivalry which, she suggests, were at the heart of Freud's hysteria, from his guilty identification with his brother Julius, who died at the age of six months, to his ambivalent friendship with Wilhelm Fliess: "Freud made everything come back to the Oedipal or pre-Oedipal parents in order to avoid the dead brother."[23] Behind the Oedipal complex was the Cain complex.

How are we to reconcile this with the idea that Freud recovered from his hysteria? Should we not conclude, according to good psychoanalytic logic, that the Oedipus complex was a symptom of the founder's *unresolved* hysteria? Mitchell shies away from drawing this conclusion, as it would obviously de-legitimize psychoanalysis in its entirety. Instead, she invites us to admit, simultaneously and contradictorily, that Freud "resolved his male hysteria by becoming Oedipus in his wishes" *and* that this "emphasis on Oedipus eliminate[d] the male hysteric" from psychoanalysis.[24] Once cured of his own hysteria, Freud no longer wanted to hear anything of male hysteria, for fear of reawakening his old demons. Hysteria, a potentiality for both sexes, became (or rather, became again) strictly a female affair. More generally, relations of lateral identification in female as well as male hysteria were neglected in favor of Oedipal relations, and soon everything in psychoanalysis came down to the mother–child relation (object relations theory) or to the impact of some non-sexual trauma (theory of traumatic neuroses of war), to the detriment of hysterical sexuality: "Hysteria 'disappeared' into its psychoanalytic 'cure' and reemerged as the trauma theories (Recovered Memory syndrome and False Memory syndrome [*sic*]) of contemporary therapies."[25]

This is an allusion to the phenomenon, well known to psychiatric historians, of hysteria's disappearance in the twentieth century: today, one hardly ever encounters the spectacular attacks, paralyses, anesthesias, hypnoid states, etc., which afflicted the hysterics in the era of Charcot, Janet, Breuer, and Freud. Other pathologies have taken over – borderline personality, depression, eating disorders, multiple personality disorder, chronic fatigue syndrome, and the rest. Psychoanalysts themselves, not wanting to be outdone, have discovered new syndromes, each school having its own (the "schizoid personality" of object relations theorists, the "narcissistic personality disorders" of self-psychology). Is not this proof, the objection goes, that the Freudian theory of the mind, despite its claims to universality, is never anything but a local theory, whose fate is tied to a "transient mental illness"[26] corresponding to very specific cultural and historical conditions? It is this constructionist objection that Mitchell's revisionist theory attempts to address, by recentering the entire discussion around Freud's self-analysis: yes, hysteria may well have disappeared from the psychiatric landscape – but this was due solely to Freud's blind spot in this regard. Once this is corrected, one realizes that hysteria was always there, patiently waiting to be seen by Mitchell's "new psychoanalytic theory."

Once again, you can only admire psychoanalysis's recuperative capabilities: not only does it integrate the facts put forward as objections to it, it even manages to make them into mere effects of the theory's own misfires. Still, this Freudocentric explanation of hysteria's disappearance will only convince those for whom the history of psychiatry begins and ends with psychoanalysis. As Mark Micale has shown,[27] hysteria's decline was a European as well as a North American phenomenon, and it occurred during the first decade of the twentieth century, at a time when psychoanalysis still involved only a small number of psychiatrists and patients. Psychoanalysis cannot, therefore, have played the historical role Mitchell attributes to it. If hysteria disappeared, this was partly due to the introduction of new diagnostic categories and to a decline in the use of hypnosis, and partly because patients followed suit, mimetically modeling their symptoms on their physicians' changing expectations.

Mitchell having a mimetic theory of hysteria, she does not ignore this second aspect. "[H]ysteria's 'disappearance,'" she writes, "is also an illustration of its mimetic ability."[28] Unrecognized, male hysteria thus left the hospital and the consultation room, only to reappear in everyday life in the guise of Don Juanism and sexual violence. Female hysteria, too, became a character trait: "femininity." Reviving, though without acknowledging it, the old theory of suggestion, Mitchell even goes so far as to admit that those hysterics who remained on the couch duly mimicked Freud's theories and those of his successors, offering up all the confirmations their analysts desired. For orthodox Freudians, they put on the great Oedipal show: "The hysteric in an Oedipal identification is only imitating."[29] For Lacanians and narrativists, they played the game of chatter and "linguistic mimesis."[30] For "object relations" theorists, they

> mimic[ked] [the object relation] in the clinical setting. It is possible that this object relationship, which is "false," may be channeled into a transference and analysed so that it can be successfully dealt with – but it may just as easily remain a perfect mimicry and be missed.[31]

Mitchell could have deduced from this that in psychoanalysis and psychotherapy one is always dealing with this kind of mimetic ("suggestive") artifact. But Mitchell makes no such deduction. If hysteria disappeared, she argues, it was not because, as a mimetic artifact, it was replaced by other artifacts. It is because it "camouflaged"[32] itself under these other artifacts, all the while remaining *the same* behind the disguise: "[A]ll it has in fact done is change color."[33] In other words, hysteria is not itself an artifact but the truth of all artifacts, enabling one to criticize all those who take the artifact for the thing itself. Mitchell does not doubt for a second that hysteria "exists." It is an absolutely universal and transcultural human "potentiality" that may well be repressed or ignored, but which cannot, as such, disappear:

> Hysteria, with its 4,000 years of recorded history and its worldwide crosscultural presence, is clearly an appropriate representative of those two *bêtes noires* of contemporary, particularly Post-Modern, thought: universalism and essentialism.[34]

How does Mitchell know this? Where has she ever encountered hysteria "itself"? Nowhere. Hysteria being in its essence mimetic, it cannot be identified, nor can it be reduced to one of its historical disguises, to this or that behavior, this or that set of symptoms. As a matter of fact, the hysteria to which Mitchell refers (the Cain complex, the reaction to the identity trauma, etc.) is not some *thing* open to observation: it is a theoretical construct intended to account for a multitude of phenomena among which some have traditionally (that is culturally) been ascribed to hysteria and others not. Specifically, this "hysteria" is the product of a psychoanalytic interpretation that infers the repressed from clues and circumstantial evidence. What assures us, then, that Mitchell's revisionist interpretation is more correct or deeper than those of Freud and/or of her psychoanalytic colleagues?

Mitchell, indeed, does not shy away from correcting Freud's and his successors' case histories, by unearthing the hysteria they failed to recognize. In her first book, she dutifully went about uncovering the hidden Oedipal structure of Laing's and Esterson's case studies in *Sanity, Madness and the Family*.[35] She repeats the same operation in her present book, except this time it is Freud's Oedipal stories that bear the brunt of her attack. Deleuze and Guattari famously reproached Freud for reducing everything to Mummy/Daddy. Mitchell, for her part, reduces everything to little brother/little sister. Dora's problem was not her father, but her brother Otto; for little Hans, it was his sister Hanna; for the Wolf

Man, his sister Anna. To demonstrate this, Mitchell marshals considerable hermeneutic resources and her interpretations are certainly as plausible and convincing as Freud's. They are hardly any *more* convincing, however: given enough biographical information, one could easily repeat the same hermeneutic feat with cousins, the uncle, the maid, or the postman. What would then have been gained? The history of psychoanalysis is one of perpetually conflicting interpretations – libido versus masculine protest, Oedipus versus birth trauma, fantasies of incest versus real sexual abuse, the pre-Oedipal mother versus the symbolic father, etc. – and it is pointless to try to find in these controversies any kind of cumulative development. What is presented as "progress in psychoanalysis" is usually just the most recent interpretation, or the most acceptable in a given institutional, historical, and cultural context.

But what of clinical practice, some will say? Does it not provide "data," "observations" that allow us to decide between competing interpretations? "My material for these reflections," Mitchell writes, "comes largely from a clinical psychoanalytical practice."[36] This is the trump card of every psychoanalyst, seemingly all the more unbeatable as the said "material" is protected by medical confidentiality and thus escapes external scrutiny. In reality, this appeal to clinical practice settles nothing at all, for analytic "observations" are never anything but interpretations transformed into facts, *interprefactions*. On the one hand, it is obvious enough that each psychoanalyst sees in his patient only what he wants to see – "signifiers" if he is Lacanian, "self-defects" if he is Kohutian, traumas if he is neo-Ferenczian. On the other hand, as Mitchell herself acknowledges, patients are only too happy to mimetically confirm their analysts' theories. How then does the hysteria she observed in her patients miraculously escape this co-production of the psychoanalytic data? How can she rule out the possibility that it is nothing but an artifact of her own theories?

Pyschoanalysts are fond of gossiping about the "professional" patients who hop from couch to couch. Mitchell is no exception. At one point, she tells how it happened that a former patient of the well-known Kleinian psychoanalyst Herbert Rosenfeld ended up in her consultation room. Rosenfeld, in a case study devoted to this very patient, had described him as a paranoid homosexual. Mitchell, however, had no trouble detecting a hysteria and an ambivalent relation to a younger brother, both of which had been ignored by Rosenfeld. "For the analyst," she charitably remarks, "the seduction of the mimetic process in which the treatment is imitated is hard to perceive."[37] One admires Mitchell's perceptiveness, but one also regrets that she applies it so selectively to her colleagues. For how can she be so sure that her patient's "hysteria" was not itself a product of the treatment's mimetic process, just like Rosenfeld's "paranoid homosexuality"? She cannot, since the facts she puts forward are produced in exactly the same way – through interprefaction.

Suppose that Rosenfeld's and Mitchell's patient has a go with a third analyst. This analyst, armed with a "brand new psychoanalytic theory," will probably have little difficulty detecting the mimetic seduction of which his colleague

Mitchell was the victim. He will write a new book, using his patient as an example, and the book will be hailed as representing a great progress in psychoanalytic theory. In the meantime, our "zero-patient" will go to a fourth analyst, who in turn . . .

Translated by JENNIFER CHURCH

Notes

1 See Eagle 1993.
2 Mitchell 2000.
3 Mitchell 1974.
4 Mitchell 2000, p. 6.
5 Mitchell 2000, p. 25.
6 The hurried reader may consult Kojève 1980, p. 6.
7 Girard 1977, ch. 7; Borch-Jacobsen 1988.
8 Mitchell 2000, p. 88.
9 Freud 1900, p. 150.
10 Freud 1914a, p. 16.
11 Borch-Jacobsen 1992, for instance p. 60: "The 'other' whose identity is thus incorporated sinks into an oblivion that precedes memory and representation, never having presented itself to any subject," etc.
12 Mitchell 2000, p. 305.
13 Mitchell 2000, p. 316.
14 Herman 1992, p. 177.
15 Janet 1919, vol. 2, pp. 272 ff; Herman 1992, pp. 37, 175, and 177.
16 Mitchell 2000, p. 295.
17 Crews 1995.
18 Mitchell 2000, p. 296.
19 Mitchell 2000, p. 137.
20 Mitchell 2000, p. 145.
21 Thornton 1983; Borch-Jacobsen and Shamdasani 2006, pp. 360–364.
22 Mitchell 2000, p. 325.
23 Mitchell 2000, p. 239.
24 Mitchell 2000, p. 52.
25 Mitchell 2000, p. 110. It is odd that Mitchell lists False Memory Syndrome among contemporary trauma theories as this notion presents itself as a *critique* of said theories.
26 Hacking 1998.
27 Micale 1993a.
28 Mitchell 2000, p. 116.
29 Mitchell 2000, p. 130.
30 Mitchell 2000, p. 122.
31 Mitchell 2000, p. 177.
32 Mitchell 2000, pp. 122, 127.
33 Mitchell 2000, p. 122.
34 Mitchell 2000, p. 118.
35 Laing and Esterson 1964.
36 Mitchell 2000, p. 135.
37 Mitchell 2000, p. 175.

PART IV

Market psychiatry

10 Science of madness, madness of science

Surprise is a rare virtue. Most often, we go about in our familiar world without asking ourselves why things are the way they are. It is only when we travel elsewhere, to another world, that we are suddenly made aware of the strangeness of our own. This is the story told in Montesquieu's *Lettres persannes*: if the Persians' mores seem to us utterly bizarre ("How can one be Persian?"), our own are no less strange in the eyes of the Persians. We need, therefore, to travel to Ispahan to realize the extent to which life in Paris is strange, foreign. This is why we have such need of anthropologists, these modern-day descendants of the explorers of yesteryear. The study of other cultures underlines not only the extent to which these cultures differ from our own, but that we too are other, different, unnatural, in brief, artificial and made. The truth of anthropology is in this moment of return, when the traveler comes back from Ispahan and begins to look at his fellow Parisians with the wide eyes of the Persians. He traveled afar only the better to see himself here, because he knows now that there are as many worlds as there are ways of seeing.

Nowhere is this anthropological lesson more striking than in the realm of mental illness. What could be more terribly real, at first glance, than schizophrenia, depression, bipolar disorder? We all know people in the grip of these afflictions, we recognize their symptoms instantly. And yet, anthropologists who have studied other cultures tell us that people there do not become mad the way we do. For instance, they attribute our "mental" illnesses to causes which to us seem absurd and childish (an evil possession, a theft of the soul, sorcery, an encounter with a certain animal). Madness in these cultures sometimes takes on forms unknown to us. (Anthropologists often cite the Malaysian *amok* and *latah*, the semen loss syndrome in south-west Asia, the *susto* of South America, the Japanese *kitsune-tsuki*.) Better yet, behavior which seems to us unmistakably pathological is considered, in some cultures, perfectly normal or is even valued, such as depression in the Sri Lankan *pilikul bhavana* or the hearing of voices after the death of a spouse among some Native Americans. And it is often from among the mentally ill (from our point of view) that shamans or healers are recruited, as if one needed to be mad, or once to have been so, in order to become a doctor.[1]

Faced with such nonsense, our first reaction is to speak of "belief systems," of a "symbolic manipulation" of the illness (Lévi-Strauss), of "culture-bound syndromes."[2] We know, do we not, that these are mere cultural representations of madness, and that these people suffer, in fact, from disorders due to psychic conflicts or to biochemical imbalances on the neurotransmitter level. But the anthropologist who has lived among these foreign cultures and who has witnessed firsthand the remarkable hardiness of these so-called beliefs knows that this will not do. The worlds of madness and healing are incommensurable, untranslatable. Just try to convince a North African attacked by a *djinn* that what he really suffers from is a fantasy of homosexual penetration. As the French ethno-psychiatrist Tobie Nathan has pointed out, to the outcry of his psychoanalytic and psychiatric colleagues in Paris, there is no point trying to treat Third World immigrants with a system of psychiatry which has no more reality for them than their healing practices have for us.[3] Viewed from a North African, Yoruba, or Bambara perspective, our scientific psychiatry is nothing but the Western ethnic group's "belief system." Hence the anthropologist's misgivings: what if the North Africans were right, after all? What if our propensity to universalize our psychiatric categories was nothing but an insidious form of colonialism?

Our anthropologist has lost his "asymmetric" certitude, to use David Bloor's term.[4] Once back home, he decides to be surprised "symmetrically" by our scientific psychiatry, by refraining from seeing in it the truth (objective, universal) of indigenous beliefs (local, cultural, and variable). He sets out to study the world of psychiatry with the same perplexed detachment that he adopted vis-à-vis the North African or Bambara worlds of madness, neither believing in it himself nor viewing it as a mere belief. He will, for example, share the life (and the medications) of the "clients" of a psychiatric outpatient clinic, as Sue Estroff has done.[5] He observes how one diagnoses (and creates) Post-Traumatic Stress Disorder in Veterans Health Administration psychiatric facilities, like Allan Young.[6] He follows how case records of schizophrenic patients are written (constructed) at a psychiatric hospital in Melbourne, as Robert Barrett has.[7] Or again, as Tanya Lurhmann has just done in a book remarkable in its scope,[8] he undertakes to describe how psychiatrists are trained in the United States.

Tanya Luhrmann's father is a psychiatrist, which leads her to describe herself at the beginning of her book as a "halfie." A "halfie," in the anthropologists' jargon, is someone who studies professionally her own ethnic group. "Being one," Luhrmann writes, "gives you a little edge, because you grew up speaking the language of the world you later describe."[9] But one could just as easily say the opposite: a "halfie" suffers in fact from a huge handicap, because she must first unlearn the language of her tribe in order to better reconstitute its grammar, its implicit laws, its rules of construction.

This is no small task. Luhrmann, then a Professor of Anthropology at the University of San Diego, spent nearly ten years studying how American psychiatrists learn to speak of madness and how in doing so they construe and construct it. She was a participant observer in residency training at two large universities, one public, the other private. She visited an elite psychoanalytically oriented treatment center, a day treatment center, and a hospital inpatient unit where chronic and underprivileged patients were treated, and many more psychiatric facilities besides. She interviewed dozens of residents at different stages of their training, as well as senior psychiatrists, psychoanalysts, hospital administrators, and scientists at elite research units. She religiously attended the annual meetings of the American Psychiatric Association, the Society for Biological Psychiatry, and the American Psychoanalytical Association. She went to lectures and participated in seminars along with other students. She familiarized herself with the admissions interview, the diagnosis, the team meeting, and the emergency room. She learned how to prescribe psychotropic medications. And because she had been assured that you cannot understand psychoanalysis from the outside, she spent three years on the analyst's couch before seeing clients herself under the supervision of no less than four trained supervisors. In brief, she became a member of the tribe.

Why focus on the training of psychiatrists, rather than on other aspects of our contemporary world of madness? Luhrmann explains it well: because in studying the way in which psychiatrists learn to see (or not to see) madness, one can follow how this "X" takes form in our culture. Indeed, madness does not exist apart from the ways of seeing it. That is to say not that madness is purely a social construction or something invented by psychiatrists (Luhrmann rightly rejects this antipsychiatric romanticism), but rather that this "X," madness, interacts with the theories and practices that deal with it.

It is not a matter of indifference for a mad person whether he is to be considered possessed by a spirit of a neighboring tribe, regarded as a shaman, or thought to be suffering from an excess of dopamine in the brain. These various theories, and the expectations that come with them (from both patients and doctors), produce, quite literally, different beings: the destiny of an American "schizophrenic" treated with Stelazine® or Risperdal® will not be the same as that of his peer, the Thonga "fool of Gods," deemed healed after having passed through a trance of exorcism;[10] nor will it follow that of the Buriat shaman, a person revered and respected by the entire community.[11] Little does it matter that we Westerners believe ourselves to have found, with our psychotropic drugs, a way of treating the real causes of psychoses. The fact is that the administration of these drugs modifies their recipients no less than do the ritualistic practices of the Thongas of Mozambique or the Buriats of Siberia.

This is what interests our symmetrical anthropologist, who has decided once and for all to no longer divide the world into true (scientific) and false (mythical) representations of reality. For her, seeing (theorizing) reality does not passively reflect it; it manipulates it and transforms it at the very moment it purports to represent it. Sometimes it even creates reality, as in these bizarre "transient mental illnesses"[12] (Ian Hacking) that appear and disappear at the whim of psychiatric theories – Charcot's "grand hysteria," multiple personality disorder, chronic fatigue syndrome, to name a few. To observe how psychiatrists learn to see madness is to follow how they make and mold it.

The problem is that contemporary psychiatry sees double. On the one hand, it views mental illness as a malady of the mind (one no longer dare say "of the soul") that ought to be treated with talk therapy, empathy, and human rapport. On the other hand, it views it as a disease of the brain comparable to other organic diseases and treatable with medication. It's an old story. Western psychiatry has always been torn between the *Psychiker* and the *Somatiker*, the psychodynamically inclined and the biologically oriented, each camp having the upper hand in turn. It all began with the "moral treatment" of the first psychiatrists, and their touching therapeutic activism. Then came the era of degeneration theory, brain anatomy, and asylums overflowing with chronically ill patients. In the twentieth century, the pendulum swung back toward psychotherapy, culminating in the stunning takeover of American psychiatry (and culture) by émigré psychoanalysts between the late 1940s and the 1960s. This was the time of Hitchcock's *Psycho*, when everyone was convinced that schizophrenia was the fault of maddening "refrigerator mothers." Then the pendulum swung back again in the other direction, when the psychopharmacological revolution of the 1950s began to bear fruits and the pharmaceutical industry flooded the market with ever more promising and specific psychotropic drugs. The latest news is that the gene of schizophrenia has been located somewhere on the chromosome 6pter-p22.[13]

When Luhrmann began her research, these two versions of psychiatry coexisted on somewhat equal terms. Some days, the residents she accompanied would attend lectures given by men in white medical coats who would teach them the alphabet of neurotransmitters and chemical compounds: catecholamines, dopamine, serotonin, reserpine, imipramine, chlorpromazine. Other days, they would listen as men in tweed jackets spoke softly to them of psychological stressors, trauma, repression, therapeutic alliance. The language of the men in white was that which was mostly spoken in hospitals, in those places where you need to be able to quickly diagnose the delusional or suicidal patients who walk in, and prescribe the appropriate drug to quiet them down. The language of the men in tweed was dominant in outpatient clinics whose clientele were more or less "stabilized" with drugs, as well as in clinics for wealthy patients and in private psychiatric practice. It is to Luhrmann's credit that she did not ask herself, as everyone else did, which of these languages is better or closer to the truth. Instead, she has described – admirably and at great length – the types of people and society they have created.

For the men in white, things are straightforward (if infinitely complex in their detail): mental illness is a disease of the brain that manifests itself in well-defined symptoms treatable with specific medications. Give chlorpromazine to a schizophrenic, and he will no longer hear the voices that persecute him. Give lithium to a person suffering from bipolar disorder, and she will no longer oscillate between periods of manic elation and bottomless depression. What more can you expect? What matters therefore is finding chemical compounds targeting the biochemical processes implicated in each disease, a task undertaken by laboratory researchers who are more likely to spend their days looking into Petri dishes or handling rats than seeing sick patients.

As for the clinicians, their role is to apply this science of the mind to actual psychiatric practice, using standard diagnostic criteria from the latest edition of the *Diagnostic and Statistical Manual of Mental Disorders* (the much referred to "DSM") to determine which medications to prescribe and in what dosage. No one worries too much that these criteria are often the product of fleeting consensus and shifting politics among psychiatrists, or that the introduction of new medications onto the market causes in turn a general reshuffling of clinical categories. The premise is that the men in white are discovering the specific causes of diseases having an established objective reality.

The relationship between the doctor and the patient is brief, distant. Once symptoms are under control, the patient is released. No stigmatization of the patient, since the disease is as distinct from him as a virus or the bleeding object that Philippine healers extract from the bodies of their clients. Admittedly, the medications will cause all kinds of very noticeable side effects that will clearly single out the patient as mentally ill, even though his original symptoms may have been alleviated; but how is this any different from other disabled persons? At no moment throughout this process does the doctor's personality come into play. Nor that of the patient, her personal history, the way she experiences and narrates her illness. Nor is any attention given to the social, familial, or professional context in which the illness occurs.

For the men in tweed, on the other hand, everything is a matter of personality and context. The patient, they say, does not *have* a disease. He *is* ill, in the sense that his illness is inseparable from his personal history, his relationship with his parents, family, and friends, his inner conflicts, the traumatic events that he lived through; in brief, all that made him who he is. The treatment is therefore long (and expensive), since it is the patient's personality that must be changed: one or even several years of inpatient care in a clinic; much longer still in the case of outpatient psychotherapy. Everything revolves around the relationship between the patient and the doctor (or the psychiatric team), conceived as the "transferential" and "countertransferential" arena where the patient's dysfunctional patterns of behavior are repeated and modified. Why did the patient react so strongly to a passing remark made by the therapist? But also, and perhaps more importantly: why did the therapist make this remark? Is it not because he knew, in the unconscious, that it would provoke such a reaction?

Convinced that their hidden motivations can play a negative role in the therapeutic relationship, the men in tweed pay as much attention, if not more, to their own feelings as to the patient's. They have strange rituals designed to purify their soul of its demons, with the idea that it is in healing the doctor that one treats the patient. They deliberately make themselves sick, somewhat in the way that certain South American shamans intoxicate themselves with tobacco juice during their apprenticeship.[14] They follow long years of treatment with an older doctor, called a training analyst, who becomes for them a strictly taboo character (they may even avoid pronouncing his name aloud) and toward whom they develop intensely ambivalent feelings that they minutely dissect with a sort of morose delight. This, they explain, enables them to better understand the lesson they hope to inculcate in their patients: whatever the difficulties of existence, we are all responsible for our own feelings. The aim of psycho-therapy is to learn to assume responsibility for who we are. As it is expressed in a case record cited by Luhrmann: "Over the course of the meetings with me over the months, Ms. Deever has demonstrated an increased capacity to experience her symptoms as the result of psychological stressors rather than biochemical imbalances."[15]

One could hardly imagine an approach more different from that of the men in white. As a matter of fact, the two camps have long battled in institutions, in professional journals, and sometimes even in court. Consider the case of Rafael Osheroff, a 42-year-old internist, who was hospitalized in 1979 for depression at the Chestnut Lodge clinic, well known for its psychoanalytic approach. Under psychotherapeutic treatment, his condition deteriorated rapidly. Faced with the clinic's repeated refusals to change the course of treatment, Osheroff's family decided after seven months to transfer him to another clinic, where he was immediately given a phenotiazine and a tricyclic antidepressant. His condition improved within three weeks, and after three months he was able to resume a normal life. (Ten years later, he had still not suffered a relapse.) Osheroff filed a lawsuit against Chestnut Lodge, which was settled out of court in 1987. According to the men in white who took his side, the doctors at Chestnut Lodge had committed malpractice in depriving their patient of the benefits of science. For the men in tweed, on the other hand, nothing proved that Osheroff's cure was due to the drugs he had been given. After all, it might well have been an expression of his negative transference toward the Chestnut Lodge medical team (in other words, a symptom). Clearly, the two sides were not speaking about the same thing.

And yet, until relatively recently, this ideological polarization did not prevent the two approaches from being taught simultaneously and coexisting in prac-tice, the same psychiatrists donning alternatively a white coat or a tweed jacket, depending on the case. There is good reason for this. One would have to be a particularly rigid Freudian not to realize that it is easier (not to mention more humane) to practice psychotherapy on a patient stabilized with medication than on someone who is in direct communication with Mars or who cuts his veins for no apparent reason. (The psychiatric historian Gladys Swain even suggests that psychoanalysis, paradoxically, would never have penetrated psychiatry as it did during the 1950s and 1960s without the covert support of psychotropic drugs.)[16] Conversely, as Luhrmann notes, a psychopharmacolo-gically oriented psychiatrist will know all the better how to prescribe the appropriate medication since he will have learned during his psychotherapeutic training to pay attention to the context and clinical details of each individual case. Moreover, psychotherapeutic follow-up of stabilized patients is indispensable to help them face their many problems and, above all, to make sure they take their medications (hated by most of them because of their side effects). It is not surprising, therefore, that most of the psychiatrists interviewed by Luhrmann told her that the biological and psychodynamic approaches work best in combination.

If this dual approach is favorable to patients, then why is it in the process of coming undone? Over a period of ten years, Luhrmann was in a position to observe how the men in white everywhere replaced the men in tweed, to the point of reducing them to an endangered tribe. Psychodynamic psychiatry is taught less and less; services offering psychotherapy are closed overnight and psychoanalysts are being sent pink slips like common steel workers; outpatient clinics are going bankrupt one after another. Here again, Luhrmann eschews the easy, asymmetric explanation that would consist in saying that the men in white won because they had science on their side. Instead, she cites the harsh law of capitalism applied through HMOs and managed care, as the cause of the demise of the men in tweed. At a time when the only thing that matters is the cost-effectiveness of health care, how can anyone justify the interminable psychoanalytic treatments (and the indirect financing of the doctor's no less interminable analysis) when a simple pill can fix up the patient within days? If you are a hospital administrator competing with other hospitals for a contract with an insurance company, you are probably not going to hesitate to get rid of your psychotherapy section. As for many psychiatrists, reduced to merely filling out prescriptions, if not to the role of secretary, hanging on the phone to obtain authorization for drug treatment, it is only too easy for them to justify their professional existence by opting for a "hard," ideological version of the psychopharmacological model. The more one treats patients with medication, the more one comes to see mental illness as just another disease like the flu, and the more the psychodynamic approach seems pointless and obsolete.

Luhrmann's analysis is undeniably accurate and convincing, but the logic of the bottom line does not explain everything. As she herself points out, in the end it would be more cost-effective for insurance companies to favor a combination of the two approaches than to cover the costs of the revolving-door hospitalizations of patients who do not take their medications because of a lack of psychotherapeutic follow-up. Besides, the statistics are very far from establishing the 100 percent success of psychotropic drugs. Even lithium, which comes closest to the model of the "magic bullet," only works in 80 percent of cases for patients suffering from bipolar disorder. Approximately 30 percent of schizophrenics recover sooner or later without their recovery being clearly related to one type of treatment or another. Conversely, the relapse rate for those schizophrenics treated with antipsychotics is 40 percent after two years – exactly the same rate, according to one study cited by Luhrmann, as that of patients being treated in family therapy!

When one turns toward depression, an illness whose explosion since the 1960s corresponds exactly to the introduction of antidepressants, the numbers are even more ambiguous: antidepressants are demonstrably more effective in only one-third of cases, the remaining two-thirds showing no improvement at all or responding as well to a placebo. As soon as one considers the shifting field of the former "neuroses" – depression, but also obsessive-compulsive disorder, panic attacks, etc. – most outcome studies show that psychotropic medications are no more effective than psychotherapy.

How is it, then, that the biomedical approach uniformly wipes out psychotherapy with the vigor of a weedkiller? The response lies in the way in which therapeutic efficacy is measured and demonstrated in modern medicine. Indeed, how does one establish whether a treatment is effective? One conducts a double-blind randomized placebo-controlled trial, or RCT as it is known in the trade: neither doctors nor patients know who is taking the medicine being tested and who is being given a sugar pill devoid of any (known) specific effect. The goal of this experimental model, which was first used to test antibiotics, is to smoke out the so-called "placebo effect," that is to say non-specific improvement caused by the mere administration of a treatment. Only if the medicine being tested is more powerful than the placebo is its effectiveness considered proven. Since 1962, when Congress mandated the US Food and Drug Administration to submit medications being placed on the market to rigorous testing, RCTs have become the universal standard for measuring potential therapies, as much in the USA as in the rest of the world. It is to RCTs that the flow of research grants is directed; it is RCTs that determine which products are going to make it onto the market (financial analysts with pharmaceutical companies call them the "pipeline"); and it is of course these same RCTs that insurance companies invoke to disqualify any treatment whose efficacy has not been proven. In practical terms, a reimbursable treatment is one that has been shown to outperform its competitors in an RCT.

In this high-stakes game, the men in white beat their colleagues in tweed each and every time. Because of the regulation of the drug market, no psychotropic medication comes out of the pharmaceutical pipeline without support from statistical analyses and rating scales. The men in tweed, on the other hand, have for a long time haughtily rejected the idea that their craft could be measured in numbers, so that they were caught flatfooted when the wave of managed care unfurled over their discipline. Since then, they have churned out outcome studies and meta-analyses in an attempt to make up ground, but the results have only been to sink even lower in the eyes of insurance managers. Overall, everyone agrees that psychotherapy is beneficial to patients and that it is better than no therapy at all. The problem is that this cannot be proven the way a medication proves its superiority over other treatments in an RCT.

Not only does psychotherapy never outdo psychotropic medications in terms of efficacy, but no one type of psychodynamic treatment – and there are plenty – appears to be better than another:[17] a classic Freudian analysis at $20,000 per year achieves no more than common or garden group therapy. The inevitable conclusion that emerges from these studies is therefore that the efficacy of these psychodynamic treatments comes from the same non-specific factor that experimenters call the placebo effect (in the old days, one spoke of "suggestion").

However, the placebo effect is exactly what these double-blind trials are designed to eliminate. In experimental logic, it matters little that people improve when taking a placebo if one cannot prove why they improve. No matter how real, these cures or improvements are purely and simply dismissed as mere artifacts, false cures (no one stops to wonder what percentage of the placebo effect enters into the "true" cures).[18] It is this process of disqualification that is ordinarily called "scientific progress": the experimental method is made to produce "hard," incontrovertible facts that present themselves as the only possible explanation and send "bad" explanations to the cemetery of pseudo- or pre-scientific theories. But when the experimental method's "all or nothing" logic is applied to a field as soft as psychiatry and is combined, in addition, with the logic of the bottom line, the result is an aberration: only medical treatments that are able to demonstrate why and how they are effective are reimbursed, and thus survive. Everyone knows that psychotherapy does yield results, but these are dismissed as mere placebo effect (read: charlatanism). Everyone also knows that antipsychotics and antidepressants are not, in practice, specific medications, because they often act on several pathologies at once and their effectiveness depends on the context in which they are administered. And yet, it is these treatments that are retained because they are the only ones to submit themselves to the same type of testing as specific medications such as antibiotics.

Viewed from the asymmetric perspective of science, this process of elimination of artifacts can only be applauded. From the point of view of the symmetrical anthropologist, who does not concern herself with the truth-value of the theories and practices she describes, the victory of the men in white over the men in tweed is quite simply an environmental disaster of major proportion. The first effect of the psychopharmacological revolution was the closing of most psychiatric hospitals during the 1970s to the benefit of outpatient clinics and community-based alternatives. As long as patients stabilized on medications were given follow-up psychotherapy, this system worked more or less (at least where these programs managed to survive the brutal budget cuts of the Reagan Administration). But at present, with psychotherapy in all its forms disappearing from the psychiatric landscape, patients are left on their own, without any safety net. Luhrmann describes a barbaric system where patients are brought to the hospital in a crisis, medicated, then returned to the streets at the end of the brief admission period authorized by insurance companies, often before having even been stabilized. In the absence of any therapeutic follow-up, the patients hasten to throw away their medications and plunge again into a state of delusion or depression, living on the streets until they are sent back to hospital (usually a different one from the first). There they are once again medicated (by doctors who do not know which drugs they have already received), and so it goes.

Suicides are frequent. Sometimes, according to Luhrmann, the police hand out bus tickets to the mentally ill to go and get treated elsewhere, in another county or another state: thus do we export the mentally ill of our times, not unlike the Renaissance practice of herding the mad into the "Ships of Fools" immortalized by Hieronymus Bosch. Very often, the mentally ill end up in jail after having stolen something to eat from a supermarket or having threatened someone in the street. Statistics recently cited on a program broadcast by Minnesota Public Radio, *Jailing the Mentally Ill*, give an appalling summary of the situation. In 1950, the average daily number of patients in US state and county mental hospitals was 592,853. In 1994, there were no more than 71,619.[19] What better proof, some would say, that the new science of the mind benefits the patients? But consider this statistic from the Justice Department: in 1999, there were 283,000 inmates with a serious mental illness in American jails, that is to say 1 in 6 prisoners.[20] The truth is that prisons in the USA have, to a large extent, replaced asylums. The psychopharmacological revolution, which was supposed to liberate the mentally ill and return them to a relatively normal life, has ended up, in a perverse paradox, creating a population of homeless people, drifters, and prisoners, just as in the days before the creation of psychiatry.

Luhrmann is shocked, and understandably so. The symmetrical anthropologist, when all is said and done, cannot remain neutral vis-à-vis her own culture, because she belongs to it. This is the ultimate truth of anthropology: once one has seen oneself through the eyes of the other, once one has become unfamiliar to oneself, one knows that one can change, become other than one is. In the last part of her book, Luhrmann drops her role of observer to caution against the evolution of American psychiatry toward an exclusively biomedical model. Patients, she argues, were much better off when psychiatrists paid as much attention to the way in which they experience their illness as to the disease itself. They were kept track of and assisted. They took their medications (most of the time). They were treated humanely, as persons, and because of this could experience themselves as free agents responsible for themselves, despite their illness, despite their dependence on drugs, despite the crippling side effects of these medications.

On this last point, however, I wonder if the "halfie" in Luhrmann does not fall into an ethnocentric trap, as if the notions of "person" and "responsibility" and "autonomy" were self-evident and were not themselves historical and transient. After all, a large number of patients support the biomedical model and make it known through their advocacy groups, such as the National Alliance for the Mentally Ill: they *want* to be considered as suffering from a disease like any other, not as people responsible (in all senses) for their illness. Why not pay attention to what they say, the same way the ethnographer listens to a mentally ill African when he insists he is possessed by a spirit? Why necessarily impose on our mentally ill the often guilt-producing model of psychological insight and psychotherapeutic self-fashioning? One can very well advocate a non-exclusively biomedical approach to illness without buying into the ideology of psychotherapy in its American version – and certainly without reducing it all to Freudian psychoanalysis, as Luhrmann tends too much to do. It is one thing to praise the psychodynamic approach for its attention to the context and the subjective experience of mental illness; it is something else entirely to credit Freud, and Freud alone, for having taught us to see humans "as complex psychological organisms who generate layers of meaning which lie beneath the surface of their understanding,"[21] to quote with Luhrmann the prose of philosopher-psychoanalyst Jonathan Lear. On that score, Stendhal, Dostoevsky, and Proust also have their claims! Psychoanalysis is only one psychotherapy among others and it does not have a monopoly over meaning, complexity, and human rapport, contrary to what many of its advocates would have us believe.

It is understandable that Luhrmann focused mainly on psychoanalysis, in view of its historical importance in American psychiatry. But there was no reason for her to absorb uncritically the Freudocentric vision of psychoanalysts; on this point the symmetrical anthropologist displayed much naivety vis-à-vis her native informers and their self-serving legends. As she herself points out, the psychoanalysts' theoretical and therapeutic claims fare neither better nor worse than those of their colleagues practicing, say, family, interpersonal, or cognitive-behavioral therapy. As the Dodo says in *Alice in Wonderland*, "*Everybody* has won, and *all* must have prizes."[22] And if all win, that means that no one wins for the reasons he invokes to stand out from the others. In the end, what matters seems to be this "non-specific" element that the men in white are trying so desperately to eliminate from their experiments: the therapeutic rapport, the (social) bond between a suffering person and another who is trying to give help to that person. It is neither more psychoanalysis nor even more *psycho*therapy that American psychiatry needs in order to become humane. It is more therapy, period.

Translated by JENNIFER CHURCH

Notes

1 Pouillon 1975.
2 Lévi-Strauss 1974 [1958], p. 221.
3 Nathan 1994.
4 Bloor 1976.
5 Estroff 1981. The reading of this book ought to be mandatory for all psychiatric students.
6 Young 1995.

7 Barrett 1996.
8 Luhrmann 2000.
9 Luhrman 2000, p. 3.
10 Junot 1936, pp. 420–455.
11 Hamayon 1978.
12 Hacking 1998.
13 Shengbiao Wang *et al.* 1995, pp. 41–46.
14 See Sebag 1965.
15 Luhrmann 2000, p. 147.
16 See "Chimie, cerveau, esprit et société" in Swain 1994.
17 See the now classic studies of Luborsky *et al.* 1975 and Luborsky 1986.
18 Philippe Pignarre makes this point in Pignarre 1997, pp. 33–35.
19 Kiessler and Sibulkin 1999.
20 Bureau of Justice 1999.
21 Lear 1995, p. 24.
22 Caroll 1970, p. 49. The reference comes initially from Rosenzweig 1936 and has been taken up by Lester Luborsky, who speaks in this regard of the "Dodo hypothesis."

11 The great depression

We all know how it happens. One day, without warning, the person feels oddly removed from things, from people, as if an invisible wall of glass were separating her from them. They go about their business but, for a reason that escapes her, none of it any longer concerns her. She could call out, but what would be the point? She isn't worth it, and the friendly overtures of others, out there, come as justified reproaches. Day by day, the wall grows a little thicker. Soon, she is no longer able to leave the house, her bedroom, her bed. The only thing she is left with is the pain of existing. She no longer eats. She no longer bathes or sleeps. She is agitated and exhausted all at once. She keeps thinking of the barbiturates, of the razor that would allow her to cut short the terrible insomnia. Life has become a waiting room for death. Sometimes she kills herself. Sometimes she recovers.

This person, we know her well. We've all read her story in recent autobiographies, or in the innumerable newspaper articles devoted to this strange illness. She is a relative, a neighbor, a colleague. Perhaps tomorrow her story will be ours: depression, it is said, strikes one woman in five, and one man in ten.[1] Its prevalence among the world's population at any given moment is of the order of 3 percent.[2] One in six depressed people commits suicide.[3] These implacable statistics toll like a funeral bell.

Fortunately, however, we are told on all sides that depression is no longer a fate. Antidepressant drugs have been around since the mid-1950s, and the new generation – the selective serotonin re-uptake inhibitors (or SSRIs) – work wonders. Under the influence of Prozac®, Zoloft®, or Paxil® (Seroxat®), people for whom existence had been an unbearable burden suddenly find renewed pleasure in life, without having to suffer the unpleasant side-effects of the older generation of antidepressants, the tricyclics and the MAOIs (monoamine oxidase inhibitors). Admittedly, SSRIs sometimes lead to diminished libido and even, among men, to impotence, but that is surely a small price to pay for a restored capacity for happiness. Not to mention that Prozac® also causes weight loss, at least at the beginning. Twenty million people worldwide are now thought to be taking Prozac® and we are hearing reports of a new era of "cosmetic psychopharmacology," in which drugs will be used to treat not only clinical depression, but daily mood swings and existential angst. Farewell Kierkegaard and Heidegger, hello "Brave New World."

There is a problem, however, with this therapeutic optimism. If it is indeed true that antidepressants cure depression, how is it that the illness is spreading ever more widely? Three books by David Healy, Alain Ehrenberg, and Philippe Pignarre[4] forcefully underscore the incongruous fact that depression was never so prevalent as it has been since the introduction of antidepressants. Make no mistake: depression has always been with us, though it went by other names and sometimes assumed different shapes, depending on the era. From Hippocrates to modern psychiatry, "melancholia" – that is, depressive *psychosis*, or "endogenous" depression – is described in remarkably consistent terms. Yet until very recently this type of depression was considered extraordinarily rare. David Healy notes that in the North Wales Psychiatric Hospital between 1900 and 1945, only fifty of one million patients were admitted for melancholia.[5] Today, by comparison, 948 of every million admissions to psychiatric hospitals are for "depresssion," of which 268 are considered severely melancholic or psychotic.[6]

Even more striking, in the mid-1950s, when the Swiss psychiatrist Roland Kuhn discovered the antidepressant effects of imipramine on some of his patients suffering from "endogenous" depression, the pharmaceutical company Geigy at first declined to finance the drug's development, judging the market to be too small.[7] Less than forty years later, in 1994, Prozac® was the second bestselling medication worldwide, just behind the ulcer drug Zantac®.[8] In the meantime, depression's rise had been irresistible. In 1971, the psychiatrist Heinz Lehmann estimated that there were 100 million cases worldwide.[9] In the USA alone, the number of consultations leading to prescriptions for antidepressants jumped from 2.5 million to 4.7 million between 1980 and 1989.[10] In France, the number rose sevenfold between 1970 and 1996,[11] and no fewer than 14 million prescriptions for antidepressants were recorded in 1994.[12] The World Health Organization predicts that depression will soon become the second largest public health problem – the largest is heart disease. "What we are witnessing," Pignarre writes, "is a veritable epidemic of depression."[13] Yet as far as anyone knows, there is no such thing as a virus causing depression. How, then, did the handful of melancholic patients in the 1950s become the millions of the 1990s?

A number of explanations present themselves, the most frequently heard being of the realist type: depression has always been around, we are told; it's just that the advances of science have enabled us to recognize it more easily. In 1956, when Roland Kuhn made his discovery, he thought he had found a molecule that acted specifically on "endogenous" or biological depression, to the exclusion of depressive neuroses attributable to an "exogenous" or psychological cause. Very quickly, however, pharmacological research called this distinction into question by showing that other molecules were just as effective in alleviating both types of depression. From there it was only a short step to the idea that one and the same biochemical dysfunction was at work in all cases of depression, and that it could be treated with well-targeted psychotropic drugs.

Simply by switching molecules and observing their effects, researchers began to discern the outlines of a new and ever-expanding psychiatric entity, "depression," side by side with schizophrenia and manic depression (also called bipolar disorder). Since the different families of antidepressants also proved effective in treating all sorts of other pathologies, it was concluded that these illnesses "masked" depression (lazy reasoning, for one might just as well have concluded that the drugs were not anti-*depressants*). Thus other conditions were successively annexed to depression: panic attacks, anxiety, bulimia, obsessive-compulsive disorders, social phobia (what used to be called shyness), autism, Tourette's syndrome, incontinence, neurological, cancerous, gastric and neck pain, migraines, Post-Traumatic Stress Disorder, alcoholism, tobacco and heroin addiction, constipation, hair loss, and hypersensitivity to cold. Under the impact of antidepressants, not only was the distinction between the psychoses and the neuroses (and, by the same token, the professional niche of psychoanalysts) erased, but also that between psychiatry and general medicine. Everything has become depression, because every condition responds to antidepressants, the new panacea.

There is, of course, another, more cynical explanation for the seemingly limitless expansion of the diagnosis: that it profits the pharmaceutical industry, the tireless supplier of new antidepressant drugs. Not so long ago, when a psychiatrist wanted to promote a new diagnostic category or treatment, he had to convince his colleagues and patients in a piecemeal fashion, with the help of a great many scientific reports and a fair amount of backslapping. These days, psychiatric disorders and their appropriate medication are packaged and sold together by pharmaceutical companies, who spare nothing to ensure that their research investments are profitable. There was no market for antidepressants in 1956? Never mind, the pharmaceutical industry would create one from scratch. In the early 1960s, seeking to publicize the antidepressant properties of amitriptyline, the pharmaceutical company Merck bought 50,000 copies of a book called *Recognizing the Depressed Patient*,[14] by Frank Ayd, a psychiatrist, and generously distributed them among other psychiatrists and doctors worldwide. Ayd's thesis was that depression, far from being confined to asylums, could equally well be diagnosed in general medical wards and primary care surgeries. As Healy puts it, "Merck not only sold amitriptyline, it sold an idea."[15]

Since then, countless public health campaigns have alerted general practitioners and the public to the necessity for recognizing the signs of depression, investigations have been conducted into its social and economic costs, special series on the subject have appeared in magazines, and TV ads unabashedly touted the virtues of the latest SSRIs – all of this financed, directly or indirectly, by the pharmaceutical industry. Doctors, public opinion leaders, and journalists have not been bought off by the depression cartel:[16] everyone is genuinely convinced that he or she is echoing the most recent advances in science. It just so happens that the industry's money is spent on researching this molecule rather than that one, this clinical trial rather than some other one, or is allotted to this particular psychiatry department, this conference, this epidemiological study.

No wonder that the only theories that survive this Darwinian process are those that interest the industry. We know, for example, that approximately one-third of all depressed patients respond positively to a placebo, no matter how serious their depression (in the case of women presenting a single episode of depression, the rate jumps to 66.7 percent).[17] Even so, no one is financing studies on the role of non-specific factors in the treatment of depression, because there is no market for placebos. It is only in establishing a strong, "specific" link between their product and this or that depressive pathology that pharmaceutical companies can claim to outdo their competitors – hence the constant redefinition of depression as one new drug after another is launched on the market. Healy summarizes the situation neatly:

> Given the many revisions of psychiatric nosology during the last thirty years, it is clearly a mistake to think that mental illnesses have an established reality and that the role of a drug company is to find the key that fits a predetermined lock ... we are at present in a state where companies can not only seek to find the key for the lock but can dictate a great deal of the shape of the lock to which a key must fit.[18]

The logic of capitalism does not explain everything, however. Indeed, why is it depression that has taken hold, rather than some other pathology? The industry might just as well have decided to promote anxiety, as it did during the 1960s, with "tranquilizers" (benzodiazepines) such as Librium® and Valium®. It is tempting, therefore, to look elsewhere for an explanation for the steady rise of depression in the market for psychiatric disorders. If more and more people are depressed, might it not be because we live in a society that is more and more depressing? Left-leaning commentators often argue that the pharmaceutical industry has over-medicalized a real social misery, created by the stress of modern life, the loss of identity markers, the isolation of the individual, unemployment, and so on. This argument is not new: at the end of the nineteenth century, George Miller Beard was already associating "neurasthenia" with the "nervous fatigue" brought on by the pressure of living in large American cities. The problem with this explanation is that it explains nothing. Even supposing that society is more inhuman than in the past, when socialized medicine and unemployment benefits did not yet exist, why would this give rise to depression rather than anguish, fatigue, "nervous breakdown," or just plain anger?

Alain Ehrenberg, a sociologist, attempts to answer this question in *La fatigue d'être soi*, subtitled *Dépression et société*. Retracing in detail the history of depression since the 1950s (mainly in France), he shows very well how it ceased to be defined in terms of sadness and psychic pain, and came to be perceived more and more as a pathology of action. The new *déprimé* lacks energy, is unable to "perform," is inhibited in his work and his relationships with others. He suffers, the psychiatrists say, from "psychomotor retardation."

And this new pathology emerges, as if by chance, in a society that values individual responsibility and initiative above all else. Just as Freudian neuroses, laden with guilt, were the pathology of a *subject* defined by prohibition and internal conflict, so contemporary depression is "the reverse of the sovereign *individual*, of the man who believes himself to be the author of his own life." [19] In that sense, depression is not directly provoked or caused by contemporary society. Rather, Ehrenberg suggests, it is the negative "counterpart" to the subjectivity created and so highly valorized in this society.

In the last analysis, however, Ehrenberg continues to interpret depression's historical progression as a simple *reflection* – even if inverted and over-determined – of changes in society, so losing sight of the link between the epidemic of depression and the marketing of antidepressants. He notes that the characterization of depressed patients in terms of inhibition and psychomotor retardation "established itself at the very same moment that new antidepressants were launched on the market, most of which were effective on these inadequacies." [20] But for him, this co-invention of the new depression and new antidepressants remains a pure coincidence, as if the development of the drugs opportunely reflected the rise of a condition that itself reflected the transformations of "*fin-de-siècle* individuality." Why not admit, inversely, that in this case something social has been *produced* by the invention of antidepressants: that if depression has spread to the point of becoming a social phenomenon, it is because *it is that on which antidepressants have an effect?*

This is the solution Philippe Pignarre proposes. If the new depression is thriving, it is because the new antidepressants that target it are effective and, above all, more practical than tranquilizers and the first generation of antidepressants. The "happy pills" of the 1960s were highly addictive, and the tricyclics and the MAOIs had all sorts of unpleasant side-effects. The SSRIs, on the other hand, are no more effective, but they have the immense advantage of presenting few side effects. [21] We should not be surprised, therefore, if general practitioners prescribe them readily, or if patients ask for more. Who cares that these drugs only mask depression if they allow the patient to be "functional"? Who would be masochistic enough to undergo a long and costly psychoanalysis, with uncertain results, when all you need to do is go to the family doctor to get your dose of well-being? As Pignarre points out, "the new psychiatry would not have triumphed so rapidly were it not for the patients' consent and silent collaboration." [22]

Antidepressants, in other words, "recruit" depressives, and do so because they work. Each new antidepressant that is launched on the market must first go through controlled trials intended to prove that it is more effective than a placebo and a competitor drug. In order to pass these tests successfully, the proposed medication must yield significantly better results among a group of patients who have been selected *because they present a pathology likely to respond to this drug*. As Pignarre shows, it is already at this early stage that patients are recruited. Each new molecule, if it is effective, creates a new group of patients, defined by the effects it produces on its members: depressives needing stimulation, depressives needing to be tranquilized, anxious depressives, aggressive depressives, etc. The creation of new pathologies begins there, before spreading throughout society as the drug penetrates the market and recruits (regroups) ever increasing numbers of "clients."

This presupposes, however, that the new medication has indeed been able to prove its efficacy: the force of Pignarre's argument is that it never reduces the epidemic of depression to a mere illusion, to an effect of marketing or a pale ideological reflection of the transformations of society. No one has been duped. If antidepressants recruit more and more depressives, it is because they *are* effective in treating this type of disorder and more successful than other medications targeting other pathologies.

Is that to say that biomedical psychiatry has at long last found the cause of depression, because it knows how to treat it? That is what the industry's advertisements would have us believe, but the researchers themselves know better. It is not because substance X produces an effect on pathology Y that one may conclude that the substance acts specifically on the cause of the illness. No one would think to say, for example, that aspirin is an "anti-flu" medication on the pretext that it relieves flu symptoms, or that whisky is an "antidepressant" because it lifts your spirits. To establish a causal relation, one would have to go beyond a simple correlation and isolate a necessary and sufficient cause, as with infectious diseases. Nothing in psychiatry allows us to affirm that we have reached this point. Healy, Ehrenberg, and Pignarre are all careful to insist that, as yet, every effort to link a biological marker to any clinical entity has ended in failure. Tricyclic antidepressants, for example, have nearly the same chemical structure as antipsychotics, and some among the latter are used in low doses as antidepressants, which well shows that you cannot establish a link between such-and-such a molecule and a specific psychiatric problem. "The antipsychotics and the antidepressants," Healy writes, "are neither specific in the sense of being specific to one disease nor specific in the sense of working regardless of the nonspecific milieu in which they are delivered."[23]

The strength of the new biomedical psychiatry does not come, therefore, from the discovery of organic causes, but from placebo-controlled trials in which the effects of molecules are measured and compared. These trials do not tell us how the medication works, but only if it works, what works best, and on whom. Biomedical psychiatry is a form of rhetoric: it knows how to produce effects without knowing how to treat causes. Pignarre proposes calling it a *petite biologie* (little biology) to differentiate it from the larger biology that it mimics. When all is said and done, nothing distinguishes it from dynamic psychiatry and the various brands of psychotherapy, which also base themselves in the end on the effects (the changes) observed among patients. The only difference is that the rhetoric of the *petite biologie* is incomparably more persuasive: how, faced with the accumulation of double-blind randomized placebo-controlled trials, could one possibly deny that antidepressants do indeed produce an effect?

The question is, however: on what? On depression? But depression, as we have seen, is nothing other than that on which antidepressants act and the proof is that its definition changes with the introduction of each new drug. It is a mistake to say that antidepressants produce an effect *on* depression, as if the illness existed independently of antidepressants. In reality, depression is itself the product of antidepressants, first in the sense that it is pinpointed thanks to the action of such-and-such a molecule on it, and then in the sense that this effect makes way for the recruitment of more and more "depressives."

So this is why so many of us are depressed: not because depression is spreading, but because we have been persuaded that "depression" exists and that it can be treated. This is what Pignarre calls the "syllogism" of depression: (1) I feel depressed; (2) I want to feel better; (3) I am going to get a prescription for antidepressants. The point is that I would not feel "depressed" if I did not know that there were drugs for treating it. That is not to say that unhappiness, fatigue, inhibition do not exist; but they would not congeal into "depression" if antidepressants were not holding this clinical entity together. Better (or worse) still, there is every reason to think that people who in another time would have felt anxious, or have had psychosomatic symptoms, now label themselves "depressed" because depression is what we best know how to treat. Exactly as in dynamic psychiatry, symptomatic demand follows the fluctuations of therapeutic supply, with patients fitting their ills to the way in which they expect to be treated.

Is that to say that modern depression is a myth, an illusion we need only dissipate in order to recover from it? Absolutely not. The distress of depressives is in every way real. But this reality is not hard-wired in their genes or neurotransmitters. It was fabricated, constructed, produced, invented by the drugs of the biomedical industry, with which it is of one piece. In that sense, it is not a fate: change the medication and the therapy, and we would have a new illness.

Translated by JENNIFER CHURCH

Notes

1 Kaplan and Sadock 1996, p. 102.
2 Lehmann 1971.
3 Kaplan and Sadock 1996, pp. 99 ff.
4 Healy 1997; Ehrenberg 2000; Pignarre 2001.
5 Healy 1997, p. 38.
6 Healy 1997, p. 251.
7 Healy 1997, pp. 57–59.
8 "Listening to Eli Lilly," *Wall Street Journal*, March 31, 1994, p. B1; cited in Shorter 1997, p. 419 n. 168.
9 Lehmann 1971

10 Pignarre 2001, p. 11.
11 Le Pape and Lecomte 1999.
12 Zarifian 1996, p. 199.
13 Pignarre 2001, p. 12.
14 Ayd 1961.
15 Healy 1997, p. 76.
16 See, however, David Healy's powerful exposé of the antidepressant industry in Healy 2004b.
17 Zarifian 1996, p. 126.
18 Healy 1997, p. 212.
19 Ehrenberg 2000, p. 292; emphasis added.
20 Ehrenberg 2000, p. 181.
21 At least, this is what was assumed for a while. We now know that this is far from being the case.
22 Pignarre 2001, p. 86.
23 Healy 1997, p. 257.

12 Psychotherapy today

What is psychotherapy? Here is a contemporary definition, proposed by Didier Anzieu in Doron and Parot's *Dictionary of Psychology*: "A method of treating psychical ills by means that are essentially psychological."[1] As I will suggest presently, such a definition probably no longer corresponds to the actual practice of psychotherapy in our advanced liberal societies, but it adequately sums up the general understanding of psychotherapy which has prevailed for almost a century. Psychotherapy, we assume, is the care of the soul by way of the soul, a psychological medication for troubles that are themselves psychical.

Let's now turn to the entry "Psychotherapeutics, or Psychotherapy" from the 1901 edition of Baldwin's *Dictionary of Philosophy and Psychology*. There we read, to our great surprise, that psychotherapy is "the treatment of disease mainly or wholly by direct and indirect appeal to or utilization of mental conditions *upon bodily states*."[2] In 1891, Hippolyte Bernheim gave a similar definition:

> Effecting an intervention of the mind in order to *heal the body*, such is the role of suggestion applied to therapy, such is the goal of psychotherapeutics . . . the mind is not a negligible quantity in our physiological and pathological life. There is a psycho-biology; there is a psychotherapeutics. The human mind is a great lever and the healing doctor should make use of this lever.[3]

Similarly, when the psychiatrist Daniel Hack Tuke launched the term in 1872, it was in a chapter entitled "Psycho-therapeutics – practical application of the influence of the mind *on the body* to medical practice."[4] The same applies to the various brands of what William James[5] called the "Mind Cure Movement" ("Christian Science," "New Thought," and so forth). There is no escaping this simple observation: before the turn of the twentieth century, psychotherapy (also called "mental therapeutics,"[6] *traitement moral, Seelenbehandlung*)[7] was for the most part a psycho-*somatics* – the practice of using the "action of the mind on the body" for medical purposes.

From this point of view, the emergence of psychotherapy did not so much constitute a rupture with prevailing medical practices; rather, it formalized some of these practices by focusing on a correlation between mind and body which was already assumed by most doctors. The idea that the mind influences the body is in no way the sensational and unique discovery of Charcot or Bernheim. On the contrary, from the Renaissance, if not before, it was taken for granted that one could both grow ill and heal through the influences of imagination, sympathy, imitation, or strong emotions. Doctors not only accepted the correlation between mind and body as a matter of course; they deliberately exploited it for therapeutic ends, whether this be by administering placebos, by trying to inspire the patient's confidence, or by psychologically manipulating him so that he might better confront his illness (this is what was called, in the eighteenth century, the "medicine of the imagination").[8] As the historian Charles Rosenberg reminds us, before the "therapeutic revolution" of the second half of the nineteenth century and the introduction of treatments targeting specific illnesses, doctors in no way separated the respective roles body, mind, and environment play in sickness and health: "All medicine was psychosomatic medicine in these generations; mind and body, sickness and health were all inextricably related."[9]

Likewise, the "psychotherapy" that spread throughout Europe and Russia during the 1890s was a holistic and non-specific form of medicine, which focused on disorders that were both psychical and somatic, "psycho-biological." To see this, one need only peruse Bernheim's case observations: there we find listed cases of neurasthenia, traumatic and hysterical neurosis, and impotence, but also of rheumatism, arthritis, neuralgia, sciatica, back pain, cephalagia, multiple sclerosis, tetanus, myelitis, pneumonia, dysentery, hepatic colic, menstrual problems, Ménière's syndrome, and so forth. One could say just the same of "mental healing," which was developing at the same time in the United States, outside the purview of the academic medical establishment. Thus Mary Baker Eddy, founder of the Christian Science movement, emphatically refused to make a distinction between organic diseases and illnesses caused by the imagination: "Mind produces what is termed organic disease, as directly as it does hysteria, and cures it as readily."[10] It is, therefore, a purely retrospective illusion to depict Tuke, Bernheim, or Eddy as pioneers of psychotherapy, at least in the specialized sense that we attribute to this term today. These people considered themselves to be doctors, and were part of a medical tradition that preceded the divorce between specialists of the body and those of the mind.

Let us now look to 1904, the year in which Paul Dubois publishes his book *The Psychic Treatment of Nervous Disorders* and Freud gives his lecture "On psychotherapy." Both declare that they do not make any use of suggestion in their respective psychotherapies, and even more remarkably, both state that their clientele is limited to those suffering from "*psycho*neuroses," meaning patients exhibiting exclusively psychical symptoms.[11] "Having eliminated the neuroses which are probably somatic in origin," Dubois writes,

> I only keep in this group of *psychoneuroses* the affections in which the psychic influence predominates, those which are more or less amenable to psychotherapy; these are: neurasthenia, hysteria, hysterical neurasthenia, the lighter forms of hypochondria and melancholia, and finally one may include certain conditions of very serious disequilibration bordering on insanity.[12]

The same thing on the other side of the Atlantic where the Reverend Samuel McComb, one of the promoters of the extremely popular psychotherapeutic Emmanuel Movement, listed in 1908 the disorders to which his half-religious, half-"scientific" treatment applied:

> neurasthenia, hypochondria, psychasthenia, hysterical pains, functional insomnia, melancholia, nervous irritability, hallucinations, morbid fears, fixed ideas ... incipient insanities, stage fright, worry, stammering, abuse of tobacco, alcoholism, morphinism, cocainism, kleptomania, suicidal tendencies – in a word, the vast and complicated field of what is technically called the functional neuroses and the psychoneuroses.[13]

No mention of organic disorders here. Within the space of a couple of years, psychotherapy had become a purely psychical treatment for purely psychical ills, which most often found its justification in some sort of "scientific psychology." What, then, had happened? On the one hand, neuroses, which owed their name to the idea of a putative derangement of the nervous system, were now being attributed to purely psychological causes. From Herbert Page's and Charcot's "nervous shock" to Janet's and Freud's "psychical traumas," the idea of a psychogenesis of the psychoneuroses had gained credence, prompting Freud to distinguish these neuroses from the "actual neuroses" which were due to somatic causes.[14] Dubois again: "Just here we find ourselves face to face with a fundamental factor: *the influence of the mind and of mental representations* ... The source of the trouble is ... psychic and it is *ideation* which causes or harbors functional disorders."[15] To treat these psychoneuroses, then, meant to act on their psychical causes, whether by means of suggestion (Forel), the recollection or abreaction of traumatic experiences (Janet, Breuer, Freud), insight into the repressed (Freud again), or persuasion (Dubois, Déjerine).[16] On the other hand, psychotherapy simultaneously ceased being the business of general practioners or internists, such as Liébeault and Bernheim, and became that of neurologists specializing in said "neuroses" and of psychiatrists open to the idea of a psychogenesis of the psychoses, such as Bleuler and Jung.[17] In short, psychotherapy was becoming a specialized field, cleanly separated from somatic medicine, which concerned itself exclusively with people suffering from psychic ills or disorders of the mind.

The century of psychotherapy had begun, and with it the era of the "psyche," a new concept that is inseparable from the idea of psychological treatment. The psyche, which is neither the soul nor consciousness, neither the brain nor the nervous system, is an entity that is partially opaque to itself as it is susceptible to all sorts of psychical causalities and influences that determine it without its knowledge. At the same time, one of the psyche's fundamental characteristics is that it is curable, or at least modifiable, with the intervention of an expert who teaches it to better take control of itself. This "psy" expert can be a neurologist or a psychiatrist, as we have seen, but also a psychologist or even someone who does not belong to the medical profession. The Emmanuel Movement, for instance, which marks the inception of modern psychotherapy in the United States, consisted of a heterogeneous alliance of Episcopalian pastors trained in philosophy and neurologists, such as James Jackson Putnam, Richard Cabot, and Isador Coriat.[18] As for the neurologist Sigmund Freud, despite his criticism of the non-medical aspect of the Emmanuel Movement during his visit to the United States,[19] we know that from quite early on he surrounded himself with non-medical practitioners such as the Pastor Pfister, Otto Rank, Hanns Sachs, Theodore Reik, and Lou Andreas-Salomé. The first psychoanalyst ever trained by Freud, Emma Eckstein, had no particular profession, while the first child psychoanalyst, the father of "Little Hans," was a musicologist. In this respect, even if Freud is far from being the first to have promoted a "lay," non-medical, psychotherapy, it is clear that the separation of psychoanalysis from medicine in favor of an autonomous mode of training and transmission[20] played a crucial role in the emergence, during the twentieth century, of psychotherapy as a distinct profession (or non-profession). Psychotherapy, whether analytic or not, has admittedly been practiced by psychiatrists (notably in the USA during the 1940s through the 1960s) and still is in a few countries such as France and Argentina, but it is no longer, institutionally, the domain of the medical school. In most Western countries today, anyone can set up shop as a psychotherapist, psychoanalyst, or counselor after receiving a training of varying duration from some school of psychotherapy – or quite simply by "authorizing himself," as Lacan famously put it.

This uncoupling of psychotherapy from academic and somatic medicine has coincided, quite paradoxically, with an ever-expanding pathologization and "psychiatrization" of domains which had previously escaped the jurisdiction of medicine. Relatively limited in the beginning, the list of conditions and disorders pertaining to psychotherapy never ceased to expand during the twentieth century. Indeed, if neuroses are "psycho-neuroses," diseases of the psyche, where are the limits of their domain? Where are we to draw the border between normal and pathological psyches? Are we not all "neurotic" to some degree – traumatized, repressed, liable to autosuggestion, engaged in some imaginary alienation? Very early on, psychotherapy extended its domain to what Freud called the "psychopathology of everyday life," that is, to problems which up to this point were not in the purview of medicine: dreams, fantasies, "Freudian slips," but also mourning, failure, traumatic experiences, marital relations, professional difficulties, family conflicts, behavioral disorders, and so forth. Starting in 1907, the Reverend McComb and his colleagues contributed a monthly column to the women's magazine *Good Housekeeping*, in which they provided "psychotherapeutic" advice on such diverse subjects as "house-keeper's anxiety," "fear of failure," "business after the business hours," the education of children, "sleeplessness," and even the "artistic temperament."[21]

Besides, the title of this advice column is eloquent enough: "Happiness and health." Max Weber said that medicine could teach us to "master life technically," but not how to lead a *good* life, a happy life in accord with ethical or religious norms.[22] Psychotherapy, on the other hand, has claimed for itself the previous domain of ethics and moral direction, while simultaneously presenting itself as a technique for happiness and mental "health." Lewellys F. Barker, professor of medicine at Johns Hopkins University, pointed this out as early as 1907:

> To-day, though many are still helped by the clergyman and priest, more turn to the physician when in psychic difficulty or when in need of mental and moral direction. And physicians, whether they like it or not, are thus being forced into the responsibilities of "confessor" and "moral director."[23]

Since psychotherapy could heal psychoneurotic phobias or paralyses with the help of suggestion, abreaction, insight, persuasion, or conditioning, there was no reason it could not also "heal" existential angst, sadness, relationships with others, low self-esteem, behavioral problems, and deviant desires. In this respect, the extraordinary expansion of psychotherapy during the second half of the twentieth century[24] corresponds much less to an unlikely increase of "neuroses" in Western countries than to a boundless extension of this psycho-technique to all aspects of life. From the askesis of pure desire practiced on Lacanian couches to stress management and business coaching through family therapy, feminist therapy, trauma therapy, interpersonal therapy, cognitive-behavioral therapy, Ericksonian hypnosis, EMDR, sophrology, existential therapy, Rogers's humanistic therapy, Janov's primal scream, or Perl's Gestalt therapy, there are today more than 400 types of psychotherapies that appeal to almost every market and need. The most recent of these therapies, Seligman's "positive psychology," unequivocally proposes making the pursuit of happiness, once and for all, into a scientific endeavor.[25]

One often speaks in this respect of an unwarranted medicalization of moral or social problems, but this is to miss the original character of this psycho-technicalization of life. In medicine, the relationship to the doctor is necessitated by illness and the patient usually has little or no say in what type of treatment is given to him. The modern psychotherapist, on the other hand, is freely chosen by a consumer who seeks him out in order to better manage her psyche, just as she would go to a dietician to better control her appetite or to a personal trainer to improve her physical performance. Admittedly, the psychotherapist is presumed to be an expert with an objective understanding of the psyche, but unlike the physician, priest, or social reformer of yesteryear, he does not impose this knowledge upon the patient in an authoritative manner. Lewellys F. Barker, again, is an early witness to this evolution: "It should be the aim of the physician … gradually to replace the medical absolutism by *self-direction*."[26] Indeed, the role of the psychotherapist is limited to assisting his client in what is essentially a self-fashioning intended to modify maladjusted emotions and behaviors, and to acquire greater psychical autonomy, the supposed source of well-being and happiness. The relationship between psychotherapist and client (the famous "therapeutic alliance") is thus a contractual one: the therapist offers his expertise, that is a theory and a technique which promise better well-being, while the client "purchases" this theory in order to refashion himself, forge a new identity, and create a new lifestyle. This explains the indoctrinating, recruiting character of psychotherapies, which can lead, in some extreme cases, to sectarian enrollment: the client is asked to adhere completely to the psychotherapist's system in order to bring about this self-transformation, something which at first glance can seem contradictory. The fact remains that initially it is the client who decides to opt for one particular psychotherapeutic system over another, based on his needs and aspirations, and he has the right, at any moment, to reject it if it does not suit him. Present-day psychotherapy is no longer, by any stretch, a matter of healing, but rather a life choice, a sort of existential shopping in the midst of a market economy where optional psyches are freely bought and sold.

And yet – and yet, we continue to speak of psycho*therapy*, as if it were a medical technique intended to treat mental, psychiatric disorders. Here we find a huge equivocation, due to the discipline's history and its initial grounding in the medical profession. This equivocation is all the more awkward as the therapeutic claims initially advertised by the founders of the discipline have evaporated during the course of the twentieth century, leading to the late Freud's pessimism and Lacan's therapeutic nihilism. We now know that, taken as a whole, psychotherapy is powerless in cases of psychoses, and that its results are disappointing when it comes to classical neuroses such as hysteria and obsessional neurosis (the list of Freud's therapeutic failures is in this regard quite edifying).[27] From this perspective, it is not an exaggeration to say that the original project of a psychotherapy of the psychoneuroses and psychoses – launched, let us remember, to the detriment of the more modest, but probably more efficacious, psychosomatics of Tuke and Bernheim – resulted for the most part in failure, even as psychotherapy pursued its triumphant expansion beyond the domain of mental disorders. Oddly enough, however, this failure has been of no consequence for the field, as the notion that psychotherapy is a treatment leading to some sort of "cure" is almost never called into question. The result is that we unduly pathologize existential problems for which there exists no cure one can properly speak of, and that we continue to offer, conversely, profoundly inadequate treatments for genuine mental pathologies such as autism and melancholic depression.

It is this ambiguity concerning the status of psychotherapy, shrewdly maintained by some of its representatives, which is the main cause of the current crisis affecting the discipline, insofar as it places psychotherapy on a collision course with the systematic evaluation of therapeutic effectiveness that has ruled modern medicine since the beginning of the 1960s. Indeed, if psychotherapy claims to be a medical, psychiatric practice and not simply a technique for personal development, it goes without saying that its effectiveness must be measured and compared to that of competing forms of therapy in order to keep patients informed of their options and to prevent the administration of inadequate treatments. Thus, when a psychoanalyst forces an analytic course of treatment upon someone suffering from stomach ulcers, drug addiction, or bipolar disorder, while other treatments have long proven their superior effectiveness, we are clearly dealing with incompetence or therapeutic abuse. Ditto for a trauma therapist who insists upon making a phobic patient repeatedly relive a hypothetical incest which occurred at the age of 2, instead of referring her to a cognitive-behavioral therapist capable of getting rid of these symptoms in about ten sessions. From this point of view, one can hardly object to some kind of regulation, governmental or other, of the profession.

But on what basis could such a regulation be carried out? Logic would have it that we remove the constitutive ambiguity of psychotherapy by reserving the title of psycho*therapist* to psychiatrists or health professionals who apply psychological treatments that have demonstrated their effectiveness for specific disorders, and by coining a new term – "psychotechnician" or "psychomanager," for instance – to refer to all of those, from psychoanalysts to yoga instructors, who offer techniques for refashioning the self and leading a better life. Such a distribution of roles would obviously have the merit of clarifying matters and of bringing an end to the ceaseless turf wars between the different schools of psychotherapy. The problem, however, is that within the "psy" field no one knows how to clearly demarcate "true" therapies from all the others, as current methods of evaluation do not allow us to trace this line with any degree of precision.

The systematic evaluation of medical treatments goes back to 1962, when the US Congress, intent on avoiding another thalidomide debacle, imposed stringent regulations on new medications put on the market by pharmaceutical companies.[28] Since then, for a new medication to be approved by the American Food and Drug Administration (which also means, practically speaking, in the rest of the world) it must be established not only that this medication is not dangerous to the consumer, but also that it is effective in treating a particular illness. This is done by submitting the medication to a randomized, double-blind, placebo-controlled trial. Why randomized and double-blind? In order to prevent the subjective biases introduced by researchers' and patients' expectations and therapeutic preferences from influencing the results of the experiment.[29] And why placebo-controlled? Because, as has become evident since the work of Henry K. Beecher, a non-specific element can always interfere with the success of any given treatment. Beecher, a professor of anesthesiology at Harvard, serendipitously discovered during the second World War that plain injections of saline solution relieved his severely wounded patients just as well as morphine injections. He concluded that placebos, far from being simply inert medications, actually had their own therapeutic effectiveness.[30] Without knowing it, Beecher had rediscovered the principle of Tuke's and

Bernheim's psychotherapy, and behind it, of the old "medicine of the imagination": the mind can relieve the body; an imaginary treatment can bring about actual healing.

However, it is not as therapeutic agents that placebos are used in modern clinical trials. Quite the opposite, the placebo effect is viewed as a pseudo-healing, an artifactual "noise" from which the treatment under consideration must be purified.[31] In order for a prospective medication to be "scientifically validated" – which is to say, emerge victorious from a clinical trial – it must demonstrate that its effectiveness is significantly superior to that of the placebo against which it is being tested; short of this, it is considered to be a pseudo-medication. What is thus established is the *specific* effectiveness of the treatment for the *specific* disorder targeted by the clinical trial: this antibiotic acts on this bacteria; this molecule acts on this neurotransmitter. The methodology of these clinical trials is clearly suitable for disorders that conform to what Charles Rosenberg has called the model of "disease specificity,"[32] which emerged with the bacteriology of the late nineteenth century and today constitutes the gospel of modern biomedicine: one gene, one protein, one illness. In these cases, the disease is a discrete and stable entity, independent of the individuals it affects, so that placebo-controlled trials indeed make it possible to determine without ambiguity whether or not the medication specifically acts on the disease in question.

It is not at all certain, on the other hand, that this method is suitable for dealing with a whole series of disorders that are placebo responsive, which is to say those in which the patient's reaction to the treatment plays a role in the healing process. In these cases, which range from skin diseases, angina pectoris, hypertension or even Parkinson's disease to most psychiatric disorders, the fact that one can establish the superiority of a given treatment over a placebo does not, in any way, prove the specificity of the treatment, or, by the same token, that of the targeted illness. Indeed, nothing rules out the possibility that this treatment may itself be a placebo, its superiority over the placebo being explained, quite simply, by the fact that it "pleases" patients more (*placebo*, we should not forget, means "I will please"). What will be measured, then, is a preference on the part of the patients, out of which a majority will have opted for one treatment over another. To conflate such patient preference with a demonstration of the specific effectiveness of a medication would obviously be a mistake.

Yet it is this mistake which lies at the source of psychotherapy's current crisis and what the French have called the "shrink wars" (*la guerre des psys*). Owing to the ambiguity maintained around the medical status of the discipline, the model of randomized, double-blind, placebo-controlled trials has been applied to all the psychotherapies, without anyone taking the time to seriously question whether these therapies are indeed specific treatments targeting clearly defined and invariable diseases, independent of the patient's reaction to the treatment. The decisive factor in this evolution was the discovery of the first antipsychotic, anxiolytic, and antidepressant drugs, which seemed to align psychiatric disorders with organic diseases. Starting in the early 1950s, several placebo-controlled trials demonstrated the superior effectiveness of chlorpromazine, reserpine, and lithium in treating, respectively, schizophrenia, anxiety disorders, and mania.[33] It was all too tempting to conclude from this that psychiatry was a matter of biochemical disorders responding to specific molecules, hence the "neo-Kraepelinian" revolution of the DSM-III. The idea behind this impressive diagnostic manual was that a neutral and atheoretical description of surface symptoms should allow for the differentiation of the various psychiatric disorders (the DSM-III counted 265 of them, the DSM-IV 297), and that a comparative and rigorous evaluation of the therapies targeting these symptoms would subsequently enable us to determine which treatment is appropriate for this or that specific disorder.[34] Such a program of comparative evaluation plainly favored pharmacotherapies and brief psychotherapies such as cognitive-behavioral therapy (CBT) that target just the type of surface symptoms listed in the DSM-III, making it easier to measure the effectiveness of treatments. On the other hand, psychodynamic and psychoanalytical therapies aiming at an in-depth restructuring of the personality have been mechanically pushed offside, owing to their diagnostic nihilism and their inability to conform to the DSM-III's standardized nosology.[35]

All this could lead us to believe that comparative evaluations of therapeutic effectiveness have provided us at last with the scalpel needed to distinguish genuine therapies for psychical disorders from vague techniques for personal development. In reality, nothing of the sort has come to pass. Indeed, the imposition of the model of disease specificity on the "psy" field comes up against a fundamental problem that may well define this field in its entirety: patients, far from being passive vis-à-vis the diagnoses and treatments administered to them, react to them in a complex fashion, thus obscuring the stable and biunivocal correspondence that we would like to establish between such and such therapy and such and such disease.

Take schizophrenia, the battle-horse of biomedical psychiatry. Anyone who has been in the presence of a person afflicted by this terrible illness can have no doubt that it is an objective and fundamentally organic disorder, whether it be genetic, biochemical, or viral in origin. And yet, we cannot rely on surface symptoms to define this disease, as the DSM-III would have it, for these symptoms vary according to time and place. As several epidemiological studies conducted by the World Health Organization have shown, the average duration of a schizophrenic episode is much shorter in developing countries than in industrialized nations, and the most severe episodes are much more pronounced. Likewise, auditory hallucinations, which top Schneider's classical list of First Rank Symptoms of schizophrenia, have evolved throughout history, both in their content and in the frequency with which they have been reported by patients.[36] This historical and cultural variability of symptoms only increases when we leave the domain of the psychoses and enter into that of the former "neuroses" – depression, anxiety, traumatic neurosis, anorexia, etc. – not to mention the whole bevy of ill-defined psychosomatic afflictions such as stress, chronic fatigue, fibromyalgia, and lumbar back pain.[37] Here we may truly speak of symptomatic fashions, certain disorders rising to prominence for a while only to disappear suddenly and be replaced by other "transient mental illnesses," as Ian Hacking calls them. Thus since the 1980s anxiety disorders have been replaced in the West by depression, while depression remains to this day quite uncommon in Japan.[38] Likewise, Multiple Personality Disorder (MPD), an extremely rare condition before the 1970s, has spread in quasi-epidemic proportions in Anglo-Saxon countries and Holland, without affecting other countries. It is today waning in favor of Post-Traumatic Stress Disorder (PTSD). One could make similar observations with respect to panic attacks, anorexia, bulimia, social phobia, and Attention Deficit Hyperactivity Disorder (ADHD).

This general lability of the "psy" field, testified to by the DSM's constant revisions, is an indication that patients interact with the theories about them, modeling their disease or ill-being on the diagnoses which are popular at a particular moment in time, as well as on the treatments being offered to them. There is, one might say, a co-adaptation, and a covariance, of "psy" therapies and "psy" pathologies. This explains the phenomenon of the placebo response which so consistently interferes with the results of clinical trials: patients – whom we might better call agents, or actors – *respond* to the treatments which seem valid to them, all the more so as they will have in part pre-formed their symptoms in order to suit these treatments. This looping effect is plain to see in the various forms assumed by what used to be called hysteria, which resists for this very reason all attempts to make it into a specific disease. But the phenomenon of placebo response cannot be reduced to a mere hysterical intrigue, for it is also found in cases of psychoses. Consider the following episode: in the 1950s, the psychiatrist Heinz Lehmann announced in his ward that he was going to test a new hormone treatment. Three deeply catatonic schizophrenics were given injections twice a week for two weeks. By the third week, two of the patients were speaking rationally again. And yet Lehmann's hormone treatment was nothing other than a placebo![39]

Depression, too, is highly placebo responsive: we now know that two-thirds of the people suffering from depression respond positively to one or another form of antidepressants, but of this two-thirds, half respond just as well to a placebo.[40] To this it should be added that antidepressants, despite their undeniable pharmacological effects, produce no notable improvements in Chinese "neurasthenics" whose symptoms are nevertheless almost identical to those of our depressed patients.[41] This seems to suggest that antidepressants are not medications targeting a specific disorder called "depression," but rather a Western placebo that is effective to the exact degree that patients incorporate it into their manner of being ill and prefer it to other forms of treatment.

This "reactivity" of patients to the diagnoses and treatments which are applied to them carries with it many consequences for the evaluation of psychotherapies and, more generally, for defining the boundaries of the "psy" field.

First of all, even when a clinical trial shows a psychotropic drug to be more effective in treating a particular disorder than a given form of psychotherapy, it does not necessarily follow that we have found *the* treatment suitable for this disorder and that we may simply disqualify the psychotherapeutic treatment. All this proves, in fact, is that a majority of patients have voted, so to speak, for the pharmacological treatments. There is nothing to guarantee that this "vote" will not change in subsequent "elections," when even more convincing treatments will have entered the race. As an old medical adage says, you should always take the latest medication on the market before its effectiveness is used up. From this point of view, pharmacotherapies and psychotherapies are all in the same boat, in the sense that their effectiveness always rests, in part, on the placebo effect, and that it is impossible to know exactly in what proportion.

Besides, outcome studies have shown, with the exception of lithium for bipolar disorders and atypical antipsychotics for schizophrenia, that neither pharmacotherapies nor psychotherapies achieve results which are demonstrably superior to those of a simple placebo. One of the most rigorous clinical trials conducted to this day, the Treatment of Depression Collaborative Research Program launched by the National Institute of Mental Health at the end of the 1970s, compared the respective effectiveness of four types of treatment on a group of 250 patients suffering from moderate to severe depression: an anti-depressant (imipramine), cognitive-behavioral therapy (CBT), interpersonal therapy (IPT), and a placebo. In both the antidepressant and the placebo groups, treatment was supplemented by a clinical management package providing minimal supportive therapy that could stand for a "psychotherapy-placebo."[42] All four groups showed significant improvement, thus verifying a constant in every outcome study made to this day: a "psy" patient following a course of treatment, *whatever this treatment may be*, will be better off than about 60 to 70 percent of the patients who are not being treated or who are placed on a waiting list.[43] The study also showed that the antidepressant and, to a lesser extent, IPT were initially more effective than CBT and the placebo in the more severe cases of depression. But if one considered the results of the overall group throughout the entire duration of treatment, one did not find any significant difference between the pharmacotherapy, the two psychotherapies, and the placebo plus clinical management. This seems to suggest that as far as depression is concerned – but this probably also holds true for most "psy" disorders – the relative effectiveness of psychotherapies *and* pharmacotherapies boils down to that of various types of placebos, that is to say of "clinical management."

The same line of reasoning holds for any comparison between psychotherapies, which in the final analysis is nothing but a comparison between placebos. Here again, the fact that one psychotherapeutic treatment obtains better results than another proves nothing, except that this therapy is more suitable for a larger number of patients at a particular moment in a particular culture. One often cites today meta-analyses indicating that cognitive-behavioral therapy has a greater effectiveness in treating phobias and anxiety disorders.[44] But what this shows, at most, is that these pathologies and CBT are particularly well suited to each other, in the sense that an increasing number of patients are seeking a brief form of therapy for discrete symptoms. Other patients, for other reasons, choose classical analysis or go to family therapy, and find these therapeutic approaches just as satisfying. Each type of therapy recruits followers who will bear witness to its benefits, whether by providing testimonials about their own improvement and the disappearance of their symptoms or by getting involved in the ideological squabbles between schools of psychotherapy. France thus recently witnesssed a very public clash between CBT and Freudian partisans, with each group of patients passionately, and with equal conviction, defending the virtues of its therapy of choice in the media and specialized publications. However, it is not because a larger number of patients bear witness to the effectiveness of a particular therapy in treating a particular condition that we can declare this treatment more valid or scientific. This would be just as absurd as claiming that soccer is more scientific than chess because more people have a passion for it.

Should we then conclude that in the "psy" field one therapy is as good as any other and that the attempt to evaluate their effectiveness is a futile endeavor? Such a limp relativism, in which all cows are grey, obviously is not satisfying. Evaluation not only is necessary for determining those cases in which a particular treatment is unequivocally superior to a placebo effect, but also is inevitable in a field where the consumer is king and demands to be informed of the benefits he can reasonably expect from the various therapies offered on the market. In 1995, *Consumer Reports* published the results of a survey conducted with 4,000 of its readers who had received psychotherapeutic treatment.[45] In other words, evaluation takes place anyway, and there is nothing wrong with that. Still, we need to be clear about exactly what it is that is being evaluated and especially *who* is doing the evaluating. Owing to the unwarranted extension of the biomedical model into the "psy" field, clinical trials have too often been conceived as a scientific and objective evaluation, performed by experts, of the effects of therapies on various mental conditions. But in fact, it is the patients (or consumers) themselves who ultimately make this evaluation by reacting in one way or another to the treatment or by testifying to the benefits they receive from this or that psychotechnique. Put differently, it is the patients who are the actual experts of their illnesses and of the remedies which best suit them.

From this perspective, the *Consumer Reports* survey – which was almost universally decried by experts in the field for its nonscientific and biased character[46] – defines, much more effectively than the most rigorously controlled clinical trials, what we can expect from an evaluation in the "psy" field. In the end, what is measured in such an evaluation is nothing but the patients' response to the therapeutic offer being made to them: "Yes, I like this treatment, it suits my symptoms"; "No, I prefer this other medication, this other placebo." Evaluations are like opinion polls or political elections, which reflect the populace's preferences at a given moment. To conflate this revocable consumer vote on "psy" therapies with proof or "scientific validation" of the effectiveness of a particular treatment would be tantamount to making an election result permanent, to preventing it from being debated and possibly rescinded in subsequent rounds of voting: a profoundly antidemocratic attitude, one which "psy" experts all too frequently adopt when trying to impose their therapy of choice on patients. This model of scientific evaluation, which seeks to establish indisputable and incontestable results, ought to give way to a model of political evaluation in which open discussions and debates allow the actors themselves to make decisions about issues that concern them directly. Gone is the time when experts could unilaterally impose the criteria distinguishing "true" psychotherapies from the others. In the world of present-day psychotherapy, as we have seen, these criteria are now negotiated on a case-by-case basis by patients/users who want to have a say in defining their own ill-being and the ways in which it should be treated. The multiplication of patient advocacy groups since the 1970s furthermore testifies to this democratization of the "psy" field: today, experts propose and patients dispose by voting for the therapy – which is also to say *the type of ill-being* – which best suits them.

Some will object to this democratization, arguing that it amounts to surrendering the psychotherapeutic field to the reign of the arbitrary and of mob psychology – and to a degree, they will be right. We are not lacking in examples from recent history of therapeutic fashions spread by patients and their advocacy groups, with help from psychotherapeutic or pharmaceutical special interest groups. The most notorious example is probably the sinister "Recovered Memory Therapy" (RMT) of the 1980s–1990s, a half-therapeutic, half-political movement which launched a veritable witch hunt in the USA and resulted in the conviction of dozens of innocent people on the basis of memories of sexual and/or satanic abuse "recovered" in therapy. So there is no denying that the democratization or "consumerization" of the "psy" field can trigger all sorts of unsavory consequences, as the patient's ill-being and the manner in which it is treated become a matter of political activism and sectarian enrollment, if not of straightforward lobbying and marketing. The more patients become full-fledged agents, the more autonomy they acquire in defining their own ill-being and in "psychotechnicizing" it, the more we can expect this self-fashioning to be influenced by fashion and by the various psychotherapeutic lobbies that manipulate the psyche market.

But these dangers, after all, are those of any democratic debate and it is through this very same democratic debate that they ought to be confronted, not by invoking an illusory "scientific" legislation which would grind all discussion to a halt. We should not be striving for fewer controversies and polemics in this field, but rather the inverse: the more of these there are, the more information freely circulates through patient advocacy groups, in the media, and on the

Internet, the better therapy users will be able to choose for themselves a custom-made self or change it if it no longer suits them. It is time for psychotherapy to stop fancying itself as a medication of the mind or as a science of the subject, and finally accept itself for what it has become, for better and for worse: a modern *politics* of the self and of happiness.

Translated by KELLY S. WALSH

Notes

1 Doran and Parot 1991, p. 562; cited in Carroy 2000, p. 7.
2 Baldwin 1901, vol. 2, p. 394; emphasis added.
3 Bernheim 1995, pp. 65–66; emphasis added.
4 Tuke 1872; emphasis added.
5 James 1961, p. 89.
6 Beard 1876.
7 See for example Freud 1890, p. 281: "'Psyche' is a Greek word which may be translated 'mind.' Thus 'psychical treatment' means 'mental treatment.' The term might accordingly be supposed to signify 'treatment of the pathological phenomena of mental life.' This, however, is not its meaning. 'Psychical treatment' denotes, rather, treatment taking its start in the mind, treatment (whether of mental or physical disorders) by measures which operate in the first instance and immediately upon the human mind."
8 See Goldstein 1987, pp. 52–54.
9 Rosenberg 2003, pp. 11–12; see also Rosenberg 1979, pp. 3–25; 1989.
10 Eddy 1875, p. 344; cited in Caplan 1998, p. 75.
11 The term "psychoneurosis" had been introduced by Krafft-Ebing in 1874 to designate mental disorders, such as melancholy, in which no organic injury could be found; see Krafft-Ebing 1874, p. 64; cited in Shorter 1992, p. 383 n. 60.
12 Dubois 1908, p. 26; Dubois's emphasis; cited in Shamdasani 2005, p. 10. See also Freud 1905b, p. 258: "And in the third place, Gentlemen, I would remind you of the well-established fact that certain diseases, in particular the psychoneuroses, are far more accessible to mental influences than to any other form of medication."
13 McComb 1908, p. 795; cited in Caplan 1998, p. 128.
14 Freud 1898.
15 Dubois 1908, p. 25; Dubois's emphasis.
16 For more on Dubois's and Déjerine's psychotherapy by persuasion, see Gladys Swain and Marcel Gauchet, "Du traitement moral aux psychothérapies. Remarques sur la formation de l'idée contemporaine de psychothérapie," in Swain 1994, pp. 237–262.
17 As for Bernheim, he firmly excluded these "diseases of the mind" from the jurisdiction of psychotherapy; see Bernheim 1995, p. 223. See also the psychologist Hugo Münsterberg: "Psychotherapy is sharply to be separated from psychiatry, the treatment of mental diseases … certainly many diseases of the mind lie entirely beyond the reach of psychotherapy, and on the other hand psychotherapy may be applied also to diseases which are not mental at all" (Münsterberg 1909, p. 1). Janet still held the same view in 1919, inviting his readers not to confuse "psychotherapy" with "psychiatry" (Janet 1919, vol. 3, p. 462).
18 For more on the Emmanuel Movement and its importance for the establishment of psychotherapy in the United States, see Caplan 1998, ch. 6.
19 In an interview granted to a Boston newspaper, Freud declared: "When I think that there are many physicians who have been studying modern techniques of psychotherapy for decades and who yet practice it only with the greatest caution, this undertaking of a few without medical training, or with superficial medical training, seems to me at the very least a questionable good" (*Boston Evening Transcript*, September 11, 1909).

20 For more on this "privatization" of psychoanalysis, see Borch-Jacobsen and Shamdasani 2006, ch. 1.
21 Cited in Caplan 1998, p. 126.
22 Weber 1999, p. 291.
23 Barker 1907, p. 16.
24 In 1955, 1 percent of the American population had consulted with a mental health professional; in 1980, that figure was already 10 percent (Klerman 1983; London and Klerman 1982).
25 Seligman 2002.
26 Barker 1907, p. 15; Barker's emphasis.
27 Borch-Jacobsen 2005a.
28 Healy 1997.
29 Marks 1997; 2000; Kaptchuk 1998a, notably pp. 427–432.
30 Beecher 1955.
31 Kaptchuk 1998b.
32 Rosenberg 2002.
33 Healy 1997, pp. 90–91.
34 The story of the DSM-III has been told numerous times: Kirk and Kutchins 1992; Young 1995, pp. 91–117; Healy 1997, pp. 231–237; Shorter 1997, pp. 295–305; Luhrmann 2000, pp. 225–232.
35 For more on the incommensurability of psychoanalytic categories and the standardized nosology of biomedical psychiatry, see the fieldwork conducted in Argentina by the medical anthropologist Lakoff 2006.
36 Hacking 1999, pp. 113–114.
37 Shorter 1992.
38 Healy 2002, pp. 66–67 and 372; Applbaum 2006.
39 Lehmann 1993, pp. 291–303; cited in Healy 1997, p. 90.
40 Stahl 1996, p. 110.
41 Kleinman 1986, notably pp. 91–95.
42 See Elkin 1994, pp. 114–139.
43 These are the figures provided by the two oldest studies of this type dating from 1938 and 1946: Landis 1938; Denker 1946. In 1994, surveying decades of subsequent outcome studies, Michael J. Lambert and Allen E. Bergin arrived at a much more optimistic figure of around 80 percent improvement due to psychotherapeutic treatment (Lambert and Bergin 1994, p. 144). However, Lambert and Bergin also noted this, which should temper the conclusions that we might be tempted to draw from their estimate: "The average patient undergoing a placebo treatment appears to be better off than 66 percent of the non-treatment controls"(1994, p. 150).
44 See the INSERM 2004 survey of psychotherapies, which in France sparked even more fierce debates than the NIMH study on depression.
45 Consumer Reports 1995.
46 Seligman 1995; Luhrmann 2000, pp. 206–207.

13 Therapy users and disease mongers

Let's start with stating the obvious: patient advocacy groups mark the irruption of the political, in its democratic form, into the medical field. Until now, at least in the West, the patient was left alone to face both his illness and the various experts – doctors, apothecaries, therapists – who were helping him to fight it. This is no longer the case today. Under the combined influence of consumerism, the self-help movement, the political activism of the 1960s–1970s and the social networking made possible by the Internet, more and more patients are organizing themselves in order to defend their interests, lay claim to their rights, lobby politicians, and weigh in for one treatment or against another medication. Once isolated and passive, the patients themselves (or their relatives, if the illness is too debilitating) have now become full-fledged social agents who intervene in the public sphere and participate as citizens in the debates and controversies that concern them.

Second obvious fact: this activism inevitably creates tension (which does not necessarily mean conflict) between patients on the one hand and, on the other, health care professionals and the various institutions or professional organizations which vouch for their expertise. If patients collectively organize, it is because they are not satisfied, for one reason or another, with the specialists' knowledge and want to assert their own knowledge and expertise of their own illness. One generally traces the history of patient groups back to 1935, with the creation of Alcoholics Anonymous in the USA. Before providing the model for countless support groups and twelve-step programs, the members of Alcoholics Anonymous first distinguished themselves by eschewing the individualistic and guilt-laden approaches which had up till then been applied to them by health-care professionals: "We alcoholics know more, collectively, than psychiatrists, psychologists and alcohologists about the experience of alcoholism and the means of recovering from it. Let's share this knowledge with each other in order to increase our chances of escaping from the bottle." In this respect, the primary characteristic of patient groups is not so much the mutual assistance that its members provide for each other as the assertion of an expertise about the illness different from that of the experts and yet just as fundamental as theirs, if not more so. It is one thing to have objective, learned knowledge of the illness; it is another thing altogether to have first-hand experience living with the illness and the difficulties it creates for patients and those around them. If patients organize, it is to have the legitimacy of their knowledge recognized and to have their say in the management of their illness, by acting as an equal party in negotiations with doctors, politicians, and the pharmaceutical industry.

This tension between the expertise of patients and that of the experts modulates markedly according to the diseases in question, and it can range, as Rabeharisoa, Callon, and Demonty have shown, from partnership to out-and-out opposition.[1] Some patient groups, like Alcoholics Anonymous for example, quite simply reject professional help in favor of self-managing their difference, which they fully assume and claim for themselves. This self-assertion can go so far as to call into question the very "disease" they are supposed to suffer from, as when gay rights groups and their allies within the American Psychiatric Association succeeded in 1974 in striking homosexuality from the list of illnesses in the DSM-III which was then in preparation, despite the opposition of psychoanalytically oriented psychiatrists.[2] In contrast, other groups closely collaborate with specialists, whether in the form of sponsoring research on a particular disease, like the French Association Against Myopathies,[3] or of acting as "lay experts" in the controversies between specialists on the subject of clinical trial protocols, as happened with AIDS activists in the USA.[4] In a fascinating study of patient electronic discussion lists, Madeleine Akrich and Cécile Méadel thus describe how the moderators of a Parkinson's listserv developed, based on data provided by its members, a software program which allowed its users to track the evolution of the disease and to adapt medication dosages to individual variations of their own condition. This is a great example of patient expertise complementing the more general expertise of the neurologist.[5]

In any case, and whatever the strategy adopted by one group or another, the incursion of patient collectives into the medical sphere has proved profoundly unsettling for the latter, as it calls into question the asymmetric relationship that has traditionally existed between doctors and patients, specialists and laypersons. Faced with the mobilization of hyper-informed patients who communicate with each other in real time on the Internet, it is becoming more and more difficult for experts to impose a treatment or clinical trial in the name of Science with a capital "S" on patients or to refuse to consider their objections under the pretext that these are a matter of irrational "resistance." This paternalistic attitude simply will not do any longer in a society where therapy users have won the right to speak and to know.

The coming together of patients has been a source of tremendous empowerment. It has given them the power to act by themselves on their own condition, a power which was previously denied to them and which made them totally dependent upon experts and bureaucrats who "knew better." The most visible manifestation of this empowerment is obviously the political lobbying of certain large advocacy groups that often compete successfully with those of the pharmaceutical industry and of medical associations. But there is also a therapeutic element to this empowerment – at least this is one of the arguments most adamantly defended by the self-help movement: to actively engage with one's own illness instead of passively submitting to it is in itself therapeutic. In a much-cited study published in 1989, the psychiatrist David Spiegel claimed that women suffering from advanced forms of breast cancer who took part in a support group lived on average eighteen months longer than those who did not.[6] This figure has since been contradicted by another controlled study,[7] which found no difference between the two sample groups of patients, but the idea lives on: taking an active part in one's own treatment by discussing it with others better allows the sufferer to confront the illness. The group, in other words, is therapeutic.

Generally speaking, this patient empowerment is a reflection of the demands for greater autonomy and individual responsibility which characterize our advanced liberal societies. Even the illness and the manner of confronting it are now a matter of responsible choice, self-management, and risk calculation with the goal of optimizing results. Once a mere recipient of care, the patient is becoming a *user* of therapy, an enlightened consumer who inquires about her options, demands transparency on the part of the professionals and the authorities, and wants to be informed about the effectiveness and side-effects of treatments in order to decide freely and with full knowledge of the facts. In this respect, groups of therapy users play a role similar to that of consumer protection organizations which, as a matter of fact, often conduct surveys of medications and/or therapies. In our day and age, experts propose and users dispose.

The fact remains, however, that this freedom of choice and of discussion depends on the diseases around which the various patient groups rally. Certain treatments are clearly less discussable and debatable than others. In their article about patient discussion lists, Madeleine Akrich and Cécile Méadel point out that the participants in the cancer list that they studied never called into question the protocols of the chemotherapy treatments prescribed to them by their oncologists, however painful they were, while they reacted with irritation to any suggestion of alternative treatments.[8] This does not mean that freedom of discussion halts in the face of scientific "hard facts," but simply that in this case, as in others, there is a consensus between experts and patients as to which treatment is the best one possible as things currently stand. Conversely, the antipsychotic medications used in psychiatry have always created debates and controversies because of their extremely debilitating side effects. In the USA, the very influential National Alliance for the Mentally Ill, which counts more than 100,000 members, argues that mental illness ought to be recognized as a biological disease like any other and therefore puts its weight behind psycho-pharmacological treatments combined with supportive counseling. Other mental health patient advocacy groups, who sometimes refer to themselves as "psychiatric survivors," adamantly reject the biomedical model and the use of psychotropic medications, which they liken to forced substance abuse.[9] If we now turn to the "psy" field as a whole, the absence of consensus there is even more marked, with each group of therapy users siding with one form of therapy against another. This dynamic was openly displayed in the recent French "shrink wars," during which patient groups supporting cognitive-behavioral therapy (CBT) clashed with members of other patient advocacy groups that are the established psychoanalytic societies and schools. The very fact that one would speak of "war" in this context is proof enough that we have entered the political realm in its rawest form, whatever its participants' appeals to the "Science-of-the-Psyche" or the "Truth-of-the-Subject" may have been.

Some of the pro-CBT patient groups called on the French Minister of Health to launch a rigorous comparative evaluation of all the various forms of psychotherapy, so that science could adjudicate the various claims and bring an end to the dissensus.[10] A very unfortunate development, as it amounted, in fact, to relinquishing the responsibility of evaluating treatments to the experts, whereas this evaluation, even in the most controlled clinical trials, is in the end always that of the patients. It is indeed the patients who make the final decision about whether a particular treatment works for them by responding to it positively or negatively. From this point of view, user collectives, by themselves, play an important role in the evaluation, one that is even more decisive and relevant than that of clinical trial experts with their narrow conception of the efficacy of a treatment. As shown by the attitude of cancer patients vis-à-vis chemotherapy treatments, a particular treatment is going to "hold up" all the better if it is capable of creating an informed consensus among its users and of silencing, even if this be temporarily, debate and controversy. Inversely, when consensus is not achieved, as happens so very often in the "psy" field, it means that the treatment does not suit everyone and that its indiscriminate generalization is unwarranted. And when a treatment is widely rejected by its users, as in the case of the psychoanalytically oriented therapies forced on French substance abusers until quite recently,[11] the case is closed: it is the experts who are wrong. As Tobie Nathan[12] quite rightly suggests, in the end it is the users and those close to them who are the actual evaluators, the true therapy "testers." One can hardly find a better control group, for it is the users who are best at judging the value of a particular treatment *for themselves*. This is another way of saying that the results of science, however armor-clad with proof and statistics, make sense only when they are accepted by the community.

One will of course object that to give the last word to therapy users is tantamount to surrendering medicine to quackery and arbitrariness, throwing out the exacting work of establishing proof to which specialists apply themselves in their laboratories and research units. We cannot, say the proponents of evidence-based medicine, trust the patients to objectively judge the treatments that are applied to them, for they are all too easily carried away by baseless enthusiasms or fears. As the historians of clinical trials Harry Marks and Ted Kaptchuk have shown,[13] it is this mistrust by the experts which is the point of departure for the various control techniques, such as blind and placebo-controlled protocols, that have been developed since the end of the eighteenth century to avoid being misled by the patients. But this methodical distrust of patients is not only misplaced, it is downright insulting. It insults the patients' intelligence, for nothing interests them more than finding the right treatment, and they will readily yield to the evidence provided by the specialists as long as this evidence makes sense for them. All they ask is to see for themselves and to be allowed to evaluate the effects of treatments prescribed to them, without being systematically disqualified as unreliable witnesses to their own condition. If no consensus is reached among patients, as is often the case today in the "psy" field, it is because we are indeed in the domain of subjective preferences, with each patient group advocating the therapy that best suits it. But then, anyway, there is little chance that the methodology of controlled clinical trials will have much success in forging the lacking consensus. The recent history of psychotherapy outcome studies proves as much.

Up to this point I have only dealt with the collective evaluation of treatments, while neglecting the attitude of patients vis-à-vis their own illness. The fact is that patients abundantly debate the treatments prescribed to them, but this discussion rarely touches on the illness from which they are suffering. There is an obvious reason for this: patient collectives, in every case, organize around a particular illness or disease that defines them as a group – sufferers of diabetes, Parkinson's disease, multiple sclerosis, and so forth. Submitting this "given" to debate would amount to calling into question the group's very existence. Moreover, who could doubt the terrible reality of diseases like cancer, myopathies, schizophrenia? This would be not only absurd, but especially cruel.

Yet the situation quickly changes if we turn to such disorders as fibromyalgia, chronic fatigue syndrome, depression, anxiety, social phobia, anorexia, Multiple Personality Disorder, or Post-Traumatic Stress Syndrome. All these disorders create controversy, with some arguing that they are psychosomatic, socially constructed, or "transient" (in Hacking's sense),[14] and others claiming that they are due to some biochemical imbalance, genetic anomaly, or real psychical trauma. In these debates, patient groups spontaneously side with the "realists" against the "constructionists" and adamantly object to any relativization of their symptoms by invoking their lived experience with the disease. For instance, Akrich and Méadel describe how fibromyalgia patients on the listserv they studied firmly oppose any psychologizing of their condition and quickly marginalize those who dare to suggest such a thing.[15] For them, even if uncertainty reigns among specialists as to the nature of their illness, there can be no doubt that it is a specific disease, along the same lines as Alzheimer's disease or Tourette's syndrome. It is just a matter of finding the right medication that will prove this once and for all by stabilizing the diagnosis of the disease.

Such an attitude makes patient groups especially vulnerable to what has been called "disease mongering." The term was coined in 1992 by Lynn Payne[16] to refer to the marketing of new diseases by various medical and pharmaceutical interest groups anxious to create a commercial niche for one of their products. And indeed, all sorts of "diseases" have recently been launched on the market, with much help from scientific conferences, alarmist press campaigns, inflated statistics, and carefully calibrated clinical trials. These include: erectile dys-function, female sexual dysfunction, social phobia, male baldness, irritable bowel syndrome, premenstrual dysphoric disorder, attention deficit hyperactivity disorder, restless legs syndrome, and many others.[17] The main characteristic of these diseases is that they allegedly respond to the treatment proposed by pharmaceutical company *X* or to the molecule patented by pharmaceutical company *Y*.

Those responsible for this incredible promotion of diseases are most often the pharmaceutical companies, which make use of the most sophisticated marketing techniques and public relations campaigns in order to achieve their goals. In his book on antidepressants, David Healy describes how the firm Merck, at the beginning of the 1960s, actively peddled the concept of depression in order to sell the antidepressive properties of amitriptyline.[18] Lilly, Janssen, and AstraZeneca similarly promoted bipolar disorders and the notion of "mood stabilizers" in order to widen the market for their antipsychotic medications olanzapine, risperidone, and quetiapine, despite the fact that no controlled trial ever established their long term efficacy, while other trials had shown a significant rise of mortality rates and suicidality associated with use of antipsychotics.[19] As for Roche and GlaxoSmithKline, they launched "social phobia," supposed to respond well to their medications Aurorix® and Paxil®.[20] The British journal *Pharmaceutical Marketing*, in its "Practical guide to medical education," cites this as an example of an especially well-managed campaign:

> You may even need to reinforce the actual existence of a disease and/or the value of treating it. A classic example of this was the need to create recognition in Europe of social phobia as a distinct clinical entity and the potential of antidepressant agents such as moclobemide (Roche's Aurorix) to treat it.[21]

More recently, Pfizer launched a television advertising campaign for its drug Lyrica®, approved by the FDA to treat fibromyalgia. It featured a middle-aged woman describing how she had "pain all over," before turning to the camera and adding: "Fibromyalgia is a real, widespread pain condition." A consultant for Pfizer commented in the *New York Times*: "What's going to happen with fibromyalgia is going to be the exact thing that happened to depression with Prozac. These are legitimate problems that need treatments."[22]

But disease mongering is not unique to the pharmaceutical industry. It is just as rampant (and has been for quite a while) in the "psy" field. George Beard, in the nineteenth century, introduced "neurasthenia" to create a market for his electro-therapeutic technique, and Freud invented the "psychoneuroses of defense" to provide more patients for his couch. Today, cognitive-behavioral therapists actively promote obsessive-compulsive disorder (OCD), anxiety disorders, stress, and social phobia, all of which are pathologies particularly well suited to the short-term therapies that they practice. One could also cite the commercial launch, at the beginning of the 1970s, of multiple personality by the publisher of the cult book *Sybil*, as well as the intense psychiatric lobbying which culminated ten years later in the inclusion of Multiple Personality

Disorder (MPD) in the DSM-III's list of illnesses.[23] Post-Traumatic Stress Disorder (PTSD), likewise, entered the DSM-III as a result of a veritable political campaign headed by Vietnam veterans' organizations and by clinicians who supported their cause, despite the fact that there was no justification for separating this syndrome from other already established diagnoses such as depression, Generalized Anxiety Disorder (GAD), and panic disorder.[24] Post-Traumatic Stress Disorder is presently at the center of a flourishing psychotherapeutic industry that ranges from trauma work to Eye Movement Desensitization and Reprocessing (EMDR).

The fact is that patient groups, far from being critical of this disease mongering, often actively collaborate in it. All pharmaceutical companies know that one of the most effective ways to introduce a new medication is to set up a patient advocacy group and launch a corresponding website. What could be more effective in terms of public relations than a group of patients clamoring for their illness to be taken seriously and for third-party payers to assume responsibility for the often significant costs of treatment? In a 1996 brochure from a professional training seminar devoted to "Creating targeted patient education campaigns," we read:

> Carefully planned education campaigns are ... becoming more widespread as pharmaceutical companies realise the benefits of added value services. At this two-day conference, you will discover how to successfully create targeted patient education campaigns which will establish your expertise in disease areas and increase company profile.[25]

Moynihan, Heath, and Henry, three Australian writers, tell how Roche, during the 1990s, worked closely with a patient group called the Obsessive Compulsive and Anxiety Disorders Foundation of Victoria to organize a conference on social phobia. They quote the foundation's chief at the time: "Roche is putting a lot of money into promoting social phobia ... Roche funded the conference to help get social phobia known among [general practitioners] and other health professionals ... It was a vehicle to raise awareness with the media too.'[26] The obvious question here is whether or not the disease existed before Roche raised awareness of it *among the patients*.

The same dynamic is also at work in the psychotherapeutic field, where certain patient groups militate, quite literally, for the recognition of syndromes introduced on the market by particular psychotherapeutic lobbies. The most striking example is undoubtedly that of multiple personality disorder in America during the 1970s and 1980s. This was a grassroots and proselytizing movement modeled on radical feminist groups, complete with newsletters, support groups, and celebrity coming-outs. The International Society for the Study of Multiple Personality and Dissociation, whose conventions, according to Daniel C. Dennet and Nicolas Humphrey, had an uncanny resemblance to a gathering of religious believers,[27] was at once a scientific society and a patient advocacy group, to such an extent that it was often impossible to distinguish the therapists from their clients. As I was able to observe in the early 1990s, while doing fieldwork with consultation groups of therapists specializing in multiple personality and satanic ritual abuse, these therapists almost always introduced themselves as incest and sexual or ritual abuse "survivors," just like their patients. Much as one becomes a psychoanalyst only after having been on the couch, dissociation experts were themselves former victims of trauma and strove with their patients for "the Cause," by bearing witness to the suffering that had been inflicted on them.

We clearly see, in this extreme case, how the expertise of patient groups, far from providing a critical counterweight to the specialists' expertise, can on the contrary simply identify with the latter and amplify the vicious circle of disease mongering. Here, to slightly subvert Karl Kraus's dictum about psychoanalysis, the illness *is* the therapy that claims to cure it, each reinforcing the other, each creating and co-producing the other: *folie à deux, folie à plusieurs.*

What can we conclude from this? I began this reflection with stating some obvious facts, but having arrived at this point I am left with only uncomfortable questions and a few half-ruminated remarks.

Remark no. 1: If it is true that patient groups mark an irruption of democracy into the medical field, we should not be shocked if this *also* brings about unpleasant consequences. Democracy provides no protection against collective errors, except the pursuit of democratic debate itself. In the USA, it was neither the psychiatrists–therapists nor the patient groups that put an end to the multiple personality epidemic and the witch hunt spurred by recovered memory therapy; it was in fact a third political agent, the False Memory Foundation formed by parents accused of incest and child abuse on the basis of "memories" discovered in therapy. So therapy users do not necessarily have the final say in their illness, since this discussion includes other groups concerned with or interested in this same illness. Thus, when the pharmaceutical company Pfizer sought to promote "female sexual dysfunction" in order to sell Viagra® to women, it was not a patient association which put up the resistance, but a group of female clinicians and feminist academics called the Working Group On A New View Of Women's Sexual Problems.[28] We should refrain therefore from exclusively focusing on the relationships between doctor–therapist collectives and users' collectives, for the illness also concerns other collectives, other agents who have a stake in it.

Remark no. 2: Disease mongering affects the medical field as a whole, but it is clearly in the "psy" field that it is most virulent and most successful in recruiting patients. The reason for this is that "psy" disorders are not specific diseases embodied in a discrete and independent entity within the individuals they affect, as is the case, for instance, with infectious or neurological diseases. Whatever their nature, "psy" disorders cannot be separated from the patients and their reaction to the diagnoses, theories, and treatments of which they are the object, as is shown by the fact that these disorders vary historically and geographically. One is not "schizophrenic" or "depressed" or "traumatized" in the same manner here as there, and this is because the people suffering from such illnesses interact with the categories that are applied to them, learn to recognize in them the nature of their suffering, and adapt to them by modeling their behavior and self-understanding on what is expected of them. Anthropologists speak in this respect of "idioms of distress,"[29] as if a quantity x of floating distress expressed itself by adopting different cultural idioms in different places. This might not be completely accurate, for the veritable epidemic of depression that we have witnessed for the last twenty years in the Western world shows that we have come to a point where it is the distress itself which is manufactured and sold with the idiom – here psychopharmacological – in which it is supposed to express itself. Disease mongering, from this perspective, is nothing but the modern, industrial form of the co-production of "psy"' diseases, which it is content to amplify, accelerate, and globalize with the cynicism that characterizes advanced liberal capitalism. As for the collectives of "psy" users, they too reveal the active participation, even if involuntary, of patients in the manufacturing and diffusion of their diseases.

Remark no. 3: This participation of therapy users in the construction of their own illnesses makes a critique of disease mongering especially difficult, and perhaps even pointless, in the "psy" field. The intentions of disease mongers are obviously detestable, but by what right can we denounce the fabrication of illnesses and the manipulation of users if the latter need these illnesses to fabricate themselves, if they construct for themselves an identity and a self with these medications and therapies that are offered to them? To criticize the false consciousness and alienation inherent to this process would assume that it is possible to posit a true consciousness, a non-fabricated self. But this is precisely what is no longer possible in a "psy" world where patients themselves choose the treatments – *which also means the illnesses* – which best suit them and organize in groups around these "life-forms," these ways of being together. Who are we to tell them they are mistaken? All we can offer them, perhaps, is another way to construct themselves, another way of fabricating themselves collectively. That is to say, another politics.

Remark no. 4: I have no idea what this "other politics" might look like. It remains to be invented. Collectively.

Translated by KELLY S. WALSH

Notes

1 Rabeharisoa, Callon, and Demonty 2000.
2 See Kirk and Kutchins 1992, ch. 4; Shorter 1997, pp. 303–304.
3 See Callon and Rabeharisoa 1999.
4 Boyd 1992; Freedman 1992; Epstein 1995; 1996.
5 Akrich and Méadel 2002.
6 Spiegel *et al.* 1989.
7 Kolata 2001.
8 Akrich and Méadel 2002, pp. 8–10.

9 See for instance the very interesting Hearing Voices Movement: Romme and Escher 1989; Martensson 1998. See as well Luhrmann 2000, ch. 7 and especially p. 269.

10 INSERM 2004.

11 Déglon 2005.

12 Nathan 2006.

13 Marks 1997; 2000; Kaptchuk 1998a.

14 Hacking 1998.

15 Akrich and Méadel 2002, pp. 8–10.

16 Payne 1992.

17 See Moynihan, Heath, and Henry 2002 as well as the articles collected in *PloS Medicine*, 3, no. 4, 2006.

18 Healy 1997, p. 76.

19 Healy 2006.

20 Moynihan, Heath, and Henry 2002, p. 888; Healy 2004a, p. 222.

21 Cook 2001, p. 17; cited in Moynihan, Heath, and Henry 2002, p. 888.

22 Berenson 2008, p. A22.

23 Hacking 1995, pp. 51–52.

24 Scott 1990; Young 1995, pp. 108–111; Shorter 1997, pp. 304–305.

25 Brochure from the training seminar "Creating targeted patient education campaigns," organized by the Institute for International Research in London, October, 29–30, 1996; cited in Healy 2004a, p. 226.

26 Cited in Moynihan, Heath and Henry 2002, p. 888.

27 "Maybe it is not surprising … that at meetings like the one we attended in Chicago [the Fifth International Conference on Multiple Personality/Dissociative States, 1988] there is a certain amount of well-meaning exaggeration and one-upmanship. We were, however, not prepared for what, if it occurred in a church, would amount to 'bearing witness'"; Humphrey and Dennett 1989, p. 93.

28 Tiefer 2006.

29 Nichter 1981, pp. 379–408.

Bibliography

Unless otherwise noted, all of Sigmund Freud's works are quoted from James Strachey (ed.), *The Standard Edition of the Complete Psychological Works of Sigmund Freud*, 24 vols. (London: Hogarth Press, 1953–74). *The Standard Edition* is subsequently referred to as *SE* followed by volume number.

Acocella, Joan (1999), *Creating Hysteria: Women and Multiple Personality Disorder*, San Francisco: Jossey-Bass.

Akrich, Madeleine and Méadel, Cécile (2002), "Prendre ses médicaments / prendre la parole: usage des médicaments par les patients dans les listes de discussion électroniques", *Sciences Sociales et Santé*, 20, no. 1, pp. 1–22.

Alexander, Franz and Selesnick, Sheldon T. (1965), "Freud–Bleuler correspondence", *Archives of General Psychiatry*, 12, pp. 1–9.

Althusser, Louis (1996[1963–64]), *Psychanalyse et sciences humaines: deux confé-rences*, Paris: Librairie Générale Française/IMEC.

   (1993[1964]), "Freud et Lacan", in Olivier Corpet and François Matheron (eds.), *Ecrits sur la psychanalyse: Freud et Lacan*, Paris: Stock/IMEC pp. 23–54.

Antze, Paul and Lambek, Michael (eds.) (1996), *Tense Past: Cultural Essays in Trauma and Memory*, New York and London: Routledge.

Applbaum, Kalman (2006), "Educating for global mental health. The adoption of SSRIs in Japan", in Adriana Petryna, Andrew Lakoff, and Arthur Kleinman (eds.), *Global Pharmaceuticals: Ethics, Markets, Practices*, Durham, NC: Duke University Press, pp. 85–110.

Aristotle (1983), *On the Art of Poetry*, in T. S. Dorsch (ed.), *Classical Literary Criticism*, Harmondsworth: Penguin Books.

Aschaffenburg, Gustav (1906), "Die Beziehung des sexuellen Lebens zur Entstehung von Nerven- und Geistes Krankheiten", *Münchener Medizinische Wochenschrift*, 53, September 11, pp. 1793–1798.

Associated Press (1998), "Psychologist says new evidence shows 'Sybil' story bogus", unpublished press release, August 16, 1998.

Assoun, Paul-Laurent (1981), *Introduction à l'épistémologie freudienne*, Paris: Payot.

Ayd, Frank (1961), *Recognizing the Depressed Patient*, New York: Grune and Stratton.

Azam, Etienne Eugène (1887), *Hypnotisme, double conscience et altération de la personnalité*, Paris: Librairie J.-B. Baillière et Fils.

Babinski, Joseph (1886), *Recherches servant à établir que certaines manifestations hystériques peuvent être transférées d'un sujet à un autre sujet sous l'influence de l'aimant*, Paris: Delahaye et Lecrosnier.

Baldwin, James Mark (1901), *Dictionary of Philosophy and Psychology*, 2 vols, New York: Macmillan.

Barber, Theodore Xenophon (1969), *Hypnosis: A Scientific Approach*, New York: Van Nostrand Reinhold.

(1976), *Pitfalls in Human Research: Ten Pivotal Points*, New York: Pergamon Press.

Barker, Lewellys F. (1907), "On the treatment of some of the functional neuroses", *International Clinics*, 17th series, 1, no. 1, pp. 1–22.

Barrett, Robert J. (1996), *The Psychiatric Team and the Social Definition of Schizophrenia: An Anthropological Study of Person and Illness*, Cambridge: Cambridge University Press.

(2000), "Le diagnostic précoce de la schizophrénie", *Ethnopsy*, 1, pp. 91–104.

Barrucand, Dominique (1967), *Histoire de l'hypnose en France*, Paris: Presses Universitaires de France.

Bastide, Roger (1972 [1965]), *The Sociology of Mental Disorder*, translated from the French by Jean McNeil, New York: D. McKay Co.

Bateson, Gregory (1972), *Steps to an Ecology of Mind*, San Francisco: Chandler Publishing Company.

Beard, George Miller (1876), "The influence of mind in the causation and cure of disease – the potency of definite expectations," *Journal of Nervous and Mental Disease*, 3, pp. 429–434.

Beecher, Henry K. (1955), "The powerful placebo", *Journal of the American Medical Association*, 159, pp. 1602–1606.

Bell, R. M. (1985), *Holy Anorexia*, Chicago: University of Chicago Press.

Benedict, Ruth (1934), "Anthropology and the abnormal", *Journal of General Psychology*, 10, pp. 59–82.

Benedikt, Moriz (1892), "Über Neuralgien und neuralgische Affectionen und deren Behandlung," *Klinische Zeitschrift*, 6, pp. 67–106.

Bennet, Abram Elting (1940), "Preventing traumatic complications in convulsive shock therapy by curare", *Journal of the American Medical Association*, 114, January 27, pp. 332–324.

Bennett, Abram Elting and Wilbur, Cornelia B. (1944a), *Narcosynthesis* (16 mm film), Omaha, Nebraska, Bishop Clarckson Memorial Hospital, Psychiatric Department.

(1944b), "Convulsive shock therapy in involutional states after complete failure with previous estrogenic treatment", *American Journal of the Medical Sciences*, 208, no. 2, pp. 170–176.

Berenson, Alex (2008), "Drug approved. Is disease real?" *The New York Times*, January 14, pp. A1 and A22.

Bergson, Henri (1886), "De la simulation inconsciente dans l'état d'hypnotisme," *Revue Philosophique*, 22, pp. 525–531.

Bérillon, Edgar (1886) "L'école de Paris et l'école de Nancy," *Revue de l'Hypnotisme Expérimental et Thérapeutique*, 1, pp. 33–41.

Bernfeld, Siegfried (1946), "An unknown autobiographical fragment by Freud," *The American Imago*, 4, no. 1, pp. 3–19.

Bernheim, Hippolyte (1891 [1886]), *De la suggestion dans l'état hypnotique et de ses applications à la thérapeutique*, Paris: Octave Doin (3rd rev. edn).

(1892), *Neue Studien über Hypnotismus, Suggestion und Psychotherapie*, translated from the French by Sigmund Freud, Leipzig and Vienna: Deuticke.

(1975 [1916]), *De la suggestion* [not to be confused with *De la suggestion dans l'état hypnotique et de ses applications à la thérapeutique*], Paris: Retz-CEPL.

(1995 [1891]), *Hypnotisme, suggestion, psychothérapie, avec considérations nouvelles sur l'hystérie*, Paris: Fayard (reprint of 2nd edn of 1903).

Bettelheim, Bruno (1956), "Schizophrenia as a reaction to extreme situations", *American Journal of Orthopsychiatry*, 26, no. 3, pp. 507–518.

Bieber, Irving, Wilbur, Cornelia B., *et al.* (1962), *Homosexuality: A Psychoanalytic Study of Male Homosexuals*, New York: Basic Books.

Binet, Alfred (1886), review of H. Bernheim, *De la suggestion et de ses applications à la thérapeutique*, *Revue Philosophique*, 22, pp. 557–563.

Bleuler, Eugen (1896), review of *Studies on Hysteria*, *Münchener Medizinische Wochenschrift*, 43, pp. 524–525.

(1910), "Die Psychanalyse Freuds: Verteidigung und kritische Bemerkungen", *Jahrbuch für Psychoanalytische und Psychopathologische Forschungen*, 2, pp. 623–730.

(1913), "Kritik der Freudschen Theorien," *Zeitschrift für Psychiatrie*, 70, pp. 665–718.

Bleuler, Manfred (ed.) (1979), *Beiträge zur Schizophrenielehre der Zürcher Psychiatrischen Universitätsklinik Burghölzli (1902–1971)*, Darmstadt: Wissenschaftliche Buchgesellschaft.

Bliss, Eugene L. (1980), "Multiple personalities: a report of fourteen cases with implications for schizophrenia and hysteria", *Archives of General Psychiatry*, 37, no. 12, pp. 1388–1397.

Bloor, David (1976), *Knowledge and Social Imagery*, London: Routledge and Kegan Paul.

Boor, Myron (1982), "The multiple personality epidemic. Additional cases and references regarding diagnosis, etiology, dynamics, and treatment", *Journal of Nervous and Mental Diseases*, 170, no. 5, pp. 302–304.

Borch-Jacobsen, Mikkel (1987), "L'hypnose dans la psychanalyse", followed by "Dispute", in Léon Chertok (ed.), *Hypnose et psychanalyse: réponses à Mikkel Borch-Jacobsen*, Paris: Bordas, pp. 29–54 and 194–217.

(1988 [1982]), *The Freudian Subject*, translated from the French by Catherine Porter, Stanford: Stanford University Press.

(1992 [1991]), *The Emotional Tie: Psychoanalysis, Mimesis, and Affect*, translated from the French by Douglas Brick and others, Stanford: Stanford University Press.

(1994a), "The Oedipus problem in Freud and Lacan", *Critical Inquiry*, 20, no. 2, pp. 267–282.

(1994b), "Sous le signe de Hyde", *Quinzaine Littéraire*, 651, pp. 24–25.

(1994c), "Who's who? Introducing multiple personality", in Joan Copjec (ed.), *Supposing the Subject*, London: Verso, pp. 45–63.

(1996 [1995]), *Remembering Anna O.: A Century of Mystification*, translated from the French by Kirby Olson in collaboration with Xavier Callahan and the author, New York: Routledge.

(1997), "Sybil – The making of a disease: an interview with Dr. Herbert Spiegel", *The New York Review of Books*, 44, no. 7, April 24.

(1998), "Neurotica. Er Freuds forførelsesteori resultatet af en hypnotisk pagt mellem ham og hans patienter?" *Kritik*, 131, pp. 9–26.

(1999a), "Much ado about nothing: a reply to Claudia Brodsky Lacour's reply", *Narrative*, 7, no. 1, pp. 120–123.

(1999b), "Die Hysterie im Zeitalter ihrer technischen Reproduzierbarkeit", interview with *Basler Zeitung*, February 9.

(2002), *Folies à plusieurs: de l'hystérie à la dépression*, Paris: Les Empêcheurs de Penser en Rond / Seuil.

(2005a), "Le médecin imaginaire", in Catherine Meyer *et al.* (ed.), *Le livre noir de la psychanalyse*, Paris: Les Arènes, pp. 72–80.

(2005b), "Un citoyen au-dessus de tout soupçon", in Catherine Meyer *et al.* (ed.), *Le livre noir de la psychanalyse*, Paris: Les Arènes, pp. 101–113.

(2006), "Qu'a-t-il vraiment découvert?", *La Recherche*, 397, pp. 40–43.

Borch-Jacobsen, Mikkel, Esterson, Allen, Macmillan, Malcolm, and Swales, Peter J. (1999), "Partisan reviewing", www.hbs.deakin.edu.au/psychology/reviewing. htm.

Borch-Jacobsen, Mikkel, Koeppel, Philippe, and Scherrer, Ferdinand (1984), "Traductions et destins de traductions," *L'Ecrit du Temps*, 7, pp. 43–52.

Borch-Jacobsen, Mikkel and Shamdasani, Sonu (2002), "Une visite aux Archives Freud", in Mikkel Borch-Jacobsen, *Folies à plusieurs: de l'hystérie à la dépression*, Paris: Les Empêcheurs de Penser en Rond / Seuil, pp. 253–300.

(2006), *Le dossier Freud: enquête sur l'histoire de la psychanalyse*, Paris: Les Empêcheurs de Penser en Rond / Seuil.

Bourru, Henri and Burot, Prosper (1888), *Variations de la personnalité*, Paris: Baillière.

Boyd, Kenneth M. *et al.* (1992), "AIDS, ethics, and clinical trials", *British Medical Journal*, 305, pp. 699–701.

Boynton, Robert S. (1998–1999), "Hidden Talents Dept.", *The New Yorker*, December 28, 1998–January 4, 1999.

Braude, Stephen E. (1991), *First Person Plural: Multiple Personality and the Philosophy of Mind*, London and New York: Routledge.

Braun, Bennett G. (1979), "Clinical aspects of multiple personality", paper presented at the annual meeting of the American Society of Clinical Hypnosis, San Francisco, November 1979.

Breuer, Josef and Freud, Sigmund (1895), *Studies on Hysteria*, SE 2.

Brodie, Benjamin Collins (1837), *Lectures Illustrative of Certain Local Nervous Affections*, London: Longman.

Brodsky Lacour, Claudia (1999), "All and nothing: a reply to Mikkel Borch-Jacobsen", *Narrative*, 7, no. 1, pp. 114–119.

Brooks, Peter (1992), *Reading for the Plot: Design and Intention in Narrative*, Cambridge, MA: Harvard University Press.

Bureau of Justice (1999), "Mental health and treatment of inmates and probationers", Bureau of Justice Statistics.

Burnham, John (1983), *Jelliffe: American Psychoanalyst and Physician and His Correspondence with Sigmund Freud and C. G. Jung*, ed. William McGuire, Chicago: University of Chicago Press.

Bynum, Caroline Walker (1987), *Holy Feast and Holy Fast: The Religious Significance of Food to Medieval Women*, Berkeley: University of California Press.

Callon, Michel and Latour, Bruno (1992), "Don't throw the baby out with the Bath School! A reply to Collins and Yearly", in Andrew Pickering (ed.), *Science as Practice and Culture*, Chicago: University of Chicago Press, pp. 343–368.

Callon, Michel and Rabeharisoa, Volona (1999), *Le pouvoir des malades*, Paris: Presses de l'Ecole Nationale des Mines de Paris.

Cannon, Walter Bradford (1942), "'Voodoo' death", *American Anthropologist*, 44, no. 2, pp. 169–181.

Caplan, Eric (1998), *Mind Games: American Culture and the Birth of Psychotherapy*, Berkeley: University of California Press.

Carlson, Eric T. (1981), "The history of multiple personality in the United States: I. The Beginnings", *American Journal of Psychiatry*, 138, no. 5, pp. 666–668.

Caroll, Lewis (1970), *The Annotated Alice*, ed. Martin Gardner, Harmondsworth: Penguin Books.

Carroy, Jacqueline (1993), *Les personnalités doubles et multiples: entre science et fiction*, Paris: Presses Universitaires de France.

(1997a), "L'effet Delbœuf", *Corpus*, 32, pp. 89–117.

(1997b), "Dédoublements. Paradoxe sur le comédien et simulation inconsciente au XIXe siècle", *L'évolution psychiatrique*, 62, pp. 501–509.

(2000), "Présentation", in "Les psychothérapies dans leur histoire" (special issue), *Psychologie Clinique*, new series, 9, pp. 7–9.

Charcot, Jean-Martin (1878), "De l'influence des lésions traumatiques sur le développement des phénomènes d'hystérie locale", *Le Progrès Médical*, 6, pp. 335–337.

(1887), *Leçons sur les maladies du système nerveux*, vol. 3, Paris: Delahaye et Lecrosnier.

(1888), "Les accidents de chemin de fer", *Gazette des Hôpitaux*, pp. 1293–1294.

(1890), *Leçons du Mardi à la Salpêtrière, Policlinique 1888–1889*, Paris: Bureaux du Progrès Médical, E. Lecrosnier et Babé.

(1892), *Leçons du Mardi à la Salpêtrière. Policlinique 1887–1888*, Paris: Bureaux du Progrès Médical, Louis Bataille.

(1991 [1887]), *Clinical Lectures on Diseases of the Nervous System*, vol. 3, ed. Ruth Harris, translated from the French by Thomas Savill, London and New York: Tavistock/Routledge.

Charcot, Jean-Martin and Richer, Paul (1887), *Les démoniaques dans l'art*, Paris: Delahaye et Lecrosnier.

Chertok, Léon (1979), *Le non-savoir des psy: l'hypnose entre la psychanalyse et la biologie*, Paris: Payot.

Chertok, Léon and Saussure, Raymond de (1973), *Naissance du psychanalyste: de Mesmer à Freud*, Paris: Payot.

Chertok, Léon and Stengers, Isabelle (1992 [1989]), *A Critique of Psychoanalytic Reason: Hypnosis as a Scientific Problem from Lavoisier to Lacan*, translated from the French by Martha Noel Evans, Stanford, CA: Stanford University Press.

Chertok, Léon, Stengers, Isabelle and Gille, Didier (1990), *Mémoires d'un hérétique*, Paris: La Découverte.

Chodoff, Paul (1966), "A critique of Freud's theory of infantile sexuality," *American Journal of Psychiatry*, 123, no. 5, pp. 507–518.

Cifali, Mireille (1988), "La fabrication du martien: genèse d'une langue imaginaire", *Langages*, 91, pp. 39–52.

Cioffi, Frank (1986), "Did Freud rely on the Tally Argument to meet the argument from suggestibility?" *Behavioral and Brain Sciences*, 9, no. 2 , pp. 230–31.

(1998), *Freud and the Question of Pseudoscience*, Chicago and La Salle, IL: Open Court.

Clarcke, John Michell (1896), review of *Studies on Hysteria, Brain*, 19, pp. 401–414.

Consumer Reports (1995), "Mental health: does therapy help?" *Consumer Reports*, November, pp. 734–739.

Cook, Henry (2001), "Practical guide to medical education", *Pharmaceutical Marketing*, 6, pp. 14–22.

Crabtree, Adam (1985), *Multiple Man: Explorations in Possession and Multiple Personality*, Don Mills, Ontario: Collins.

(1993), *From Mesmer to Freud: Magnetic Sleep and the Roots of Psychological Healing*, New Haven: Yale University Press.

Crews, Frederick (ed.) (1995), *The Memory Wars: Freud's Legacy in Dispute*, New York: A New York Review Book.

(1997), "The legacy of Salem. Demonology for an age of science", *Skeptic*, 5, no. 1, pp. 36–44.

Crocq, L. and Verbizier, J. de (1989). "Le traumatisme psychologique dans l'œuvre de Pierre Janet", *Bulletin de Psychologie*, 41, no. 385, pp. 483–484.

Croes, Shelley (1999), "Researcher: Sybil a sham", *Mankato Free Press*, April 27.

Danto, Arthur (1965), *Analytical Philosophy of History*, Cambridge: Cambridge University Press.

Danziger, Kurt (1990), *Constructing the Subject. Historical Origins of Psychological Research*, Cambridge: Cambridge University Press.

Déglon, Jean-Jacques (2005), "Comment les théories psychanalytiques ont bloqué le traitement efficace des toxicomanes et contribué à la mort de milliers d'individus", in Catherine Meyer *et al.* (ed.), *Le livre noir de la psychanalyse*, Paris: Les Arènes, pp. 616–637.

Delbœuf, Joseph (1886a), "La mémoire chez les hypnotisés", *Revue Philosophique*, 21, pp. 441–472.

(1886b), "De l'influence de l'éducation et de l'imitation dans le somnambulisme provoqué", *Revue Philosophique*, 22, pp. 146–171.

(1891–92), "Comme quoi il n'y a pas d'hypnotisme", *Revue de l'Hypnotisme Expérimental et Thérapeutique*, 6, pp. 129–135.

(1993 [1879–93]), *Le sommeil et les rêves, et autres textes*, ed. Jacqueline Carroy and François Duyckaerts, Paris: Fayard.

Denker, Peter G. (1946), "Result of treatment of psychoneuroses by the general practitioner. A follow-up study of 500 cases", *New York State Journal of Medicine*, 4, pp. 2164–2166.

Derrida, Jacques and Roudinesco, Elisabeth (2001), *De quoi demain. . . Dialogue*, Paris: Fayard/Galilée.

Devereux, George (1956), "Normal and abnormal: the key problem of psychiatric anthropology", in J. B. Casagrande and T. Gladwin (eds.), *Some Uses of Anthropology: Theoretical and Applied*, Washington, DC: Anthropological Society of Washington, pp. 23–48.

(1967), *From Anxiety to Method in the Behavioral Sciences*, The Hague: Mouton.

Dhorme, Etienne (1959), "Introduction", in *L'Ancien Testament*, vol. 2, ed. Etienne Dhorme, Paris: Gallimard, pp. xi–clxxix.

Doron, Roland and Parot, Françoise (eds.) (1991), *Dictionnaire de psychologie*, Paris: Presses Universitaires de France.

Dubois, Paul (1908 [1904]), *The Psychic Treatment of Nervous Disorders*, translated from the French by Smith Ely Jelliffe and William A. White, New York and London: Funk & Wagnalls.

Eagle, Morris (1993), "The dynamics of theory change in psychoanalysis", in J. Earman (ed.), *Philosophical Problems of the Internal and External World: Essays on the Philosophy of Adolf Grünbaum*, Pittsburg and Konstanz: University of Pittsburgh Press and Universitätsverlag Konstanz.

Eddy, Mary Baker Glover (1875), *Science and Health*, Boston: W. F. Brown.

Edinger, Dora (1968), *Bertha Pappenheim, Freud's Anna O.*, Highland Park, IL: Congregation Solel.

Ehrenberg, Alain (2000), *La fatigue d'être soi: dépression et société*, Paris: Odile Jacob.

Elkin, Irene (1994), "The NIMH treatment of depression collaborative research program: where we began and where we are", in Allen E. Bergin and Sol L. Garfield (eds.), *Handbook of Psychotherapy and Behavior Change*, New York: John Wiley & Sons (4th edn), pp. 114–139.

Ellenberger, Henri Frédéric (1970), *The Discovery of the Unconscious: The History and Evolution of Dynamic Psychiatry*, New York: Basic Books.

(1973), "Freud in perspective. A conversation with Henri F. Ellenberger", interview with Jacques Mousseau, *Psychology Today*, March, pp. 50–60.

(1995), *Médecines de l'âme: essais d'histoire de la folie et des guérisons psychiques*, Paris: Fayard.

Epstein, Steven (1995), "The construction of lay expertise: AIDS activism and the forging of credibility in the reform of clinical trials", *Science, Technology and Human Values*, 4, pp. 408–437.

(1996), *Impure Science: AIDS, Activism, and the Politics of Knowledge*, Berkeley: University of California Press.

Erichsen, Sir John Eric (1866), *On Railway and Other Injuries of the Nervous System*, London.

Erickson, Milton H. (1967), *Advanced Techniques of Hypnosis and Therapy*, New York: Grune and Stratton.

Esterson, Allen (1993), *Seductive Mirage*, Chicago and La Salle, IL: Open Court.

(1996), "Grünbaum's tally argument," *History of the Human Sciences*, 9, no. 1, pp. 43–57.

(1998), "Jeffrey Masson and Freud's seduction theory: a new fable based on old myths", *History of the Human Sciences*, 11, no. 1, pp. 1–21.

Estroff, Sue E. (1981), *Making It Crazy: An Ethnography of Psychiatric Clients in an American Community*, Berkeley: University of California Press.

Falzeder, Ernst (1994), "My grand-patient, my chief tormentor: a hitherto unnoticed case of Freud's and the consequences", *Psychoanalytic Quarterly*, 63, pp. 297–331.

Farr, Robert M. (1978), "On the social significance of artifacts in experimenting", *British Journal of Social and Clinical Psychology*, 17, pp. 299–306.

Favret-Saada, Jeanne (1977), *Les mots, la mort, les sorts*, Paris: Gallimard.

Fischer-Homberger, Esther (1975), *Die traumatische Neurose: vom somatischen zum sozialen Leiden*, Vienna: Hans Huber.

Fish, Stanley (1986), "Withholding the missing portion: power, meaning, and persuasion in Freud's 'The Wolf-Man'", *Times Literary Supplement*, August 29, 1986.

Flammer, Ilan (1994), *La mémoire abusée*, TV documentary, Arte.

Flournoy, Théodore (1903), "F. W. H. Myers et son oeuvre posthume", *Archives de Psychologie*, 2, pp. 269–296.

(1911), *Esprits et médiums: mélanges de métapsychique et de psychologie*, Geneva: Kündig.

(1994 [1899]), *From India to the Planet Mars: A Case of Multiple Personality with Imaginary Languages*, ed. Sonu Shamdasani, Princeton, NJ: Princeton University Press.

Forel, August (1919 [1889]), *Der Hypnotismus oder die Suggestion und die Psychologie*, Stuttgart: Ferdinand Enke (8th–9th, augmented and revised edn.)

(1968), *August Forel: Briefe/Correspondance 1864–1927*, ed. Hans H. Walser, Berne and Stuttgart: Hans Huber,

Forthomme, Bernard (1999), *De l'acédie monastique à l'anxio-dépression: histoire philosophique de la transformation d'un vice en pathologie*, Paris: Les Empêcheurs de Penser en Rond / Synthélabo.

Foucault, Michel (1965 [1961]), *Madness and Civilization: A History of Insanity in the Age of Reason*, translated from the French by Richard Howard, New York: Pantheon Books.

(1978 [1976]), *The History of Sexuality*, vol. 1: *An Introduction*, translated from the French by Robert Hurley, New York: Pantheon Books.

(2003 [1999]), *Abnormal: Lectures at the Collège de France, 1974–1975*, ed. Valerio Marchetti and Antonella Salomoni, translated from the French by Graham Burchell, New York: Picador.

Freedman, Benjamin (1992), "AIDS and the ethics of clinical trials: learning the right lessons", *Controlled Clinical Trials*, 13, pp. 1–5.

Freud, Sigmund (1884), "Über Coca", *Centralblatt für die Gesammte Therapie*, 2, pp. 289–314; reissued as a separate volume, Vienna, Perles, 1885.

(1885), "Über die Allgemeinwirkung des Cocains", *Zeitschrift für Therapie*, 3, no. 7, April 1, pp. 49–51.

(1888), "Hysteria", *SE* 1, pp. 37–57.

(1888–89), Preface to the translation of Bernheim's *Suggestion*, *SE* 1, pp. 71–87.

(1889), Review of August Forel's *Hypnotism*, *SE* 1, pp. 89–102.

(1890), "Psychical (or mental) treatment", *SE* 7, pp. 281–302.

(1987 [1892]), "Über Hypnose und Suggestion", *Gesammelte Werke, Nachtragsband*, Frankfurt am Main: S. Fischer Verlag.

(1895a), "A reply to criticisms of my paper on anxiety neurosis", *SE* 3, pp. 119–139.

(1895b), "Über Hysterie", original account in the *Wiener Medizinische Presse*, 36, pp. 1717–1718.

(1896a), "Heredity and the aetiology of the neuroses", *SE* 3, pp. 141–156.

(1896b), "Further remarks on the neuro-psychoses of defence", *SE* 3, pp. 157–185.

(1896c), "The aetiology of hysteria", *SE* 3, pp. 189–221

(1897), "Abstracts of the scientific writings of Dr. Sigm. Freud 1877–1897", *SE* 3, pp. 223–257.

(1898), "Sexuality in the aetiology of the neuroses", *SE* 3, pp. 259–285.

(1900), *The Interpretation of Dreams*, *SE* 4–5.

(1901), *The Psychopathology of Everyday Life*, *SE* 6.

(1905a), *Three Essays on the Theory of Sexuality*, *SE* 7, pp. 121–245.

(1905b), "On psychotherapy", *SE* 7, pp. 255–268.

(1906), "My views on the part played by sexuality in the aetiology of the neuroses", *SE* 7, pp. 269–279.

(1907–08), *Original Record of the Case of Obsessional Neurosis (the 'Rat Man')*, *SE* 10, pp. 251–318.

(1908), "Character and anal erotism", *SE* 9, pp. 167–175.

(1909), *Notes upon a Case of Obsessional Neurosis*, *SE* 10, pp. 153–249.

(1910), *Five Lectures on Psycho-Analysis*, *SE* 11, pp. 1–56.

(1911), *Psycho-Analytic Notes on an Autobiographical Account of a Case of Paranoia (Dementia Paranoides)*, *SE* 12, pp. 9–82.

(1912), "A note on the unconscious in psycho-analysis", *SE* 12, pp. 255–266.

(1913), "On beginning the treatment. (Further recommendations on the technique of psycho-analysis I)", *SE* 12, pp. 121–144.

(1914*a*), *On the History of the Psycho-Analytic Movement*, *SE* 14, pp. 7–66.

(1914b), "On narcissism: an introduction", *SE* 14, pp. 67–102.

(1915a), "The unconscious", *SE* 14, pp. 159–215.

(1915b), "Instincts and their vicissitudes", *SE* 14, pp. 109–140.

(1916–17), *Introductory Lectures on Psycho-Analysis*, *SE* 15–16.

(1917a), "A difficulty on the path of psycho-analysis", *SE* 17, pp. 135–144.

(1917b), "On transformations of instinct as exemplified in anal erotism", *SE* 17, pp. 125–133.

(1918), "From the history of an infantile neurosis", *SE* 18, pp. 3–122.

(1920), "A note on the prehistory of the technique of analysis", *SE* 18, pp. 263–265.

(1921), *Group Psychology and the Analysis of the Ego*, *SE* 18, pp. 65–143.

(1925), *An Autobiographical Study*, *SE* 20, pp. 1–74.

(1926), "The question of lay-analysis: conversations with an impartial person", *SE* 20, pp. 179–258.

(1933), *New Introductory Lectures to Psycho-Analysis*, *SE* 22, pp. 1–182.

(1937), "Constructions in analysis", *SE* 23, pp. 255–269.

(1954), *The Origins of Psycho-Analysis: Letters to Wilhelm Fliess, Drafts and Notes, 1887–1902*, ed. Marie Bonaparte, Anna Freud, and Ernst Kris, translated from the German by Eric Mosbacher and James Strachey, New York: Basic Books.

(1985), *The Complete Letters of Sigmund Freud to Wilhelm Fliess 1887–1904*, ed. Jeffrey Moussaïef Masson, Cambridge, MA: The Belknap Press of Harvard University Press.

Freud, Sigmund and Abraham, Karl (2002), *The Complete Correspondence of Sigmund Freud and Karl Abraham 1907–1925: Completed Edition*, ed. Ernst Falzeder, translated from the German by Caroline Schwarzacher, London: Karnac.

Freud, Sigmund and Ferenczi, Sándor (1993), *Correspondence 1908–1914*, ed. André Haynal, Ernst Falzeder *et al.*, Cambridge, MA: The Belknap Press of Harvard University Press.

Freud, Sigmund and Jung Carl Gustav (1974), *The Freud/Jung Letters: The Corres-pondence between Sigmund Freud and C. G. Jung*, ed. William McGuire, translated from the German by Ralph Manheim and R. F. C. Hull, Princeton, NJ: Princeton University Press.

Freud, Sigmund and Zweig, Arnold (1970), *The Letters of Sigmund Freud and Arnold Zweig*, ed. Ernst L. Freud, New York: Harcourt, Brace & World.

Fromm-Reichmann, Frieda (1948), "Notes on the development of treatment of schizo-phrenics by psychoanalytic psychotherapy", *Psychiatry*, 11, no. 3, pp. 263–273.

Fuller, Robert C. (1982), *Mesmerism and the American Cure of Souls*, Philadelphia: University of Pennsylvania Press.

Garfinkel, Harold (1967), *Studies in Ethnomethodology*, Englewood Cliffs, NJ: Prentice Hall.

Gauchet, Marcel (1992), *L'inconscient cérébral*, Paris: Seuil.

Gauchet, Marcel and Swain, Gladys (1997), *Le vrai Charcot: les chemins imprévus de l'inconscient*, Paris: Calmann-Lévy.

Gauld, Alan (1992), *A History of Hypnotism*, Cambridge: Cambridge University Press.

Gaupp, Robert (1900), Review in *Zeitschrift für Psychologie und Physiologie der Sinnesorgane*, 23, pp. 233–234.

Gay, Peter (1988), *Freud: A Life for Our Time*, New York: Norton.

Gesell, Arnold and Gesell, Beatrice (1912), *The Normal Child and Primary Education*, London: Ginn.

Gillin, J. (1948), "Magical fright", *Psychiatry*, 11, no. 4, pp. 387–400.

Girard, René (1977 [1972]), *Violence and the Sacred*, translated from the French by Patrick Gregory, Baltimore: Johns Hopkins University Press.

Goldstein, Jan (1987), *Console and Classify: The French Psychiatric Profession in the Nineteenth Century*, Cambridge: Cambridge University Press.

Good, Byron (1994), *Medicine, Rationality, and Experience: An Anthropological Perspective*, Cambridge: Cambridge University Press.

Goodman, Louis Sanford and Gilman, Alfred Goodman (1965), *The Pharmacological Basis of Therapeutics*, London and Toronto: Collier-Macmillan (3rd edn).

Gravitz, Melvin A. and Gerton, Manuel I. (1981), "Freud and hypnosis: report of post-rejection use," *Journal of the History of the Behavioral Sciences*, 17, pp. 68–74.

Greaves, Georges B. (1980), "Multiple personality: 165 years after Mary Reynolds", *Journal of Nervous and Mental Disease*, 168, no. 10, pp. 577–596.

Grivois, Henri (1992), *Naître à la folie*, Paris: Les Empêcheurs de Penser en Rond / Synthélabo.

     (1998), "Coordination et subjectivité dans la psychose naissante", in Henri Grivois and Joëlle Proust (eds.), *Subjectivité et conscience d'agir: approches cognitive et clinique de la psychose*, Paris: Presses Universitaires de France, pp. 35–73.

Grünbaum, Adolf (1984), *The Foundations of Psychoanalysis: A Philosophical Cri-tique*, Berkeley: University of California Press.

Habermas, Jürgen (1971 [1968]), *Knowledge and Human Interests*, translated from the German by Jeremy J. Shapiro, Boston: Beacon Press.

Hacking, Ian (1995), *Rewriting the Soul: Multiple Personality and the Sciences of Memory*, Princeton, NJ: Princeton University Press.

     (1998), *Mad Travelers: Reflections on the Reality of Transient Mental Illnesses*, Charlottesville: University of Virginia Press.

(1999), *The Social Construction of What?*, Cambridge, MA: Harvard University Press.

Hale, Nathan G., Jr. (1999), "Freud critics: a critical look", *Partisan Review*, 66, no. 2, pp. 235–254.

Haley, Jay (1965), "An interactional explanation of hypnosis", in Ronald E. Shor and Martin Orne (eds.), *The Nature of Hypnosis: Selected Basic Readings*, New York: Holt, Rinehart and Winston, pp. 267–287.

(1973), *Uncommon Therapy: The Psychiatric Techniques of Milton H. Erickson*, New York: Norton.

Hall, Stanley (1909), "Evolution and psychology", in *Fifty Years of Darwinism: Modern Aspects of Evolution. Centennial Addresses in Honor of Charles Darwin before the AAAS*, New York: Henry Holt, pp. 251–267.

(1923), *Life and Confessions of a Psychologist*, New York: D. Appleton & Co.

Hamayon, Roberte (1978), "Soigner le mort pour guérir le vif", *Nouvelle Revue de Psychanalyse*, 17, pp. 55–72.

Hansen, Bert (1992), "American physicians' 'discovery' of homosexuals, 1880–1900: a new diagnosis in a changing society", in Charles E. Rosenberg and Janet Golden (eds.), *Framing Disease: Studies in Cultural History*, New Brunswick, NJ: Rutgers University Press, pp. 104–133.

Harding, Courtenay *et al.* (1987), "The Vermont longitudinal study of persons with severe mental illness, I: methodology, study sample, and overall status 32 years later", *American Journal of Psychiatry*, 144, pp. 718–726.

Harrington, Anne (1988), "Hysteria, hypnosis, and the lure of the invisible: the rise of neo-Mesmerism in *fin-de-siècle* French psychiatry", in William F. Bynum, Roy Porter and Michael Shepherd (eds.), *The Anatomy of Madness*, London: Tavistock, vol. 3, pp. 226–245.

Hart, Bernard (1929 [1927]), *Psychopathology: Its Development and Its Place in Medicine*, Cambridge: Cambridge University Press.

Hart, Onno van der and Horst, Rutger (1989), "The dissociation theory of Pierre Janet", *Journal of Traumatic Stress*, 2, pp. 397–412.

Healy, David (1997), *The Antidepressant Era*, Cambridge, MA: Harvard University Press.

(2002), *The Creation of Psychopharmacology*, Cambridge, MA: Harvard University Press.

(2004a), "Shaping the intimate: influences on the experience of everyday nerves", *Social Studies of Science*, 34, no. 2, pp. 219–245.

(2004b), *Let Them Eat Prozac: The Unhealthy Relationship between the Pharmaceutical Industry and Depression*, New York: New York University Press.

(2006), "The latest mania: selling bi-polar disorder", *PLoS Medicine*, 3, no. 4. www.plosmedicine.org.

Heidenhain, Rudolf (1888 [1880]), *Hypnotism or Animal Magnetism: Physiological Observations*, translated from the German by L. C. Wooldridge, London: Kegan Paul, Trench & Co.

Herman, Judith Lewis (1981), *Father–Daughter Incest*, Cambridge, MA: Harvard University Press.

(1992), *Trauma and Recovery*, New York: Basic Books.

Heusch, Luc de (1971), "La folie des dieux et la raison des hommes", in *Pourquoi l'épouser?*, Paris: Gallimard, pp. 245–286.

Hilgard, Ernest R. (1986 [1977]), *Divided Consciousness: Multiple Controls in Human Thought and Action*, New York: Wiley-Interscience (2nd edn).

Hillman, Robert G. (1965), "A scientific study of mystery: the role of the medical and popular press in the Nancy–Salpêtrière controversy on hypnotism", *Bulletin of the History of Medicine*, 39, pp. 163–182.

Hirschmüller, Albrecht (1989 [1978]), *The Life and Work of Josef Breuer: Physiology and Psychoanalysis*, translated from the German by the author, New York: New York University Press.

(1993), "Freud, Meynert et Mathilde: l'hypnose en question", *Revue Internationale d'Histoire de la Psychanalyse*, no. 6, pp. 271–286.

Hoche, Alfred (1910), "Eine psychische Epidemie unter Aerzten", *Medizinische Klinik*, 6, no. 26, pp. 1007–1010.

(1913), "Über den Wert der 'Psychoanalyse'", *Archiv für Psychiatrie*, 51, no. 3, pp. 1054–1079.

Hollister, Leo H. *et al.* (1961), "Withdrawal reactions from chlordiazepoxide ('Librium')", *Psychopharmacologia*, 2, no. 1, pp. 63–68.

Humphrey, Nicholas and Dennett, Daniel C. (1989), "Speaking for our selves: an assessment of multiple personality", *Raritan*, 9, no. 1, pp. 68–97.

INSERM (2004), "Psychothérapie: trois approches évaluées", Expertise collective INSERM, Paris: INSERM.

Israëls, Han (1999 [1993]), *Der Fall Freud: Die Geburt der Psychoanalyse aus der Lüge*, translated into German from the Dutch by Gerd Busse, Hamburg: Europäische Verlaganstalt / Rotbuch Verlag.

Israëls, Han and Schatzman, Morton (1993), "The seduction theory", *History of Psychiatry*, 4, pp. 23–59.

Jackson, Stanley W. (1986), *Melancholia and Depression: From Hippocratic Times to Modern Times*, New Haven, CT: Yale University Press.

Jacobsen, Paul B. and Steele, Robert S. (1979), "From present to past: Freudian archeology," *International Review of Psychoanalysis*, 6, no. 3, pp. 349–362.

James, William (1892), *Text-Book of Psychology*, London: Macmillan.

(1961 [1902]), *The Varieties of Religious Experience: A Study in Human Nature*, New York: Collier Books.

(1984), *William James on Exceptional Mental States: The 1896 Lowell Lectures*, ed. Eugene Taylor, Amherst: University of Massachusetts Press.

(1999), *The Correspondence of William James*, vol. 7, *1890–1894*, ed. Ignas K. Skrupskelis and Elizabeth M. Berkeley, Charlottesville: University of Virginia Press.

Janet, Pierre (1886), "Les actes inconscients et le dédoublement de la personnalité pendant le somnambulisme provoqué", *Revue Philosophique*, 22, pp. 577–592.

(1891), "Etude sur un cas d'aboulie et d'idées fixes", *Revue Philosophique*, 31, pp. 259–287 and 382–407.

(1901 [1894]), *The Mental States of Hystericals: A Study of Mental Stigmata and Mental Accidents*, translated from the French by Caroline Rollin Corson, New York: G. Putnam's Sons.

(1904), "L'amnésie et la dissociation des souvenirs", *Journal de Psychologie*, 1, pp. 417–453.

(1919), *Les médications psychologiques*, 3 vols., Paris: Alcan.

(1929a), *L'évolution psychologique de la personnalité*, Paris: Maloine.

(1929b [1907]), *The Major Symptoms of Hysteria: Fifteen Lectures Given in the Medical School of Harvard University*, London and New York: Macmillan.

(1989 [1889]), *L'automatisme psychologique: essai de psychologie expérimentale sur les formes élémentaires de l'activité humaine*, Paris: Société Pierre Janet/ CNRS.

Jastrow, Joseph (1932), *The House That Freud Built*, New York: Greenberg.

Johnson, Steve and Norris, Monty (1975), "Sybil: a shocked Dodge Center thinks she grew up there", *Minneapolis Star and Tribune*, August 27.

Jones, Ernest (1953), *The Life and Work of Sigmund Freud*, vol. 1, New York: Basic Books.

(1955), *The Life and Work of Sigmund Freud*, vol. 2, New York: Basic Books.

(1957), *The Life and Work of Sigmund Freud*, vol. 3, New York: Basic Books.

Jung, Carl Gustav (1906), "Freud's theory of hysteria: a reply to Aschaffenburg," in *The Collected Works*, vol. 4, ed. Herbert Read, Michael Fordham, and Gerhard Adler, Princeton, NJ: Princeton University Press, Bollingen Series XX, pp. 3–9.

(1912), "The theory of psychoanalysis," in *The Collected Works*, vol. 4, ed. Herbert Read, Michael Fordham, and Gerhard Adler, Princeton, NJ: Princeton University Press, Bollingen Series XX, pp. 83–226.

Junot, Henri (1936), *Mœurs et coutumes des Bantous: la vie d'une tribu sud-africaine*, vol. 2: *Vie mentale*, Paris: Payot.

Kaplan, Harold and Sadock, Benjamin (1996), *Pocket Handbook of Clinical Psychiatry*, Baltimore: Williams & Wilkins.

Kaptchuk, Ted J. (1998a), "Intentional ignorance: a history of blind assessment and placebo controls in medicine", *Bulletin of the History of Medicine*, 72, no. 3, pp. 389–433.

(1998b), "The powerful placebo: the dark side of the randomized controlled trial", *The Lancet*, 351, no. 9117, June 6, pp. 1722–1725.

Kardiner, Abram (1977), *My Analysis with Freud*, New York: Norton.

Kempe, Henry C. *et al.* (1962), "The battered-child syndrome," *Journal of the American Medical Association*, 181, no. 1, pp. 17–24.

Kenny, Michael (1986), *The Passion of Ansel Bourne: Multiple Personality in American Culture*, Washington, DC: Smithsonian Institution Press.

(1995), "The recovered memory controversy: an anthropologist's view," *Journal of Psychiatry and Law*, autumn, pp. 450–452.

Kiell, Norman (1988), *Freud without Hindsight: Reviews of His Work (1893–1939)*, Madison, WI: International Universities Press.

Kiessler, C. A. and Sibulkin, A. E. (1999), "Resident patients in state and county mental hospitals", 1994 survey, Center for Mental Health Services, US Department of Health and Human Services.

Kirk, Stuart and Kutchins, Herb (1992), *The Selling of DSM: The Rhetoric of Science in Psychiatry*, New York: Walter de Gruyter.

Klein, Milton I. and Tribich, David (1982), "Blame the child", *The Sciences*, 22, no. 8, pp. 14–20.

Kleinman, Arthur (1977), "Depression, somatization and the 'new cross-cultural psychiatry'", *Social Science and Medicine*, 11, no. 1, pp. 3–10.

(1980), *Patients and Healers in the Context of Culture*, Berkeley: University of California Press.

(1986), *Social Origins of Distress and Disease: Depression, Neurasthenia and Pain in Modern China*, New Haven, CT: Yale University Press.

(1988a), *The Illness Narratives: Suffering, Healing, and the Human Condition*, New York: Basic Books.

(1988b), *Rethinking Psychiatry: From Cultural Category to Personal Experience*, New York: The Free Press.

Klerman, Gerald L. (1983), "The efficacy of psychotherapy as the basis for public policy," *American Psychologist*, August, pp. 929–934.

(1982), "Varieties of hypnotic intervention in the treatment of multiple personality", *American Journal of Clinical Hypnosis*, 24, no. 4, pp. 230–240.

Knorr, Cetina Karin (1999), *Epistemic Cultures: How the Sciences Make Knowledge*, Cambridge, MA: Harvard University Press.

Kojève, Alexandre (1980 [1947]), *Introduction to the Reading of Hegel*, ed. Allan Bloom, translated from the French by James A. Nichols, Jr., Ithaca, NY: Cornell University Press.

Kolata, Gina (2001), "Cancer study finds support groups do not extend life", *New York Times*, December 13.

Krafft-Ebing, Richard von (1874), *Die Melancholie: eine klinische Studie*, Erlangen.

(1891), "Zur Verwerthung der Suggestionstherapie (Hypnose) bei Psychosen und Neurosen," *Wiener klinische Wochenschrift*, 4, October 22, pp. 795–799.

(1893 [1888]), *An Experimental Study in the Domain of Hypnotism*, translated from the German by Charles G. Chaddock, New York and London: G. Putnam's Sons.

(1894 [1886]), *Psychopathia sexualis, mit besonderer Berücksichtigung der conträren Sexualempfindung: eine klinisch-forensische Studie*, Stuttgart: Ferdinand Enke (9th edn).

(1895), "Über Unzucht mit Kindern und Pädophilia erotica", *Friedreich's Blätter für gerichtliche Medizin*.

(1896), "Zur Suggestivbehandlung der Hysteria Gravis," *Zeitschrift für Hypnotismus*, 4, pp. 27–31.

(1897–99), *Arbeiten aus dem Gesamtgebiet der Psychiatrie und Neuropathologie*, vol. 4, Leipzig: Barth.

Lacan, Jacques (1977 [1966]), *Ecrits: A Selection*, translated from the French by Allan Sheridan, New York: Norton.

(1984 [1938]), *Les complexes familiaux dans la formation de l'individu*, Paris: Navarin.

(1988 [1975]), *Freud's Papers on Technique, 1953–1954*, vol. 1 of *The Seminar of Jacques Lacan*, ed. Jacques-Alain Miller, translated from the French by John Forrester, New York: Norton.

Laing, Ronald D. and Esterson, Aaron (1964), *Sanity, Madness, and the Family*, New York: Basic Books.

Lakoff, Andrew (2006), *Pharmaceutical Reason: Knowledge and Value in Global Psychiatry*, Cambridge: Cambridge University Press.

Lambert, Michael J. and Bergin, Allen E. (1994), "The effectiveness of psychotherapy", in Allen E. Bergin and Sol L. Garfield (eds.), *Handbook of Psychotherapy and Behavior Change*, New York: John Wiley & Sons (4th edn), pp. 143–168.

Landis, C. (1938), "Statistical evaluation of psychotherapeutic methods", in S. E. Hinsie (ed.), *Concepts and Problems of Psychotherapy*, London: Heineman, pp. 155–165.

Laplanche, Jean and Pontalis, Jean-Bertrand (1964), "Fantasme originaire, fantasme des origines, origine du fantasme," *Les Temps Modernes*, 215, pp. 1833–1868.

(1971), *Vocabulaire de la psychanalyse*, Paris: Presses Universitaires de France.

Latour, Bruno (1987), *Science in Action: How To Follow Scientists and Engineers through Society*, Cambridge, MA: Harvard University Press.

(1996), *Petite réflexion sur le culte moderne des dieux faitiches*, Paris: Synthélabo.

(1999), *Pandora's Hope: Essay on the Reality of Science Studies*, Cambridge, MA: Harvard University Press.

Latour, Bruno and Woolgar, Steve (1979), *Laboratory Life: The Social Construction of Scientific Facts*, introduction by Jonas Salk, Beverley Hills, CA: Sage Publications.

Laurence, Jean-Roch and Perry, Campbell (1988), *Hypnosis, Will, and Memory: A Psycho-Legal History*, New York and London: The Guilford Press.

Le Pape, Annick and Lecomte, Thérèse (1999), *Prévalence et prise en charge de la dépression. France, 1996–1997*, Paris: CREDES.

Lear, Jonathan (1995), "The shrink is in", *The New Republic*, December 25, pp. 18–25.

Lehmann, Heinz E. (1971), "Epidemiology of depressive disorders", in R. R. Fieve (ed.), *Depression in the 1970s: Modern Theory and Research*, Amsterdam: Excerpta Medica, International Congress Series, p. 239.

(1993), "Before they called it psychopharmacology", *Neuropsychopharmacology*, 8, pp. 291–303.

Lévi-Strauss, Claude (1974 [1958]), "L'efficacité symbolique," in Lévi-Strauss, *Anthropologie structurale*, Paris: Plon, pp. 205–226.

(1987 [1950]), *Introduction to the Work of Marcel Mauss*, translated from the French by Felicity Baker, London: Routledge and Kegan Paul.

Lewes, G. H. (1877), *The Physical Basis of Mind*, London: Trübner & Co.

Liégeois, Jules (1889), *De la suggestion et du somnambulisme dans ses rapports avec la jurisprudence et la médecine légale*, Paris: Doin.

Loftus, Elizabeth and Ketcham, Katherine (1994), *The Myth of Repressed Memory: False Memories and Allegations of Sexual Abuse*, New York: St. Martin's Press.

London, P. and Klerman, Gerald L. (1982), "Evaluating psychotherapy", *American Journal of Psychiatry*, 139, pp. 709–717.

Lothane, Zvi (1989), "Schreber, Freud, Flechsig, and Weber revisited: an inquiry into methods of interpretation," *Psychoanalytic Review*, 76, no. 2, pp. 203–262.

Löwenfeld, Leopold (1895), "Über die Verknüpfung neurasthenischer und hysterischer Symptome in Anfallsform nebst Bemerkungen über die Freudsche Angst-neurose," *Münchener Medicinische Wochenschrift*, 42, pp. 282–285.

(1899), *Sexualleben und Nervenleiden: die Nervöse Störungen sexuellen Ursprungs*, Wiesbaden: J. F. Bergmann (2nd edn).

(1901), *Der Hypnotismus: Handbuch der Lehre von Hypnose und der Suggestion, mit besonderer Berücksichtigung ihre Bedeutung für Medizin und Rechtspflege*, Wiesbaden: J. F. Bergmann.

(1904), *Die psychischen Zwangserscheinungen*, Wiesbaden: J. F. Bergmann.

Luborsky, Lester B. (1986), "Do therapists vary much in their success? Findings from four outcome studies", *American Journal of Orthopsychiatry*, 56, pp. 501–512.

Luborsky, Lester B. *et al.* (1975), "Comparative studies of psychotherapies: is it true that 'everyone has won and all must have prizes'?" *Archives of General Psychiatry*, 32, pp. 995–1008.

Luhrmann, Tanya M. (2000), *Of Two Minds: The Growing Disorder in American Psychiatry*, New York: Knopf.

Lunier, L. (1874), *De l'influence des grandes commotions politiques et sociales sur le développement des maladies mentales*, Paris: F. Savy.

McComb, Samuel (1908), "Christianity and health: an experiment in practical religion", *Century*, 75, March.

Mach, Ernst (1976 [1905]), *Knowledge and Error: Sketches on the Psychology of Enquiry*, ed. Brian McGuinness, translated from the German by Thomas J. McCormack and Paul Foulkes, Dordrecht and Boston: D. Reidel.

McHugh, Paul R. (1993), "Multiple personality disorder", *Harvard Mental Health Letter*, 10, no. 3, pp. 4–6.

(1997), "Foreword", in August Piper, Jr., *Hoax and Reality: The Bizarre World of Multiple Personality Disorder*, Northvale, NJ: Aronson.

Mackinnon, D. W. and Dukes, W. F. (1976), "Repression", in L. Postman (ed.), *Psychology in the Making*, New York: Plenum, pp. 702–703.

Macmillan, Malcolm (1977), "Freud's expectations and the childhood seduction theory," *Australian Journal of Psychology*, 29, no. 3, pp. 223–236.

(1979), "Delbœuf and Janet as influences in Freud's treatment of Emmy von N.", *Journal of the History of the Behavioral Sciences*, 15, pp. 299–309.

(1997 [1991]), *Freud Evaluated: The Completed Arc*, Cambridge, MA: MIT Press (2nd edn, revised and augmented).

Mahony, Patrick (1984), *Cries of the Wolfman*, New York: International Universities Press.

(1986), *Freud and the Rat Man*, New Haven, CT: Yale University Press.

(1996), *Freud's Dora: A Psychoanalytic, Historical, and Textual Study*, New Haven, CT: Yale University Press.

Maître, Jacques (1993), *Une inconnue célèbre: la "Madeleine Lebouc" de Pierre Janet*, Paris: Anthropos.

Makari, George J. (1992), "A history of Freud's first concept of transference," *International Review of Psycho-Analysis*, 19, no. 4, pp. 415–432.

(1997), "Towards defining the Freudian unconscious: seduction, sexology and the negative of perversion (1896–1905)", *History of Psychiatry*, 8, no. 32, pp. 459–485.

Marett, R. R. (1920), Review of Freud, *Totem and Taboo, The Athenaeum*, February 13.

Marie, Pierre (1925), "Eloge de J.-M. Charcot," *Presse médicale*, May 27, pp. 689–692.

Marks, Harry M. (1997), *The Progress of Experiment: Science and Therapeutic Reform in the United States, 1900–1990*, Cambridge: Cambridge University Press.

(2000), "Trust and mistrust in the marketplace: statistics and clinical research, 1945–1960", *History of Science*, 38, pp. 344–355.

Martensson, Lars (1998), *Deprived of Our Humanity: The Case against Neuroleptic Drugs*, Geneva: Associations Ecrivains, Poètes & Cie.

Masling, Joseph (1960), "The influence of situational and interpersonal variables in projective testing", *Psychological Bulletin*, 57, no. 1, pp. 65–85.

(1965), "Differential indoctrination of examiners and Rohrschach responses", *Journal of Consulting Psychology*, 29, no. 3, pp. 198–201.

Masson, Jeffrey Moussaïeff (1992 [1984]), *The Assault on Truth: Freud's Suppression of the Seduction Theory*, New York: HarperCollins (3rd edn).

Méheust, Bertrand (1999), *Somnambulisme et médiumnité*, vol. 1: *Le défi du magnétisme*, Paris: Les Empêcheurs de Penser en Rond / Synthélabo.

Meige, Henri, *Étude sur certains névropathes voyageurs: le Juif-errant à la Salpêtrière*, Paris: Louis Bataille.

Merskey, Harold (1991), "Shellshock", in German E. Berrios and Hugh Freeman (eds.), *British Psychiatry's Strange Past: 150 Years of British Psychiatry, 1841–1991*, London: Gaskell, Royal College of Psychiatrists, pp. 245–267.

(1992), "The manufacture of personalities. The production of multiple personality disorder", *British Journal of Psychiatry*, 160, pp. 327–340.

Meyer, Catherine, Borch-Jacobsen, Mikkel, Cottraux, Jean, Pleux, Didier and Van Rillaer, Jacques (eds.) (2005), *Le livre noir de la psychanalyse*, Paris: Les Arènes.

Micale, Mark S. (1990), "Charcot and the idea of hysteria in the male: gender, mental science, and medical diagnosis in late nineteenth-century France", *Medical History*, 34, no. 4, pp. 363–411.

(1993a), "On the 'disappearance' of hysteria. A study in the clinical deconstruction of a diagnosis", *Isis*, 84, pp. 496–526.

(ed.) (1993b), *Beyond the Unconscious: Essays of Henri F. Ellenberger in the History of Psychiatry*, Princeton, NJ: Princeton University Press.

(1994), "Charcot and *Les Névroses traumatiques*: historical and scientific reflections", *Revue Neurologique*, 150, no. 8–9, pp. 498–505.

Micale, Mark S. and Lerner, Paul (eds.) (2001), *Traumatic Pasts: History, Trauma, and Psychiatry in the Modern Age, 1870–1930*, Cambridge: Cambridge University Press.

Mink, Louis O. (1965), "The autonomy of historical understanding", *History and Theory*, 5, no. 1, pp. 24–47.

Mitchell, Juliet (1974), *Psychoanalysis and Feminism: Freud, Reich, Laing and Women*, New York: Vintage Books.

(2000), *Mad Men and Medusas: Reclaiming Hysteria and the Effects of Sibling Relationships on the Human Condition*, London: Penguin.

Moll, Albert (1889), *Der Hypnotismus*, Berlin: Fischer's Medizinische Buchhandlung, H. Kornfeld.

(1913 [1909]), *The Sexual Life of the Child*, translated from the German by Eden Paul, New York: Macmillan.

Moynihan, Ray, Heath, Iona, and Henry, David (2002), "Selling sickness: the pharmaceutical industry and disease mongering", *British Medical Journal*, 324, pp. 886–891.

Mulhern, Sherrill (1991), "Satanism and psychotherapy: a rumor in search of an inquisition", in James T. Richardson (ed.), *The Satanism Scare*, Hawthorne, NY: Aldine de Gruyter, pp. 145–174.

Münsterberg, Hugo (1909), *Psychotherapy*, New York: Moffard, Yard and Company.

Nathan, Tobie (1994), *L'influence qui guérit*, Paris: Odile Jacob.

(2006), "Pour une psychothérapie enfin démocratique", in Tobie Nathan (ed.), *La guerre des psys: manifeste pour une psychothérapie démocratique*, Paris: Les Empêcheurs de Penser en Rond / Seuil, pp. 21–27.

Nathan, Tobie, Stengers, Isabelle and Andréa, Philippe (2000), "Une ethnopsychiatrie de la schizophrénie?" *Ethnopsy: Les Mondes Contemporains de la Guérison*, 1, pp. 9–43.

Nichter, Mark (1981), "Idioms of distress: alternatives in the expression of psychosocial distress", *Culture, Medicine and Psychiatry*, 5, no. 4, pp. 379–408.

North, C. S., Ryall, J. M., Ricci, D. A., and Wetzel, R. D. (1993), *Multiple Personalities and Multiple Disorders: Psychiatric Classification and Media Influence*, New York: Oxford University Press.

Numbers, Ronald L. (1976), *Prophetess of Health: A Study of Ellen G. White*, New York: Harper & Row.

(2003), "Sex, science, and salvation. The sexual advice of Ellen. G. White and John Harvey Kellogg", in Charles E. Rosenberg (ed.), *Right Living: An Anglo-American Tradition of Self-Help Medicine and Hygiene*, Baltimore: Johns Hopkins University Press, pp. 206–226.

Nunberg, Herman and Federn, Ernst (eds.) (1967), *Minutes of the Vienna Psychoanalytic Society*, vol. 2: *1908–1910*, translated from the German by M. Nunberg, New York: International Universities Press.

Obeyesekere, Gananath (1985), "Depression, Buddhism, and the work of culture in Sri Lanka", in Arthur Kleinman and Byron Good (eds.), *Culture and Depression: Studies in the Anthropology and Cross-Cultural Psychiatry of Affect and Disorder*, Berkeley: University of California Press, pp. 134–152.

Obholzer, Karin (1982 [1981]), *The Wolf-Man Sixty Years Later*, translated from the German by Michael Shaw, London: Routledge and Kegan Paul.

Ofshe, Richard (1992), "Inadvertent hypnosis during interrogation: false confession due to dissociative state; mis-identified multiple personality and the satanic cult hypothesis", *International Journal of Clinical and Experimental Hypnosis*, 40, no. 3, pp. 125–156.

Ofshe, Richard and Watters, Ethan (1994), *Making Monsters: False Memories, Psychotherapy, and Sexual Hysteria*, New York: Scribner.

Orne, Martin (1962), "On the social psychology of the psychological experiment: with particular reference to demand characteristics and their implications", *American Psychologist*, 17, no. 11, pp. 776–783.

(1965 [1959]), "The nature of hypnosis: artifact and essence," in Ronald E. Shor and Martin T. Orne (eds.), *The Nature of Hypnosis: Selected Basic Readings*, New York: Holt, Rinehart and Winston, pp. 89–123.

(1969), "Demand characteristics and the concept of quasi-control," in Robert Rosenthal and Ralph L. Rosnow (eds.), *Artifact in Behavioral Research*, New York and London: Academic Press, pp. 143–179.

(1970), "Hypnosis, motivation, and the ecological validity of the psychological experiment," in William J. Arnold and Monte M. Page (eds.), *Nebraska Symposium on Motivation*, Lincoln: University of Nebraska Press, pp. 187–265.

(1977), "The construct of hypnosis: implications of the definition for research and practice," in William E. Edmonston, Jr. (ed.), *Conceptual and Investigative Approaches to Hypnosis and Hypnotic Phenomena*, special issue of *Annals of the New York Academy of Sciences*, 296, pp. 14–33.

Osgood, Charles E. and Luria, Zella (1954), "Case report. A blind analysis of a case of multiple personality using the semantic differential", *Journal of Abnormal and Social Psychology*, 49, no. 4, pp. 579–591.

Page, Herbert (1883), *Injuries of the Spine and Spinal Cord without Apparent Mechanical Lesions and Nervous Shock, in their Surgical and Medico-Legal Aspects*, London: Churchill.

Paget, Sir James (1873), "Nervous mimicry", in *Selected Essays and Addresses by Sir James Paget*, ed. S. Paget, London: Longman, Green & Co., ch. 7.

Pankejeff, Sergius C. (1957), "Letters pertaining to Freud's 'History of an infantile neurosis'," *Psychoanalytic Quarterly*, 26, pp. 449–460.

Parker, Ian (2000), "Obedience," *Granta*, 71, pp. 101–125.

Parker, Neville (1980), "Personality change following accidents. The report of a double murder", *British Journal of Psychiatry*, 137, pp. 401–409.

Pattie, Frank A. (1937), "The genuineness of hypnotically produced anesthesia of the skin," *American Journal of Psychology*, 49, pp. 435–443.

Payne, Lynn (1992), *Disease-Mongers: How Doctors, Drug Companies, and Insurers Are Making You Feel Sick*, New York: Wiley and Sons.

Peirce, Charles Sanders (1986), *The Collected Works of C. S. Pierce*, Bloomington: Indiana University Press.

Pendergrast, Mark (1996 [1995]), *Victims of Memory: Sex Abuse Accusations and Shattered Lives*, Hinesburg, VT: Upper Access (2nd edn).

Pickering, Andrew (1995), *The Mangle of Practice: Time, Agency, and Science*, Chicago: University of Chicago Press.

Pignarre, Philippe (1997), *Qu'est-ce qu'un médicament? Un objet étrange, entre science, marché et société*, Paris: La Découverte.

(1999), *Puissance des psychotropes, pouvoir des patients*, Paris: Presses Universitaires de France.

(2001), *Comment la dépression est devenue une épidémie*, Paris: La Découverte.

Plummer, Kenneth (ed.) (1981), *The Making of the Modern Homosexual*, Totowa, NJ: Barnes and Noble.

Polgar, Franz J. (1951), *The Story of a Hypnotist*, New York: Hermitage House.

Pollack, Richard (1997), *The Creation of Dr. B: A Biography of Bruno Bettelheim*, New York: Simon and Schuster.

Popper, Karl (1963), *Conjectures and Refutations: The Growth of Scientific Knowledge*, London: Routledge and Kegan Paul.

Porter, Roy (1985), "The patient's view: doing medical history from below", *Theory and Society*, 14, no. 2, pp. 175–198.

Pouillon, Jean (1970), "Malade et médecin: le même et/ou l'autre? (Remarques ethnologiques)", *Nouvelle Revue de Psychanalyse*, 1, pp. 76–98.

Prince, Morton (1905), *The Dissociation of a Personality: A Biographical Study in Abnormal Psychology*, New York: Longmans, Green and Co.

Putnam, Frank W. (1989a), *Diagnosis and Treatment of Multiple Personality Disorder*, New York and London: The Guilford Press.

(1989b), "Pierre Janet and modern views on dissociation", *Journal of Traumatic Stress*, 2, pp. 413–429.

Putnam, James Jackson (1883), "Recent investigations into the pathology of so-called concussion of the spine", *Boston Medical and Surgical Journal*, 109, pp. 217–220.

(1906), "Recent experiences in the study and treatment of hysteria at Massachusetts General Hospital", *Journal of Abnormal Psychology*, 1, pp. 26–41.

Rabeharisoa, Volona, Callon, Michel and Demonty, Bernard (2000), "Les associations de malades et la recherche. II. Les formes d'engagement des associations de malades dans la recherche en France", *Médecine/Sciences*, 16, no. 11, pp. 1225–31.

Reynolds, Sir Russell (1869), "Paralysis and other disorders of motion and sensation, dependent on idea", *British Medical Journal*, pp. 483–485.

Ribot, Théodule (1921 [1885]), *Les maladies de la personnalité*, Paris, Alcan (18th edn).

Richet, Charles (1884), *L'homme et l'intelligence: fragments de physiologie et de psychologie*, Paris: Alcan.

Ricoeur, Paul (1981), "The question of proof in Freud's writings", in Ricoeur, *Hermeneutics and the Human Sciences*, ed. and translated from the French by John B. Thompson, Cambridge and Paris: Cambridge University Press / Editions de la Maison de l'Homme, pp. 247–73.

(1983), *Temps et récit*, vol. 1, Paris, Seuil.

Roazen, Paul (1975), *Freud and His Followers*, New York: Knopf.

Romme, Marius and Escher, Sandra (1989), "Hearing voices", *Schizophrenia Bulletin*, 15, no. 2, pp. 209–216.

Rosario, Vernon A. (1997), *The Erotic Imagination*, New York and Oxford: Oxford University Press.

Rosenberg, Charles E. (1979), "The therapeutic revolution: medicine, meaning, and social change in nineteenth-century America," in Morris J. Vogel and Charles E. Rosenberg (eds.), *The Therapeutic Revolution: Essays in the Social History of American Medicine*, Philadephia: University of Pennsylvania Press.

(1989), "Body and mind in nineteenth-century medicine: some clinical origins of the neurosis construct", *Bulletin of the History of Medicine*, 63, no. 2, pp. 185–197.

(2002), "The tyranny of diagnosis: specific entities and individual experience", *Milbank Quarterly*, 80, no. 2, pp. 237–260.

(2003), "Health in the home. A tradition of print and practice", in Charles E. Rosenberg (ed.), *Right Living: An Anglo-American Tradition of Self-Help Medicine and Hygiene*, Baltimore: Johns Hopkins University Press, pp. 1–20.

Rosenthal, Robert (1966), *Experimenter Effect in Behavioral Research*, New York: Appleton-Century-Crofts.

Rosenthal, Robert and Rosnow, Ralph L. (eds.) (1968), *Artifact in Behavioral Research*, New York and London: Academic Press.

Rosenzweig, Saul (1936), "Some implicit common factors in diverse methods of psychotherapy", *American Journal of Orthopsychiatry*, 6, pp. 412–415.

Ross, Colin A. (1989), *Multiple Personality Disorder: Diagnosis, Clinical Features and Treatment*, New York: Wiley.

Roudinesco, Elisabeth (1986), *La bataille de cent ans: histoire de la psychanalyse en France*, vol. 1, Paris: Ramsay/Seuil.

  (1990), *Jacques Lacan & Co.: A History of Psychoanalysis in France, 1925–1985*, translated from the French by Jeffrey Mehlman, London: Free Association Books.

  (1991), "Obituary notice, Léon Chertok," *Libération*, July 10.

  (2001 [1999]), *Why Psychoanalysis?*, translated from the French by Rachel Bowlby, New York: Columbia University Press.

Rouillard, A.-M.-P. (1885), *Essai sur les amnésies principalement au point de vue étiologique*, Paris: Le Clerc.

Roustang, François (2000), *La fin de la plainte*, Paris: Odile Jacob.

Rush, Florence (1977), "The Freudian cover-up" *Chrysalis*, 1, pp. 31–45.

Sal y Rosas, Federico, (1957), "El mito del Jani o Susto de la medecina indigena del Perú", *Revista Psiquiátrica Peruana*, 1, pp. 103–132.

Sarbin, Theodore Roy (1965 [1950]), "Contributions to role-taking theory: I. Hypnotic behavior," in Ronald E. Shor and Martin T. Orne (eds.), *The Nature of Hypnosis: Selected Basic Readings*, New York: Holt, Rinehart and Winston, pp. 234–254.

Sartorius, N. *et al.* (1986), "Early manifestations and first-contact incidence of schizophrenia in different cultures", *Psychological Medicine*, 16, no. 4, pp. 909–927.

Sartre, Jean-Paul (1956 [1943]), *Being and Nothingness*, translated from the French by Hazel Barnes, New York: Simon and Schuster.

Schafer, Roy (1980), "Narration in the psychoanalytic dialogue", *Critical Inquiry*, 7, no. 1, pp. 29–53.

Scharnberg, Max (1993), *The Non-Authentic Nature of Freud's Observations*, vols. 1–2, Uppsala Studies in Education 47–48, Uppsala: Uppsala Universitet.

Schimek, Jean G. (1987), "Fact and fantasy in the seduction theory: a historical review", *Journal of the American Psychoanalytic Association*, 35, pp. 937–965.

Schivelbusch, Wolfgang (1979), *The Railway Journey: Trains and Travel in the 19th Century*, translated from the German by Anselm Hollo, New York: Urizen.

Schneck, Jerome M. (1976), "Freud's 'medical hypnotist'," *American Journal of Clinical Hypnosis*, 19, no. 2, pp. 80–81.

Schreiber, Flora Rheta (1963), "I was raising a homosexual child", *Cosmopolitan Magazine*, January, pp. 61–64.

  (1974 [1973]), *Sybil*, New York: Warner Books (2nd edn).

  (1983), *The Shoemaker: The Anatomy of a Psychopath*, New York: Simon and Schuster.

Schrenck-Notzing, Albert von (1892), *Die Suggestions-Therapie bei krankhaften Erscheinungen des Geschlechtssinnes: mit besonderer Berücksichtigung der conträren Sexualempfindung*, Stuttgart: Ferdinand Enke.

Schur, Max (1966), "Some additional 'day residues' of the specimen dream of psychoanalysis", in R. M. Loewenstein, L. M. Newman, M. Schur and A. J. Solnit (eds.), *Psychoanalysis: A General Psychology*, New York: International Universities Press, pp. 45–85.

(1972), *Freud: Living and Dying*, New York: International Universities Press.

Schusdek, Alexander (1966), "Freud's 'seduction theory:' a reconstruction," *Journal of the History of the Behavioral Sciences*, 2, pp. 159–166.

Scott, Wilbur J. (1990), "PTSD in *DSM-III*: a case in the politics of diagnosis and disease", *Social Problems*, 37, pp. 294–310.

Sebag, Lucien (1965), "Le chamanisme ayoréo", *L'Homme*, 1–2, pp. 106–113.

Seligman, Martin E. P. (1995), "The effectiveness of psychotherapy. The *Consumer Reports* study", *American Psychologist*, 50, no. 12, pp. 965–974.

(2002), *Authentic Happiness*, New York: The Free Press.

Shakow, David and Rapaport, David (1968), *The Influence of Freud on American Psychology*, Cleveland, OH: Meridian Books.

Shamdasani, Sonu (1990), "A woman called Frank", *Spring: Journal for Archetype and Culture*, 50, pp. 26–55.

(1994), "Encountering Hélène. Théodore Flournoy and the genesis of subliminal psychology", in Théodore Flournoy, *From India to the Planet Mars: A Case of Multiple Personality with Imaginary Languages*, ed. Sonu Shamdasani, Princeton, NJ: Princeton University Press, pp. xi–li.

(1997), "La folie du jour: Jung et ses patients", paper presented at the conference "Histoire de la psychiatrie. Nouvelles approches, nouvelles perspectives", Lausanne, February.

(2001), "'Un magnétiseur à l'ancienne'? Note sur Théodore Flournoy et l'hypnose", *Ethnopsy*, 3, pp. 113–122.

(2005), "'Psychotherapy': the invention of a word", *History of the Human Sciences*, 18, no. 1, pp. 1–22.

Shaw, Horace J. (1981), *The Bishop: The Story of A. A. Leiske and the Unique Telecast – "The American Religious Town Hall Meetings"*, Mountain View, CA: Pacific Press.

Sherwood, Michael (1969), *The Logic of Explanation in Psychoanalysis*, New York: Academic Press.

Shorter, Edward (1986), "Paralysis: the rise and fall of a 'hysterical symptom'", *Journal of Social History*, 19, pp. 549–582.

(1992), *From Paralysis to Fatigue: A History of Psychosomatic Illness in the Modern Era*, New York: The Free Press.

(1997), *A History of Psychiatry: From the Era of the Asylum to the Age of Prozac*, New York: John Wiley and Sons.

Skues, Richard (2001), "On the dating of Freud's *Aliquis* slip", *International Journal of Psychoanalysis*, 82, no. 6, pp. 1185–1204.

(2006), *Sigmund Freud and the History of Anna O.: Reopening a Closed Case*, Houndmills, NY: Palgrave Macmillan.

Spanos, Nicholas P. (1986), "More on the social psychology of hypnotic responding," *Behavioral and Brain Sciences*, 9, no. 3, pp. 489–502.

(1996), *Multiple Identities and False Memories: A Sociocognitive Perspective*, Washington, DC: American Psychological Association.

Spanos, Nicholas, Gwynn, M. I., and Stam, H. J. (1983), "Instructional demands and ratings of overt and hidden pain during hypnotic analgesia", *Journal of Abnormal Psychology*, 92, pp. 479–488.

Spanos, Nicholas and Hewitt, E. C., (1980), "The hidden observer in hypnotic analgesia: discovery or experimental creation?" *Journal of Personality and Social Psychology*, 39, pp. 1201–1214.

Spector, Jack J. (1972), *The Aesthetics of Freud: A Study in Psychoanalysis and Art*, New York: Praeger Publishers.

Spence, Donald P. (1982), *Narrative Truth and Historical Truth: Meaning and Interpretation in Psychoanalysis*, New York: Norton.

Spiegel, David *et al.* (1989), "Effects of psychosocial treatment on survival of patients with metastatic breast cancer", *The Lancet*, 2, pp. 888–891.

Spiegel, Herbert, Shor, Joel and Fishman, Sidney (1945), "An hypnotic ablation technique for the study of personality development", *Psychosomatic Medicine*, 7, no. 5, pp. 273–278.

Stahl, Steven (1996), *Essential Psychopharmacology*, Cambridge, MA: Cambridge University Press.

Stengers, Isabelle (1992), *La volonté de faire science: à propos de la psychanalyse*, Paris: Les Empêcheurs de Penser en Rond / Synthélabo.

(2001), "Qu'est-ce que l'hypnose nous oblige à penser?", *Ethnopsy*, 3, pp. 13–68.

Stepansky, Paul E. (1999), *Freud, Surgery, and the Surgeons*, Hillsdale, NJ: The Analytic Press.

Stone, Martin (1989) "Shellshock and the psychologists", in William Bynum, Roy Porter and Michael Shepherd (eds.), *The Anatomy of Madness: Essays in the History of Psychiatry*, vol. 2, London: Tavistock, pp. 242–271.

Strümpell, Adolf von (1892), *Über die Entstehung und die Heilung von Krankheiten durch Vorstellung: Rede beim Antritt des Prorectorats der ... Universität Erlangen*, Erlangen.

(1896), review of *Studies on Hysteria*, *Deutsche Zeitschrift für Nervenheilkünde*, 8, pp. 159–161.

Sulloway, Frank J. (1992 [1979]), *Freud, Biologist of the Mind: Beyond the Freud Legend*, Cambridge, MA: Harvard University Press (2nd augmented edn).

Suls, Jerry M. and Rosnow, Ralph L. (1988), "Concerns about artifacts in psychological experiments," in Jill G. Morawski (ed.), *The Rise of Experimentation in American Psychology*, New Haven, CT: Yale University Press, pp. 163–187.

Swain, Gladys (1994), *Dialogue avec l'insensé*, Paris: Gallimard.

Swales, Peter J. (1982a), "Freud, Johann Weier, and the status of seduction: the role of the witch in the conception of phantasy," New York: privately published by the author.

(1982b), "Freud, Minna Bernays, and the conquest of Rome. New light on the origins of psychoanalysis," *New American Review*, 1, no. 2–3, pp. 1–23.

(1983), "Freud, Krafft-Ebing, and the witches. The role of Krafft-Ebing in Freud's flight into fantasy", New York: privately published by the author.

(1986a), "Freud, his teacher and the birth of psychoanalysis", in Paul E. Stepansky (ed.), *Freud, Appraisals and Reappraisals*, vol. 1, Hillsdale, NJ: The Analytic Press, pp. 2–82.

(1986b), "Freud, Breuer, and the Blessed Virgin", paper presented at the Richardson History of Psychiatry Research Seminar, Cornell University, New York.

(1988), "Freud, Katharina, and the first 'wild analysis'", in Paul Stepansky (ed.), *Freud: Appraisals and Reappraisals*, vol. 3, Hillsdale, NJ: The Analytic Press, pp. 79–164.

(2000), "The creation of Sybil: a tale of three women", paper presented at the Richardson History of Psychiatry Research Seminar, Cornell University, New York.

(2003), "Freud, death, and sexual pleasures. On the psychical mechanism of Dr. Sigmund Freud", *Arc-de-Cercle: An International Journal in the History of the Mind-Sciences*, 1. no. 1, pp. 6–74.

Taylor, W. S. and Martin, M. F. (1944), "Multiple personality", *Journal of Abnormal and Social Psychology*, 39, no. 3, pp. 281–300.

Thigpen, C. H. and Cleckley, H. (1954), "A case of multiple personality", *Journal of Abnormal and Social Psychology*, 49, no. 1, pp. 135–141.

(1957), *The Three Faces of Eve*, New York: McGraw-Hill.

(1984), "On the incidence of multiple personality disorder", *International Journal of Clinical and Experimental Hypnosis*, 32, no. 2, pp. 63–66.

Thornton, E. M. (1983), *Freud and Cocaine: The Freudian Fallacy*, London: Blond and Briggs.

Tiefer, Leonore (2006), "Female sexual dysfunction: a case study of disease mongering and activist resistance", *PLoS Medicine*, 3, no. 4. www.plosmedicine.org.

Tissié, Philippe (1887), *Les aliénés voyageurs: essai médico-psychologique*, Paris: Octave Doin.

(1888), *L'hygiène du vélocipédiste*, Paris: Octave Doin.

(1890), *Les rêves: physiologie et pathologie*, Paris: Alcan.

Tuke, Daniel Hack (1972), *Illustrations of the Influence of Mind upon the Body in Health and Disease Designed to Elucidate the Action of the Imagination*, London: Churchill.

(1892), *Dictionary of Psychological Medicine*, 2 vols., Philadelphia: Blakiston, Son.

Veith, Ilza (1965), *Hysteria: The History of a Disease*, Chicago: University of Chicago Press.

Veyne, Paul (1971), *Comment on écrit l'histoire: essai d'épistémologie*, Paris: Seuil.

(1983), *Les Grecs ont-ils cru à leurs mythes?*, Paris: Seuil.

Vogt, Oskar (1899), "Zur Methodik der ätiologischen Erforschung der Hysterie," *Zeitschrift für Hypnotismus*, 8.

Walton, G. L. (1883), "Case of typical hysterical hemianesthesia in a man following injury", *Archives of Medicine*, 10, pp. 88–95

(1884), "Case of typical hysterical hemianesthesia, convulsions and motor paralysis brought on by a fall", *Boston Medical and Surgical Journal*, 111, pp. 558–559.

Wang, Shengbiao *et al.* (1995), "Evidence for a susceptibility locus for schizophrenia on chromosome 6pter-p22", *Nature Genetics*, 10, pp. 41–46.

Warner, Richard (1985), *Recovery from Schizophrenia: Psychiatry and Political Economy*, Boston: Routledge.

Watzlawick, Paul, Beavin, Janet Helmick and Jackson, Don D. (1967), *Pragmatics of Human Communication: A Study of Interactional Patterns, Pathologies, and Paradoxes*, New York: Norton.

Webb, E. J., Campbell, D. T., Schwartz, R. D., and Sechrest, L. (1966), *Unobtrusive Measures: Nonreactive Research in the Social Sciences*, Chicago: Rand McNally.

Weber, Max (1999 [1918]), "Science as a vocation", in *Max Weber: Sociological Writings*, ed. W. Heydebrand, translated from the German by Hans H. Gerth and C. Wright Mills, New York: Continuum, pp. 276–303.

Webster, Richard (1995), *Why Freud Was Wrong: Sin, Science, and Psychoanalysis*, New York: Basic Books.

White, Hayden (1974), "The historical text as literary artifact", *Clio*, 3, no. 3, pp. 277–303.

Wilbur, Cornelia B. (1944), "Uses of barbiturates intravenously in neuropsychiatry", *Diseases of the Nervous System*, 5, no. 10, pp. 293–297.

(1947), "Convulsive shock therapy in patients over seventy years of age with affective disorders", *American Journal of Psychiatry*, 104, no. 1, pp. 48–51.

(1960), "Age regression by hypnosis", *Diseases of the Nervous System*, 21, no. 9, pp. 520–526.

(1964), "Female homosexuality", in Arthur Burton (ed.), *Modern Psychotherapeutic Practice*, Palo Alto, CA: Science and Behavior Books, pp. 339–357.

(1965), "Clinical aspects of female homosexuality", in Judd Marmor (ed.), *Sexual Inversion*, New York: Basic Books, pp. 268–281.

(1970), "Homosexuality on the college campus", *College Health Journal*, Evanston: American College Health Association.

Wilbur, Cornelia B. *et al.* (1967), "Homosexuality in women", *Archives of General Psychiatry*, 17, no. 5, pp. 626–634.

Wilbur, Cornelia B., Michaels, Joseph, and Becker, Arnold H. (1947), "Atropine pre-medication in electroshock therapy", *Diseases of the Nervous System*, 8, no. 3, pp. 74–76.

Wilcocks, Robert (1994), *Maelzel's Chess Player: Sigmund Freud and the Rhetoric of Deceit*, Lanham, MD: Rowman and Littlefield.

Wohlgemuth, Adolf (1923), *A Critical Examination of Psycho-Analysis*, New York: Macmillan.

Woodworth, Robert S. (1917), "Some Criticisms of the Freudian Psychology," *Journal of Abnormal Psychology*, 12, pp. 174–194.

World Health Organization (1973), *The International Pilot Study of Schizophrenia*, Geneva.

(1979), *Schizophrenia: An International Follow-Up Study*, Chichester.

Wright, Lawrence (1993), "Remembering Satan", *The New Yorker*, May 17 and 24.

Young, Allan (1995), *The Harmony of Illusions: Inventing Post-Traumatic Stress Disorder*, Princeton, NJ: Princeton University Press.

Zarifian, Edouard (1996), *Le prix du bien-être: psychotropes et société*, Paris: Odile Jacob.

Index

255